Harold

Harold

Hal Holbrook

The Boy Who Became
Mark Twain

Farrar, Straus and Giroux

New York

FARRAR, STRAUS AND GIROUX
18 West 18th Street, New York 10011

Copyright © 2011 by Hal Holbrook
All rights reserved
Distributed in Canada by D&M Publishers, Inc.
Printed in the United States of America
First edition, 2011

Library of Congress Cataloging-in-Publication Data
Holbrook, Hal.
    Harold : the boy who became Mark Twain / Hal Holbrook. — 1st ed.
      p.   cm.
    ISBN 978-0-374-28101-4 (alk. paper)
    1. Holbrook, Hal.   2. Actors—United States—Biography.   I. Title.
PN2287.H57A3 2011
792.02'8092—dc22
[B]
                                                        2010053555

Designed by Abby Kagan

www.fsgbooks.com

1   3   5   7   9   10   8   6   4   2

For the girl of my dreams . . .

Harold

1

I'm trying to remember being held by my mother. Those memories are all so dreamy now, as if none of them ever really happened. I could have dreamed my memories and they would be as real to me. I'm told she was just a young girl and that she left when I was two. I have a picture of her, a little brown-tinted photograph in a gold frame, and she is, indeed, a young girl with a shy smile. But there is some other message in her eyes. Something tired, the eyes of a girl who has had enough and wants it to be over.

All I have are two drifting memories of her. The first is on the enclosed porch in the big Cleveland house, green wicker furniture. A baby is stumbling around, knocking into the sharp stub ends of wicker and crying, and a young woman reaches for this baby, but Grandma moves in ahead of her and the baby never gets inside the young woman's arms. That would be me.

The other memory is a few years later, in the cigar-scented den off Grandpa's bedroom in the South Weymouth house when I was about six years old. My mother and father have come out of the blue to visit us. They are tap-dancing in the archway of Grandpa's den and she is smiling, but there is no beginning or ending to this memory. It is just a vision, connected to nothing, two young people dancing in limbo. I revisited that house many years later because I was told the people who live there now had sometimes seen the ghost of a young woman with blond hair when they went down into the basement. They were very matter-of-fact about it. They told me I wouldn't feel afraid of her, because she was not threatening. They had a young son, and he agreed. She was friendly, he said.

When I descended, I told myself that I would *like* to see her, that if I could believe in this apparition, I would know my mother. The basement was larger than I had remembered, much larger, so clean and dry, the paint so fresh and shiny after all these years. It stretched away around a corner to the right, where the laundry and shop tools were. To the left was the coal room for the furnace, with the coal chute slanting down into it. It gave me a shock of remembrance, the glistening chute. I remembered crouching there as a little boy. They said she would be in this part of the cellar. That I would probably see her here. I waited. I made myself still, my heart and my body. Did I feel a presence? Was someone there? I wanted her to appear.

"Mother?"

In my heart I felt a tiny shock. Was it her I felt? Or was it the word I don't remember ever saying that sent a thrill through me?

"Hello, Mother. It's me, Harold."

I hung on to the feeling as long as I could but finally had to let it go. I don't believe in ghosts. Maybe that had something to do with it, maybe not. I don't know.

I would never see her again after she and my father suddenly appeared and danced in the archway of Grandpa's den. Nowadays, at night when I turn out the lights in the living room before going up to bed, I look at her little picture in the gold frame under the lamp where my dear wife has placed it, and I say, "Good night, little girl." She was just a little girl, that's all she was, those years ago when last I saw her.

My name is Harold. The year after my mother disappeared for good, they sent me away to boarding school to make a man of me. I was seven years old. The junior school was run by the Headmaster, a short, round man who told stories about a turtle that lived under a rock beside the path to the dining hall. That was his good side.

Harold

One afternoon I was playing halfback in football practice and I got a shoe full of cleats in the face. Baam! I started to cry. The coach banished me for not being tough enough. I was already in disgrace from the Saturday before, when I caught a pass and ran eighty-eight yards for a touchdown. I couldn't understand why no one was chasing me, until they told me I'd gone the wrong way.

I was ashamed. I decided to run a mile. I'd never done it before. Across from the football field was a cinder track—five times around for a mile. I hobbled over there, pulled off my helmet, and drew a line in the cinders. Five times around. No stopping. My football shoes and shoulder pads were pretty heavy, but I didn't think about that right away. Soon I was gulping the fall air of Connecticut and it bit down into my lungs like slivers of ice. By the end of one lap the shoes felt like hunks of pig iron and the shoulder pads were flopping around, banging my ears.

"Please, God, don't let me fail! Maybe the Headmaster is watching me up on the hill, from the window in his office, where he likes to punish us. Maybe he will be proud of me if I keep going all the way."

Five laps. Now only three and a half. I was beginning to cough up stuff and my lungs were filling up with the ice slivers. Maybe the coach was watching me, too, and he would think, "That Harold has guts, after all. Look at him go." I began to think I was going to make it. A sensation of air spread through my chest, and it seemed to me I could even breathe better. The far turn was coming up again, where those big fall leaves were letting go, and then came the homestretch and I had run four laps. Or was it three? Maybe it was only three. I didn't want to cheat. I could *say* four, but if it was only three, that would be cheating. They're probably watching me anyway. If I can really make it to a mile without stopping, that will be something big. Very big. My legs were beginning to feel as if they were attached to swivels, and I couldn't see anything past the sweat in my eyes. There was no sound outside my head except the awful gasping that erupted from somewhere in my chest. I yearned to walk a few steps. Just a few. No cheating! Gotta keep moving or it's not *running* the mile, it's *walking* it. It's being *weak*. There's that far turn again, with the harsh smell of brittle autumn leaves. If I can just keep moving until I see that line in the cinders, I will have run the mile.

I stopped. There was a great thumping sound in my ears and my eyes were stung shut from the sweat, but I had done it. I had run the mile. It got quiet and I rubbed at my eyes, and when I looked around, I was alone. The football field was empty. Away up the hill I could see the last of the team rounding the corner of the white junior school building, and I could imagine them disappearing into the darkness of the basement, where the Headmaster would be waiting. I would be late.

The hill was going to be tough. In winter we built a ski jump on it out of wet snow, so it was steep. There were cement steps along the left side of the hill, under the three big maple trees we climbed when we were playing Tarzan of the Apes. I could go up the steps. But cutting across the slope of the hill was more direct, and that's where I was already heading. Breathe! Lean forward into the hill so you don't fall and roll down it. Maybe the Headmaster won't be waiting in the basement today.

It must be adrenaline that keeps you going when you want to stop. Adrenaline or something. I made the hill, and I made the corner of the wooden building where we slept and went to school all year long except for vacations at Thanksgiving and Christmas. And there were the steps, three of them, down into the big, dark space you had to cross before you entered the locker room. And he was there in the dark. Coming out of sunlight into the darkness blinded me, so I couldn't see him. All I heard was a voice.

"Holbrook, you're late." The Headmaster was using my last name, not Harold.

"Yes, sir. I'm sorry . . ."

"Come here."

"Sir, I was running a mile . . ." Whack! Whack! His hand flew out like a whip and lashed the right side of my face and then the left in one smooth, beautiful move. Perfect aim. I tried to get by him toward the locker-room door, but he caught me and drove his knee between my legs. I saw stars. The blow pitched me toward the whitewashed wall of the locker room with all those black hooks on it, and I saw that my head was going to land right between two of them. Clunk!

"Get showered."

I must have closed my eyes. When I opened them, he was gone. I heard a sob fly out of me and the tears came quick and hot. "If Grandpa knew what you did to me, he would come down from South Weymouth and kill you, kick you, murder you, beat you until the blood spurted out of your nose and ears. You would be dead!" Grandpa would be wearing his big overcoat with the smell of cigar smoke in it and he would pat me on the head and say, "Don't cry, Buddy, we're going home." Then we would walk away and leave the Headmaster dead on the ground.

I was not going into that locker room with my eyes red. I was going to let the pink go away first and get my breathing right. Maybe I was only seven, but I was not a sissy. I was not going to walk into that locker room crying, even if my name was Harold.

The mind flows back. We enter memory, and events and people pour out like little swaying creatures, saying, "Here I am, here I am." The plot is there, the road your life has taken, and those little creatures appear faint and whimsical because you've traveled so far from them. But some of these creatures—certain crippled ones—do not speak out to you. They limp gravely across the past with hard, dead eyes and they stare at you with a question: What do you think of me now?

The Headmaster is a crippled figure. After seventy-six years I cannot love him. Something having to do with the awful sorrow of life has helped me forgive other people, and that helps me to forgive myself. But I haven't been able to forgive him.

I can see him sitting behind the yellow oak desk in the large classroom after the last class of the day, sitting on a platform slightly above us. It gave his dwarfed height a stature in front of the room full of young boys who waited. We assembled in that classroom before going out to the playing fields, and we waited for our name to

be called out. It meant we were going to be punished. The Headmaster enjoyed this ritual. He played his role like a cat, staring at us
for the longest time without blinking. His pale blue eyes and round
face were almost expressionless, but not quite. Something was there,
a faint emotion. Sometimes it suggested a hint of friendship. Maybe
today he wouldn't call out names, he'd tell a little story and we would
laugh and feel relief and gratitude. He liked telling little stories.
Then he called out a name.

"Holbrook."

He didn't say the name harshly. It was more like the sound of
someone who wanted to share something nice with you. A friendly
thing. It meant you had to line up outside his office and be punished. He never told you why.

When you entered his office, he would move about quietly in a
familiar way. He was not an imposing figure. He was short and ro-
tund and balding, and perhaps he thought of himself as benevolent,
a twin version of the mother and father you didn't have.

"You know what to do, Harold. Take down your pants." You
unbuckled your pants and let them fall.

"Both of them." You pulled down your underpants.

"Assume the position."

You took hold of the arms of a chair that had been neatly placed
for you and bent over. Meanwhile, he would be searching in the
closet for something. It was a one-by-three flat stick from a packing
crate, about three feet long. Probably pine. You waited while he got
this stick and then you held your breath while he moved across the
room toward you. Whack! Whack! Whack! Three. Whack! Four.
Whack! Five. You tried not to cry out, because the boys waiting
outside would hear that. Whack! Six. If you cried, he'd stop, but—
Whack! Seven. Am I bleeding? Maybe he'll stop if I cry—Whack!
Eight. A sob. Whack! Nine. Tears. Tears. Crying. It's over. He just
wanted the sound of crying.

"All right, Harold. You can go now. Pull up your pants."

Once, when I came out of the room, humiliation blinding me,
the piano teacher was waiting down the hall past the line of boys. I'd

Harold

forgotten about our lesson, and there she was in a doorway, searching my face with her eyes as I got close. Brown eyes, pools of softness. I could tell she had listened to my punishment. She held the door for me, and while I walked over to the piano and sat on the bench, she closed it. Then she sat beside me on a chair pulled up close. There was a pause, an emotional one, while she waited for me to balance myself on the brink of breaking down. I had been learning to play "America" two-handed, and I placed my hands on the keys and tried to remember the first note. Then I started to cry. The piano teacher put her arms around me and held me to her. It was an act of kindness I have remembered all of my life.

2

My father was at the front door and Grandpa wouldn't let him in. Their voices were strident, and my sister June and I sat on the floor of the living room, our play interrupted, holding our breath. Only a few days before, we had seen our father when he and our mother suddenly stepped out of our world of dreams and tap-danced for us in the archway of Grandpa's den. They were smiling and young and graceful, these strangers who lived in our heads, beautiful, carefree strangers to whom we belonged in some curious, embarrassing way.

And now one of them was shouting at Grandpa: "You son of a bitch, I'll kill you!"

The door slammed, the world lurched off center, and the hole of silence echoed with the fear that was thumping in our hearts. We sat in stillness and waited. Grandpa disappeared. There was no explanation.

Years later my sisters and I learned that soon after this explosion Grandpa had committed our father to the insane asylum in Taunton, Massachusetts. Our mother needed an operation, and he was asking Grandpa to give him the money. He was refused.

Grandfather was the spitting image of General "Black Jack" Pershing, the commander of the American army in World War I who'd got his name leading the cavalry of black troopers up San Juan Hill in the Spanish-American War. Grandfather looked like him, tall and straight and stern. He was our Rock of Gibraltar, and my sisters and I obeyed him. He had grown up in the little town of South Weymouth, a few miles south of Boston, and had just finished building this house for his mother when my sisters and I became homeless because our mother disappeared one day and our father followed her. We didn't know why they left. We were not told. At first they said we were "too young" to know, and as time went by, no one seemed to remember, but there were rumors, and they floated from one cousin to another in the quiet knowing of New England. Meanwhile, it was up to Grandma and Grandpa to raise us.

Grandma was very stylish. She and Grandpa lived in separate bedrooms in the big twenty-room house on Lake Avenue in Cleveland. My sisters and I were one, two, and three years old when our parents suddenly went away and our grandparents had to take us in. I'm told I was Grandma's favorite: "My blue-eyed baby boy," she called me. Grandma was famous for her hats, and she always sent her food back at Stouffer's restaurant because it was never done right. She had more than twenty pairs of shoes in her closet, but she did not want to repeat the experience of being a mother. She had done that and once was enough. Now she wanted to travel and drive around in her Buick and be complimented for her looks, especially her legs. So Grandpa took June and Alberta and me down to South Weymouth to raise us in the house he had built for his mother. Then he commuted between South Weymouth and Cleveland because he had shoe stores in Cleveland and Boston. Grandma stayed in the big house in Cleveland.

Grandpa's chair in South Weymouth was brown and the upholstery had a velvety feel, but tougher, more like a brush. It was near the fireplace in the small living room, and he would sit alone in that brown chair at night after we went to bed, smoking his cigar and sipping whiskey. He was born one year after the Civil War ended. As a boy of eleven he had quit school to help support his family and had secured a job in Boston at the United Shoe Machinery Company, cleaning spittoons and other things for a salary of fifty cents a week.

He had to ride the train into Boston and back every day and yet he was able to save enough out of the fifty cents to help the family. His goal was to become a salesman, and as he grew out of boyhood and began to work for the Stetson Shoe Company as a stock boy, he hounded his employer for a chance to prove himself. One day a salesman who was supposed to go on the road right away reported sick. My grandfather stepped forward, ready to go, so they sent him out. In 1919, I'm told, he became the first traveling salesman in America to sell a million dollars' worth of shoes.

He built a park across the street from our house in South Weymouth, just for my sisters and me. It had a goldfish pond, swings, a seesaw, a summerhouse, a tennis court, and a flagpole. On June 14, my sister Alberta's birthday and Flag Day, Grandpa would take us across the street holding the folded American flag and one of us would be given the privilege of raising it. Then we would place our right hands over our hearts and repeat after Grandpa,

> I pledge allegiance to the flag
> of the United States of America,
> and to the republic for which it stands,
> one nation, indivisible,
> with liberty and justice for all.

We would remain silent for a while, learning the meaning of reverence. It would stay with me for a lifetime.

The chain-link fence around the park was covered with red roses. The street came to a dead end at our house, and beyond it were woods and a field where we picked blueberries. Grandpa encouraged us to achieve things, so we set up a lemonade stand in front of the house, which also offered blueberries, but since it was a dead-end street the only customers we had were Pete Pillsbury's mother and Helen Vinal, whose mother gave her a nickel to spend on us. We went out of business fast, which did not please Grandpa.

Breakfast was at 7:00 a.m. It consisted of yellow cornmeal mush and milk. You were not late. Grandpa was dressed and freshly shaved, the odor of his shaving tonic spicing the morning. His hair was brushed into place, and so was ours. In the winter he wore tweedy things with little bristling fibers in them that were rough to the touch but gruffly friendly and warm. He favored knickers, big, full ones with high argyle stockings. In the summer he wore cotton suits and brown and white wingtip shoes. You did not talk at the table unless to respond to Grandpa. Sometimes Henry, our chauffeur, would be summoned right into the dining room and reprimanded for some off-course behavior. He was always in uniform, and I think he was a second or third cousin. In New England everyone seemed to be related distantly, and Henry looked a lot like my father, which was strange because it blurred my image of him.

Sometimes Grandpa would have too much Scotch whiskey for even his historic deeps to hold, and after Henry had driven him home from Boston he had the dangerous task of putting Grandpa to bed. Henry got battered up pretty bad sometimes and Grandpa would end the wrestling match by firing him. "You're fired, damn your soul!" would ring out in the sheltered stillness of night, but it was the Great Depression and jobs were scarce and Henry was back again in the morning ready for the breakfast-time court-martial.

"Henry, I've thought the matter over, and while your behavior last night was a disgrace, I have decided to hire you back for the good of your family. Warm up the LaSalle, we're going into Boston."

Sometimes Grandpa would take me into Boston with him, to the Copley Plaza Hotel on Copley Square, where he was given a shave and a manicure on Tuesdays and Thursdays in the formality of the hotel barbershop. As Henry swung the green LaSalle, ablaze with chrome and bearing Grandpa's initials on its doors, up to this elegant entrance, the uniformed doorman's hand would land on the door latch at precisely the moment the LaSalle's wheels paused, and his voice would boom out, "Mr. A.V. Welcome to the Copley, sir." Grandpa would push me gently out and shake the doorman's hand, leaving a large bill in it. "Make sure your children all have good shoes," he'd say. I stood there in awe of the doorman, a magnificent gold-braided creature whose face and hands were black, and he would peer at me with the smile of an old dog and say, "Harold, are we riding the merry-go-round today?"

The bar in the Copley was actually a merry-go-round. The bar was in the center and you sat on the perimeter while it spun around. Grandpa would leave me there with my counterfeit Scotch and soda (ginger ale) and I would sip it sagaciously and try not to fall off as the bar revolved. It was just a game, of course, but fun. The bartender would keep a wary eye on me in case I needed to be carried out, as some of his patrons did. Grandpa would be gone for quite a while (two Scotch and sodas for me) and then reappear looking fresh and trimmed, and we would drive home.

At night when I got into bed in my small room, Grandpa would come in and lower the top half of the window all the way down. He believed in fresh air. Then he would lean over my bed and lightly touch me on the head. "Good night, Buddy," he'd say. Later in the evening, when the night had grown still and every tiny sound was in the air, I felt his presence at the window, pushing it up again so that only a small opening was left. Then he moved silently away.

On Memorial Day, Grandpa would take us to Mount Hope Cemetery, on a rocky hill where his first wife and our great-grandfather and the rest of our people were buried. It was like that cemetery in the play *Our Town*, "on a hilltop, a windy hilltop." It was quiet up there, with the tender foliage of spring all around us and the sky above our heads a long way off, and this was the only time I saw Grandfather cry. As he stood by his father's grave, the tears rolled down his face while the silent agony of his life clutched at him. It was then I saw that life was not going to be a spring day. There was suffering ahead. It did not require that any words be spoken for me to see the face of what life had in store. I saw it in the anguish of Grandfather's tears.

When I look at pictures of me as a little boy I see a happy child with an impish look. It surprises me. Where did it come from? How could I have lived through the deprivation of having no mother and father, never knowing why they left, and then being sent away among strangers and the beatings in that school, and still look happy in those pictures? What was going on that made this possible? By today's standards I was what people call "an abused child." Were we tougher then? Did we expect less of life's honey on our daily bread? Is that it? A while ago my wife and I were watching some Hollywood toy person, fresh off drugs, pouring his heart out on television about being an abused child. I said, "My God, it just hit me! I was an abused child!"

"Yes, you were," said my wife.

"I never thought of it before."

"You were too busy surviving," she said.

Was it the image of my grandfather that kept me going? A survivor himself. Or was it the little acts of kindness that saved me? When the piano teacher put her arms around me and held me close—those moments? I saw the face of kindness then and perhaps that gave me hope. My sisters were to suffer much more than me.

3

In the summer of 1937, when I was twelve, Grandpa became ill. We never knew it because we were sent away to the Spalding farm in South Woodstock, Connecticut. Dr. Spalding was Grandpa's physician in South Weymouth and the Woodstock Spaldings were his cousins, and it was closer to home than the camp we'd been going to in Maine. We suspected nothing.

I loved the farm. Bare feet and bib overalls, cows to milk, cornfields, and a swimming hole. The farmhouse was already two hundred years old when we got there and had only two electric lights, a pump for water in the kitchen sink, and a big iron woodstove. There was a cold room where sides of meat and bacon hung and a crock to store the doughnuts Aunt Ruby served up out of a cast-iron cauldron of boiling oil on the stove. She'd pluck the glistening doughnuts out with a long, charred stick and drop them into our outstretched hands, and we'd bounce this scalding, greasy delight around until it wouldn't burn our mouths and then we ate it. There is nothing in this world I have ever tasted in the finest restaurants around the globe that could match the heavenly taste of those doughnuts.

That summer on the Spalding farm came to an alarming end when we arrived home and found the door to Grandpa's room closed to mute the sounds of his agony. The doctor and nurses would open his door and for one frightening moment we would hear the full-out cries of our great soldier in the grip of battle with death, and then the door closed again. He faced that dark angel with curses and disbelief. His bedroom had twin beds and he was moved from one bed to the other all day and night as he drenched the sheets with the sweat of his relentless torture. Sometimes he slept. Or the pain receded for a brief term. We lingered outside the door, sick with fright, listening for the sounds of our champion at bay.

June and I were sent away before Grandpa died. Only Alberta stayed, with our housekeeper, Nettie Wigton, in charge of her. June and I were to go to Cleveland and stay with strangers while Grandma came to South Weymouth to oversee those last days, to make preparations, and to search for the will.

Before we left I was brought in to say goodbye. It was not put to me like that, but when I stood outside the door of Grandfather's room and waited, I knew what this moment would mean to me for the rest of my life. Goodbye, Grandpa. Goodbye, my captain. He was lying on the closer twin bed, his head propped up on a pillow, and he was not smiling. He was past any effort of dissembling. He was looking toward me, and he reached out his hand.

"Come here, Harold."

I went and took it. It was hard and smooth. His eyes burned into mine, fierce with intent.

"Promise me something."

"Yes, Grandpa."

"I want you to promise me that you will go to Culver Military Academy. Will you promise me?"

"Yes, Grandpa. I promise."

"You're a good boy." His grip on my hand was so powerful it was as if he never let go. Then they took me out of the room. I know now why Grandpa wanted me to make that promise. It was to save my life.

In Cleveland, June and I were enrolled for the year at St. Augustine Academy, a Catholic school far down Lake Avenue near Lakewood Park. And while Grandma remained in South Weymouth for Grandfather's last days, we were sent to live with some people who were friends of Grandma's housekeeper, Francis. I forget their names. They lived in a substantial but much more modest home than Grandma's twenty-room mansion, not in a fancy part of town, and perhaps this was the source of the sourness with which the man of the house received us. He made it clear we were unwelcome. His wife was kind enough, considering the burden our coming had laid upon her home, and their young son was a decent boy. But the man was a bear trap ready to spring, so we crept around him.

The new school was a major diversion. I had to put in my eighth grade there before I could go to high school at Culver, and since we were not Catholics I noticed a lot of strange things about St. Augustine. The grounds were very nice and there were buildings on them that looked like castles, but I kept seeing so many statues of a woman with her head tilted down, sometimes looking at a baby, that it gave the whole place a feeling of sadness. She seemed to be slightly unhappy, this woman, although if you got close enough, there might be a tiny, sweet smile lurking under the stone cloth that hung over her head. I was twelve, and I remember thinking, Could this be my mother?

There were real people called nuns all over the place, with real cloths over their heads, black cloths that hung over stiff white picture frames resembling starched collars that covered everything except their foreheads, eyes, noses, mouths, and chins. Everything else was black from the shoulders down. Not exactly a dress, more like a tent cinched in at the waist, and there would be a long, beaded chain around their necks with a cross at the bottom of it. Some of these women appeared to be pretty ferocious. Since all that showed was their faces, I learned to read their disposition from their eyes and mouths. They were called Sisters and I had to learn to say that to them, too.

There was a young one named Sister Ernestine and her face was kind. It was pretty, too. It made calling her "Sister" a pleasant experience, not awkward at all, because the look in her eyes took all the awkwardness away. I wished she really was my sister or maybe my mother, because I could see in her face that she was a very nice, kind, soft person. I found out that Sisters couldn't be mothers, but I'll bet she could have been a nice one.

One evening at the house where we lived with the strangers, it was the seventh of October, we were having dinner and the man of the house was angry at June. An empty jar of chocolate sauce had been found under her bed and the man was accusing June with very near to white fury in his voice.

"You will be punished. This is stealing! You will stay in your room for a week on bread and water."

A silence followed, with embarrassment in it. June's head was unbowed. She did not apologize. The man picked up his evening newspaper and said, "Oh, by the way. You'll probably be interested in this. 'Stetson Shoe Dealer Dies.'" Then he read Grandpa's obituary to us.

June began to scream. Her screams were horrible, torn out of her heart. She broke from the table and ran into the night, disregarding the man's furious orders to "Get back in here!" I ran past him and called for her to wait for me, but she was lost in the neighborhood shadows. The man ordered me inside. I turned on him with an authority I didn't know I had: "I'm going to find my sister!" I sounded like Grandfather. I would have killed the man where he stood. He saw it and retired.

I looked for June in the maze of neighborhood streets, under a cold moon, and I finally found her. She would not stop sobbing. We wandered together until the terrible shock began to go away and silence took over.

"Look at the stars, Harold," she said. "You see how bright they are? Grandpa is up there and he sees us."

That is how we found out Grandpa died. The next morning my first class at St. Augustine was with Sister Ernestine. She always started it off with a prayer. When the class was assembled, she waited until it was quiet. Then she said, "This morning we are going to say a prayer for Harold's grandfather who has gone to heaven." It was another act of kindness I would remember.

I never got a chance to grieve over Grandfather's death. The cold hearth ruled over by the man did not allow for it. This haunting grief stayed inside me. Nor did I ever learn, beyond rumors hinted at by ancient aunts, what took place down there in South Weymouth when Grandpa died. We were not brought up to ask such questions. Nettie was quickly dismissed by Grandma, and my father's brother, Uncle Al, and his wife, Aunt Merce, arrived. There was some problem about the will or finding it, something like that, but nobody ever discussed it with us. We were too young.

Our father never showed up at the deathbed, of course, having been put away in the insane asylum. Our mother didn't seem to exist at all. She had tap-danced her way into infinity. Or Hollywood, which is where she was last sighted. Our father eventually got out of the asylum, since he'd never been pathologically insane in the first place, whereupon he took to the road, riding the rails to California in search of my mother. He nearly froze to death under a boxcar going over the Rockies. From time to time he sent a message by Western Union, like the father in that Tennessee Williams play who fell in love with long distance. It usually read "Am broke. Send $50 General Delivery Phoenix. Harold." We had the same name, all the way through, too: Harold Rowe Holbrook. I'm Junior. I hoped that was as far as I would follow in his footsteps. The telegram came to Grandma, who always sent him the $50. There was a picture of him in her room. He was tall and thin and handsome, with dark eyebrows like Henry Fonda's, and he was wearing white flannels and a white sweater and his dark hair was slicked down. He had one hand in his pocket. He looked clean, not like someone who sent a telegram requesting $50. I didn't know what to make of this movie star father who looked like Henry Fonda and was dressed in white. Where was he? Did I look like him? Did I want to see him? Every time a telegram came from Phoenix, Fairbanks, or Juarez, I told myself, "Don't go crazy or you'll end up like him."

Once, I remember seeing him outside the house in Cleveland fighting with my uncle Al. I must have been very young, because I was playing with my brown teddy bear. Grandpa sometimes took us to Cleveland for a visit when we were young children still living in South Weymouth and I played with Teddy in the linen closet, where

Harold

I loved to hide in one of the cabinets. The closet had a window at the end and on this particular day I heard shouting, so I got up and peered out the window and there was my father throwing punches at Uncle Al and cursing him. My father was winning because he was wildly aggressive, like a crazy person, his arms swinging like windmills, and Uncle Al couldn't get out of the way. Then the police came and took my father away. Back to the asylum? All I knew was that he was gone. We were not encouraged to ask questions.

Now Grandpa was gone, too, and we were back in Cleveland. Francis was there with her gray hair combed straight back and her mouth a straight line from side to side. The house was big and empty and there was no more grief in it for Grandpa than there had been at the man's house. All I could do was go upstairs to Grandpa's big bedroom and bath and the friendly den that still smelled of his cigar smoke and remember him. On the other side of the wide balcony above a formal staircase was Grandma's bedroom and closets and bathroom, and beyond that, down a long hallway past the linen closet, were two maids' rooms over the garage. Francis, the prison guard, occupied one and the other was mine. Back in the middle of the house, opposite Grandma's room and facing Lake Erie, was a large room with a heavy four-poster bed. This was June and Alberta's room. It was here that Grandma assembled us when she returned with Alberta from the funeral in South Weymouth. An air of suspense tainted the room.

"I want to tell you children something. I do not like girls. I have loved this little boy ever since I saw him in the hospital, my blue-eyed baby boy. I will do the best I can for you, but I do not like girls."

I remember the shame and disgrace I felt for all of us. I suppose she was trying to be honest with us, and she must have felt frightened and overwhelmed, but it was the worst thing she could have said. A sense of survival set in from that moment on. Survival of the fittest. It was a furtive thing, a layer of desperation underneath our daily existence, like quicksand. We were bound together in the name of brother and sisters and the knowledge we had of one another's fears and sorrows, but on that day we were sent forth upon our private journeys, looking for safety and looking for love.

June and Alberta were also at St. Augustine that year, but I don't remember spending much time with them. They were girls, and when they were with other girls they became different people. Girls laughed too much and looked as if they had secrets against boys and that made boys nervous, so for my sisters and me it was almost like going to different schools. But there was one girl who was different. She was quiet. She had dark, interested eyes and dark hair and her face was in repose most of the time. She had small curves on her body and I found it hard not to look at her a lot. Sometimes I saw she was looking at me. One time she smiled. I noticed she walked home in the same direction as I did and one day we happened to leave at the same time, so we walked together. I had begun to consider the idea of asking her to go to the movies. I'd never had a date with a girl and I had just turned thirteen years old. It was time. Now or never.

"Uh."

She smiled at me. "Yes?"

"Do you like the movies?"

"Sometimes."

"Would you go to a movie with me?"

"When?"

"Saturday."

"I think so, but I have to ask my father."

I hadn't thought that far ahead. I had to ask Grandma, and that took a measure of courage, too. I was her blue-eyed baby boy and wise enough at thirteen to know she did not expect competition.

She was taking me out to Stouffer's with her that night. The girls had misbehaved and were being punished by not being allowed to go, which was no punishment at all to June and Alberta. They made their own fun. So I sat in a chair in Grandma's room while she preened herself in front of the mirror, dressed in a flimsy kimono, and curled her hair with the hot iron, spitting on her fingers to test its heat.

"Grandma, I want to go to the movies this Saturday."

"Which movie do you want to see?"

"I mean with a girl."

"A girl? What girl?"

"A girl at school."

"Who is she?"

"She's a nice girl. She said she had to ask her father, so I'm asking you, too."

"What's her father's name?"

"I think it's Mr. Rodzinski."

"That sounds Jewish. What does he do?"

"I think he's a bandleader. He has a band."

"You want to go to the movies with the daughter of a kike bandleader?"

"Yes, Grandma."

"Well. We'll see."

It turned out that Mr. Artur Rodzinski was the conductor of the Cleveland Philharmonic Orchestra, a civic resource beyond the cultural summits of my family's adventuring, but clearly on a higher social plane than Harry James, so I was allowed to go.

This brings me to the astounding realization that nobody ever read books in my family. If they did, books were never mentioned. Nor did they go to concerts or the theater and certainly not the ballet. They lived in a limbo world apart from such foolish fancies, and as I was to learn years later, so does much of America. Our mother and father danced for us and must have gone to the theater and done all kinds of exciting things, but that was never talked about. They were strangers. Our mother was never mentioned. Was it because she was in show business? Because she danced? Because she was different and that was an embarrassment? And so was my father, because he did not want to go into the shoe business. Did they put him away because he was different?

The creative urge is an impish shadow that falls across a child's path as if by accident, giving some credence to the notion that it is subversive. Thus it was that I began to dance like Fred Astaire. My performances were secret and took place in the basement. A recreation room was down there with a shiny varnished floor thirty feet long and a windup Victrola sitting alone on the dance floor. And there was a spooky, impish bonus: an album of records belonging to my mother. The day I made this discovery I plucked one out of its sleeve, put it on the turntable, and cranked up His Master's Voice. The glorious sound of a man singing "My Blue Heaven" poured out of the horn-shaped speaker that spread like a crown above this magic box.

There was no one around. I started to move, spinning and pirouetting in wild arcs across the polished floor. As I gave myself up to the thrill of it, I performed feats of creative contortion that would have been impossible had anyone been watching. It was just me, Fred, and "My Blue Heaven."

Since the recreation room was at the far end of the enormous cellar running the length of the house, my clandestine recitals remained secret for some time. Then June caught me at it and started to riffle through our mother's record collection in wonder and sober delight. When this secret trove was revealed to Alberta, they both spent hours listening to the collection, knowing that our mother's hands had held these records and that she had danced to them.

The recreation room became a kind of hiding place for us, a place to dream things and pretend, where we spent time alone or with each other. Grandma never came down there, nor did Francis.

There was a door in one wall. It was always locked and we never gave it a thought. One day I found it open. So I went in, and when I snapped on the light I saw that it was a trunk room and right in front of me was a wardrobe trunk standing open. It was upright, with clothes on one side hung on special little hangers, a woman's clothes. On the right side were drawers, gray and quite deep. I stared at this strange sight for a while, wondering whose trunk it was and why it was open. Then I pulled out one of the drawers.

Baby shoes, baby clothes, little silver spoons and forks, two little silver cups. On one cup was engraved the word "Sunshine." Could that be me? I opened another drawer and found some long, rolled-up pictures of pretty women in a chorus line onstage. They were bending over, holding their knees, and smiling. They didn't have much on. Under one of the women was a little arrow. More pictures unrolled. The woman above the arrow was onstage with a man and she was holding a guitar. The name Joe Penner was written in a margin and that had a familiar sound. One of the big pictures had a caption: "George White Scandals." There were letters, a batch of them tied together with a blue ribbon. The reality of what I had discovered began to dawn on me. I slipped a letter out and read "Dear Aileen . . ." That was my mother! I looked for my father's name at the bottom of the letter and it wasn't there. There was another man's name. Russ.

These were my mother's things. This was her trunk. She was on the stage. She was in a big show about "Scandals" and I had never been told. She was in show business. That's why she had danced for us in the archway, because she was on the stage! Our mother! Was our father on the stage, too? Who was the man who wrote these letters my mother kept with a blue ribbon around them? I started to read the one in my hand. It was very personal, about love, and I was embarrassed so I stopped. I felt like a thief stealing into my mother's life. These people were strangers.

4

Our curiosity had been let loose and we dared to ask questions and Grandma loved to talk. She began to tell us stories about these strangers who brought us into the world. The problem for me was—should I believe them?

We had lived in a house on Chase Avenue in Cleveland that Grandpa had bought for our mother and father. They were just kids when they married, my mother eighteen and my father twenty. A first child, a boy, died. Then in fast succession came June, me, Alberta. By the time she was twenty-four our mother had three children, but it was the Roaring Twenties and my parents wanted to have fun. Grandpa got them a car with a rumble seat, and they bought a little pig, put it in the rumble seat, dropped their three young babies off at our grandparents', and left for a Florida vacation. Finally our grandfather became fed up with his youngest son's irresponsibility and sent him to Pittsburgh to work in the shoe store he owned there. He was put to work in the stockroom, and when the manager went down there to check on him, Dad was pushing a Stetson shoe around in a bucket of water to see if it would float. That sent him back to Cleveland.

And then one fine day our parents disappeared. According to Grandma, they left us in our playpen in diapers and little pants, which were full when she discovered us. We had been discarded. I was two, Alberta and June were one and three, so she hauled us over to the big house and the Chase Avenue version of our lives slid away.

Harold

Beyond those revelations Grandma's memory closed down. We knew there was more stuff hiding away, but we were to spend the rest of our lives looking for pieces that would complete a picture. I found out years later from our mother's brother in Opa-locka, Florida, that she went to New York and landed a job with the Ziegfeld Follies. When the stage manager began messing with her body, she quit, went around the block, and got a job with George White's Scandals. She must have been pretty irresistible, our mother. I saw our uncle Dick only a couple of times and his collection of missing puzzle pieces didn't connect more than a couple of strays, so that trail disappeared, but I always wondered if he knew where she was. Of course he did.

We did find out from him that our mother's last name was Davenport and she came from Columbus, Ohio, where she and Dick were born. My father was born there, too, and so was his older brother, Uncle Al, and there was a rumor, whizzing like a bee you aren't sure you heard go by, that my mother was Uncle Allen's property first and that our father stole her away from him, and I think the fight on the front lawn when the police dragged Dad away adds a stroke of credibility to the story. Uncle Al was a kindly and patient man and my father was clearly a wildcat. There must have been some hot times going on there in Columbus, and why no one has ever seen fit to describe them to us is a mystery so sad it is foolish. Or so foolish it is sad. What in hell were they hiding?

It would be fair to ask why I didn't spend a lifetime hunting for my mother. Because very early on I let her go. She was a ghost, she had chosen to disappear. She had a mission, mysterious though it was, and I had a mission, too. Mine was to save Harold, and that sometimes demanded risk, which was okay because some of our father's wildness had found its way into his children's genes, particularly June's and mine. Like our father, we hopped freight trains. This could seem a bit off balance for kids living in a twenty-room mansion on Lake Avenue, but that's what we did and it was no doubt the origin for what would become my "suicide impulse." We climbed on the Nickel Plate Railroad boxcars on our side of the high trestle across the gorge of the Rocky River when the engine stopped to take on water on the other side, and we hung on to the iron ladder rungs as the train lurched forward over the two-hundred-foot-high chasm, picking up speed. Then we jumped off when we cleared the gorge. We had to hit the cinders running and roll. Alberta rarely joined us, but June's wild spirit inspired me to go along. One time we hung off the trestle itself while the train went by above us. If it seems strange that I would embrace these wild impulses while fearing to follow in my father's footsteps, you have to remember that insanity leaks down from generation to generation, no matter how sober you try to look later on.

Around my thirteenth birthday our father reappeared in Cleveland for an extended stay. His new address was the insane asylum on Carnegie Avenue, east of downtown. He was lodged on the third floor in a very large room lined with cots perpendicular to the walls, and his immediate family were a crew of awkward-looking men, partially shaved, who mumbled or grunted or stared silently at something called Space. We always visited Dad with Grandma and had to pass through two locked doors made of prison bars to get to him. Standing there with Grandma while the guard unlocked the barred doors, I wondered if I would end up behind them someday, like him. Then we walked down the length of a big room where he had his bed by the window and gave him his carton of Lucky Strike cigarettes. That quickly felt like the purpose of the visit, so there wasn't much conversation and he seemed as detached as we were and quite normal. Grandma treated the encounter as if we were in a college instead of an asylum. When we left I hoped insanity was not hereditary and wondered why my father sometimes seemed so sane.

While Dad was in the asylum I went off to Culver Military Academy. Off among the boys again, and behind gates, too. Grandma got the 1938 dark green Buick Special coupe packed up with our bags and we pulled out of the driveway and onto Lake Avenue. The Buick purred beautifully, proud that it had never gone a week without having its engine dusted and inspected for flaws. At the first intersection, traffic stalled while she cautiously rolled across no-man's-land, carefully observed by nervous motorists who had dared once to challenge her for the right-of-way. We crawled across the state of Ohio, stopping for the night at Bowling Green. The next day we entered the state of Indiana and completed our journey to Culver, covering 178 miles in eight hours.

Once again I was fated to be the youngest boy in school. We rolled through the academy's gates and into a world of massive brick buildings resembling fortresses with openings on the roof for people to shoot at you. They were decorated with stonework and carved quotations from Chaucer, Shakespeare, and other giants of history. The place had a serious look. We were supposed to locate South Barracks. Grandma drew up alongside a young man in uniform who cantered a step to the left for safety and snapped off a salute.

"Ma'am?"

"Young man, could you direct us to South Barracks?"

"Yes, ma'am. It's directly in front of you."

"Thank you. This is Harold, my blue-eyed baby boy. He's going to live in South Barracks."

"Grandma, could we—"

"We've driven all the way from Cleveland. Harold's father and his uncle went to Culver quite a while ago—"

"Grandma, let's just go—"

"But they did not graduate, because of the war, I think. Harold's father played the bugle here—"

"Grandma—"

"To wake the boys up in the morning."

"Yes, ma'am."

"Grandma—"

"Do you play an instrument?"

"No, ma'am, I'm in the cavalry."

"Goodbye, young man."

"Goodbye, ma'am. Goodbye, Harold."

The cavalry. My God. I had shrunk about nine inches by the time he took his merciful departure and allowed us to proceed to South Barracks.

"Grandma, promise me something."

"Yes, Harold."

"Don't call me your blue-eyed baby boy again in front of any of these cadets. You'll ruin me."

"I want them to know who you are and to be nice to you."

"Okay. But don't say the blue-eyed baby stuff, please!"

At the entrance a short, round man in a different kind of uniform, a brown one that looked more like the real army, introduced himself as Colonel Johnson. He was in charge of South Barracks. I understood that meant he was in charge of me. He had awfully round blue eyes, but they looked friendly.

"Harold, you will be known as Cadet Holbrook from now on, and when you address me you will say 'sir' and salute."

"Yes, sir."

"Do you know how to salute, Cadet Holbrook?"

I had been practicing this, so I said, "Yes, sir."

"Let's see you do it."

I snapped off the best salute I had, but nearly scooped my eye out.

"We're going to have to practice that, Cadet."

Grandma wanted to come up and see my room and meet all the boys. My heart sank like a dying swan until Colonel Johnson told her that she was not allowed in the barracks and we could say our good-byes now. Then he discreetly moved away. Grandma began to cry.

"Please, Gram, don't cry. I'll be fine. Don't worry."

"Will you miss me?"

"Yes, I will." I gave her a hug and she clung to me as if I were going into battle, and then I followed Colonel Johnson inside.

I think it was then that I began to know with an absolute certainty that there was not going to be anyone I could safely count on. I was a soldier now on a solo mission of survival. My sisters had already begun to kick up their heels, and I sensed they were headed for trouble while I would be caged in a military school and beyond help to them. Grandma herself was a subtle threat. Her need to be admired and courted was not exactly healthy for a young boy. I suspected it had weakened my father. Before we went out to dinner or a movie together, she liked to have me sit in her bedroom and wait on her while she finished her makeup. I was her date. I waited in a chair under the fringed standing lamp while she cavorted around her bedroom in a flimsy flowered robe over her pink corset and bloomers and then perched on the little bench before her makeup table and its mirror. She lovingly curled her hair with a hot iron, rouged her face and powdered it, and smeared on a layer of red-on-red lipstick with a twisting motion that looked as if she were garroting herself. I was trapped there, sometimes for nearly an hour, while she mused with pursed lips about this and that. Grandpa was right. "Promise me you'll go to Culver."

At Culver I was a plebe, a first-year nonperson subject to the tongue-lashing and simple sadism that teenage boys in charge of younger teenage boys take pleasure in. You had to slam yourself against the wall at stiff attention, eyes straight ahead, when one of them passed by. If it was a first classman he could crack you on the head with his heavy first class signet ring right on the bone at the very apex of your skull. As in the case with the Headmaster, there never seemed to be a reason for the punishment except one so flimsy as to be a mockery.

In chapel on Sunday mornings we sat on metal folding chairs during the service, upperclassmen behind the rows of plebes, who were required to sit upright, shoulders down and back, and your spine could not touch the chair. If it did, if you relaxed and let it touch, the hard toe of a shoe cocked behind you dug into your spine. If a vertebra was dislodged a little, we would not notice it until we grew up.

Our rooms at Culver were small and efficient, not unlike a ship's cabin. It was you and your roommate. I was in Company C, Infantry. The rest of the cadet corps were in Company A, B, or D and Artillery and Cavalry. Cavalry was famously represented by the Black Horse Troop, which paraded down Pennsylvania Avenue at the inauguration of every president of the United States. The school was on a lake, a beautiful big lake with the Indian name Maxinkuckee, and had tennis courts, a ski jump, a golf course, an indoor polo field,

and a landing strip for airplanes. Our school was not training ama-
teurs. There was a big war on the horizon. In my freshman year, our
Regimental Commander was Willis Maxon, star of the football team,
boxing team, and track team. Maxon was killed in the war and cited
for bravery. His brother, Danny, became our Company Commander
and finally Regimental Commander himself. He was killed in the war.
Many of these boys would be killed in the war. Culver was not a
place for sissies.

I joined the cross-country team. The mile I had run five years
before when the Headmaster rewarded me with a slug to the face
and a kick in the balls had never left my mind. I signed on to be a
distance runner, and from that moment on, endurance became a
part of my life. It probably saved my life, too.

Our coach was Mike Carpenter, not a man you forgot. Tall, for-
mer football star from fabled Alabama, steel-blue eyes that shrouded
his inner life—a man who measured you and waited. I wanted to do
well for him. He was also coach of the undefeated track team and I
wanted to run the mile for him come spring.

Meanwhile, the cross-country course was a two-mile endurance
run in which you became your own torture chamber. It started and
finished between the halves of the football game on Saturday. We
sprang out in a jagged line from under the far goalposts and swarmed
across the football field with long, easy strides, unless you were
short, and shouldered each other for early positions while crossing
the far playing fields of Culver and heading for ski jump hill and the
upland golf course. As a freshman runner leaned into that hill, the
realization dawned on him that he should have joined the golf team.
After the sand traps and trees came the airfield, and here comes the
ski jump hill again. Going down was dangerous. Waning strength
caused the legs to flop around like beheaded hens, and if a spiked
shoe hit the edge of a deep rut, snap went the ankle.

Now came the playing fields. This was the crucible. In the distance was the football field, the final hundred yards where the halftime football fans enjoyed watching you gasp out your last breath. If
you were way behind, this was where you dared not let the last run-

ner in the race pass you before you passed the finish line and then passed out. I never passed out. That may be why I didn't win.

In the spring I went out for track. I knew Mike Carpenter was pleased about that because he kept his eye on me while I ran, even when I finished a full lap behind everyone in the mile. But I kept running, a skinny, long-legged version of Ichabod Crane, ribs sticking out, hair flying, giving what I thought was my all. When I finished, Mike gave me a wordless cuff and studied me a bit. He began taking me on the road trips when we ran at other schools and still I came in a lap behind. I got my own applause while my teammates were putting on their sweat suits. Our team captain, MacIntyre, a tall, thin, elegant athlete, began to talk to me. He liked me. I belonged to the team. I was part of something. This had never happened before.

We had cultural events at Culver, too. Rather famous people came and talked to us about One World or some other thoughtful topic, and one day the Indianapolis Symphony Orchestra came to play for us. Being bored to death by classical music was something we looked forward to with dread, a dread compounded by the vision of being kicked in the spine when the torture got to be so tedious that we slumped back in our folding chairs. But then I heard there were a hundred of them. One hundred musicians all in one place, banging out thunderclaps of music—that could be a funny sight!

When the time came, we filed into the gymnasium, which doubled as the school chapel and concert hall, and sat on the metal folding chairs. There they were, one hundred of them dressed in black, like crows gathered to plunder a cornfield. Two women were among them; the one embracing a big harp was pretty. The other one had a big violin between her legs. My attention was captured by them until a little man came out, dressed in black, with long tails on his coat and a thin white stick in his hand. Someone snickered and you could hear the toe of a shoe striking solid vertebrae, followed by a groan. The man with the stick bowed. A rattling applause spread through our ranks. Then he turned and raised his white stick. You could hear a pin drop. Then the stick moved.

Music began. Gentle and soft and strangely grand. I had never heard anything like it before. It rose and floated like visions in a dream, pouring over me sounds that took my boyish heart and held it like a bird. I soared with it, I flew in great arcs and circles, I rose higher and higher and then swooped down. I hovered and waited. With one more burst of purest flight the music brought me gently down and landed. That evening a desire awoke in me. I had danced to my mother's records secretly, out of sight. Now I secretly began to write poetry. The man with the little stick and his hundred musicians had offered me one more act of kindness.

5

The year I entered Culver, June was enrolled at Laurel School in Shaker Heights. It was the premier all-girls school in Cleveland and for that year June did well. Alberta continued at St. Augustine and they saw each other on weekends when June came home. It looked as if things might work out.

In the summer Alberta and I went back to the Spalding farm in South Woodstock. June was to stay with Great-aunt Anna at her two-hundred-year-old farmhouse in Halifax, down toward Cape Cod. When Aunt Anna and her chauffeur drove Alberta and me to South Woodstock I was already wearing my new farmer overalls. Aunt Ruby came out of the house with a large pair of scissors. She cut off one pant leg below the knee, then cut off the bottom of the other one so it would unravel, and I gave her my shoes. I never wore shoes again all summer. It was a chicken farm with eight thousand chickens on it, so I gave up worrying about where I was stepping. My feet were part of the earth.

We called the Spaldings Aunt Ruby and Uncle Sabe. Aunt Ruby was a small, wiry woman with a hornet's temper and a well-worn ruddy face. But her brown eyes could smile so nice. She worked hard from dawn till night, cooking and housekeeping, and she stood for no nonsense from anyone, including her husband. Uncle Sabe worked in the mornings, milking the cow and wringing a chicken's neck and plucking it for dinner, but in the afternoons he sat next to the radio with his glasses way up on his weathered forehead and listened to the Boston Red Sox play baseball. He was a big man with blue eyes that twinkled when he was not mad at Aunt Ruby or over a defeat of the Boston Red Sox.

Their son, Paul, was six years older than me, with a medium but powerful physique. He could lift one end of a car by himself. Paul worked from dawn to dinnertime in the fields, often on a homemade tractor assembled from a Model T Ford and spare parts. If he wasn't in the cornfields or mowing hay, he was in the chicken coops or incubator barn or fixing something. He was a taskmaster when he allowed us to help, but he taught us by leading and he was never unkind. I don't think he knew how to be unkind. Uncle Sabe was hard on him sometimes and Paul spoke his mind, but he always did the job. I learned how to work from watching Paul.

In those days a new Ford cost $666, which the Spaldings could not afford. Paul built what he needed out of secondhand cars. He bought a 1928 Buick for $25, cut the top half and the backseat off, then built a truck bed and attached it behind the front seat. That was our farm truck. I learned to drive on it and the Model T tractor, which has worried people ever since.

We shopped very rarely in stores, except to buy flour and sugar and such, because we lived off the land and ate like lions. In the morning we had plate-size flapjacks with melting butter and maple syrup, plus eggs and bacon or sausages. Alberta had a room to herself upstairs and Paul and I slept in the attic. My bed was under the eaves near a window. We climbed up there by a narrow little staircase off the kitchen and if there were mice running around, we paid them no heed as long as they kept out of the way. We rose early and went to bed early; our day was defined by the sun. In the evenings before bedtime we all sat out on the porches that ran around two sides of the old farmhouse and waved at people in the cars as they passed by. They were all friends. The sun fell slowly, the dusk crept in, and then the dark took over and we went to bed. These memories would fill up my actor's well in later years. Huckleberry Finn was no stranger to me because I felt a kinship with people who came from the backcountry and from villages on a river or a stream.

We had a dog named Spot, a lanky white English setter with black spots, and a swimming hole made by nature and the spring floods. At spring thaw when the ice broke up, the brook rose and surged mightily, and all that ice and debris chewed into a bend in the lower pasture, tore at it, and gouged it out deeper and deeper, and having spent its fury, it spilled out over a gravelly bar where you could sit in the summer sun and pick up brown pebbles. The hole in the bend, dug in the wildness of March, was twelve feet deep, a wonderful place to dive into. Paul built us a diving board, a long, limber plank a foot wide, sawn from a length of fallen timber. Sometimes bloodsuckers hung from us when we surfaced and we scraped them off each other with our fingernails. But that was all part of a summer's day.

On the Fourth of July and Labor Day we had a big family feast outdoors to which cousins, uncles, aunts, brothers and sisters, and their children were invited. We ate outdoors on long planks laid across sawhorses and covered with rolls of white butcher paper. It was not allowed to rain. Everyone brought some portion of the dinner and you had to roll over and die in place when the meal was over.

On one of these holiday extravaganzas Aunt Anna and Cousin Aaron dropped by to observe how Alberta and I were getting along in the country. Paul was all dressed up for the holiday in white pants and a clean white shirt. I decided that a swimming exhibition would be the most impressive way for me to show off in front of Aunt Anna and Aaron, and I had an evil little plan in mind to climax the event. I was very good at holding my breath. I'd gone two minutes and fifty seconds sitting on a log at the bottom of the swimming hole. That log had a vertical limb with a point on it sticking straight up, just a wee bit to the right of the diving board, so your dive had to be aimed straight or you would be forever impaled at the bottom of the swimming hole. I bounced on the end of the board for a bit, to show them how high it could fling me, and did a few jackknifes and somersaults and plowed a foamy wake across the hole to give them a look at my speed.

"That's enough, Harold," said Aunt Anna. "That's very good, but you should come out now. You're making Auntie very nervous."

I scrambled up the bank and leapt onto the diving board. "Just one more dive, Aunt Anna. Aaron, watch this."

Paul edged closer to the water's brink, having felt the cool shadow of a disaster passing over him, and Aaron sidled up near him, sensing the same. I took a running start and catapulted off the board like the ball from a howitzer, spreading my arms in a beautiful swan dive. Then I knifed into the water. Ripples spread out in repeating circles from the point of entry and stillness began to reign. No sign of me. I was down below sitting on the log and holding on to the vertical spear to keep my movements to a minimum. I knew Paul was up there quite aware of what I was doing, but I had taken a very big breath.

"Where is Harold?" said Aunt Anna.

"Hasn't come up," said Paul.

"He should have come up by now," said Aaron.

"I'm so-o-o nervous," said Aunt Anna.

They waited some more while the ripples disappeared and only the black surface of the swimming hole remained for contemplation.

"Don't worry," said Paul, "there's a log down there and he's sitting on it."

"Why?" said Aunt Anna.

"Why is he sitting on a log underwater?" said Aaron.

"I think Harold wants to show you how long he can hold his breath," said Paul.

"Harold!" cried out Aunt Anna. "Come up, come up. You're making Auntie much too nervous, dear."

"How long has he been under?"

"Maybe a minute and a half. He'll be up soon," said Paul.

"What if he doesn't come up?" said Aaron.

"He will. He can hold his—"

"Harold!" shrieked Aunt Anna. "Come up out of there right now. Auntie is going to leave if you don't come up!"

Other people had drifted close. Paul was out on the end of the board, splendid in his white shirt and pants.

"What's the matter?" said an uncle.

"It's Harold. He might be drowning," said a cousin.

"Isn't anybody going to jump in and get him?" said someone's sister.

"Harold, Harold, Harold!" shrieked Aunt Anna.

"Somebody go in after him," said an uncle or an aunt.

"He's been down there for two minutes now, he's caught on something."

"Harold, get out of there," shouted Paul. "This is not a joke anymore."

"Help! Harold! Harold!"

"He's drowning for sure."

A grim decision settled over Paul's countenance. He was out on the end of the diving board and there was only one thing left for him to do. Aunt Anna was going into hysterics, falling backward into Aaron's arms. Aunt Ruby stepped forward like a sergeant major, her face a mask of anxiety being stalked by the certain knowledge that I was down there, ready to pop to the surface, smiling. But better safe than sorry, as the saying goes.

"Jump in, Paul," she said. And in he dove. When the impact hit the surface above me, I let go of the log and rose to the land of the living.

I did not get a hero's welcome. I was blasphemed pretty hard by everybody, especially Paul when he dragged himself out of the water with his clothes mulched around his body.

"Harold, you're going to pay for this," he said. But I don't think he ever collected.

Those summers on the farm were the happiest times of my youth. The surroundings offered me the grandest opportunity to open up my imagination, to invent things with simple tools, and to dream. Looking back now, I see something else I've been unaware of all these years: I was a mischievous child. I liked to shock people. Show off. I think the acting bug first bit me back there on the farm where I was free. I wanted to attract attention when pursuing my adventures because it added the elements of excitement and danger and hunger for approval. Aunt Ruby's was hard to win and I tried to win it. She could be critical and abrasive. June disliked her and this dislike became mutual, so June did not return to the farm the second summer. June gave the world a clear message about where she stood and she did not waver when she took a stand. I wavered. I wanted people to like me so much that I experimented with behavior that would make that happen. With Aunt Ruby, something clicked between us because I refused to be put off by her sandpapery nature. I praised her food by eating lots of it. I hugged her whenever I could whether she liked it or not, and I knew she liked it, and I sought her praise for my projects around the farm. She became my friend.

When I got back to Culver that fall I trained hard for cross-country. Sometimes with one or two others I ran five and ten miles at a time. It all seemed more serious now. I felt stronger and I did better in the weekly races. Mike Carpenter also coached the boxing team and his star 125-pounder was Luis Carlo, one of three students from Cuba. He'd been some kind of a champion boxer back there and when we watched him defeat his opponents week after week, his hands moved so fast you couldn't see them. One evening as we were forming our company ranks, preparing to march to the mess hall, I got into an argument with another cadet and we started shoving each other around. Luis Carlo stepped between us and held my arms. I pushed him away, and then the suicide impulse bit me and I threw a punch at him. The same impulse, I suppose, that had me hanging off the railroad trestle. It startled him as much as it did me. We stood facing each other while motion stopped around us and the cadets of

C Company stared at this face-off with disbelief. I had made the move, and now I had to back it up.

"Who are you pushing around?" said I.

Luis Carlo regarded me with some amusement, but no scorn. Everyone waited for those hands to start moving.

"Okay, Harry," he said.

That was it. Luis hadn't just let me off the hook, he'd given me a new name. Harry. I liked it better than Harold. My father's name.

6

There was trouble back in Cleveland. When Grandma tried to en-
roll Alberta in Laurel School, the headmistress warned her, "June is
doing well here. She's a difficult girl, but she is doing well. If you
bring her sister here, it will be bad for her." I don't know how
thoughtfully Grandma received this advice or whether she couldn't
think of an alternative, but she sent Alberta to join June. In a few
months they ran away and were expelled. They were then placed in
a private school near our favorite railroad trestle, but they ran away
from that one, too.

I was fifteen years old then, June and Alberta were sixteen and
fourteen. Our fate was in the hands of Grandma with some counsel
from Uncle Al. Our father was in the insane asylum, our mother had
disappeared in the wilderness of Hollywood, and I was at Culver
Military Academy. My actions were tuned to the art of survival.
Grandpa was right. Culver saved me. In Cleveland the ground was
constantly shifting, like a roving earthquake rumbling underfoot,
and Culver was the only steady place I knew.

At "home," disaster was the order of the day and I never knew
from what quarter it was coming. Zoom! Look out! "Harold, June
has run off with Bill Meyer and I think he's a Jew." If I allowed these
crises to push my nervous system to the edge of eruption, if my voice
rose and my emotions began to shred, Grandma had a sure method
of quieting me down. She would look at whoever was with us, point

her finger at her brain, twirl it, and say, "Just like his father, just like his father." It's possible that my chief aim in life was to stay out of the nuthouse.

All the mysteries and uncertainties that hid in the darkened corners of my growing up caused me to smile without pleasure, living each day with the nervous anticipation of nameless disaster. But somewhere in the boy Harold a pact was made: I would survive even if no one else did.

June did run away with Bill Meyer. He was a tall, dark-haired young man from the other side of the tracks, but an irresistible guy who even won over Grandma, briefly. And after the roller-coaster ride of enrollments and expulsions, June longed for California, the land of the lost into which our mother had disappeared. So she and Bill hopped the boxcars on our side of the trestle and never got off. June dressed as a boy in some of my clothes, pulled her hair back under a hat, and she and Bill headed for the Golden State with their hobo act.

Now what to do with Alberta? She was hanging loose with no companion, no sister or brother nearby. Enter Nettie Wigton again. The veils of family silence have closed over the origins of this idea, but Nettie offered to take Alberta and raise her down in Zanesville, Ohio. It was to foment rumors in years ahead, rumors that slipped out of hiding in New England and bred connections with other rumors. Grandma had never liked Nettie, but Grandpa had kept her close.

Meanwhile, Dad had somehow "escaped" from the insane asylum on Carnegie Avenue. On one of my visits back home—Zoom! "Harold has escaped from the asylum. I just had a postcard from Kansas City. Send fifty dollars." Such news only fed my determination to wall myself off from that queer circus in Cleveland. How this magical character called Dad managed to get out of a locked and barred facility was never explained. All I needed to file away was the news that our father had joined the boxcar battalions along with his eldest child.

When nobody knows who you are, you have to do something to

show them, so June attended Hobo College, an educational experience beyond the wildest dreams of Laurel School. She learned to go
without food, to exist on water until hunger drove them off the train
when it slowed down entering a town and they could jump off and
get some pea soup. Or a watermelon. Watermelons were on the high
end of the menu because they contained water.

She and Bill entered the City of Angels at the freight yards and
found their way to Alvarado Street and MacArthur Park. After a
night or two in this teeming playground, edgy with the sweaty hunger of illegal Mexican immigrants and other drifters in search of the
next chance, Bill was told by one of them, "Don't stay here. It's too
dangerous for June." So they headed downtown near the Biltmore
Hotel and found a rooming house off the small park there.

Bill would not work. He charged shirts on Grandma's account at
Bullock's and sold them on the street. June didn't like that and said
so, and responded by getting a job. She headed for Sunset and Vine
to get closer to the movie stars and maybe a chance encounter with
her mother. We all courted the illusion that our mother was out
there, secretly watching us and keeping up with our progress, and
that someday she would show up and say, "Here I am, children!"
Her great-looking seventeen-year-old daughter landed a job in the
traditional pipeline of "discovery" in Hollywood—the hot dog stand
near the corner of Vine. She was costumed, too, in a sailor suit with
a little sailor hat to set off her Ginger Rogers looks. In this rig she
must have attracted the admiration of the male half of the population of Hollywood, and she could eat all the hot dogs she wanted,
free. June had graduated from Hobo College.

One of the roving eyes she captured belonged to Gion Fenwick.
The name Fenwick was an invention in the Hollywood tradition to
disguise his country of origin, which was due east of Switzerland. He
took note of June in her sailor suit and little hat as he lounged on his
Hollywood balcony, and he approved of her. So he waved and June
waved back. Gion continued to smile and wave when he walked by
the hot dog stand to have his shoes polished around the corner. Not
the ones he was wearing, the ones he carried—a measure of sartorial

distinction some yardage beyond anything June had encountered since our grandfather passed away—and it caused her to view Gion with the respect he was seeking. He was a handsome man with a mustache, twenty years older than June, a man to whom the mannerly shows of life were a pleasure. And he was patient. When Bill appeared he invited them both to dinner. He listened and drew conclusions. Gion recognized quality and he recognized spoiled goods and he bided his time.

The police caught up with Bill at the rooming house and arrested him for illegally charging shirts to Grandma's account at Bullock's. June was taken into custody as his accomplice. They put him in jail and June in a holding tank for underage girls, where they were held for six weeks before being sent back home. But a Samaritan appeared in the tradition of Pat O'Brien and said, "This girl doesn't belong in there. Put her downstairs with the little kids and let her teach them." So they did and June became a teacher. My hobo sister was once again enrolled in a house of learning.

They were abandoned children, very small, and June became attached to a three-year-old boy. She would hold him so he could look out the window and see the trees and she would hug him. They came to adore each other. When it was time for her to be discharged, she didn't want to leave. She liked it there. As she was escorted away from the building, one of the women held the little boy up so he could wave goodbye to June and she could wave to him. They waved at each other until she couldn't see him anymore. Then they put her on the train alone and she headed back to Cleveland.

In the cocoon of Culver, I knew nothing of all this sad adventure. The zoom would hit me when I got home. When it did, I jammed it into the attic of my mind and let it lie there because it was too wild a problem for me to solve. I spent the summer in Cleveland working in the men's shirt department of the May Company because in those days teenagers were expected to learn the rules of the real world before it smashed them in the face all unprepared. I don't ever remember thinking that anyone was going to give me a free ride. I was sixteen years old and it was time for my senior year at Culver.

Harold, now known as Harry, had flunked algebra. I had managed to shrink myself through the knothole of a D minus in Latin, but taking algebra all over again loomed like a mastiff in my path. I did not want to run this problem past anyone with a military mind, so I sought advice from the least dedicated cadets I knew. With the help of these crafty advisers, I padded my requirements with the softest choices available until I had arrived at twenty hours of credit a semester, one shy of the magic number to graduate. A one-hour course was needed. Astronomy was out of the question and I had used up all of my chapel credit. Along came Perry Warren Fiske.

"What about dramatics, Harry?" Perry was in the dramatics class and he was not thought of as a model cadet. No one in the dramatics class was thought of as a model of anything except weird. There was Oliver Rea, who had been at Culver for five or six years and showed signs of wanting to live there the rest of his life. A strange, rather high-voiced cadet named Walter Collins had gone on to New York and was in some play called *Junior Miss*. But these were not subjects of discussion for the men of Culver. Dramatics was a mongrel.

"Nah. Thanks, Perry."

"There's no homework, Harry."

"What?"

"No homework." A ray of light appeared and then it vanished again.

"But I'd have to go on a stage."

"Aw, it would be nothing. Major Mather would give you a little walk-on part, so all you'd have to do is just stand there."

"I wouldn't have to talk?"

"Naw."

The light appeared again. A way out of darkness, and I took it. I was pretty embarrassed and kept as quiet as I could about it. I certainly hid it from Coach Carpenter. Talk about sissies! I approached my first dramatics class with a heart of lead, but Perry had adopted me as a friend now and he kept chirping away in his extravagant theatrical manner, assuring me in tones of liquid grandeur that I would like it. Fat chance.

The first thing Major Mather did was play us records of Lionel Barrymore's brother, an actor named John Barrymore, who used the words like knives and daggers and small bouncing balls, sometimes covering them all over with syrup to disguise his meaning. He was reciting Shakespeare, something called soliloquies, which meant he did all the talking. It was pretty ripe stuff, almost like half singing, but sometimes he would suddenly spit the words out in such a vicious tone you knew he was really angry at the king who had married his mother before the food got cold. He was an angry man and some of his anger got inside me and stirred up feelings I didn't know were there. He felt betrayed. So did I. He wanted to give his mother hell and then let her know he loved her, and I found I had those feelings, too. I especially liked " 'tis naoww the verry whitcheeng tyme of nite when churrch yarrds yawwwn and helll itself brreathes out contage-eon to this warold. Naoww cood I drrink hot bllud and dooo such bitturr bizness as the dey would *quayke* to look awn." I felt like doing bitter business myself and giving people holy hell for the lies they told and the secrets they hid, and Hamlet was good at telling them off. Damn good. Better than me. That was clear as a bell the more I listened to him.

Perry Fiske could imitate John Barrymore really well, except he didn't have the threat of insanity I heard in Barrymore. Barrymore was dangerous. Perry was good at making the words sound similar, but he didn't have the danger.

The people in the dramatics class weren't as weird as I thought they were. Mostly they were just not military. They laughed a lot and made fun of things, and they had secrets they kept among themselves. But they weren't mean. The new people, like me, were quiet and we listened while these real actors talked mostly among themselves. But sometimes they would smile at us and make us feel part of their gang. That was it. They made us feel we could belong.

Major Mather was so unmilitary it felt awkward to call him Major.

He seemed a little absent sometimes, as if his mind were whirring around a different planet, but he talked like one of us without losing his authority as our teacher. He said our first play would be *Seven Keys to Baldpate*, a melodrama by George M. Cohan, and I did not have the shred of an idea what the title meant, what Baldpate was, or why Cohan spelled his name with an *a* instead of an *e*. I was given the part of an old caretaker because when Major Mather asked me to read the lines I imitated Grandpa. Another new boy like me played the other caretaker and he was very good at it. His name was Evans. You could see he'd done acting before. But the really scary part was this: we were going to be the first ones to go out on the stage.

We didn't have a stage to practice on—that had to be set up in the small gymnasium when the time came to do the play—so we pretended the end of the classroom was a stage and one wall was the audience. It didn't give you much of a feeling for what the real thing would be like, but it made me nervous anyway. Major Mather let us kind of wander around and then he would do what he called "set it." That meant "stay where you are!" So you tried to remember what you had said when you were in that place and then you had to get there every time those words came around again. It was pretty confusing, and I kept bumping into Evans, who chattered away like a little old man, and then the rest of the actors would laugh at us, so Major Mather called out, "Keep it in." That meant bump into him on purpose. I began to enjoy this after a while because it gave me something to do besides just standing there and reciting my lines; and it made me think of old people who couldn't see well and didn't know where they were going, so I pretended I couldn't see chairs and tables and began to walk into them, too, and then the actors laughed at *me*. I don't think the other caretaker liked that, but Major Mather shouted, "Leave it in!" That was a command and I wasn't going to disobey it. This play took place in Maine in the dead of winter and we were opening up a hunting lodge, so it was freezing cold on the stage and we had to add shaking to everything else we were doing, bumping and chirping and shaking, and it was a lot to remember.

The day for dress rehearsal came and I was so anxious to see the stage that had been built for us in the small gym that I got there too early, while work was going on behind the curtains. But there was the hunting lodge, much more real than I had thought it would be, with windows and doors and a big moose head on the wall. I heard a voice shouting, "Goddamn electricity! Damn electricity!" I looked behind the curtain and it was Major Mather swearing at a radio. He was trying to hook it up. A teacher swearing! Just like a real person outside Culver. I liked Major Mather even more hearing him swear and watching him perspiring over that radio, and I never felt afraid of him again. He was like a friend in disguise.

The dress rehearsal that night was pretty horrible. Lights went on and off, an actor fell off the stage in the dark, and Major Mather damned this and that regularly. I got so hot in my heavy winter jacket and fur hat with earmuffs and gloves that perspiration ran down my spine like a brook and made me forget my lines. I was glad to have them, but when I forgot them Evans kept chattering away, saying things that were not on the page, and I didn't know where I was half the time. It was a mess.

The next night, the audience came. I could hear them out there, banging their shins into the metal folding chairs and laughing, but there wasn't anything funny going on backstage. It was grim back there, quiet and grim. All except Evans. He was whispering his lines to himself, chattering, chattering in a whisper until I wanted to bash him in the head with my key chain. They'd given me this big bunch of keys on a chain at the last minute. No one had ever told me I was supposed to have keys and now I didn't know which hand to carry them in or what I was supposed to unlock except the front door, and the audience couldn't see me do that, so why have keys? Why not put them in my pocket? I wanted to ask the old character lady what I should do. She played the older female parts in our plays because it was all boys at Culver, and she was sitting backstage in the dark and saying nothing. The real actors called her Mother Bays, but she was Colonel Bays's wife, which meant her husband was second-in-command at Culver. Just the thought of talking to her made me more nervous, what with the keys and the audience to think about.

She saw me looking at her and smiled at me and—Whoosh!—what a relief that was! She'd been a real actress before she married Colonel Bays, an actress on the stage in vaudeville, and got paid for it, so she was a pro. To smile at me like that, it made all the difference. I decided to carry the keys in my left hand, open the door with my right hand, and put the keys in my pocket out on the stage. That would be natural.

The lights were going down in the gym. There was an awful hush out there where the audience was and I began to shake all over. Mrs. Bays smiled at me again and Evans pushed me and said, "We're on!" I tried to get the key in the lock but it was only painted on the door, so I kept jabbing at it in the dark until Evans opened the door and went on the stage in front of me.

The first thing I felt was the silence. Then the lights. They were like moonlight shining through the windows. In front of me, where the audience was, something waited. Something immense and powerful, like God. I spoke my first line and then another and another, and they felt real to me. Bold and scary but real. I wasn't so frightened anymore because a marvelous thing was happening. People were listening to me. Listening to *me*.

Nothing went awry. I put the keys in my pocket while the audience laughed at the other caretaker, then I said my line and they laughed at me. I didn't even know it was funny. The whole scene turned out to be funny, the other actor chattering and chattering and me bumping into tables and chairs and shivering, and when we went off, the audience applauded. What a sound! It wouldn't leave my head. I stood there in the dark offstage, breathing great gulps of air, the sweat pouring off me and my heart thumping like a running horse, and I looked at Mother Bays and she smiled.

"You're hooked, sonny," she said. I don't think I realized what had happened, but the old vaudevillian knew.

In cross-country, Teasdale was leading the way home, but I was getting closer. We were cocaptains of the team now, in our senior year, and I came in second to Teasdale most of the time, but I couldn't seem to pass him at the end. I always went out first and took the lead early if I could get it from the other team, but I couldn't hold it. By the time I had staggered down the hill and hit the playing fields, Teasdale would run right past me, and I couldn't overtake him. He was shorter than I was and barrel-chested, but his shorter legs pumped like pistons while my long ones flailed around numb with exhaustion. The last football game was just before Thanksgiving vacation. Our final race was at the halftime period. Our opponents were boys from Niles, Michigan, and their best runner was a tough, hard-edged boy we could never beat. He had a powerful, ground-eating kick at the end and he waited for the flats of the playing fields to unleash it. His face when he blew past us was like determination carved in stone. Teasdale and I were desperate to beat him and we talked over a strategy: I would stay right on this guy's shoulder and try to egg him on to speed up early and waste himself so Teasdale could shoot past him at the end.

The race began pretty smoothly and I felt that I was taking it easy by not going out in front. It wasn't a pleasant way to run. I worried that the four runners in front of us would get too far ahead and I wouldn't be able to finish well myself, and hearing Teasdale's steady pounding strides behind me set my nerves afire. I felt trapped.

We stayed this way up the hill and across the golf course to the landing strip, and then I couldn't stand it anymore so I passed the runner from Niles and the four others. Let him catch up, I thought. We'll wear him out that way. As we came to the brow of the ski jump hill I heard the stride behind me change, a new one, familiar, like piston legs, and Teasdale was suddenly past me. Now what? He had moved too soon. I shot a look over my shoulder and there was Determination Carved in Stone moving along, steady and expressionless. At the bottom of the hill Teasdale was getting too far ahead, so I pushed myself to come closer to him, about seven or eight yards behind, so I could call out to him when Carved in Stone made his move.

And here he came! We had just broken out onto the far green

playing fields about three hundred yards from the finish line across the football field. The band had played its last flourish and now all was silent except for the nasal intake and expelling of air as our chests pumped and our spikes reached out. I heard our nemesis, steady as an engine, and took a quick look. God, he'd gained on us already, seven yards behind and coming.

"Get going, Teasdale," I shouted. Teasdale didn't speed up, so I put on a burst to get closer, where he'd be sure to hear me.

"Teasdale, he's gaining!" Teasdale didn't move out. What was the matter with him? We were only a hundred yards from the football field now and this guy was gaining on us. I felt a desperate panic seize me. All I could think of was getting Teasdale to pour it on. I sped up to just a stride behind him and gasped, "He's coming! Go!" Then I snapped a quick look over my shoulder and there he was, four yards behind, his blue eyes beaming past us to the finish line. We flew under the first set of goalposts and were on the football field, and the crowd was going nuts. I thought, I'll get right next to Teasdale and force him to go faster to beat me and that way we'll win, and I came up even with him. Seventy yards to go. I heard Niles, Michigan, breathing on our necks. Here he comes! I thought. Do something!

I was past Teasdale! I was running alone, in front, and there were the goalposts. I was in the clear! The crowd was going crazy and I realized I could win. And I did. I won. For the first time, I won! Then I fell down and passed out.

One Sunday early in December we had returned to the barracks from chapel and were marking time before lunch. Since my second year at Culver I'd had a new roommate, George Livingston. It was a friendship that would leave its mark on how I viewed the human race. George was a Jew. I didn't even know it at first and it didn't move me when I found out. What I did understand right away was that his was an older head than mine. I think he knew the face of deception. And he understood survival. We had a premier corner

Harold

room on the third floor of South Barracks. It had two windows, one looking east, the other south. If the breathtaking vision of a girl was walking on campus, we could track her progress longer from our own room than from any other. The room across the hall was occupied by Lee Winchester from Memphis and his roommate, Tom Scofield. Lee had his radio on, and presently some sensory shadow caused me to prick up my ears at the words "Pearl Harbor." The voice was distant but familiar. George and I moved toward Lee's doorway and heard the voice say, ". . . a date which will live in infamy." It was FDR. As we listened to the declaration of a global war that would end with the massive carnage of the first atomic bombs, four Culver cadets heard the world turn upside down and the life we had taken for granted blown to smithereens. In a year to a year and a half, at the age of eighteen, we would each be training for war. Would we be alive in four more years?

7

Shortly after the declaration of war, Grandma decided that Christmas would be spent in California because my father was out there. She was going to pick me up at Culver and drive us to Los Angeles at the start of my vacation, a perilous adventure to contemplate: two thousand miles with Grandma in the 1938 Buick coupe. Route 66 had never seen a more careful driver. She curved herself over the wheel and squinted through her glasses at every adversary to let them know who was boss. As the green of the east was thinning out I began to see new colors and shapes: the brick-colored clay of Oklahoma, treeless vistas that stretched out level to merge with the sky, the deep-cut arroyos of the Texas Panhandle, and the sentinel buttes of the ancient Indian lands in New Mexico and Arizona, waiting there under the great sky, mysterious markers of times gone by. I would see these sights again and again as the years added up, but at this first sighting I was mesmerized by the unfinished beauty of our western lands.

But California was the heaven of this enchanted kingdom, and when we reached the pearly gates of Needles, the guards were there to look us over before we were allowed to enter. They said they were searching for fruit and bugs, but they looked like policemen to me. We were told to drive the desert at night so the car radiator wouldn't boil over, and to gas up first because there would be no gas stations or anything else for miles and miles. The trip took on a pioneering tone. Once in a while we passed a struggling ancient vehicle, loaded high with goods and furniture and children, the radiator shooting steam and the face behind the wheel a wilderness of broken dreams and hope. I would read about them on a troopship in a book entitled *The Grapes of Wrath*.

As the desert stretched on and on, I kept looking for California. It was supposed to be a green place with palm trees beside a sparkling ocean. Where was it? The mountains rose up before us, past San Bernardino, and we started to climb. The needle on the temperature gauge was climbing, too. We had to stop every little while to cool the engine off. Higher and higher we rose, great pine trees closing in around us, the road snaking this way and that. This was no place for a flat tire or to run out of gas. The wolves would pick our bones clean. We crested the top of a snowbound ridge and I caught my breath. There it was! California! Spreading below us, a great valley bathed in sunlight. Carpeted with the greenest green orange trees and here and there the red tile roofs of small white ranch houses. Above it all a sky of purest blue. The colors were the freshest I had ever seen. We got out of the car and took in this mirage of perfection come to life. The Garden of Eden must have looked like this.

Grandma and I checked into the Normandie Hotel. It was very near the Ambassador Hotel, site of the famous nightclub, the Coconut Grove. Across the street from the Ambassador was the Brown Derby, where all the movie stars ate. We were in the heartland of Fame. The Ambassador was so big, with such endless lobbies and corridors, you could stay there all day long, even if you lived at the Normandie, and not a soul would be the wiser. A little tea or coffee here and there, and maybe a sandwich, and you had bought your way into a tropical castle. That's where Grandma strutted her stuff when she wasn't at Bullock's, where she bought me my first grown-up suit with a vest. California was so exciting it stirred up not only envy and longing but also the intimidating thought that you were trespassing. These happy people in tieless shirts and pastel-colored clothes were another race, and you, with your gloomy midwestern ways, did not belong to it.

Then the one true original appeared. My father. He was wearing a battered cowboy hat with a bullet hole in it, and he had no upper teeth. He was as skinny as a carved table leg, just a lot of bones for six feet two inches off the ground, even higher because of the rounded-over cowboy boots. He was driving an Austin, a miniature car that forced his knees up level with his chin. To corkscrew himself into this vehicle he had to take his hat off. That revealed a head of hair cut off like a brush, and it was white. Grandma explained that his hair had turned white from fright, but she never explained what had scared him, and I didn't think I wanted to know. This was my father? God! Where could we hide him? Not a chance. He drew every eye to him as surely as any ostrich would if it sauntered into the Ambassador Hotel among all the movie stars. To make things even worse—could they be?—he acted as if he owned the place. He was quiet about it, no yelling or throwing ropes, nothing like that. It was more like an unconcerned manner, as if there wasn't anyone else around.

"Hi, Harold. Hi, Momma. How ya doin'? Hey! Let's sit down here and have some iced tea or some kind of tea. How ya doin', Harold? California, huh? I'm building a house out in Calabasas. Ought to see it. Pure redwood, 'cause that don't rot. Even got a redwood toilet seat, but I gotta get the toilet first. How ya fixed for cash, Ma?"

People were taking him in and moving away. I wanted to move away, too, all the way back to Ohio. The California shine was tarnished now. How could I be the son of this boyish nut?

Ventura Boulevard is a very long road. We were driving to Calabasas in two cars because the Austin would seat only two midgets or one boy with a gymnast behind the wheel and no room in back for more than a dachshund. I had declined to share the bumper car with Ichabod, happy to risk my life with Grandma, so we followed Dad. What a procession! If only we could just get there and hide in the redwood experiment, or behind a tree if the termites had proved Dad wrong. The trouble was, there were no trees. They were thinning out, just an occasional dry-looking coast live oak—*live*! Hold it. If they were live oaks they were just hanging on, because there was no water in sight, no water anywhere, just a wilderness of lumpy brown. And no houses. They had thinned out way back there, right after Sherman Oaks, and now there was nothing. Not a store, not a house, not a human being in sight. Dad had found a safe place all right. No insane asylum was going to find him here.

There it was. Nestled in the palm of a dusty brown depression, off on a little trace of path within sight of Ventura Boulevard, which name had now become hilarious. The place was red all right, definitely redwood from the floor to the roof, which was only partly finished. One wall was open to the bounties of nature, too. Bugs, bears, wolves, coyotes, bears, bugs, wolves. There was a canvas fold-up cot in the living room, which was the only room, and the bathroom was a space with nothing in it but a hole in the floor. Where did he go? I wondered.

"Do you live here, Daddy?"

"Yep."

"Gosh."

"Is it safe out here, Harold?" said Grandma. "I mean the animals . . ."

"Won't hurt ya. Smell scares 'em away." Okay. That's fair enough, but what about going to the bathroom? There was not a bush in sight and that hole was worrisome.

"Just hunker down outside, Harold. The coyotes don't mind. Hey, how 'bout you spending the night out here with me, son?"

"Oh . . . uh . . ."

"I don't think Buddy would be comfortable, Harold. There's only one . . . Is that a bed?"

"Yep. I'll sleep on the floor."

"But how will we get him back?"

"Drive him back in the morning in the Austin."

My first and only night alone with Dad was in a cabin with one wall missing and half open to the sky, away out in the empty hills of Calabasas. Empty except for the animals.

"Dad, was that a wolf?"

"Won't hurt ya."

I had been lying on the canvas cot with a piece of blanket over me, listening to the howling cries of wolves or coyotes, I didn't know which. The anthropological listing didn't matter. Having either one of them join us through the bare two-by-fours of an unfinished wall was a portent that kept me on guard throughout my night with Dad. He had lost interest and gone off to sleep. I was alone. I listened sharply for the soft padding of four feet until the sun rose like a savior, and then Dad rose and went outside.

Our trip back to town was largely uneventful, except for one startling moment. We were humming along Ventura Boulevard in the Austin, Dad filling every inch of space behind, above, and below the wheel, and it was pretty clear he'd been trained to drive by Grandma. He had a nonchalant attitude about it. By this time I had learned that what had turned his hair white was a car accident. I had let my attention waver for a moment when he suddenly shouted "Whaaah!" and started pounding the tiny dashboard in front of me. The car careened to the side and he flung my door open. "Out, out, Harold. Get out." He kept beating with his hat at the seat I had recently been daydreaming in until he plucked a hairy black thing from under the brim of his hat and mumbled, "Black widow."

"A spider?"

"Yep. Wanna watch out for them, Buddy."

You said it, pal. I watched out for them all the way back to the Ambassador Hotel. I watched out for them in bed that night and I watched out for them every time my father took off his hat.

Before I left Culver for California, a fellow cadet had invited me to be his sister's date for New Year's Eve at—guess where!—the Coconut Grove. He told me that his father, Clarence Brown, directed movies for a living. He said it in such an offhand way, without mentioning any of his father's movies, that I let it go. Quite a few sons of famous and wealthy people went to Culver: the heir to Phillips Petroleum,

Harold

General Jimmy Doolittle's son, and Johnny Knight of the newspaper family, who was captain of the boxing team. But we paid little attention to who sired them. So I was taking a famous movie director's daughter to a famous nightclub in Hollywood, dumb as an ox about her lineage, and perhaps that was just as well. I was scared enough already. Girls were like Venetian vases to me. Having been emotionally sheltered by imprisonment in one male lockup after another, paroled only for a one-year stretch with the nuns, I was even frightened of my younger sister, who was getting mature awfully fast. I couldn't keep my eyes off her and I knew I was treading the edge of perdition there. So I did a lot of worrying about what Miss Brown was going to look like and what would happen when I touched her.

We met at our new hangout, the Ambassador Hotel, and this girl was a beauty. I didn't know which way to look, and when I touched her hand to say hello, I thought mine had caught on fire. Grandma had not trained me to handle girls, just old people, so I was out there in Hollywood breaking new ground. Miss Brown turned out to be a girl of quality. She knew how to pour life into the evening even though her brother had lashed her to a cement post for a date on New Year's Eve. She was well-mannered, but fun. She was blond, of course, it being California, and had obviously been in training. I could imagine her throwing the javelin very far and looking good every step of the way. God's gift to California, was the way I thought of her, and I dreaded the moment we would have to get on the dance floor and perform in front of Artie Shaw and his band.

Prior to God's gift, I'd had one date at Culver, with Mary Alice Henderson, daughter of the commandant, Colonel Henderson. Mary Alice walked across the campus once in a while, which was why George and I fought for that corner room with the two windows. And why South Barracks had a permanent tilt to it, owing to the weight of so many cadets rushing to the southern windows at the same time. I had worked my courage up for two years watching the great sight of Mary Alice waltzing by, and I finally called her up to ask if she would go to the Friday night movies in the gym with me. Her father answered the phone. Very terse. He also answered the door, still very terse, and looked me over slowly. I was perspiring when he finished. Then Mary Alice appeared and lightened things up.

We started out for the gym. I had said hello to her, but now I couldn't think of what to say next, so it was a silent walk, more like the last mile kind of walk when there's an execution on tap and you are going to star in it. When we sat on the metal folding chairs I accidentally touched her and reared like a horse that had spied a rattler in the brush. But Mary Alice pretended I'd just seen an old friend, so we both waved at somebody we didn't know. We watched the movie in silence but my mind was active. I kept watching her hand. Had she laid it there on her leg for me to hold it? That would mean touching her leg. Are you nuts! Her dad would expel me if I touched her leg, and since the hand was there on the leg, better forget it. But I couldn't. I thought about it for 109 minutes, which was the length of the movie, whatever movie it was. I didn't pay much attention. I experienced dramatics enough watching her hand, and I was emotionally spent when I walked her wordlessly home. Her dad was waiting up and I thought he smiled at me. It could have been pity.

At the Coconut Grove the maître d' led Miss Brown and me to a seat at ringside, where everyone could see us. Everyone. When drinks were mentioned, I had a Cuba libre first and then a whiskey sour. I'd had two drinks before in my entire life, both Tom Collinses, and had thrown them up. But experimentation was the name of the game tonight for this sixteen-year-old, especially since I was going to get on the dance floor with a blond princess from Hollywood in front of a bunch of movie stars and Artie Shaw. I needed to become a daredevil right away. Those two drinks would have to turn the trick.

"Shall we drance?"

"Now?"

"Better nate than lever."

Other than my fling with Fred Astaire in the basement of the Cleveland house, my dancing had been limited to being pushed around a dance floor once by my little sister.

"Would you like to lead?" I said.

"Oh, I'd love to. I like to lead." She had to use her strength on me to get us started, but we began to move.

"Do you ski?"

"I'm sorry. What?"

"Isn't skiing like drancing! You slee your feet around, don't you?"

"Oh, yes. I see what you mean. It's very much the same."

"It's probably better to shluffle them."

"To what?"

"Shluffle them. I'm sworry."

"For what?"

"For slepping on your foot."

"Oh. I didn't feel a thing."

"You will if we kleep drancing."

This was a game girl. She was somehow amused by my clumsiness and the effects of the two drinks, so we laughed a lot and began to enjoy ourselves. I lost my fear of her as the evening went on and sobriety returned, and I began to see her for what she was—an attractive, intelligent young woman who knew how to handle a tenderfoot. Miss Brown was a good sport. She enrolled at Reed College in Oregon the following year and we corresponded for a while. I liked her. I hope she's had a wonderful life.

Grandma was staying on in California with Dad, so I headed back to Culver by railroad. The Union Pacific Railroad station in downtown Los Angeles was meant to welcome you to a land far different in character from the one you'd left back east. This land was Spanish before General Frémont and the army claimed it for the immigrants flooding west across America, and Spanish colors and designs, the tiles and clean stucco surfaces glorified an architecture that defined the place. It could knock your eyes out. And it could make you wistful upon leaving it. I looked forward to the great adventure of crossing the Rocky Mountains in a train, but I took my last look at California with a sore heart and wondered if I would ever see it again.

I tried to sleep that night on the train, but the excitement of this magnificent trip would not let my nervous system alone. The deserts, the mountains, the snowfields high in the sky, the breathtaking precipices on one side of the train as it clung to the wall of a canyon, this was a moving picture show to fill my dreams. When we stopped at Salt Lake City for a scheduled two-hour layover in the dead of night, I had to get off and look for Mormons. I had never seen one and I wanted to find out if they were different from me, on account of having so many wives in the house.

The conductor cautioned me to get back to the train by 3:30 a.m., that would be mountain time, and he told me I should not miss the Mormon Tabernacle right up the hill a ways. I walked up that hill in the bright, cold night, a young pioneer entering a new land, my boy's heart ablaze with the thrill of discovery, and there it was in the moonlight, that miraculous great meetinghouse built by people with a belief in dreams. I was inspired. I wanted with all my heart to be a part of a miracle.

8

The next play at Culver was *Room Service*. It was a farce, a big success on Broadway, about some theatrical producers locked in a hotel room with no money to pay the bill, trying to raise the dough to put on a play by a young man from Oswego. Perry Fiske played the producer, Ollie Rea a bellicose character named Harry Binion, and I was given the part of Faker Englund, a kind of hanger-on and gofer. I was surprised to have been given such a good role. Right away I decided I'd have to paint on a mustache and wear a hat indoors. I was really beginning to feel a part of the gang now, and since I was acting in scenes with the real actors I began to feel like one myself. And farce was fun! Great fun. You exaggerated emotions a bit and there was great energy in it, almost breathless sometimes. You didn't ponder things, you kept it moving, almost like an athletic event, and pretty soon you felt a kind of tempo on the stage, which Major Mather called "timing." You timed your lines to make them funny, but it had to be natural so the audience never knew you were trying to make them laugh. You could describe it as being deadly serious to the point of looking ridiculous. I liked that. Somewhere I had learned a knack for it.

And this character, Faker, he was from New York, of course, and I had seen movies with New York people in them so I imitated the way they spoke and that was great fun. I liked pretending to be someone else, so I had him move fast, in a kind of breathless way all the time, but dumb. He was a dumbbell and didn't know it.

The play felt like a real hit. People laughed so hard that I almost laughed myself. My heart was singing with excitement, and when I got too eager, when I started to speak my lines too soon while the audience was still laughing, Ollie Rea would take my arm and whisper, "Hold it, hold it. Now!" There was so much to learn and it was all fun. But the best part was getting a laugh from the audience. That was like drowning in candy.

Perry Fiske and I were becoming good friends. I enjoyed his theatrical ways, and offstage I began to mimic him, to ham it up and try to get laughs. The imp got loose in me again—where did it come from? Not Grandfather. My father? Was it my mother's voice rising in me? It moved me to conspire with Perry to do some crazy stunts. One of them was crawling through the ventilation system at night, after lights-out and final inspection, and scaring cadets in the other rooms. My roommate, George, was only half amused when I balanced on the top of our door and removed the wall vent to the air-conditioning system and squeezed myself through the hole into the duct beyond. I would crawl down the airway duct above the hallway to a room whose occupants I'd selected for terrorizing and pause there a moment to make sure they were asleep. Then I began moaning, very low at first, but building to a crescendo. Then a pause while the startled occupants rose up in bed listening keenly. Now another moan, very low and guttural, and the two roommates leaped out of their beds and scooted from the room in search of this moaning shrike that had to be right around somewhere. But where? They dashed up and down the hall, waking everybody, in a sweat to find the source of this moaning creature, and I had to hold my breath to keep from exploding with idiot laughter.

One night, after Colonel Johnson had made his rounds, making sure that all lights were out and his prize group of cadets in Company C were commencing a long night of health-giving sleep, I crawled down the air duct toward Perry's room to moan at him. He would know who it was, but his roommate wouldn't. This nocturnal moaning sound was the subject of edgy speculation up and down the hall: a rat in labor or the wind were two theories that had been advanced along the corridor. So when I paused at Perry's vent and began to moan, there was a good deal of mutual merriment between us that had to be suppressed if the joke was going to play out on his roommate. I began to build up the moaning sound and Perry could barely control himself.

"What's that?" he whispered hoarsely to his roommate.

"Huh? What's what?" said his roommate, slowly coming awake.

"Listen."

"Moooaaann."

Perry began to choke on suppressed hysteria. "What's that?"

"What the hell . . ."

"Moooaaann."

"It's coming from the vent," said his roommate.

"How could it be?" said Perry.

"Because there's some damn fool up there."

"No," said Perry, sputtering mirth like a teakettle. "Who could it be?"

"Moooaaann."

"Who else? Holbrook."

Then Perry and I exploded with laughter while his roommate put a chair under the doorway and removed the vent.

"Holbrook, come out of there, you idiot. If Colonel Johnson catches you up there, you'll walk the quadrangle until commencement day."

I crawled out onto the top of the door, shrieking with laughter, and presently I noticed a bald head below my feet with a uniform under it and silver lieutenant colonel insignia on each shoulder. A pair of round blue eyes rolled up at me. There was a quite deadly pause while the doomsday clock ticked away.

"Hello, Colonel Johnson."

There were more dreadful seconds on the clock while I saw the outside corners of his eyes flutter and twitch. A suppressed moan rose out of Perry.

"I was just investigating something up here, sir. A moaning sound—"

"Please, Cadet Holbrook, don't stretch my patience."

"I'm coming right down, sir." I lowered one foot to the doorknob and catapulted off the door at attention. I saluted. Colonel Johnson's eyes had begun to water and his mouth was twisting up in some kind of an awful grimace.

"Will you get back to your room, Cadet Holbrook? I don't know what I'm going to do with you."

The next day he called me into his office and we had a little talk. At the beginning of senior year I had been raised to the rank of PFC. When I left his office I was a private again.

For three years at Culver I had run the mile. From those early days as a plebe—when Mike Carpenter had taken me on road trips even though I finished a lap behind—to my third year on the team, I had trained hard and was now in contention for first place. There was a runner from Iowa named Baxter with a great stride and a killer finishing kick, and I had come in second to him the year before, running my best time for the mile in just over 4 minutes and 35 seconds. In 1934 Glenn Cunningham had set the world's record at 4 minutes 6.8 seconds and Sydney Wooderson of England had lowered it 0.4 of a second in 1937. The high school record was about 4 minutes 20 seconds, and Baxter had done 4:29. Before the acting bug bit me I had dreamed of being another Glenn Cunningham. I had the long legs and the thin frame that seemed to be a standard for most milers and I had gained confidence in how to pace myself. Mike Carpenter was counting on me to come through for him in my senior year.

Then in the spring Major Mather cast me in a leading role. It would require a great deal of rehearsal and I was not going to be able to train for the mile and do the play. It was the toughest decision I had ever faced and to this day I can feel the heat of it. For the first time I was about to make my own choice about the future path my life would take. The acting bug was new, the bite might not last. If I chose it, I would be turning my back on the dream of winning for Mike Carpenter and turning toward a dream that had no clear shape.

Harold

We were on the edge of the quadrangle outside the Canteen, where cadets at liberty got Cokes and hamburgers, when I told Mike Carpenter I would have to quit the track team to rehearse a play. I hoped to make it a private confrontation, but cadets drifting out of the Canteen were caught in the coils of tension winding around us. Mike was tall. The tip of his nose and patches of his face turned white when he was angry. They were white now. A crowd began to gather.

"You're yellow."

"No, I'm not—"

"You're yellow. You're a coward—"

"I'm not a coward. I know this is the right—"

"You've trained for three years and now you're going to quit?"

"I have to make what I think is the right choice. I've thought a lot about—"

"You're a quitter! A yellow-bellied quitter!" He walked away.

I felt only naked, naked shame. How could I have thought the wound would not go deep in him? I stood nailed to the ground. The cadets around me silently drifted off. Was I a yellowbelly? Did I quit because I was losing confidence that I could beat Baxter? I had already been stalked by doubts that I had truly beaten Teasdale. How could I have gone past him like that when I'd never been able to do it before? We were cocaptains of the team, maybe he had let me win that last race.

I wish I could go back sixty-nine years and watch the turning point of that choice inside my head. Was I a yellowbelly? Or was it an escape? The choice to join the weirdos. To be an actor. It had not occurred to me that someone would care about me that much. Since then there have been times in my life when I have made choices as cruel as this because I felt I had to save myself. To choose me over everyone else, to be brutal no matter what the cost in guilt and self-loathing and sadness. But the choice at Culver did not bring me sadness, it brought relief. I didn't have to win. I chose to belong to a bunch of people who were eccentric and daring and fun to be with, show people who had taken me in. And there was something irresponsible about it, too. Doing the unexpected, hanging off the railroad trestle, showing off. Watch me now! Acting may have been the high board.

I put the guilt and self-loathing to use in the play. I'd been given the role of the maniac in a Grand Guignol drama from the French called *Murder in the Foyer*. I wore a great black cape and used it like a scythe, and all the anger and suppressed emotions inside me gathered together in a crazy ball and erupted in the climax of the play. At that point I had my hands around Ollie Rea's neck and I was choking him to death. In rehearsals I often got carried away and had to be warned to ease off because Ollie's neck was turning a little purple, so he was on edge when opening night came. He knew the signs of an actor possessed by his role, especially one playing a maniac whose father really was one. As I advanced upon him, I could see concern and even fear in his eyes. "Here comes that damn Holbrook again," he was thinking. "I've survived the rehearsal period but what about tonight? With an audience out front and Holbrook getting loonier by the minute—here he comes! Oh God!" I had put my hands around his neck and begun to squeeze, trying to follow instructions about not shutting down his windpipe, but Ollie was taking no chances, not on this night with an untrained actor smelling stardom and blood. He clawed at my hands with a desperation way past acting, sweating to release the pressure on his Adam's apple before it was crushed to dust. Ollie was normally a rather elegant and sophisticated fellow, but this was no time for appearances or style. When he was down to a last, small puff of air he gasped, "Holbrook! It's only a play!!!"

In the summer of 1942, after graduation from Culver, it was time to go to work. I inspected the want ads in the Cleveland *Plain Dealer* and applied for a position in the hat department at Halle Brothers. By three o'clock in the afternoon of my first day I felt I'd been imprisoned there for the best part of my life and what was left of it was not worth living. A few customers wandered in, stared awhile at the stacked hats, and then left. The hats sat there in lonely piles, waiting for Cleveland to want them and give me a reason for not leaning against the display cases. I got scolded for it often by Mr. Thunderstorm, the floor manager. My friend Milton, a twenty-year veteran of the hat department, would warn me of his approach. "Here comes Adolf Hitler. Atten-shun!" And we would pretend to be busy counting hats or twitching them into better alignment as Thunderstorm lifted an eyebrow at us while we beamed confidence that a big sale was on the elevator and heading our way.

"Harold," Milton would say, "I see a speck of dust on that one, blow it off quick before Myron Millionaire gets off on our floor."

Milton was more like a soft-shoe dancer than a salesman. He was always sliding around, busy as a nervous bird looking for bugs. If a customer did approach, say a middle-aged lady, he would say, "Excuse me, madam. Harold, would you check out that white straw? I think I saw a centipede dash across the brim. Yes, madam?"

I was not cut out to be a salesman. I believe Uncle Al had an early premonition of this, so he did not try me out in the stockroom of the shoe store on Sixth Street, risking a repetition of my father's sailing-the-shoe experiment. One cruise was enough to last several generations of Holbrooks, and I was edging dangerously close to the antics of my father. I was threatening to become an actor. An unstable profession. Look what happened to my mother!

It's odd to look back now and realize that at this same time we were six months into a world war and that our troops in the South Pacific were facing disaster. They were trying to hang on at Corregidor, and here I was, only a year away from induction into the army, fooling around in Cleveland, feeling sorry for myself because I couldn't lean on the counter. Young men almost my age were bleeding to death in defense of the flag my grandfather had taught us to salute, but in Cleveland that summer the conflict seemed far away.

One night on the streetcar on my way home from Halle's I read a small newspaper item headed "Casting at Cain Park." They were casting for a play called *The Man Who Came to Dinner* at a theater on the east side of Cleveland. On an impulse I decided to try out for it and switched to a streetcar going east. I knew nothing about the play or the theater, nor had I ever been to a casting tryout, but inspired by my success as a maniac, my confidence was at high tide: I took the plunge. When I joined the people in a crowded room at Cleveland Heights High School, someone handed me a copy of the play and said, "Read Richard." I hadn't a notion who the character was, but the people sitting next to me cleared that up. He was the son in the family. I was scared, so I was nervous and certain that no one else in the room was as nervous as me. When my turn came I heard my voice speaking the lines, but in a disembodied way. A few people looked at me and said nothing. I was going to leave, but someone asked me to go to the next room and read for Paul Randall. He was directing *Ah, Wilderness!* and he asked me to read the part of a young man who was "the friend of Richard." There seemed to be a lot of Richards. I got the idea that Richard was the big part in this one, and he was being read by a fellow about my age named Morgan, but they called him Ace. He had the part already. I think I kind of resented that, that he had the part and didn't have to do anything more to get it and that meant I couldn't get it. But when we started to read, he was good. There was something special about him.

As I was finding my way out of the room, a small, wiry man about thirty-five years old with lots of lines in his face stopped me and introduced himself as Ed Wright, a teacher at Denison University in Ohio. He said he was acting and directing at Cain Park that summer. The name of Denison University rang a bell because I had applied there. My first choice was the University of Michigan at Ann Arbor because it had a celebrated theater department headed by a well-known teacher. But in my final months at Culver I'd been chosen to read the Scripture in chapel one Sunday. The guest preacher was Dr. Kenneth Brown, president of Denison University, a place I'd never heard of until then. I'd always been irritated by the way preachers read the Scripture, mashing the life and passion out of it, so I worked hard on the performance I was going to give. This was after I had strangled Ollie Rea to death and I wanted to leave Culver with a more humanitarian memory of Harry the cutup. Just before graduation I'd been caught brewing gin with Perry Fiske on the roof of South Barracks. The chapel reading went off without any failure of memory (I had memorized it) and then Dr. Brown gave the sermon. Not bad, I thought. Afterward he commented on my biblical performance and asked, "Have you applied to a college, Harold?"

"Yes, sir. I've applied to the University of Michigan."

"My college is Denison University. Have you heard of us?"

"No, sir. But I'm interested in studying theater and Michigan is tops."

"We have a fine department of theater run by a man named Edward A. Wright. You'd like him. I wish you would think about us."

It was so kind of him to take this much interest in me that I did apply, as a backup to Michigan in case they didn't take me. Now here was Ed Wright magically in the flesh at Cain Park.

"Dr. Brown told me about you. You read the Scripture for him at Culver."

"Yes, I did."

"Have you made up your mind where you're going to go this fall?"

"No, I haven't. Not yet. I've been accepted at Michigan."

"Well. We have a small department, much smaller than Michigan's. But we could use you."

I liked Mr. Wright. He wasn't afraid to come right out and be friendly and say he wanted me for his student. That meant a lot. It was personal. The next day they called me and said I was going to play Richard in *The Man Who Came to Dinner*.

I never dreamed it would be so easy. And when I heard they were going to pay me $15 a week, I was astonished. Paid to act? That was unbelievable. I was getting only $18.75 a week selling hats at Halle's, and since we rehearsed in the evenings I could keep my day job. Suddenly I was rich. Rich—$33.75 a week! If I weren't living with Grandma, I could have rented a small apartment and supported myself for the two weeks the Cain Park job would last. I was a person. I was free!

"I knew it," Milton said. "I knew you wouldn't last here. Now I suppose you'll become a movie star and leave me here all alone with Rolling Thunderclap."

"No, no, Milton. It's just for this one play and I'll be working every day here."

"A likely story."

The two weeks of work stretched to six when I was cast in two more plays, *The Vagabond King* and *In Time to Come*. We rehearsed a week for each play and then performed it a week at the outdoor theater in the leafy wonderland of Cain Park. It sat three thousand people in seats planted in concrete within the curve of a graceful hillside bordered by trees. Below this sylvan grandstand the actors performed on a large stage lit by spotlights from towers above the audience. It was a magical place, humming with life, and for this raw recruit who was getting paid to act in his fourth play, it was like going to heaven. I had the sensation that I was being lifted aloft on a lovely balloon, way above the life I had lived until now.

The actors were all practiced hands. I was eager to make a good impression on everyone, but there wasn't much opportunity to show off in the role of Richard, no monologues like John Barrymore's and no chance to strangle anyone. However, in *The Vagabond King* I was to play the role of Captain of the Scotch Archers, and this had heroic possibilities, especially when I dashed onstage with the archers behind me. I forget why I was dashing onstage and it's possible I didn't know at Cain Park why I was dashing on, but that didn't matter. It was the dashing on that was the whole acting job as far as I was concerned. We came on through double doors upstage center, in full view of the audience, just after a stagehand behind each door had opened them wide. Then I dashed on, followed by five Scotch Archers waving bows and arrows and shouting, "Here we come, the Scotch Archers!" or something like that. By opening night I had worked myself into a Scotch swivet about this heroic entrance and I wanted it to be memorable. And it was. The stagehands yanked the doors apart and in so doing they raised the iron strap holding the partition together at floor level. This little bow didn't rise very high above the floor, but it rose high enough to snag my boot as I came dashing through in my forest primeval outfit, full tilt, blood up, and waving my bow. Crash. That was the sound of me hitting the floor. Tramp, tramp, tramp. That was the sound of my Scotch Archers tramping over me before they dropped onstage like coconuts. Ho, ho, ho! That was the sound of the audience trying not to have heart attacks from laughing themselves to death. This was my memorable moment at Cain Park Theater in the summer of '42.

But I had one other memorable moment that summer in the role of Captain Stanley, the naval aide to President Wilson in *In Time to Come*. The play centered on Wilson, Lloyd George from England, Clemenceau from France, someone from Italy, and Ed Wright as Senator Henry Cabot Lodge of Connecticut, all of them fighting over the League of Nations treaty that would banish war forever. My most important entrance was when I dashed on once again at a crucial moment with a telegram that would change the course of this summit meeting.

The backstage area is usually very dark, even one under the stars. At Cain Park it was also very large, about the size of Buffalo around 1750. There was a separate house for costumes, one for props and offices, one for dressing rooms—a sort of theatrical Williamsburg back there in the dark. I had become interested in makeup. While playing the madman at Culver I had discovered collodion. It inspired me to glue a network of scars around my face. Then I discovered false hair, which I used at every portal above the neck—ears, nose, and a heavy bush above each eye. I hadn't stopped there. I had brought my Max Factor makeup kit home with me to Cleveland that summer, and one night I decided to scare the neighbors. Quasimodo was my choice. I managed to close over one eye with half a Ping-Pong ball and some adhesive tape painted with makeup. The eyebrows were there, of course, though a bit askew. The mouth had a dreadful droop to the side, created by cementing one corner in a crease to the south with collodion, and there were several acres of warts and moles sprouting hair tentacles. Surmounting this out-of-control masterpiece was a canopy of false hair jammed under a bandanna from

Grandma's scarf collection. There was the hump, of course. And a limp, made more grotesque by an inward turning of the foot.

In this disguise I, Quasimodo, crept down the back staircase and stole into the quiet neighborhood to test my creation. At the first house whose bell I rang there was no one home but the dog. He flung himself repeatedly at the side window until a roar from me sent him wheeling away into the interior. At the second house a lady opened the door a crack and screamed, "I don't want any! Help, oh help!" and slammed the door. I was afraid her husband would come out and club me, so I slunk quickly away into the night. Mostly I had the thrill of screaming women and men running for their guns and baseball bats, but at one door the lady just looked me over and said, "Young man, go home." This was a downer. I limped toward my own house, a chastened Quasimodo, and that's when I remembered Grandma. If I could convince her, success was mine.

I decided to use the front door because it was more isolated in our big house and no one ever went there, especially at night when it was dark. I could hear her coming, and I slipped behind a clump of privet so she wouldn't see me. When she peered out the narrow window beside the door and saw no one, she vanished. I rang the bell again and ducked behind the privet. This time she opened the door and looked out.

"Aaarrh."

"Hah! Hah! Help! Hah! Help! Go away!" She tried to close the door, but I saw she was terrified and stopped her.

"It's me, Grandma!"

She ran into the house shouting, "Help! Police! Help! Harold, come quick—"

"Grandma, it's me . . ."

"Harold," she shouted up the stairs, "call the police!" I pursued her into the kitchen, grabbing at her, trying to convince her it was her boy.

"It's me, Grandma!"

"Go away, you nasty thing! Help! Police! Police!" I tried shedding the limp and backed her against the stove.

Harold

"Please go away! Oh, you nasty thing. Harold, come quick! Poleeece!"

"Grandma, it's me. Harold."

"No it isn't. Poleeece!"

"It is. It's me. I have makeup on. See?" I raised one hand to point at my face, but the ringlet of hair I had added to the back of my hands ruined the appeal.

"Poleeeeeece! Poleeeeeece!"

When I took the Ping-Pong ball off, I managed to quiet her down and convince her that I was her blue-eyed baby boy with a Ping-Pong ball over one of those eyes. It was this experience that showed me how effective makeup could be, though I believe it crushed any seedling of love for the theater that might have bloomed in Grandma.

The makeup room at Cain Park was on the second floor of one of those backstage buildings in Buffalo and I had acquired the nervous habit of running across the backstage acreage and climbing the stairs between my entrances and exits to check on my makeup. In my mind the naval captain had to be at least forty years old, so I had been busy hunting over my face for any depression that a brown pencil could deepen into a wrinkle. There weren't many, so I had to add some. This may have had something to do with the long look President Wilson always gave me when I dashed in with the telegram and threw him my best Culver salute. Something about my appearance seemed to unsettle him, possibly because my makeup kept sweating off, which was why I constantly checked it out in the mirror of the makeup room. It turned a simple role into a cross-country event.

One night as I was deepening a line in the mirror I heard running feet hit the stairway and start bounding up.

"Holbrook! Holbrook! You're on!" My blood froze. Then I started running. I dove down the stairs and ran across the back streets of Buffalo, past the prop table, yanked open the president's door, and dashed in. I saluted. There was that long, quizzical look from Wilson, only this time it got longer.

"Well," said Wilson finally.

A horrible reality began to flood my head with the thought that I might have forgotten something. Clemenceau and the fellow from Italy, Orlando I believe, looked at me with European disgust and Senator Henry Cabot Lodge (Ed Wright) seemed on the verge of breaking into an impromptu oration.

"Do you have something for me, Captain?" said Wilson, his voice beginning to crawl with desperation. My God, I thought. The telegram!

"I forgot something, sir. Be right back." A quick salute and I was gone, leaving the League of Nations on hold while I dashed to the prop table. There were about ninety-nine objects on it. One of them was a telegram, but where was it? In the darkness backstage it could have been anywhere. I pawed wildly at this forest of objects, desperate for anything even distantly related to paper, until I heard the prop girl breathing heavy behind me and clawing at the table, too. She pushed me aside, plucked a piece of paper into my hand, and hissed, "Get on the goddamn stage!"

I felt much less like a naval captain on this entrance than I had on the first, because my makeup had sweated off.

"A telegram for you, sir," said I.

Clemenceau was having some kind of wheezing seizure now and the audience had grown aware that a screw was loose in the Oval Office. That would be me.

"Well?" said the president, looking at the telegram in my hand.

"Sir?"

"May I have it?" A dreadful pause in which Lodge turned away from the audience and covered his mouth.

"What, sir?"

"The telegram," he said drily. "The one in your hand."

"Oh, of course, sir. I was bringing it to you." That brought down the house. Wilson, Lloyd George, Clemenceau, Orlando from Italy, and Ed Wright lost control of themselves along with the hillside of people. I retired from the stage and searched for an alley where I could hide myself.

That summer I decided to go to Denison. Maybe this choice was influenced by the discovery that I needed a lot more practice before I could ask an audience to expose itself to me. Maybe it was the good humor in Ed Wright's eyes, which forgave anything. Maybe it was the example of Ace Morgan, the wonderful young actor in *Ah, Wilderness!* who had spent his freshman year at the University of Iowa and was going to switch to Denison.

9

When June got back to Cleveland, she married Bill Meyer to spite Grandma. In the fall she went to work for the war effort, standing at a punch press all day while carrying her first child. Alberta had spent a year on the farm in Connecticut. She'd been shipped down there when Grandma and Uncle Al were at a loss over what to do with her. Alberta was by now a beautiful young girl in the ripe flush of life and Paul was a vulnerable young man. He fell in love with her. It ignited a proposal that Alberta should stay on the farm and marry him. The details are scattered in the mists of history, but we know my sister did not want to become a farmer's wife, and she left. I believe it would be honest to say that Paul carried the wound for a long time.

When I look back so many years down the line, after I have finally come to understand the word "family" and realize that my sisters and I never sat down and discussed what was happening to us, it seems unnatural. But we were never a family from the moment Grandpa died. At that moment we began to live separate lives. The journey each of us took had its own set of rules and its separate destination. I didn't know how to reach across the unnatural space between us and join hands to help my sisters, because we were going it alone on our personal journeys of survival.

That summer before I left for Denison, Alberta told me I was going to be her date for the night. She was going to take me to a bar out near the airport, she said, and teach me to dance. "You need to get relaxed, Harold," she said. She was acting like an older sister, more worldly than me, and it made me nervous, but it was also exciting. When we got to the roadhouse she knew everybody, including the bandleader, and all of a sudden there she was at the microphone, singing. I was astonished. She was good! Where did she learn to sing like that? I wondered. And to have the confidence to get up and do it? While we were dancing she told me she'd been offered a job singing with the band and was thinking it over. She was revealing to me a life I'd never heard about before, a wildly different and seductive life, the forbidden one my sister was living. More than anything else it told me we were strangers.

Now it was time for me to go to college. Another dark forest to enter alone. Uncle Allen and Aunt Merce drove me down to Granville, a languid Shangri-la resting among the Welsh hills of central Ohio, one block long, with three churches and the Opera House on its main intersection and not a bar in sight. Uncle Al took great pride in making this trip with me. He felt he was serving as a substitute father, taking the white hope of the family to college. I was to live in Curtis Hall, a big redbrick dormitory, with a hundred or more freshmen. Back with the boys again after the blessed luxury of having a room to myself at home all summer. George Livingston had enrolled at Denison, too, but he was not rooming with me. Perhaps he figured the dormitory would have a ventilation system, and between that and having me catapult out of bed at night to write another poem and insist he listen to it, the cost was too great.

It was rush week. That was when you sold your personality to a Greek fraternity. The idea of surrounding myself with even more buddies was as attractive to me as exploring a limestone cave, but George wanted to join up. He took it seriously, studying each fraternity with care, and halfway through the week he made his choice, the most macho fraternity on campus, crawling with football players. I couldn't believe it, but the bigger surprise came when he told me they wanted him.

"But there's a problem."

"Whadya mean?"

"I'm Jewish."

"So . . . What does that mean?"

"It means they have a rule in the national office about Jews. They're going to make a special petition to the national office for me. They really want me."

I saw how much this meant to him and held my breath. On the last night of rush week I went looking for George. I found him sitting in his room alone.

"George . . ."

"They turned me down."

"George . . . Goddamn it—"

"They didn't want me. The fellows wanted me. But the national office—"

"George—"

"They said they were sorry. Because they really wanted me."

I had never seen him cry before. He was struggling against it, but the tears finally came and they kept coming, and I have never forgotten it. It was a terrible sight to see this young man's hopes destroyed by prejudice.

George joined the American Commons Club, a quasi-fraternity created to catch the fallen, the Jews, our one black student, the crippled and disfigured and strange. Anyone who didn't have the winning ticket. I joined them, too. At the end of the first semester George joined a much larger fraternity, the United States Army. He went to Europe and fought the Nazis.

I found my brotherhood at the Opera House. Brothers and sisters working together. It had been a church once upon a time, so that intersection in Granville had been a gridlock of sanctity until Ed Wright came along and turned one corner into a theater. But Ed did not take the sanctity out of that corner. Nor did he welcome us into the theater to be strange or weird or even rebels. He inspired us to serve a quietly sanctified purpose and to work hard for it. To begin with, you had to put in one hundred hours backstage before you could audition for a play. There was a chart on the wall backstage in the Opera House where we recorded the number of hours we put in, and I wanted to be the first one to hit the mark. Our theater sat about four hundred people, but that was the grandest thing you could say about it. Ingenuity made it run. We built our own scenery, of course. One-by-four battens for the frames, canvas tacked over them, shrunk and painted. Our lighting expert, a senior student named Inky, made most of his spotlights out of discarded cans. Maxwell House coffee for the overheads and the tall Del Monte tomato juice cans for the spots out front. These were mounted on pipes hung from the ceiling by chains dropped through holes punched in the plaster and lath. Nothing about the place would have qualified under the codes of corporate America, but we were lucky enough to be learning our trade before corporate America came along and smiled the life out of everything.

The first play was *Brother Rat*, a comedy about a military school, which George Abbott had directed on Broadway. I painted the scenery and myself with various hues of paint, and right away I could see that Denison was turning into a good choice, because I was impressed with the quality of the acting and Ed's production. For the second play, *Thunder Rock* by Robert Ardrey, Inky put me on his lighting crew and introduced me to the mysteries of the dimmer board rheostats and the art of smoothly guiding the handles up and down. Now I felt a part of the play because my hands were helping it. Standing just offstage at the dimmer board, I felt the magic of stage lighting, how it stirred the drama of a scene with visual poetry. The Opera House was a wonderland of excitement and fun and slow-growing comradeship. I couldn't wait to get down the hill and go to work so I would be the first to reach a hundred hours. Then up came a problem. My fraternal order, the Commons Club, wanted me to rake the fall leaves around the house on Saturday mornings, but this would deduct four hours from my Saturday total backstage every week. Before the leaves gave out, I quit the fraternity for the Opera House. Best switch I ever made.

Ed Wright was no theatrical holy roller. He just pointed out your mistakes and let you do the holy part, and if you got too passionate he calmed you down. His idea was that the audience should understand what you were raving about because the reason you were there was because they were there. He did not teach self-indulgence, nor did he discourage passion and sincerity. The technique of the stage and its rules of the road were what he wanted to offer you. And respect for the theater.

I hadn't been at Denison more than a few days when I got a call from Ed. "Can you come over to the house for dinner? Louise is cooking up something and a few other theater kids will be here."

That was the beginning of a friendship that was going to last fifty-four years, until we spread Ed Wright's ashes on the Pacific Ocean. Louise was his partner and protector all his life, until she passed quietly into the great beyond one night by his side. He was from Marshalltown, Iowa, this small, sprung-wire man who lived just a little off the ground and had fallen in love with the stage as a boy when traveling theatrical companies came through Iowa's rural towns, playing under canvas. Ed turned pro at the age of fourteen as the Boy Impersonator on the Chautauqua circuit. His idol was Elias Day, an older monologist of supreme skill and dedication who saw in this young powder keg a talent of extraordinary promise. He agreed to take Ed on and teach him everything he knew. Ed drank at this well with earnest dedication until Elias Day gave him permission to use his own creations. The prize jewel in that treasure chest was a character called Elmer Wartz, the Champion Hog Caller of Indiana. Now suspend judgment and even belief for a bit here because this was not the kind of entertainment you would run across today. It's long gone. You could've seen it in Shakespeare's comedies, maybe, if his back was turned, and there may be a shred or two of it left in the provincial vaudeville houses of England.

Imagine watching a small fellow with a rubber face who has just impersonated a woman's club president (weird as a soap bubble) introducing the young hero of the day, Elmer Wartz, who has returned from the Indiana State Fair after a triumphant performance in the hog-calling contest. Don't leave, this is going to be worth it. The small man we just saw as this woman's club nutcase with the fluttering hanky has turned his back for a brief moment and is doing things to his face while he describes Elmer's advance to the stage to receive the accolades of the homecoming crowd and deliver his victory oration. You pretty much cringe in anticipation because if what has gone before seemed excessive, you figure this will blast it out of the park. He seems to be pulling some red thing over his head—could it be a dry mop?—and then he is silent for a moment while we hear him stuffing something in his mouth. With a final flip at his lapels, which stands them straight up, he turns toward us. Round, awfully round blue eyes, carrot-red hair fresh from a riot, and the blank look of a farm boy who ought never to have left the barn. He stares at us a moment while we chuckle and wonder if the performer can possibly survive what he has created so far. And then he smiles. It's a slow smile and it reveals a set of teeth that look big and then get bigger and bigger as the smile widens, until you are looking at a row of molars that would be the pride of a Missouri mule. Long in the tooth does not do them justice. You can hardly believe your eyes now because they are watering up pretty bad from the hysterics that have started to shake you all over. Then he swings that leg. You think you've seen a leg swing before? Not like this one. This one carves an arc in the air that would put to shame an F-86, and it lands with a thump, foot first, on the table beside him. You're a goner now. You've given up the sophisticated notions you had about art and all that stuff and you have caved in before the hilarious creature Ed Wright has planted in front of you.

"Waaal, folks!" The speech has begun. It's not going to stand up with the Gettysburg Address or even the speech your frightened seven-year-old gave at the graduation ceremony for the first grade. It has to do with calling hogs. In fact, the joy of calling them. You get the whole picture from when the hogs start running toward another hog-caller contestant and then Big Tooth lets loose with his adenoids and those hogs turn around and come trotting right up to him as happy as eeny, meeny, miny, and moe. By this time you've turned to jelly and given up any claim to sanity. The wee portion of it you've got left is busy admiring this man's shameless exhibition of pure theatrical wizardry. He knows exactly how to control an audience.

Ed Wright never learned to drive. I don't know why, because he had a car. But he always asked a student to drive him to his engagements around central Ohio, so we got to watch him do his show. If at first you felt it was beneath you to enjoy this sort of thing, you gave up that fantasy before very long. You were being treated to a lesson in playing an audience like a fiddle and a primer in the art of timing a laugh line, given by a superb performer. I was one of his drivers.

A beginning class Ed gave for freshmen was Oral Interpretation. You stood up in front of the class at a lectern and performed a story or a poem or a dramatic passage, but you were not allowed to act it out. This was only a waypoint to acting. It was interpreting a text for its sense and dramatic substance *with your voice*. We were being trained for the stage, not the whispering realm of television and film. I chose to do Edgar Allan Poe's "The Telltale Heart" and I made a hit with it, which gave me the kind of ego boost that is useful to a newcomer. I also did Poe's poem "Ulalume." Why I was drawn to these morose, here-comes-the-madman selections I do not know, beyond the fact that having scared the living lights out of Grandma and being familiar with the insane asylum, I felt this might be my calling. Apparently Ace Morgan thought so, too, because he cast me as a Nazi officer in the play Ed had given him to direct, *Letters to Lucerne*.

Ed had been mesmerized when he happened upon Ace directing a production of *Rio Rita* at Cleveland Heights High School that summer in Cain Park. He convinced Ace to leave the University of Iowa, where E. C. Mabie was a highly respected head of Drama (Tennessee Williams went there), and transfer over to Denison. The catnip Ed used to seduce Ace away was an offer to let him direct one of the major plays at Denison in the coming year. Ace took the bait and we got ourselves an uncertified genius. Ed felt he was the most gifted young theatrical talent he had ever seen. A natural genius, a private inferno housed in a small, friendly person who listened to you intently. He was not too busy being a genius to hear what you said and to embrace your feelings with sympathy and understanding. He was a friend. I had never had one like him before.

Harold

When I think back on those days and remember that we had only that one school year together, plus a few meetings in the army, it bewilders me that I still have such a deep well of affection for Ace. I think he ignited a flame in me that has never gone out. The flame he lit has glowed not just for the theater but for tracking down what is true. It may be that this is what prepared me for the role that has defined my life. We were young idealists together. I never knew I was one until I met Ace, probably didn't even know what an idealist was. I'm not the disciple type, my ego is too prickly for that, but he opened up my mind to the battleground of curiosity and skepticism. Yet he was not a destroyer. His soul was active. Take Shostakovich, for instance. When Ace asked me to sit down on the floor and listen to this Russian guy's Fifth Symphony, I thought, Oh God, he's gone too far; but as I loosened my grip on the security of ignorance and let this new thing descend on me, the room filled and expanded with the roar of passion resounding in those giant chords. I was hooked on it. He told me he was going to use it in *Letters to Lucerne*.

This was the second production of that fateful year when the war loomed over us, penetrating even the quiet hills around Granville, Ohio. Hitler's motorized gangs had rolled across Europe and Jews were being slaughtered like diseased animals. Ace brought the war to us in *Letters to Lucerne*. This play centers on the invasion of a girls' school in Lucerne, Switzerland, by Nazi troops who want to take it over. The headmistress will not yield in her defense of the sanctity of the school and this brings her into confrontation with the German officer in command, the role played by me.

At the height of this face-off Ace gave me a peculiar piece of direction. He asked me to turn my back on the headmistress, who then turned her back on me. It was an awkward move that was sure to get a laugh. I felt passionate about the seriousness of the moment and argued with Ace that this odd staging would destroy it. He listened and asked me to try it out. On opening night the audience laughed. I felt humiliated. I believed I had ruined the scene and I went back to my room feeling disgraced. I took a piece of paper out of my desk and wrote on it, "They laughed."

I hung that paper above my desk where I would always see it and be goaded by it. At every performance I tried to make the laugh go away, but I couldn't. Ace wanted the laugh because it ridiculed the German officer, and I was too far gone into the characterization to see anything funny in it. If this had happened with a hundred other directors I would have lost faith in them. I didn't with Ace and I think it had to do with the quality of our friendship and my respect for him. The truth is, we didn't spend that much time hanging around together. He involved himself in his fraternity and the theater, and he made straight A's without appearing to study. I was staggering around with chemistry and Spanish and could hardly keep my head above a water-level average of grade C. The only subjects I enjoyed were Oral Interpretation and English. I liked writing and even won the poetry prize that year. But my overall grade average had a big dent in it.

Yet when an emotional crisis came, Ace responded. I had fallen in love with Carol Jacquet, a young actress in the Theater Department, and one night something had gone wildly wrong between us. I was in an agony of distress. I had moved downtown at the end of the first semester to a room in a house on Broadway and that night I left my room in a desperate condition, blindly forcing myself to walk the quiet streets of the village. I wound up at a bridge over the river on the Columbus road and began to sob in awful snatches of anguish. I felt I had lost her, and the loneliness that smote me was so frightening that I began to wonder if I would lose my mind and end up like my father. I teetered on the edge of this obsession until it frightened me so much I walked away from the bridge and the river below. The little savior of sanity in my head cautioned me that I must talk to someone. Call Ace, it said. Even though it's one o'clock in the morning, go back to your room and call him. When he answered the phone I managed to croak his name out, and then my voice shut down. "Hal . . . Hal, is something wrong?" I couldn't speak, because I didn't know how to say "Help." Ace said, "I'll be right there."

I met him on the road and we went walking. I began to tell him about my father and the fear I had that I might end up in an asylum, how we had been abandoned and that it could happen again, and he listened and asked questions. Finally he said, "I don't think you have to go into the asylum right now. You're going to be inducted into the army in three months." We laughed and then laughed at ourselves for laughing, because the idea of getting killed in the war was not very funny. Then he gave me a bear hug and went east to the Kappa Sig house and I went west to my rooming house at the other end of Broadway.

Carol Jacquet gave me the name Hal. I grabbed hold of it and hung on because I didn't like Harold and seemed to have outgrown Harry. She was a talented actress, a sensitive one whose emotions rose easily to the role. We had begun going around together. It was intense. The hunger we felt for each other was held at bay only by her religious principles, which made the hunger worse. She was a Catholic, and that saved us from leaping headlong into a union that the war would have sundered. I was a vulnerable young man with emotions that had just been let out of school, and that freedom made them untrustworthy.

Gordon Condit had played Robert Browning in *The Barretts of Wimpole Street* the year before and every girl in the college had swooned over him. Now he had written a play. Its name was *The World Within*. Its heroine is a famous novelist whose career has become so cyclonic that her younger sister, who lives with her, is left alone to search for a life, and she creates a world within her imagination. In this world is a friend, an imagined friend, more real to her than her older sister. The novelist callously uses the girl's imaginary relationship in her novel. I was thrilled to be given a role in the play as the mercurial author's uncle, a sophisticated observer of the tattered relationship between the sisters. But I had trouble with the role because I was playing a straight character with no disguise. Close to myself, in other words. No beards, no hump, no limp, no eye obscured by half a Ping-Pong ball, and that always scared me. It continued to shake my confidence for years and was to become my Achilles' heel: This person named Hal Holbrook, who was he? Was he my father? No thanks. My mother? Who? My uncle? I liked him but he wasn't the role model I sought for myself. The person I wanted to be was a dream with no dimensions. I didn't have a person to grow into.

Ed's pride in Gordon, his faith in this shy, handsome young man with a sensitive, almost fragile talent, was justified in his production of *The World Within*. It was a home run. The newspapers in Columbus and nearby towns signified this, and now Ed reached out further. He sent the play to Brock Pemberton, the New York producer who had scored high on Broadway. Pemberton acknowledged receipt of it and then no word came for weeks. Ed contacted Pemberton again. The message came back that he was trying to get to it. Months passed and Ed wrote him again: respond or return the play. The response came. "The idea of an imaginary character leaves me cold." It was a disappointment, but the real knockout drop came a year later when Pemberton produced a comedy called *Harvey* by the playwright Mary Chase. The imaginary rabbit at the center of Chase's play became a classic character in the lore of American theater.

10

In the month of May, Granville, Ohio, blooms in the misty air. The mist is more a vapor caused by the sun's heat settling on the Welsh hills and encouraging the buds to come out. The maples and elms peek out first, then the tulips stretch forth with glorious pride, and suddenly the cherry blossoms lining the brick walk to Swasey Chapel put everything else to shame. Photographers catch their breath. I have called Granville a Shangri-la because that's the feeling of it. A New England town that picked itself up in the early 1800s and moved to the graceful hills of central Ohio. A small college was established by the Baptists. It grew over the next century to a larger liberal arts institution, joining the pantheon of Oberlin, Kenyon, and others hidden away in the surprising beauty of rural Ohio. From the celibate cocoon of Granville have come statesmen, giants of industry and invention, scientists, artists, and Woody Hayes. Denison is not quite dismissable by the eastern establishment and it regards the West with amusement. Granville goes its own way because it knows what it is and is cheerful about it.

From this sheltered nest I entered the United States Army on May 28, 1943, the day after the conclusion of freshman classes. The rules of the wartime draft permitted us to finish our freshman year if we turned eighteen in the middle of it and that was my case. Ace had left a few weeks before me. Very early on the morning of the twenty-eighth I was driven away from Granville to Fort Hayes in Columbus and dumped into the rawboned melting pot of the armed forces. Stripped naked, pushed, poked, bent over, stuck with needles, glowered at, given a number. Back with the boys again.

"Fuck you! You ain't never seen no motherfucking still, you fat-assed fucking city boy. You ben drinkin' yer pappy's piss and goin' down on yer shiteatin' momma."

I had heard the words before but never in a barrage like this, one that went on for hours. Never from the mouths of 90 percent of the human animals surrounding me like beasts in a swamp. And the swamp was riddled with quicksand. I was an outsider, that was as clear as the bells of hell. I wouldn't last another day in this place if I didn't alter my behavior, forget poetry and politeness, and try to fit in, because I neither saw nor heard another human being who could possibly have come from Granville. I was trying to write to Carol Jacquet, but every decent thought was blasted out of my head by the filthy verbal onslaught from my new buddies out of the hills of Kentucky and West Virginia. I was vaguely aware that they were as insecure as I was, most of them, but they weren't the kind of guys who wanted to talk about that. Until it became clear who was going to be head dog in this big kennel, a punch in the jaw and a fuck-you was going to be their mantra for getting through the day.

By rights, the head dog could have been me because I was from Culver Military Academy. Three years of senior ROTC qualified me for a rating of sergeant after six weeks of training in the U.S. Army. It said so on the slip of paper I had in my hand when I was in that line of naked bodies. I was clutching it and I was also sweating on it because all the faces I saw behind the desks did not look friendly. They didn't have that warm, brotherly look; it was more of a look that said "Christ, you're hopeless." So releasing hold of my slip, even daring to place it in front of one of these mean-looking bastards, was going to require an act of bravado reminiscent of Nathan Hale. "I have but one life to give for my country." However, the old suicide impulse was still pumping inside my naked body, so when I got to the last desk in the nudist parade and saw a great, hulking mastiff sitting behind it with sergeant stripes on his sleeves, my mission was clear.

"Sir." A red-eyed glance was all I got. "Sir, I have this paper."

"Uhh?" He was checking out my body parts like a fellow who had got tired waiting for a bus.

"I have this paper from Culver Military Academy that says—"

"Whah?"

"What, sir?"

"Whah 'camedy?"

"Culver Military Academy, sir. It's in Indiana—"

"Pass."

"No. I have this paper here that says I'm a sergeant." A surprised look would not describe what he gave me, as well as the piece of paper. Beyond surprised.

"I mean, I know this is . . . probably it doesn't mean . . . but it says right here—Sergeant. See?" And I laid the sweaty paper in front of him. He didn't even touch it, just looked at it as if I'd laid a turd on the table. Then his red eyes hopped up to me.

"Whaa-th-hell-iz this?"

"Never mind, sir. It's okay. It just says I should be a sergeant after six weeks' training." He seemed to get the idea now. I could see it racing around the fortifications of his brain.

"I'll take care o' this. Pass."

I saw it slide off the table as I backed away in the manner of a supplicant leaving the royal chamber. Where that little wet slip of paper wound up, only the real sergeant knows and he ain't never told nobody. The truth is, I didn't want to be a sergeant. The idea of trying to control those boys from the hills with very pale blue eyes and a tendency to violence scared me off. I wanted to be the quiet one.

After a cautious review of my educational background and usefulness to the war effort, I was assigned to the Amphibious Engineers. Basic training was at Camp Edwards on Cape Cod. The only thing they got right by sending me there was my New England genealogy. Engineering was as alien to me as Afghanistan. However, this bewildering assignment had one very powerful consolation, which came in the form of paratrooper boots. The Amphibious Engineers was the only other outfit in the army that wore those high boots with the pants tucked into them. The probable reason for this gesture of romance to the amphibians was that we would be in the advance wave of an invasion. Paratroopers came out of the air. We came out of the water, where we were supposed to clear it of mines, barbed wire, and other obstacles resting below its surface and then hit the beach if we hadn't been blown up first.

The idea behind army basic training in wartime is to scrape the civilian out of you and make you want to kill people. Most of us do not hanker for the life of a murderer. We want to live in peace. That, however, does not serve the requirements of war. You have to get the civilian mad. So, first you humiliate him by taking away his clothes. Then you stuff him into a hot railroad car and send him to a godforsaken prairie of sand dunes on Cape Cod. The civilian's first thought is: Where's Falmouth? Where's the beach? They're still there, but guard gates shut the captured civilian away from all that happy stuff. He is now a prisoner. His lockup is a two-story wooden barracks with opposing rows of iron cots running the length of each floor. There's a wooden footlocker at the end of each bed where he stores what's left of his life. And there's the latrine. That's the army's word for where he washes the sand off and eliminates the food he has scraped from a tin plate three times a day. The latrine has a cement floor for general drainage; the little amenities of civilian life, like privacy, have been left out. The only possible point of admiration about a latrine is that it's clean and the imprisoned civilian knows that because he has cleaned it.

Rising at 5:30 a.m. is no problem because the platoon sergeant announces the dawn as if it had just come up like thunder. The latrine also figures into one's zeal for rising because if the civilian-now-a-soldier doesn't get there quickly, he lines up. Lining up is a way of life now. Lining up, waiting, and staggering forward, those are the three main activities of the day. There's calisthenics—hup two three four—out there in the damp dawn between the barracks, and then there is chow. Chow is food. No. It's army food. He wolfs that down by getting into the habit of not looking at it. If he dislikes lima beans, he'll starve.

Harold

There's a good deal of stress put on movement in the army, but always after the soldier has been standing still for a while. The movement takes many forms. Marching and drilling are two of them. That's when the civilian learns the squad right, squad left, to the rear, and halt ballet for men. There are some who were never meant to dance and these recruits leave the platoon and return like boomerangs every time a change of direction is called out.

There are two other activities during basic training that are not easily forgotten: the twenty-mile hike and the obstacle course. The twenty-mile hike is led by the platoon sergeant, who announces it with a half smile on his face because he knows that if the civilian has not yet developed an appetite for murder, he will have one when the hike is over. In fact, his appetite begins to sharpen when the sergeant tosses in the news that the civilian is going to make this trip with a seventy-pound pack on his back. By the time he has covered those twenty miles, the civilian is disappearing and a mad dog is taking his place. Now he is ready for the obstacle course. This is where he crawls along the ground with real lead flying over his head. The lead is from machine guns aimed just a tad above the ground, so he naturally tries to get his head as low as he can while still performing the approved crablike crawling motion that elevates his buttocks and never allows him to cover enough ground to put his mind at ease. He has to drag his rifle with him, of course, and there's a good deal of barbed wire to nip at his clothes, face, hands, ears, knees, buttocks, and the dragging foot. By this time it begins to dawn on the civilian who he wants to murder first. It's the sergeant.

Since I had graduated from military school, some of this stuff came easy and I knew how to break down the Springfield rifle. This early in the war we had not yet been given the M1. I was still trying to be a model cadet, so it shouldn't have come as such a shock to me when, after eight weeks of training, I was chosen by the army as a potential candidate for West Point. I hadn't relaxed my character enough by then to become a human being and drink beer with the boys. I was holding myself aloof, still looking for someone who could spell C-A-T. In other words, in my cowardly way I was pretty arrogant.

There were a couple of guys I talked it over with and they looked at me as if I'd won the raffle. "West Point? Shit, boy, you're home free. Grab it! In four years this motherfucking war will be over."

"What if it isn't?"

"So you'll get shot at. That's four years from now."

I was in a quandary. I wrote to Uncle Al and Grandma and I wrote to Ed Wright. Uncle Al saw it as a plum toward real advancement in life and he did have a powerful argument. It was an honor. The problem was, after four years at West Point I would be required to serve at least four more years in the regular army. That would make me twenty-six years old before I could become an actor, if I was still alive and the war had ended. Ed made those points to me and suggested I should think it over. He was writing me every week, in fact writing the same letter to Ace Morgan at Fort Benning, Georgia, and Gordon Condit, who had gone into the navy. So one of us got the typewritten original every third week and a carbon copy the other two weeks. Ed never missed. He chose the three of us for that special weekly letter, and it tied us together.

I couldn't make up my mind. Taking a side trip to West Point seemed less than brave to me, so when the time came to go before the board of big-time officers representing the Northeast Army Command, I was still unsure about what to do. The guys in my platoon who were going to face the Germans in France and Belgium and Mussolini's pals in the Italian boot were not bothered by any illusions, romantic or otherwise, and they voted for West Point. I felt like a fool to worry about losing my acting career, because the war would surely be over in four years and I could get out of it with my life. I think General Patton had hit the beaches of Africa by this time and was heading for Rommel, so hope was rising.

I met the other three candidates who were vying for the two positions at West Point and we were taken to an island off the coast of Cape Cod with a lot of pine trees on it. They drilled us in the precise procedure for entering the army hut and presenting ourselves to the general and three colonels inside. Squad left, squad right, halt, salute.

Harold

"Private Holbrook reporting, sir."

There was a pause. They were all looking down at my records on the table in front of them and I was desperately trying to decide what I was going to say. I still had not made up my mind, because no one had ever asked me the question that the general now spoke.

"Private Holbrook, I guess the first thing we have to know is, do you want to go to West Point?"

There was another pause, awesome to me because this was going to be a choice that would alter my life or perhaps end it. It was the high board again, and I let my suicide instinct take the dive.

"No, sir."

The heads popped up. All four officers had been studying those records, which I don't think included my damp piece of paper from the nudist line, but now four pairs of eyes looked at me in disbelief. No, maybe not; I think the general had the shadow of a smile at the corner of his mouth. He studied me for a long moment and said, "Well, I guess that's all, Private."

"Thank you, sir." I saluted him, did my about-face, and left West Point to join the boys with the pale blue eyes.

The experience seemed to uncork me. Culver drained away. I began to drink beer at the PX with some of my bunkmates and relaxed into a tentative companionship with them. I found them interesting. It was fun to join in the litany of complaints and cusswords that built our conversations into small mountains of distemper as the sandy days dragged on. At the same time, I was creating a character for myself, one that fit in with the boys but showed only a part of me. The rest I protected. I was hiding behind a character again.

I hid my feelings for Carol Jacquet, too, so they would not be tainted by the ugly sexual references splattered like mud in almost every bragging exchange between the competing males in our pack of mustangs. Locker rooms at schools were nurseries compared with the animal farm that war had created on fashionable Cape Cod. At the end of eight weeks we were given a pass to go into town, and we spread out through the streets of Falmouth like crazed predators who'd just been let out of a cage. We prowled the town in search of the females we'd imagined in those bragging fantasies back at the camp, but those women weren't in town. Real women were. Real girls who were polite and said hello. They looked so decent and wholesome that our posturing embarrassed us. We were privately ashamed. These females were somebody's sister.

Though West Point was out, the army was not going to give up on me. It still had plans to remodel me, so they sent me—hold your breath—to Harvard! My IQ scores had somehow slipped through the fingers of Sergeant Mastiff at Fort Hayes and they showed me to have a mental capacity above his. So they sent me to Harvard. I was forcibly enrolled in a program of excellence called the ASTP, the Army Specialized Training Program. I never found out what they were trying to specialize me into, but that didn't matter because if they were sending me to Harvard, it meant I had to be some kind of a genius, according to the army. I should have said, "Stop! My freshman grade average at Denison was D plus." But then I got the news that Ace had been collared for this program at Syracuse University, so I let it slide.

Harvard! Talk about unreal. To be plucked off the scrub pine acres of Cape Cod and ushered into a three-bedroom suite with parlor in Dunster House was electrifying. There was the Charles River right across the road where Grandpa had directed Henry to drive us after a wild ride on the merry-go-round at the Copley Plaza. How was I going to turn into a killer in a place like this?

I now had only five roommates. Two of us in each room plus me and we could all spell C-A-T, but the conversation still drifted toward girls. The references were more refined, not so many eff-you-see-kays, and we were all dazzled by the news that we could go into Boston on the weekend. But the bad news came in the titles on the textbooks: chemistry, trigonometry, calculus. I was in deep, deep water here and the addition of English to the curriculum did not sew up the death wound this Fright Brigade of higher learning inflicted on me. The whole setup was surreal. I was supposed to become a killer and shoot Germans and Italians, not march around Harvard Yard and fight it out with higher learning. There was only one thing left for me to do. Fuck off.

Harold

There were wrought iron bars on the first-floor windows of our suite in Dunster House and the screws could be easily removed. Five of us decided to remove them and slip away into Boston after bed check at night. The sixth man was a serious Polish guy who wanted to stay home and study. He is probably a general now. The rest of us walked to a subway stop away from Harvard Square and scouted the streets of Boston all night long. We followed girls around and went to the burlesque show at the Old Howard in Scollay Square. Then to save carfare we walked back to Cambridge before dawn and removed the bars, climbed in the window, and screwed the bars in place. We lay down on our bunks fully clothed until reveille sounded and then rolled onto our feet in a semi-torpor and lined up with the troops of the rear guard who had stayed behind to study and rest up for classes. We took breakfast, of course, to help settle our stomachs, and then went back to the suite and crawled into bed for our proper ration of sleep. We were on a campaign a little offset from the one the army had plotted out. Sure, the education we got in downtown Boston did not necessarily support the war effort *at that time*, but it was going to pay off when we got to France. Our specialized training program was designed to clear the streets and fool the enemy, emphasizing the arts of concealment, reconnaissance, and seeking women.

And let's not forget the exercise of the mind. When I suggested a Saturday night at the theater the other troops broke away to outflank the female locals in Boston Garden while I took shelter at a pre-Broadway tryout in the Wilbur Theatre. *Voice of the Turtle* was playing there, with the leggy Margaret Sullavan, whose husky voice could raise the hair on the back of your neck, so I campaigned there. The set was a marvel of reality—Miss Sullavan's apartment (her name was Sally in the play) with a kitchen and real running water. Elliot Nugent was Bill, the young soldier who had fallen in love with her just like me, and the big question was, What were they going to do about it before he shipped out for France? Thumping big decisions had to be made right there on the stage, and young men like myself were onstage with Bill and Sally, holding hands with them in our hearts. Since

Sally wasn't available, my thoughts dwelled on Carol Jacquet. My efforts to be unfaithful to her and thus raise my standing among the mustangs had been rendered hopeless owing to a lack of expertise in search and destroy. So when the first act was over I went into the lobby flushed with romantic feeling and eager to know what would happen next. That's when I heard the voices in the Wilbur's crowded little lobby passing judgment on what we had just seen.

"Simplistic, wouldn't you say?" "Oh, yes, I give it no chance at all." "Maggie and Elliot are charming, of course, but the premise is old hat." "The running water will get the *Times* review."

Who are these fools? I thought. Are they nuts or what? Then it dawned on me that they had come up from New York and probably knew more than I did. They were the Broadway crowd. But I, the simpleminded soldier, loved the play and saw it again in New York six months later on its way to a run of more than fifteen hundred performances. Just an early lesson in the fragility of showbiz opinion.

I have two eloquent memories of my time at Harvard. The first was at the Stage Door Canteen, the refuge for men in the service run (I think) by the USO. I heard Paul Robeson was there and he might sing for us. He did. It was in an upstairs room and this great tall man stood up on a heavy chair and out of his powerful body began to pour the ancient emotions of "Ol' Man River." Torn from the soul of a man who could have been there. I can feel it yet. It laid a hand on me for a lifetime.

The second memory was brief, and it was out of tune with the usual melody of my days at Harvard. It was an English class held outside in the yard, under the trees, with the tall-spired church nearby. We were assigned the task of writing down our feelings about what we saw around us. I wish I had that paper now so that I could revisit the moment more intimately, but what I recall clearly about that little interlude of sweetness is the freedom that was in it. My spirit was freed. For that wee space of time it flew back to where it came from and carried the message that I was still me. That's what I wrote about. Then it returned to hide again behind the macho charade I was playing to survive.

Harold

That moment of reacquaintance with myself was my swan song at Harvard. The first term was coming to an end and I flunked out of higher learning and was sent to Fort Belvoir, Virginia. I had been in the army for almost seven months. I'd been trained and haphazardly educated through no fault of the army and now I was going to be trained again. My friend Bill West from Camp Edwards and Harvard ended up going to Belvoir with me. We were now old hands at the army and we just wanted to get it over with and get on the boat. Or out of the army, if the war would end, but that prospect was a very dim light in the future. One day at the rifle range I walked off through some brush to be alone for a spell and found a paved two-lane road. It stretched to the right and left as far as I could see. The road to freedom. I stayed there for a long, long time, staring down the road until the heat waves off its surface blurred my eyes.

There were some newly drafted GIs who couldn't stand the mental and physical imprisonment of the army and sixteen weeks of basic training. They grew desperate. Some went AWOL, some took a quicker escape route. One morning when our platoon fell out for calisthenics, someone shouted, "Look!" He was pointing toward the obstacle course where a soldier was hanging by the neck from a crossbeam. And there were the old men, the men over thirty-five who were caught in the net of the draft when the age limit was raised to thirty-nine. Death was cutting into the supply of manpower for fighting a war on two fronts, and now the out-of-shape inductees whose bellies hung over their belts were stumbling along in our marching ranks. We had one in our platoon, a rather small red-faced man who was thirty-nine going on forty and overweight. Eddie. Our platoon sergeant ragged the guy all the time, cussed and belittled him until we felt ashamed to be witnesses to such cruelty. The sergeant was proud of his physical prowess. Bill West and I disliked him, but now it turned to hate.

The day of the twenty-mile hike arrived. The one with the seventy-pound packs on our backs. Eddie asked the sergeant if he could please be excused because he knew he couldn't walk the twenty miles even without a seventy-pound pack on his back. The sergeant told him to stop complaining and get his ass in gear. When the call came to "fall in," Eddie struggled out of the barracks with his pack, bouncing off the doorjamb and stumbling on the steps, and then he veered into place in the platoon. He was sweating already.

The twenty miles were long and dusty and the Virginia sun beat down. The shoulder straps on our backpacks cut deep into each shoulder and the weight of seventy pounds bore heavily on the rise just below the smalls of our backs. Stealthy sweat crept into every crevice of our bodies, and itching was a constant torture. Blisters formed and broke on the feet less hardened to army shoe leather. The shoes became fiery ovens carried forward yard by yard on legs as numb and heavy as stones. By the halfway point, when the sergeant called a break, old Eddie was way out of sight. A jeep was sent back to check on him and reported that he was still moving but very slowly. By the time he came in sight, the rest period was declared over and the sergeant ordered us to move out. Eddie was shuffling after us in the distance, his face contorted and red.

When our platoon made it back to the barracks, we were bone-tired men. We sprawled hunched over on our footlockers or flung ourselves on our bunks. An hour passed with no sign of Eddie and then a jeep arrived with him and his backpack. The color of his face was alarming, it was beet red. He moved in a trance, disoriented and mute. His bunk was on the second floor of the barracks and as he approached the stairs a defeated look passed over his face and then he started to climb. Before he reached the top, he fell. By the time his body came to rest, he was dead.

Maneuvers. This is when the army puts you through the final exam phase of basic training. The Blue Ridge Mountains of Virginia do not qualify as unpleasant at any time of the year except winter, say February and March, in a pup tent. That's a piece of canvas stretched taut in an inverted V over two men in sleeping bags, with snow on the ground, ice sculpture on the trees, and the temperature around eighteen degrees.

Harold

Our battalion was bivouacked on top of a sizable mountain following a bumpy slog up frozen dirt roads on the back of army trucks. The sergeant told us to pick out our tent sites in a grove of birch and alder trees and haul ass. That meant make camp. Once Bill West and I figured out how to set up the pup tent so it wouldn't sag too bad when the ice clung to it, we were assigned to latrine duty. Dig a long trench in the frozen earth about eighteen inches wide that could be aimed at or straddled, depending upon which duty the soldier was performing up there in the arctic weather. Speed and balance were the two main talents required in the safe performance of this duty. You did not want to stumble or fall in or freeze permanently in that position.

That first night, we were routed out of the tents at midnight and ordered to climb onto the trucks. Our orders were to build a pontoon bridge across the river in the valley below. The trucks heaved and grunted down the mountain, around rough switchbacks carved into its side, and as we went down it got warmer. That raised our spirits. But when we saw the river our spirits dropped. It was forty yards across, with cakes of ice tumbling in the moonlight along its surface. It was March and the ice was breaking up. How were we supposed to span that angry piece of river with a bridge? A cardinal rule in the army is that you do not ask questions. That's why the army and I never got along.

"Sarge, how 'n hell are we s'posed to put a bridge across that mean-looking river?"

"That's what you're going to show us, smart-ass. You and West."

"Yeah? How's that?"

"You're going in first."

At this point the lieutenant called us together and explained the procedure for getting the pontoons into the water and joining them together. Three-man teams would go into the water and work five-minute shifts. No team would stay in the water longer than five minutes because hypothermia would set in, the water being around thirty-five to forty degrees. Then he disappeared and left us to the discretion of the sergeant.

"Holbrook, West, and McNeeley, in the water." The sergeant had us now, right where he wanted us. We'd have to beg to get out. We waded into the stream and waited for our bodies to go numb.

We worked by moonlight. No light was allowed at night lest the enemy detect us. It was hard to keep our footing; the pontoons were cumbersome and wanted to break away from us and go with the current. Staying upright was a nimble trick and we were growing numb right up to our necks. But we were young and tough and this was a challenge, and in a crazed way we enjoyed it. We wanted to show up the sergeant, but after five minutes had come and gone a grim message began to drain away our confidence: hypothermia was tougher than we were. No word came from the sergeant. Our legs began to lose control and there was a loss of feeling in our hands. They were like clubs. Movements became slow and dreamy. We were sure the sergeant would have to give in first and bring us out, but no word came. Then McNeeley went under. We had managed to secure two pontoons and were working to move another into place when Bill saw McNeeley's head bobbing downstream. He yelled at me and we started swimming. We caught up with McNeeley's head and dragged him over to the shore, where some GIs pulled him out. He was practically unconscious and shivering bad so they threw blankets over him and called for the medics. His feet were frostbit, hard and white, and his whole system was out of synchronization. The major rolled up in a jeep from headquarters, looking grim, and took charge of things.

"How long was this man in the water?" There was a fitful silence, Bill and I adding to the drama because our teeth were going like castanets.

"West, you and Holbrook were in there with McNeeley?"

"Y-yes, sir."

"How long?" There was a big, mean pause. West said, "F-fifteen m-minutes, sir."

"Holbrook?"

I figured what the hell. "M-more like t-twenty, sir." The major's eyes roved around the circle of men. Nobody looked up.

Harold

"I want to see the sergeant. The rest of you go back to work."

The sergeant came forward and they had a little conference while McNeeley, West, and I were trucked over to the field hospital. We figured the major would chew the sergeant out, period. But we were wrong. He broke him to private. Old Eddie must have got a laugh out of that.

I was now fully trained, ready to get on the boat and go fight for my country. I was ready to be a killer. My plan was to kill the sergeant turned private first and then turn my gun on the Germans. But somewhere in a dreary office a GI clerk looking to fill a quota let his finger pause at my file. "Harvard," he mumbled. "Hmmmm." That's no doubt how the orders arrived for electrical school. No burst of genius tripped on the question of whether I was qualified to be an electrician. The army was desperate *not* to send me overseas to Italy or France or the Pacific Islands or wherever the fighting was taking place, that was clear, so they grabbed at this one last nutty detour. I was in the arms of a giant and I went where the giant told me to go. With a few other candidates I headed for New York.

11

The army had taken over the Broadway Central Hotel on West Broadway, off the southeast corner of Washington Square. The huge building had become an army barracks. We all assembled in a ballroom with soldiers from several army camps along the eastern seaboard and I was surprised to see a lot of black faces. The army had not been integrated yet, so what were they doing there? Silence lay over the room. The sergeant gave us some information about what we were there for and then he started handing out room assignments. The white soldiers would occupy the lower floors and the black soldiers the top floor. The name call droned on, two men to a room, and then an unwelcome crisis laid its embarrassing egg right there in the sergeant's lap. There was one white man left over and one bed available on the top floor. Uh-oh. An awkward silence fell while the numbers were checked and rechecked and the assembled multicolored troops stood waiting in poleaxed wonder. Someone was going to have to make one hell of a decision for crystal-clean America. Someone was going to have to go up there and sleep in the slave quarters. Certainly not me. Not this boy from the white west side of Cleveland, the blue-blooded descendant of criminal immigrants out of Plymouth, England. My folks referred to these dark-skinned people as niggers, unless they lived in our homes and picked up after us; then we called them by their names and often hugged them because there was something lovable in them. Or maybe it was because they dassn't be critical of us.

Anyway, there we stood, the United States Army in miniature, faced with an enemy we couldn't shoot down, because it had no speakable name. White boys and black boys together, trying not to be ashamed while the sword of humiliation raised its mighty question over our heads: Who was going to volunteer? I watched the black faces. They did not look back at us with either humor or scorn. Their eyes were lowered. I felt sorry for them. I couldn't help it. I looked slyly at the white faces around me and saw variations of concern, grimness, and uncertainty. The grandstand was waiting for one of us to step forward.

"I'll go."

There was an awkward moment while a lot of eyes from black faces drilled into me, along with the sergeant's. That was it. Onward Christian soldiers. I moved to the top floor with a quiet, intelligent guy who had an easy smile and didn't seem to feel awkward about the arrangement. That made it easier for me. I can lay some of my heroic choice to the look-at-me grandstand devil rising, but it was more than that. The pledge of allegiance my grandfather had taught us on Flag Day said "with liberty and justice for all." Plain, but not so simple. And there was Paul Robeson. Couldn't get him out of my mind.

We rode the Third Avenue El uptown to our classes at electrical school. I had enjoyed working the light board backstage for Inky at Denison, so maybe electricity would be fun, and I tried to gather my curiosity into a crouching frame of mind, but as our teachers' voices droned on, I lost interest. The army had made electricity boring. These were civil servants, tired-looking men, and I had been spoiled by much better teachers than these.

A miracle hand of fate had brought Ace Morgan and Gordon Condit to New York, too—Ace in another Specialized Training Program and Gordon at Columbia's Midshipmen's School. Ace and I met in the middle of Seventh Avenue, ignoring the New Jersey drivers lunging at their brake pedals, and headed down Grove Street to his girlfriend's apartment. She was Pat Hudson, a long-legged, dark-haired girl with a great-looking pixie face. She had become Ace's "Sally." I watched them together and noted that they were not a pair of stargazing lovers, but two individuals, affectionate but also outspoken. It looked to me like a more mature relationship than the one I had with Carol Jacquet. Somewhere in me I was beginning to feel trapped. The world of Granville was rocking out of focus. I needed to stay loose, primed and ready for the next move.

The shadow of loneliness was with me most of the time. When my thin wallet could handle it, I saw plays alone or with Ace and Pat, but I was reluctant to intrude on their precious time. *Life with Father* was at the Empire, trying to catch up with *Tobacco Road*, which had fooled every critic and stowed more than three thousand performances in the box office bank. John Barton played Jeeter Lester, the foul old redneck daddy on a dead Georgia farm, and it was a miracle of characterization. *Life with Father* was a wonderful evening. Unforgettable. I would see it three times over the next few years with different actors playing Father and Mother Day, but Howard Lindsay and his wife, Dorothy Stickney, were the ones I remember with most affection. Fifty-seven years later I can hear Lindsay's Father Day, the accents and tone of voice as clear as a bell, saying, "Vinnie . . . Where's my necktie? . . . Oh, damn!— Damnation!" And there was *Angel Street* with Leo Carroll's brilliant Sergeant Rough, *One Touch of Venus* with the glowing Mary Martin, and *Jacobowsky and the Colonel* with Louis Calhern.

Ace and I saw our friend Gordon from time to time at a bar on upper Broadway. We drank beer and wondered where the war would take us in the months to come, and all the while the specter of death sat with us in its ghostly way, unspoken but waiting and listening, preparing itself for the big surprise. Our men in the Pacific were beginning to step from island to island on beaches washed with blood. Gordon was a handsome, shy young man, sensitive and modest, so modest you wanted to shake him until his talent jumped out and took a bow. But he remained forever a modest man. Years later I asked him to refresh my memory about his wartime career.

"Where did you end up after Midshipmen's School at Columbia, Gordon?"

"Oh. The Pacific."

"Where, Gordon?"

"Oh. The islands."

"What islands?"

"Well. A lot of them."

"You mean those islands where the fighting was?"

"Yes."

"You landed on them?"

"Well. Yes."

"What kind of a ship were you on?"

"An APA attack transport with those little landing craft."

"You mean, you went in on those landing craft?"

"Yes."

"You led one?"

"Yes." I was having trouble matching Gordon up with the horror stories about those blood-soaked landings in the Pacific.

"What islands did you land on?"

"Lots of them."

"Well, which ones?"

"Oh, islands like Iwo Jima and Okinawa."

"You landed on Iwo Jima and Okinawa?"

"Yes."

"In the invasion?"

"Yes."

"Jesus. Gordon . . . I can't—"

"On Iwo Jima it was the first day. On Okinawa it was the second." I had spent years in his company and never knew what he went through. He never talked about it.

There was an outbreak of spinal meningitis at the hotel where our troops were housed, and I came down with a fever. The captain moved me off the premises fast and sent me to the Governors Island army hospital. By midnight I was a human oven, and when the nurse put a thermometer in my mouth and stepped outside to whisper something to the doctors, I pulled it out and looked at it. It read 104.8. Holy smoke! I was going to die. Someone came in and pulled the nightgown thing up and stuck a needle in me. I lost my grip on the situation after that and slid off to sleep.

I woke up to sunshine. It was flooding into the room and I felt fine. I even got up and went to the bathroom. The nurse came in looking kind of strange and excited and asked if I wanted some breakfast. Sure, I said. I asked her what was in the shot someone gave me. "It was penicillin," she said. "It's a new drug, very powerful." I was one of the first to get it.

From my window I could see the Statue of Liberty on the next island. It was quite a sight this close up, that Lady with the Torch of Hope. Ace and I had both volunteered for the paratroopers, hoping to get overseas in the same unit, and we were waiting for our orders to come through, telling us to report to Fort Benning, Georgia. The bombs were falling on London, the Germans were losing ground in Italy, and in England the army camps were filling up with Americans. And George Patton was there. Everyone knew what the next step would be—the invasion of France. The great Nazi army was waiting for the Americans and the British to step up to the plate, and the question on everyone's mind as the season turned to spring was where and when the slaughter would begin.

Meanwhile, I was taking the Third Avenue El to electrical school. I tried to be interested in the classroom work, but I don't remember anything about it. Not a volt, ohm, or watt. I sat in the back, as near to the windows as I could, because spring was sweetly wearing away at the stone fortress of New York. Through the open window the scented air of April carried my mind away and my eyelids began to fall. Our teacher had one talent: hypnotism.

"Holbrook!" The sound of my name woke me up.

"You are a disgrace to this class and to your uniform! Your behavior is un-American."

My return to consciousness had a dreamlike clarity, as if I had come from a better world to this one. "What did you say?"

"I said your behavior is un-American, Holbrook."

Something dangerous moved in me. "Don't call me un-American, sir."

"I'll call you what you deserve—"

I had risen to my feet as if pulled up by some stealthy force and the small hairs on the back of my neck rose up. "Nobody calls me un-American." I started toward him down the aisle.

"There are men dying overseas—"

The killer the army had planted inside me was uncoiling itself. "Don't call me un-American."

"It's what you are . . ."

"Nobody calls me that. Nobody . . ." I was reaching for him and my fist was on its way when the sergeant grabbed me from behind and pulled me out of the classroom.

"Nobody calls me un-American! You son of a bitch! Nobody! Nobody calls me un-American." The sergeant dragged me across the hall into the locker room and ordered me to calm down, but something had cracked open inside me and I began slugging the steel doors of the lockers and sobbing. There had never been any good feeling between the sergeant and me, but his tone of voice changed.

"Okay, Holbrook. Take it easy. Take it easy, kid." He pulled me down on a bench and waited for me to quiet down. "Let me see your hand." It was bloody. "Stay here for a while." And he left me alone in the locker room until the class was over. Then we rode the el back to the Broadway Central Hotel and I was ordered to report to the captain. He quietly listened to what I had to say about the incident and told me it might mean a court-martial for me. He would let me know in the morning. Meanwhile, I was confined to barracks.

I heard nothing for a day or two. Then I was shipped out to Fort Belvoir again to join a company of engineers still in training. I was not court-martialed. But neither did I get into the paratroopers, because my orders came through to report to Fort Benning's paratrooper school two days after I left New York. They were superseded by the orders to ship me to Belvoir, so my chance to jump out of a plane over France with Ace was gone.

I was finally headed overseas to fight the enemy. Camp Shenango in far western Pennsylvania, snugged up near the Ohio border, was where troops assembled from different camps before shipping out to the debarkation ports of Boston or New York. Our battalion was thrown in with troops from all the other camps, we were no longer Company B of any outfit, and our busted sergeant was gone. Drill sergeants were often separated from their outfits for the boat trip overseas so they wouldn't happen to fall overboard in the middle of the ocean.

The stay at Shenango could be three or four days or longer; meanwhile, we hung around the barracks and got acquainted with the new GIs we might end up getting killed with someday soon. The hours were suddenly empty. We just waited. Sometimes we lay down on our bunks and thought about things, but the bunks were three tiers high and I had the unwisdom to choose one on top. It was like scaling the Matterhorn, so I didn't lie down much.

There were no passes into town. However, the guard posts were wide apart, there were no fences, and the town of Sharon was only about seven miles away, so one night I sneaked out of camp with my newfound friend Keating from Boston and two other guys. Officially we were AWOL, but there weren't any straight-backed noncoms around, so . . . We walked the railroad tracks into town and fate brought us to the Little Brown Jug.

The Jug was brimful of soldiers, drunk and noisy, topped off by a small group of sailors over by the bar. The four of us got a booth, and a thin, worn-out girl-woman took our order for beers. Real beer, not the 3.2 variety the PX served up on army posts. The noise level pitched higher at the bar, something was going on over there, something involving the six sailors. They were encircled by a small crowd and it looked like one of them was punching a soldier sitting on a stool. Our waitress came back with more beer. "That poor guy," she said, and slammed the bottles down. "That soldier was wounded at

Guadalcanal. He has a medical discharge, and that guy is just punching him. He can't defend himself. Makes me sick."

We looked toward the bar again and could see the soldier swinging back and forth on the stool every time the sailor slugged him. Something stirred in me, the suicide impulse rising. I looked at Keating, the Irishman from Boston, and without pausing to think things over said, "Let's go."

When I stood up, nobody followed. I was vaguely aware that this trip was going to be a lonely one, but I had made the move. Just as I reached the outskirts of the group, fate turned the sailor around and he started to leave, followed by his five navy buddies. I was in the way. He shoved me aside and moved past. "Hey!" I said. He stopped, turned, and looked me right in the eye. He was stocky and had a bullet head with a blond crew cut.

"Who do you think you're shoving?" I said.

The next thing I saw was stars. I think they were different colors. I came to right away and tried to get up. Bang!—something hit me behind the ear and I went down again. Must have turned my head. Luis Carlo, where are you? I thought. I tried to get up again, but shoes were kicking me all over—black shoes, sailors' shoes. Where were my buddies? By this time I was being run over, people bouncing off each other and stepping on me trying to get away. I was getting mad. I grabbed at sailor uniforms wherever my hands could find them and heaved myself up again. Bang!—behind the ear again. Damn! Was I keeping my head down? Maybe so, because I don't remember that I saw anything until then, but now I looked up from the floor, in the middle of the moving mass of people and black shoes, and I focused on Bullethead's confident blue eyes. He was enjoying this, cool as ice and having fun. I wanted to kill him. I grabbed the tunics of Bullethead and one of his buddies in a fury and hung on to them like a trapeze, jerked this way and that until their weight shifted back with the moving mob and the counterweight action lifted me off the floor. Then I swung at them. Missed. Bang!—that one spun me around and launched me into space. My hands landed on the back of a chair and I lifted it over my head, turning, and hurled it with all my might at Bullethead. He plucked a table off the floor as calm as a juggler and lobbed it into the path of the chair, which splintered like confetti. Then he calmly took a beer bottle off the bar and broke off the end of it and handed it to one of his mates.

People started running fast now. The bartender was shouting at us to stop, tables and chairs were tripping over like ducks in a shooting gallery, and the six sailors started moving toward me with the broken bottle. I heard a voice say, "MPs, MPs! Get outta here!" Then the bottle slashed at me and the blows started to land over and over. I lost control of my body and what was left of my brain, and when I saw blood flying around, it turned me into an animal. I grabbed at his hand and tried to rip it open with my teeth, but it never fazed him. I couldn't seem to land a blow. Every time I swung at him, he wasn't there, and then his fist landed behind my ear. Or on my face or body. I was going backward all the time, trying to get out of the way of the bottle, crashing into tables and tripping over chairs that I couldn't see. The place had cleared out now, leaving just the sailors and me and the bartender screaming at us, going around the room. When we passed the bar again, one of them broke off another beer bottle. The sound of a siren stopped everybody in their tracks and in that split second I saw his face waiting there for me. I hauled off and smashed him in the mouth. I hope it broke his tooth, because it broke my finger. I think it was the only blow I landed.

That was it. They turned and ran. I felt someone grab me by the arm and drag me backward. It was the pale girl-woman waitress. "Come with me," she said. "Come on!" She dragged me behind the bar, through the clutter of shattered glass, into a hallway and opened the door of a big freezer. "Get in," she said. She put a piece of meat over my eye. "Hold this there and keep quiet." Then she closed the door.

I could hear the MPs' voices and heavy feet tromping around, crushing glass and moving chairs and tables, and after a while it went quiet. The waitress opened the freezer door.

"They've gone. Lemme see your eye." She took my hand with the meat away. "That's pretty bad. There'll be a bruise, but keep the meat on it. It'll help." The bartender came up.

"Jesus, the place is ruined."

"We'll clean it up," said the girl-woman.

"I'm sorry—"

"You better get going. Wait. Here are your friends." It was Keating and the other two guys. They were back and trying to look humorous.

"You ought to pick on someone your own size," said Keating. Nobody smiled, so he said, "We'll get him back to the camp."

It was quite a walk, those seven miles. We followed the railroad tracks leading back to Shenango, stepping from one railroad tie to the next until it made us dizzy, and then we tried the cinders on the shoulder. Everything was hurting in me. My ribs, my ears, my head, my shoulder, my hands. I was one massive ache. We didn't talk too much. It was an endless, awful hike, but we finally crept across the field between the guard posts just as the sky was lightening up in the east and made it to the barracks. I wanted to lie down so bad I could almost cry, but first I had to get up the Matterhorn to my bunk. My muscles had stiffened up, my joints were sore, and there was something wrong with my ribs. I went up one end of the beds very slowly and let myself down on the mattress. Soft. I eased my body out full length. It was heaven. Heaven. Then the bugle blew reveille.

I didn't quite know what to do next. I knew I was hurting, but how could I explain it and still get a medical checkup instead of the guardhouse? I was carefully lowering myself down the end of the beds when the sergeant in charge of our barracks stopped and watched me.

"What's the matter with you, soldier?"

"I'm okay."

"You don't look it."

Keating came up the aisle and said, "He needs to see the doctor, Sarge."

"Yeah?" He studied me a minute. "What's your name?"

"Holbrook."

"You'd better report to sick call."

I limped over to the medical building with Keating and stood in line until my turn came. The doctor looked me over. "What happened to you, soldier?"

"Sir, I was attacked by six sailors."

"Sailors? Where was this, Private?"

"Right here on this post, sir."

"Say that again?"

"Right over there in that field between the guard posts."

"You were attacked by sailors on an army post?"

"Yes, sir!"

"Uh-huh."

"Yes, sir. Six of them."

He looked at Keating, who was trying to look sad. "You're telling me that six sailors came on this army post and beat you up?"

"Yes, sir."

"We're all going to have to watch our step from now on, I guess."

"Yes, sir!"

"Yes. Well, we'll have to put you in a hospital bed and look you over. Give the orderly your name and serial number."

I was going to be in that hospital for seventy-nine days. I would miss the boat again. The only war I'd been waging was against the armed forces of the United States.

They decided to experiment with me. They cleaned me up, plucked glass shards out of me and sewed up the cuts, taped up a dislodged rib, and worked over a clavicle until it slid into home base again. Then they started on my broken little finger. An orderly assembled materials: gauze, plaster, a wire coat hanger, tape, a rubber band, a drill, a little horseshoe thing, and a tiny silver pin. First he built a plaster cast along my left forearm all the way down to the first joint in my fingers. It had a special hole for my thumb. Then he opened up the coat hanger and bent it into a U shape, with another little *u* in the middle of the big *U*. Then he took the two ends of the big *U* and embedded them in the cast and let it dry. Then he took a hand drill and bored a hole through the bone of my broken little finger, near the end, and slipped the tiny silver pin through it, with the ends sticking out on each side of my finger. Then he attached the horseshoe thing onto the ends of the silver pin, and *then* he strung a rubber band through a hole at the top of the horseshoe, all the way up to the little *u* in the coat hanger, and pulled it tight enough to ache. My broken little finger was now stretched out as stiff as a stick. They called it a tension splint. In every doctor's office in America a tongue depressor and some tape is all you need for a broken finger. I was special.

The tedium of captivity in the hospital was almost toxic. We could wander around the corridors in our pajamas or play games of chess and checkers or read books. I decided to take on a master-piece. The Bible. I had never read it. I began with an eager spirit but wore down early in Genesis. All those people begetting children and grandchildren by the peck; it was like having dinner with a southern family and trying to keep track of the relatives' names being hurled across the table. So I tracked down the chaplain and tried to get some religious revelations from him, but he was a young man trying to be one of the fellas and that effort had sandpapered most of the revelations off of him. He put me to work scrubbing down the chapel with ammonia and soap and stuff. My tension splint got wet and banged around quite a bit and it felt more and more as if the edge of the cast was cutting into my little finger, so I started to pick away at it and some yellow stuff began seeping out. When the captain stopped by my bed at inspection, I showed him what was leaking out of the cast.

"We'll get that off now. Report to the orderly in room 102, then report back to my office." The cast had been on for six weeks. When it came off and the pin had been pulled out, there was a leaking wound at the first joint and the finger was stiff and straight. It barely moved. I showed it to the captain.

"You'll need to exercise it, Holbrook. We'll get you a ball to squeeze and you'll report to rehab in the morning."

The finger was not going to flex again, because the tendon sheath had rotted out on the edge of the cast, but I had to find that out much later. All the ball squeezing and soaking in rehab was a sham. At the end of three or four more pointless weeks the captain called me in.

"Holbrook, you're not cooperating. We're discharging you back to regular duty."

"What about my finger, sir?"

"What about it?"

"I can't have my finger sticking straight out like this, sir. I'm going to be an actor."

"How would you like it?"

"Well, maybe bent in. Curved."

"Lemme see it." He took my hand in both of his, pressed his palm against my finger, and squeezed. *Rrrrr-Ah!!* The sound was like a rusty door hinge groaning shut, and the finger was bent in the curved position for life.

One fine day we were loaded into the railway cars and headed east. Rumor was we were going to the port of debarkation in Boston. It was true. We stood on the docks and stared up at the vast hull of a Liberty ship, built by the industrial minuteman Henry Kaiser. When a world war that was being fought across two oceans landed on the unprepared shoulders of America, Kaiser found a way to build troopships fast, simple, and good enough to float. Ours was ready to go. The Red Cross was there with the uniformed ladies and their gorgeous doughnuts and hot coffee. They were so welcome. Then we climbed the gangplank, the moorings were cast off, and the great iron monster headed out to sea.

12

I was three decks down, next to the vegetables and the screw. The screw was noisily pushing the ship, and the vegetables smelled bad because they had mated with the odor of diesel oil. I had two weapons against seasickness in the colon of the ship—the Bible and *The Grapes of Wrath*. The Bible was going to be for when they started shooting at me, but for seasickness I chose *The Grapes of Wrath*. The Joad family, Tom and Ma and the whole bunch of them, Grandpa and Muley, they told me a story about America I had not known, and it would alter my feelings about the America I had grown up in, the privileged end of it. The Joad family were the faces of hope and courage, and they saved me from seasickness.

By that time Ace was moving across France with the 87th Infantry Division. George Patton had broke loose. The game of war was turning. In the South Pacific, Gordon Condit's landing craft were surfing onto the beaches. It was December 1944, and I'd been in the army a year and a half and gone nowhere. As we plowed through the cold mist of the North Atlantic, hoping the German subs would leave us alone, I tried in my letters to say a goodbye to those I loved. My sisters were in Cleveland. June had married Bill, and their daughter, Cheryl, was two years old and walking. June was still working in the war plant. Bill's occupation was vague. Alberta had married a handsome young man from Cincinnati named David Drazil and—

like our mother—at the age of eighteen was carrying her first child, Diane. The ties that bound us to one another had stretched so far they had lost tension and gone slack, and war was pulling us further apart.

I felt the slack in my connection with Carol, too. Her letters were dear and loving, but I felt distant. It wasn't just the thought of getting killed; I felt cut loose. Abandoned. I was crawling back into the solitary survival harness in which I had spent most of my life. Survival. That is what I faced, but now it had a keener edge to it. The thrill of the unknown excited me. In this frame of mind I saw a dark gray line ahead of us. Land! Only four days out and we're stopping somewhere? For what? Rumors raced around the deck like pinballs: Greenland! Iceland! Nova Scotia? No. Couldn't be. The wintry outlines of a bay opened up; we passed between its cold arms and saw pine trees, snow, and rocks. The ship ghosted to a halt and a voice came over the loudspeaker.

"This is Argentia Bay. Newfoundland. We will disembark here." Good God. Eskimos! My spirits dropped like a stone.

The name Argentia had a familiar ring. It was the bay in which Roosevelt and Winston Churchill had rendezvoused aboard a naval ship for their historic first meeting, but there were no Eskimos onshore or in St. John's or anywhere in the ancient British colony of Newfoundland. Captain John Cabot had planted the English flag here in 1497, long after the Vikings and the Portuguese had made their landfalls, but the Norsemen didn't stay and the Portuguese were hunting for codfish. They found them on the Grand Banks. Now there were other fish in the sea off the eastern shores of Newfoundland, fish made of steel, on the prowl for the convoys carrying American and Canadian troops to fight the war in Europe. On the horizon off St. John's harbor Canadian destroyers met troopships like ours and formed an escort for them on the eastward journey along the Gulf Stream to England and France. Artillerymen standing watch beside their cannons on Signal Hill saw the convoys form, then saw plumes of smoke smudge the horizon and watched the ships go down, torpedoed by German submarines. There is more tonnage on the bottom of the ocean off St. John's harbor than John Cabot ever dreamed of.

The first American troops sent "overseas" went to St. John's to stop the Germans from establishing an air base there, and Fort Pepperell was established—regular army men, good old boys who had joined up during the Depression, mostly for bed and board, and they were friendly, especially to the female population. The customs of this isolated British colony went back to the nineteenth century: civility, honesty, church twice on Sunday and again on Wednesday. Our boys married them and gave them children, and when orders arrived to send them home they disappeared. The Church of England got pretty mad about that. Now Fort Pepperell was opening its arms to us, the replacements for departing members of the 58th Engineer Battalion, and we bundled into the back of army trucks and headed into the snowy woods, clearing trees from meaningless places and followed by our Newfie mascot, a dog the size of a bear. Actors in Hollywood war movies saw more action than I did.

I had made two special friends in the platoon, Blackwood and Boyd. Blackwood was a tall, stringy guy from the Baltimore shipyards and Boyd was a railroad conductor from Philadelphia who was shaped for drinking beer. They were guys I would never have known at Denison. On New Year's Eve we got a booth at the PX and took turns in the beer line. Two cans per trip to a soldier was the rule, so we had to run relays from the table to the line in order to build an Everest of 3.2 beer, which was going to fuel our salute to the arrival of 1945. The salute was a contest to see who could drink the most. When we had seventy cans on the table we started drinking in earnest.

"You gotta go kinda slow," said Boyd. "You don't want to push the bladder too hard. Drain it when you feel like you're starting to drown."

There was a conga line to the latrine that snaked around one side of the room, but it moved fast because everyone was trying to set a record. The seventy cans disappeared by 11:00 p.m. and we had to line up for more. Boyd won with forty-two.

A person's character changes in the army. I was creating a new person who would fit into this provisional world of men I would never have gotten to know back home, a college boy like me. Most of the GIs were from the other side of town, and conversation did not come easy. The first stage of communication was territorial, like dogs measuring each other, sniffing, stepping aside, or holding still. Eye contact was avoided. Within this masquerade, a new person evolves. Someone not quite you, more like an actor playing a role, and this new character could be a strain because once I put him onstage I had to keep him there. Walking down the aisle past the double bunks: "How's it hanging, Harry?" "Low, asshole." Or standing at the urinal in the latrine: "I knew a guy back home could hit a fly on the wall ten feet away, but his pecker was five feet long." Stuff like that. Bringing up Keats and Shelley would've marked me for a "faggot." This was the new face of survival for Harold.

Sometimes I tried to escape this person by walking outside and standing in the shadows. Going into town was another escape. Our job at Pepperell was mostly from eight to five, so I could ride the bus into town at night and walk the streets like a civilian; but that's when my thoughts turned to Ace over in Belgium dodging machine-gun fire.

St. John's was an ancient town, older than Boston. There were massive stone buildings and walls, even cobblestone streets that rose in terraced levels within the curving arc of the harbor, a perfectly shaped refuge from the sea. The wood siding of the houses was gray and etched with age and flaking paint, giving no hint of the cleanliness inside. There were churches everywhere, mostly of ancient weathering stone that the sea air worked upon in its unrelenting way. The town seemed medieval to me. Letters came from Ed Wright. Gordon was in the Philippines. Ace was slogging toward Germany with the 87th Division. I was riding the bus into town. I walked around the streets for a while, feeling hopeless, bought the *Evening Telegram*, and sifted through it for some ray of excitement. Nothing. I boarded the bus for Pepperell. As we neared the gate I was still reading the newspaper when I spied a small item tucked into the upper-right-hand corner of a page.

ST. JOHN'S PLAYERS

There will be a casting session this evening for the St. John's Players' next scheduled production, "Lady Precious Stream." Mr. Christopher Frere of the Winnipeg Little Theatre will direct this production. He describes "Lady Precious Stream" as a Chinese play to be performed in the Kabuki tradition. Among the roles being cast is the young lover, a prince . . .

The young lover? Chinese? Kabuki? What in hell was Kabuki? *Lady Precious Stream.* What a name for a show!

"You getting off?" We were at the Pepperell gate, where the bus turned around and went back to town.

"Uh. I don't know."

"Make up your mind. We're going back now." I could never have guessed this was a critical moment in my life. I thought of Ed. What would he do?

"I'll stay on."

The address in the casting notice turned out to be Memorial University, a large stone building with a walkway that curved around one corner. At the end of it was a half-open door, and inside it was warm. Down the hallway was an open door with a sign pinned on it: CASTING. Under it two ladies sat at a table.

"An American. How nice. You've come to read for the young prince?"

"Well, I guess so."

"Your name, please?"

"Holbrook. Hal."

"Prince Hal." She smiled. "You can go in now. Christopher will read you." They both smiled.

It was not a large room and the chairs were half empty. Most of the young princes in town were off fighting the war. A small man sprang forward, almost half a midget with the face of a cherub. He was on the further side of forty and his skin was soft and pink and minutely wrinkled.

"Ah! We're glad to have you. Glad to have you. Yes. American, eh? Yes. Well. I'd say the prince, and would you mind reading for us, Holbrook?"

"No. Yes. Fine."

"Do you know the play?"

"No, sir."

"Lovely play. It's Chinese, you know, quite a famous one out there. And it's done in an exciting style. Kabuki. Rather formal, with silks and flags, very stylized and a smashing love story." Brother, I thought, what have I got myself into? "And this is your princess, Miss Johnston, Lady Precious Stream."

I hadn't noticed her over there in the corner. Her face was pale, shaped like a heart, and her eyes in the shadowy corner were large and dark. Quiet and vulnerable, a striking face. Wouldn't it be something if she could act? I went back and sat beside her. We shook hands briefly. She was nervous. I got the impression of a doe, poised and listening. We began to read. Her voice was low and a little husky, an actress's voice. The lines seemed stilted coming out of my mouth, but on her they fit. I tried to listen to her and talk back. Something was happening beneath the surface of the scene that felt exciting and mysterious.

"Ah, yes, that's rather good, isn't it? Suppose you read the final scene on page—Ah—"

"Seventy-eight." It was Miss Johnston. We turned the pages and she gave me a quick look with those big eyes and started off. The scene was a love scene, formal and touching. She seemed very nervous.

"Well, I do think we've found our prince. Would you like to be in our play, Mr. Holbrook? May I call you Hal?"

"Yes. Hal, yes. And I would like to be in the play. I can get out most every night for rehearsal."

"That's lovely. We'll make it work. Yes. Just lovely."

Harold

Miss Johnston gave me a bit of a smile and I staggered out of the place with a big crush building for Miss Johnston. Some Eskimo.

Rehearsals let me return to the person I used to be, the young man named Harold who was polite and didn't curse and could afford to have a heart. I used to get there early because there was an upright piano in the room that I liked to play when no one was around. I didn't know how to play anything on the piano except "Clair de Lune" with one finger; mostly I just made sounds on it that expressed my feelings. Chords that reverberated in the room. Sometimes Miss Johnston came early, too, and I would let her catch me playing my private sounds because I felt she would understand them. Or "Clair de Lune." It was a form of showing off, but also a form of wooing. I wanted her to get interested in me. There was a quality about her that was absolutely rare. It was a tremulous joining of dignity and vulnerability held a little aloof. She seemed to be expecting something, which lent mystery to her behavior. The accents of her speech were different from other Newfoundlanders. They were pure English accents without the affectation. Her name was Ruby.

I was standing near my bunk, kidding around with some guys, when I opened a letter from Ed.

"Dear Hal and Gordon, it breaks my heart to tell you that Ace was killed on February 7."

At the end of the barracks there was a door to the roof, and I found myself pushing it open and climbing the stairs. I finished the letter standing on the roof's gravel surface.

It happened near Roth, Germany. It was snowing. Three men started out to bring in a wounded comrade. Two were driven back by machine gun fire but Ace went on. He did not come back. His body was identified and he was buried in Belgium with a cross at his head. His mother and father have been informed that he will receive the Bronze Star and the Purple Heart posthumously.

I wanted to cry but I couldn't. Come on, cry, I thought. Please. Cry. I couldn't. "But Ace went on." *He went on.* In the face of machine-gun fire he kept going forward with his wonderful eagerness for life. He must have been frightened. At the end of a letter written on February 5, two days before he died, he spoke of an attack on the Siegfried line: "Our first swallow of the bitter pill and the anticipation is terrifying." He was not made for war. He believed passionately in this war and that is why he directed the anti-Nazi play *Letters to Lucerne* just two years before, but his spirit was too eager for the battlefield. He would not retreat.

I went downstairs and stopped talking. I remained silent for two months, except when responding to an order or when speaking was required to carry one out. It was like a weapon, the silence, to strike back at fate. Or me. Would I have gone on? When my bunkmates tried to find out what was the matter, I refused to tell them, and finally they got angry and left me alone. I wanted to chop myself in two.

Something had closed up inside me like a trapdoor. My feelings were down there, but they were mute except for a wild echo that rose up and said, "Are you glad to be alive?" He went on. "Would you?" I had to shut that voice away. The bitter silence was broken only by rehearsals for *Lady Precious Stream*. I always went early to play my chords and hear them tremble in the air. I always looked forward to seeing Miss Johnston because there was a silence in her, too. Her eldest brother, Clifton, had been killed in the war.

The rehearsals were an escape for me. It was an odd play, with movements almost like a ballet. The movements had a special meaning, a formalized message in the Kabuki tradition, so rehearsals were strange and interesting. But I found Miss Johnston more interesting than the play. I invited her out on a date five times before she agreed to go, unaware of the weight of disapproval she was going to risk by taking a chance on me. There were several social cannons trained on her. One piece of artillery was her boyfriend, whom she had joined the St. John's Players to get away from. Another was the firehouse fear of becoming involved with an American soldier, because they deserted Newfoundland girls. But the big howitzer was Dad. He had pretty well thrown the fear of God and Armageddon into his youngest child. Ruby was the fifth of five children. Her mother had produced one every two years, and by the time Ruby came along Mrs. Johnston was ready for a nervous breakdown, so she had one. Ruby was put in charge of her sister, Beryl, who was not much older and possibly untrained in the ways of motherhood. Ruling over this family battalion was "General" Johnston, often called Dad or Father. He probably loved his family, but so did God, and look what he did to Adam and Eve.

I was surprised to discover that this was Ruby's first play. She seemed natural on the stage and gave off that hint of mystery within, which is the mark of an exceptional talent. She had appeared on-stage once before in a Gilbert and Sullivan operetta, when she sang in the chorus and had one line to speak; as soon as she left the stage she threw up. The plot of *Lady Precious Stream* is not a vivid memory for me, its climax having something to do with crossing a bridge, which I believe took a very long time and was accompanied by considerable amounts of colored cloth waving around to indicate our passage. I was Prince Hsieh Ping-Kuei, and I believe the prince and Lady Precious Stream got married after the bridge crossing, because it certainly would have been an anticlimax if we didn't.

Once the play was over, an abyss was waiting for me. I felt useless. The war in Europe was closing out, Patton had carved a highway across Germany's southern tier, and Clark and Montgomery had reduced the rest of the German army to a militia. I felt guilty as hell stuck in Newfoundland while Ace and a million others were under the ground, and the shame I felt was intensified by the "Dear Carol" letter I wrote to end my broken promises to her. I was lonely company for myself, and when the isolation became unbearable I started talking again. Slowly the platoon took me back into its confidence. They seemed to have figured out what went wrong, and they let me go through it on the crippled path of silence I had chosen. Blue-collar guys.

If at this point the army had sent me home or to Germany for cleanup duty, life would have taken a different trail. But we stayed in Newfoundland and Ruby and I began seeing each other, mostly on the weekends because she had a job. Her silence attracted me, the mystery of it. She seemed wounded and I felt wounded, too. That drew me to her. The ties I had formed with Miss Jacquet had unraveled in the eighteen months of living the life of a character put on for survival. The college boy who considered suicide on a bridge in Granville did not belong to the world a war had handed us, and a pattern of personal survival I had learned from twenty years of clinging to lifeboats and debris was taking over. I was going to save Number One. If that meant looking straight ahead, right past people I had loved, I would do it. I walked the streets of St. John's with Ruby and we climbed up Signal Hill. There I kissed her. I was made welcome in her home on Fleming Street—a wary welcome from her father, Emanuel, whose name was biblical, and so was the threat of wrath that always seemed to be warming up in the bowels of his Old Testament soul. I toiled hard at being accepted, agreed with everything Emanuel said, and tried to tickle her mother's funny bone while we awaited news of the invasion of Japan and the order to head for the Pacific. Survival there was going to be chancy.

The platoon was terracing the north side of St. John's harbor with long-handled shovels when we heard about the bomb. A place called Hiroshima had been wiped out with one bomb. One bomb? We didn't know how to react to that. We knew it meant we might be going home instead of getting massacred in Japan, but still . . . one bomb? Was that possible? Hundreds of thousands of people dead? Then they dropped another one on Nagasaki to prove it, and the war was over. We were going home.

But you don't hurry the army. It would be another month or so before our troops left Newfoundland and eight months before I would be discharged. Ruby and I decided to get married. I requested a meeting with the captain to get the nuptials under way and was handed ninety-one forms to fill out.

"I have to fill out all these papers, sir?"

"Right, Holbrook. You can't get married here unless you fill 'em out."

"But why . . . I mean, how long—"

Harold

"It could be quite a wait. The Church of England is not happy with the way some GIs have treated the local females. Married them and then disappeared to the States when their hitch was done, never left a forwarding address. A lot of the girls have babies."

"That's terrible."

"You're sure you want to do this? I mean, once you get back to the States you could change your mind."

"No, I won't."

"Okay. If you want my advice, you'll send for her once you get back. No forms to fill out that way."

Now I had to wait and think about it. I had written Uncle Al and Aunt Merce to tell them about the happy event and received the following reply:

Harold, Merce and I feel you're making a big mistake to marry an Eskimo. She's not going to fit in down here. They have different ways, you know, different habits and all that, and you must consider how you'll feel when you get back home among your own people. I'm sure she's a lovely person, but you've been up there in the snow for months and you're lonely.

I wrote them again, explaining Ruby more carefully, that we wouldn't be rubbing noses and eating whale blubber, that kind of thing, but they remained worried. They had reason to be. I was not yet twenty-one years old and had three years of college to finish before getting a job. I reviewed my prospects: no sure way to earn a living yet, but I could get through college on the GI Bill, which meant free tuition and $90 a month to live on. And there was the $100 a month Grandpa left me, that would last a few more years. Ed wrote that Ruby could get a job at the school to pay for her tuition if she wanted to go to college. A great idea. He also said we could live with him and Louise until the prefabricated Enchanted Cottages for married veterans were completed. Still, it was a long shot.

Was it a mistake to get married? I loved Ruby. But what exactly was love? Had I ever loved anyone? I was lonely, that was true. I had been lonely most of my life and perhaps I wanted some kind of a home and my own family, not a substitute one. Some kind of safety beyond surviving. I knew I was taking a chance, and it was going to be awkward for us going back to Granville, because Carol was still there. The girl I had jilted.

That was a distant hurdle. First there was a big one right at hand. I had to get Ruby's father's permission. This was going to be high noon, six-guns on an empty street. Having defied the throne of authority before—at Culver with my track coach and before the high brass at the West Point interrogation—going off the high board was not unfamiliar to me. And having been brought up with a respect for civility, I understood that Mr. Johnston would require this formality, chilly as it promised to be, and that it was his due. So there was a tremor of expectancy in the house when I walked into the small front parlor and said, "Mr. Johnston, I would like to marry your daughter. Ruby."

Ruby was crouching at the top of the narrow front stairway and her mother and Beryl were hiding in the kitchen, waiting for the twin to Nagasaki, but my announcement was followed by a cool pause.

"And how do you expect to support her?" His large blue eyes were fastened on me. I told him about the GI Bill and the idea that Ruby could go to college; surely that would excite him. It didn't. "You're leaving here. How do we know we'll ever hear from you again?"

"You will. I promise." He judged me carefully. The odds were not in my favor.

"You'll send for her?"

"Yessir."

"When would that be?"

"Right away."

"You'll be married immediately? You won't be living in sin?"

"Nosir. I mean, yes, we'll get married in New York. Maybe at the Little Church Around the Corner. My teacher at college, Ed Wright, thought that would be—"

"Your intention is to become an actor, I suppose."

"Yes, sir."

"In Hollywood?"

"No, sir. In the theater. I want to be a stage actor in New York."

"Well . . . be that as it may. I am not comforted by the thought that my little girl should leave here and face the perils that will await her in America."

I thought of Ruby waiting at the top of the stairs. "I will take care of her. I promise."

He stood up. His face had whitened. "If I ever hear that you have gone to Hollywood and abandoned my child I will come to America and kill you." He walked out. I had been handed a death sentence if I screwed up. My mother and father had abandoned me. How could I do that?

Before she left Newfoundland, Ruby sent me a telegram: "SEP-TEMBER 14, 1945. I HAVE TAKEN MY LAST LOOK, DARLING. AM LEAV-ING BY CLIPPER 9:00 AM ON SUNDAY THE 16TH. ARRIVE AT LAGUARDIA FIELD 5:00 SAME DAY. RUBY." On it I had written: "This is the beginning. God bless us."

The army's gift upon returning to the States was a twenty-eight-day furlough for everyone. It gave me time, time to go home to Cleveland and explain to Grandma and Uncle Al and Aunt Merce that I was marrying a pure white woman who looked just like us and spoke better English. Ed and Louise were coming to New York to attend the wedding and Ed was to be my best man. Ruby's sister, Beryl, was coming to stand up for her. The Little Church Around the Corner on East Twenty-ninth Street in the lower part of Manhattan Island had legitimized the nuptials of actors for generations, which excited us. The big time. When Ruby arrived at La Guardia Airport, it was the first time she had ever gone more than twenty miles outside of St. John's, Newfoundland.

The wedding was scheduled for 11:15 a.m. When we got there at 10:45, there was a crowd. A clerical attendant explained that this was for another wedding. "There will be one more before yours."

The Little Church Around the Corner was in a big hurry. We were going to have fifteen minutes to get married. Fifteen minutes to concentrate our distracted emotions and nerves and brains into one solemn trance for a lifetime commitment. It made the marriage ceremony feel like a parachute drop. When we entered the church and had to pass through a turnstile and pay up in advance, our illusions about a beautiful ceremony slid away. We could have been going to a ball game. We made the trip down the aisle as fast as we could to save time for the ceremony, but the clergyman hardly looked at us. This was business. How I hated the bastard. We poured the best of our eager souls into those few precious minutes while he droned on, and then it was over and we were all laughing and crying and hugging each other until the attendant told us to move out of the way for the next couple. That night we boarded the New York Central sleeping car for Cleveland, where Ruby would meet her new family. The Holbrooks.

I had tics. Not bugs, but twitches and sometimes jerks. My hands would jerk spasmodically sometimes and I think I did something with my chin, a sudden lurching to the left as if dodging a right cross. But the real acrobat was my nose. I twitched it beyond the dreams of a rabbit. My nerves were on edge during most of my growing up, never being too sure what was coming next, and when Ruby and I stepped off the train in Cleveland and were greeted by Uncle Al in his golf knickers and two-toned golf shoes my nose got loose again. Where were we going? To a golf course? We had settled on the expectation that Grandma was going to take us in, but a golf course? "Where are we headed, Uncle Al?"

"I'm taking you over to Mother's house. You'll stay there with her, but Merce and I want you to come to dinner soon. I've just played eighteen holes."

I was nervous about Grandma and I had tried to prepare Ruby. She knew all about the blue-eyed baby boy stuff and the wet kisses and how I had to keep moving all the time to keep from being fondled, which would make anyone's nose twitch. At least she didn't have to meet Dad. A phone call had come in from the police chief in Houston saying that my father was in custody for vagrancy. He was safely behind bars in Texas with his bullet-hole hat.

We wanted to have a honeymoon, but we had no car to go anywhere nor the funds to pay for hotels. Uncle Al came to our rescue. In a gesture of trust that did not run wild in the Holbrook family he loaned us his car. This was a heroic act of faith because I had very little experience in driving an automobile. You had to go back to the farm in Connecticut, and that had been on short runs to the chicken coops in a Model T Ford that had been converted into a tractor. There was already some sweat on his forehead when he made the offer and more when he gave me the keys. Since the $29 a month pay I got for trying unsuccessfully to go to war would not get us over the Ohio state line, he gave us $200 to pay for a honeymoon. That was a generous sum then and a kind offering from a good-hearted man. I don't know why my father always wanted to box him.

Uncle Al suggested we go up into the Canadian woods north of Lake Ontario to a fishing resort. He'd been there once himself and said even if we caught no fish it would be restful. "Restful" was the best he could come up with. We drove away while he stood on the front lawn, watching his car disappear. It was a long way up above Lake Ontario, with me practicing and Ruby gripping the edge of the seat, and it was cold in early October in the north woods. We managed to get a fire going in our cabin fireplace after a session of cursing and mutual recriminations and then climbed into bed under a shedding buffalo robe and clung to each other for warmth. It was more a survival embrace than a romantic one. The next day we went fishing. I knew about oars and rowing from summers on the farm and I spent a good deal of exasperated time trying to get Ruby to row the boat while I fished. She did not have the God-given talent for rowing and she tried to explain this to me, at first with an effort at kindness and then with expletives heretofore absent from her vocabulary. Finally

I took the oars and she fished. We had a can of worms and dragged each one of them around the lake until they disintegrated.

I was ordered to report to Fort Belvoir, Virginia, at the end of my furlough and was assigned to clerical work in Special Services, helping to organize entertainment for the base. Ruby landed a job as secretary to a colonel. It was October 1945. *The Army Engineer Show* put me on its weekly radio program and I played Leo Davis, the author from Oswego, in a production of *Room Service*. Then just before my discharge orders came through in March, my boss, a lieutenant, asked me to stay on for a while after the 6:00 p.m. leaving time. That seemed strange. The captain was also there, at the other end of the large office. I was standing by my desk examining some papers the lieutenant had handed me when I felt something weird going on behind me. He was pressing against me and starting to put his hands on me. Jesus! A homo! I pushed him away and said, "What the hell are you doing? Are you nuts?" and grabbed my cap and walked out. I had never thought of the lieutenant being anything but a skinny, bland guy who got to be an officer and out of the blue he turns into a homosexual with a yen for me. It was a shocker. Was there something about me that attracted these guys? I went home to our army apartment and told Ruby about it. We figured there might be consequences.

The next day the lieutenant was cool as a doily, but the captain called me into his office and assigned me to cleanup duty in the Service Club on Saturday night after the blitzkrieg of dancing and drinking had turned the place into a trash heap. When I found out I was supposed to do this all by myself, Ruby said she would help me so we could spend the night together. We started after midnight with push brooms and mops and pails of water and trash cans. The first layer of stuff was easy—newspapers, toilet paper streamers, cigarette butts, and the occasional cigar. The latrines were subhuman places, vomit and stray urine making queasy patterns on the cement floor. But the real challenge was the tiny bits of torn paper lodged in the cracks of a wooden dance floor the size of a basketball court whose seams had been battered open by too many Saturday night hoedowns. Soldiers without dates stood on the balcony that ran around the circumference of the place, and tore up newspapers into little bits of confetti and floated them down on the dancers. The brooms could not dislodge them from the cracks, so we went over the place like a couple of crows, picking the stuff out of the cracks by hand. It was dawn when we got out of there.

On Monday morning I was called into the captain's office and stood at attention before his desk, hating his guts and trying to hide it.

"What happened on Saturday night? You never showed up?"

"Never showed up!" I laughed. "What do you mean, sir?"

"I mean you never cleaned the place."

"That is not true."

"You were ordered to clean the Service Club Saturday night after the dance and you never showed up."

"Yes I did. I cleaned the place for hours."

"You did not."

"My wife cleaned it with me. We worked all night, until five a.m. You can ask her."

"The place was never cleaned, Holbrook. This is a serious offense. You could be court-martialed for this. The lieutenant will verify that you never cleaned the Service Club on Saturday night." Whatever shred of respect I might have brought into the room left my face.

"Anyone who says that my wife and I did not clean up the Service Club on Saturday night is a fucking liar."

"You will hear from me. Dismissed."

What I wanted now was a machine gun. In the early afternoon a few days later I was called into the captain's office again. He handed me my discharge orders from the United States Army. They said I should report to Camp Atterbury, Indiana, for my separation from the service, and a railroad ticket was included with the order.

"You're pretty lucky, Holbrook. The orders for your court-martial hearing came in an hour ago. Your discharge came in this morning. Pack up and leave." In the army the first order to come in stands and the later one is negated by it. Was I saved by the bell of coincidence or did the lieutenant and his pal the captain ring it themselves to get me out of there? I'll never know. My service in the U.S. Army ended with a hatred for corrupt authority: the sergeant who killed Eddie and put us in the cold water to die and the lying captain who disgraced me to hide the disgraceful behavior of his weird pal.

It was a long trip to Atterbury, and then I got on a highway and hitchhiked all the way back to Washington, D.C., to save money and got the bus to Belvoir and Ruby. On the way through Ohio in the dead of night, dozing in the cab of an eighteen-wheeler, I passed only twenty miles south of little Granville, that peaceful village, a pearl of honor and decency.

13

Grandma had sold the big redbrick house and gone east on Lake Avenue to the first-floor apartment of a duplex house opposite Lakewood Park. There were two bedrooms, and we had one. It was rather tight quarters. Ruby and I got jobs and kept careful watch on the money we earned. It would be five and a half months before the fall term began at Denison and for the time being a free room in Grandma's home was a life raft.

One of our first social calls was to Ace Morgan's mother and father. They lived across town in Cleveland Heights, opposite a graveyard. They had requested that their son's body be returned from France, and now he was buried there, a stone's throw away from where his life began and a mute presence for his grieving father and mother to remember every day of their lives. They had fitted out the upstairs portion of their house as a separate apartment for Ace's brother, who had married and moved away. The Morgans offered it to us. We thanked them and said we would come to them if the bivouac with Grandma did not work out.

It didn't. For a while we all performed our delicate dance in step, more or less, we being grateful for the housing and aware of Grandma's need to be admired a lot. But nervousness was on the loose pretty much all day and all night in this den of lovers and the blue-eyed baby boy's nose was in a constant flurry of action, as was the neck jerk and arm spasm, and when I came home one evening to find Ruby quietly crying in our bedroom I knew we had to get out of there and find a home of our own. I called the Morgans.

The twitches went into second gear. Vernon and Mrs. Morgan were a middle-class couple still in shock from their stunning loss and balancing on the bitterness consuming Mr. Morgan. I couldn't escape a feeling that I was a kind of temporary replacement for the boy who could never be replaced. This unspoken presumption lurked there, an unrevealed danger. We were too happy and we had too much to look forward to, a whole wonderful life that the Morgans would always know could never belong to their son.

I was impatient to get on with life. The summer of 1946 was at hand. Once college was over I would have to earn a living, and I saw a way to shorten the three years of higher education standing before me. I could pick up twelve hours of credit, one-third of a year's load, by enrolling in the summer program at Western Reserve University in downtown Cleveland. When added to the six hours of credit I had managed to eke out at Harvard by rarely going to class, that would raise the total to eighteen, half a college year. And Western Reserve had a good theater program, somehow connected to the Cleveland Play House, which was the first permanent regional theater company in the nation. Ruby agreed to work through the summer to help keep us afloat. For the first time in my life I got very good grades. All A's. Equally unexpected was the request from a young man in the directing class that I play Hamlet in a scene he was directing. This was a surprise. Why me? I had no experience with Shakespeare or the classics and the only loony I had ever played was the maniac in the commencement play at Culver. The idea scared me, but I said yes. The high board again; it could become a habit. The young director's name was Ted and he raised the stakes for me.

Ted had chosen the closet scene for his class project, the one in which Hamlet rips into his mother for betraying his father and then pleads with her to renounce her new husband's bed. The scene begins with bloody impulsiveness when Hamlet spears the court spy, Polonius, hiding behind a curtain.

HAMLET: "How now? A rat! Dead for a ducat, dead!"
QUEEN: "O me, what hast thou done?"
HAMLET: "Nay, I know not. Is it the King?"
QUEEN: "O, what a rash and bloody deed is this!"
HAMLET: "A bloody deed! Almost as bad, good mother
　As kill a King and marry with his brother."

The words did not seem as obscure as I thought they would be. Maybe Shakespeare wasn't so mysterious after all. I seemed almost to be talking to my own mother, wherever she was, far away somewhere, hiding from me. I had not experienced such a direct line to emotions before. It was personal. For the first time, acting became real for me without makeup and wigs.

". . . Peace! Sit you down
and let me wring your heart . . ."

The voice of John Barrymore was in my ear, those recordings we had heard at Culver, his wildness and daring telling me it was all right to use the words like knives and let my own feelings explode.

"Nay, but to live
In the rank sweat of an enseamed bed,
Stew'd in corruption, honeying and making love
Over the nasty sty."

What was spewing out of me was raw and amateurish, but it was me speaking and Ted was surprisingly patient with my awkwardness and inexperience. The director of the Cleveland Play House, Frederic McConnell, came to our performance. They were casting for the role of Mio in Maxwell Anderson's poetic drama *Winterset*, which had made Burgess Meredith a star. McConnell liked what he saw well enough to give me an audition, and Ruby did the scene with me, playing Miriamne, the girl Mio loved. I hoped to nail down McConnell's interest on the future chance that he'd take me on after

I got out of Denison, so it was a shock when he offered me the role. I wasn't prepared for that. My plan was all laid out: go to college at Denison, Ed would teach me, and maybe then the Play House. This was turning things around, it was out of sequence. If I skipped college now I might never return, and in the back of my mind was a lifeline: if the acting dream failed, I could always be a teacher. I could earn a living and survive. But to be a teacher I had to go to college and for that I needed a diploma. I turned down the role in *Winterset* and went to Denison. Survival if the acting dream failed was too important, but I wonder where the role of Mio would have taken me? He was young. Like me.

On Mulberry Street in Granville, Ohio, there was a table, not round and not surrounded by ancient knights. It was the dining table in Ed Wright's small house, and sitting around it were Ed and Louise, Leah Ashbrook, Gordon Condit, June and Hartley Ferguson, Ruby and me. We ate dinner together around this table for nine months. These knights were our new family.

We took turns cooking the meals, cleaning up, and laughing at all the funny things people snatch at to laugh about when they're having a good time. Anything was fair game, even an alteration on the front end of Hartley's name. Leah was the house Republican, but with a wild and chancy streak. She dyed her long johns red in the winter and said she was going to start a revolution. She got me to put on red long johns, too. Except for the Fergusons, we were all attached to the Theater Department, and Ed was our guardian while Louise quietly played out the angel part. In a stunning act of generosity, these two people slept on a pullout sofa in the living room for nine months because they had given up both of their small bedrooms upstairs to provide a home for the Holbrooks and the Fergusons. By the end of the school year we would move up the hill to the married students' cottages that were feverishly being built.

The phrase "up the hill" was familiar to all. The college was perched up there, a hell of a climb straight up, and the beauty of the campus was breathtaking—lush trees, brick walks, the worn buildings and elderly architecture, the undulating sea of autumn leaves, the feminine curves of fallen snow, and in the spring the cherry trees along the chapel walk were so heavenly it could make you cry. We called it Shangri-la. At the far end of this long and magical hill would sit the Enchanted Cottages for the married veterans. Downhill, Broadway stretched for a whole block, with the Opera House at the near end. People said hello on the street, young and old. Visitors from the big cities were rattled by this surprising overture, sometimes losing their cool entirely, owing to an inability to cope with simple civility.

The older returning veterans put their imprint on the quality of the college productions. Many actors were well into their twenties now. Some, like John Collison, were almost thirty and his advanced maturity greatly added to his performance in *The Late George Apley*. My first play that fall was *You and I* by Philip Barry. Gordon Condit directed it for the small Studio Theatre and cast Ruby and me as the young lovers. It should have been simple enough, playing ourselves, but this was a high-bred, sophisticated comedy that spun its epigrams around people I knew nothing about. I had no beard or wig, no limp, not even a mustache to hide behind, and I made matters worse by using a silver cigarette case and tapping my cigarette on it. I must have been crazy.

For *The Enemy* by Channing Pollock I clamped on a beard the size of a hedge and put white shoe polish in my hair. My character was a pacifist German professor, so there was the accent, too. Nobody knew who I was. This became something of a mantra with me, to make myself disappear, a strange attitude for an actor; and later in the season I accomplished my dream scenario in the silent role of a waiter whose only appearance was in the epilogue of *The Late George Apley*. I arrived at the theater to start the makeup before anyone in the cast got there and spent the two-hour duration of the play growing old. I'd got hold of an old gray wig with a canvas front that I had to blend into a crease in my forehead that hadn't appeared yet. I drew a liberal amount of lines and creases in my face where there weren't any, and of course I had a large mustache. It helped cover my face. I made sure the costume was too tight, so as to give me the wasted Ichabod Crane look, and eighty was the year I chose for my age. This meant move slowly. Since my entire performance consisted of entering the library of Apley's private club with a glass of whiskey on a tray, walking to his chair and mutely offering Mr. Apley his whiskey, and then walking out again, the slowness of the walk was crucial. Maybe I was ninety. It was one arthritic step after another, with a wince or two thrown in, all the way into and all the way out of the room. Dialogue ceased while I executed this painful march, because no amount of talk could compete with me or the trembling tray.

On the street the next day I had my reward: "Oh. Were you in the play last night?"

When Ruby applied for admission to Denison, the English-style education she'd received in Newfoundland was so superior that she was given a scholarship. Score one for the Eskimos. Since the start of the school year she had been going to classes and working in the administration offices to help pay our way, and she'd appeared in only one play. But her appearance caught people's attention. Her face and eyes and voice were made for the stage. In January, Ed began casting for an exciting project, a new play by Gordon Condit. He asked Ruby to audition for the leading female role and she got it. *Thank You, Stranger* became her launching platform.

The play was about loneliness and isolation. A blind veteran and a doctor share an apartment in New York. Dick Welsbacher was the veteran, Ruby his secretary and friend, and Parnell Egan was the doctor. I had a minor role. The music of Franz Liszt from a stranger's apartment next door haunted the play. Welsbacher was a small, underfed-looking young man with a worn-out face, a resonant voice, and a quietly confident intellect, and he may have been the best actor in the school.

Then a strange thing happened in the chapel as the first semester ended. Dr. Brown, the president of the school, was in the middle of a speech about the returning veterans when I heard something that sounded familiar.

"There is a young man in this audience who spent his freshman year with us before going into the service. He made such poor grades that we were not going to have him back again. But we took a chance on him, and I'm pleased to tell you that young man has finished the first semester with straight A's." It was me. Ed Wright had gone to bat for me again and I never knew it until then.

A letter came from Rochester telling me that my great-uncle George H. Rowe had died. In the ambulance on his way to the hospital Uncle George told his wife he wanted his costume trunk and play scripts given to me. Until then I never knew he'd been an actor. It is astonishing to realize that even after I had begun aiming myself at the acting profession, his career in the theater was hidden from me. What the hell was the matter with my people? From 1886 to 1905 George H. Rowe was an itinerant actor whose experience in countless plays moved him from town to town in New England and New York state until he became the actor-manager of the Utica Stock Company. I have a picture of that acting company, handsomely framed, a formal group portrait in which you can identify the job of each actor in it: the leading man, the leading lady, the character man, the character woman, the ingenue, the juvenile, and all the other supporting actors. Uncle George was the character man.

His trunk was a meticulously arranged tomb of acting memorabilia. Its tray contained his makeup, with sticks of old greasepaint and liners, red, yellow, and blue, and a powder brush of soft bristles; there were sections in the tray for hand properties, rings, a watch chain with a pendant, eyeglasses. There were wigs in fine condition; and beneath the tray were his period costumes, beautiful ones of satin and lace and fine worsted, each one folded in sheets of tissue paper, fresh smelling and lovingly preserved. It was clear to me that this man, who had been forced to give up the life of an actor and become a furniture salesman in order to marry Aunt Pauline, must have opened this trunk every year and carefully refolded each costume in fresh tissue paper. Uncle George had silently passed on to me his respect for tradition and the tools to disguise myself, and it was up to me to carry on. I used one of his wigs in *The Late George Apley*.

There were two major productions left in the season and I wanted to be in one of them. My eye was on *The Hasty Heart* and the role of the young Scottish soldier, but Ed had invited an Englishman named Bertram Tanswell to come from New York and direct the outdoor production of *Much Ado About Nothing*. Shakespeare. That would be a challenge, too. Bert Tanswell had the face of Joe E. Brown and stood not much higher than a magnum of champagne on a stool. He was Puck in modern disguise. He'd come over from England in the 1930s with the B. Iden Payne Shakespearean company to perform at the Old Globe Theatre, which was built for them in San Diego's Balboa Park. Bert was all actor in motion, the quick wit, the limber face and road-worn voice of the ageless itinerant thespian.

Ed and Bert thought I should audition for Dogberry and it was tempting. I could wear a stomach, sagging tights, a nose and a beard, and carry a cane. A cane! I decided to do both auditions and see what happened. If I got one of them, that would settle it. But when I was offered a choice of either role, it was an awful quandary for an eager young man in search of a career. The Scot in *The Hasty Heart* would be a leading role and I had yet to play one. On the other hand, Shakespeare offered a new experience, but a scary one. What if I wasn't funny? Dogberry was the low-comedy kingpin in *Much Ado*. I talked it over with Ed, and although he said nothing to push me either way I knew what the choice had to be. The scary one and the challenge. So I gave up *The Hasty Heart*.

The good news was that Ruby was cast as Hero and Dixie Campbell would play Beatrice. Dixie was a ripe choice, a great curvy young woman with a tart tongue and a sense of humor that might have been deadpan or just innocent, you couldn't tell. When I heard that Dick Welsbacher was set to play Verges I knew we would get laughs as a comedy team, but it worried me that he would get most of them. He did. I was dizzy trying to get out of his way when he darted out from behind my knees in a low crouch and dislodged my cane to add his two cents to Dogberry's magisterial idiocy and collect howling approval from the audience. Bert helped a lot with physical stuff, though when he showed me how to do something he was so funny I could never imitate him well enough and I found out that imitating the director was hard for me because it took away something personal. Our Benedick was a magnificent blond Adonis from Chicago, Ken Telford, so we had a fine cast.

Shakespeare was done under the night sky on a large brick plaza cut into the deep slope of the college hill, and on opening night it poured rain. Bert got us all together: "We're moving down the hill to the high school. I'll tell the audience to follow us. There's a stage and that's all we need." So we moved and so did the audience, the whole crowd. Just like that, and we did the show on a bare stage. It's amazing how well a play can go off with the scenery missing. Those magnificent troupers Alfred Lunt and Lynn Fontanne proved this more than once when a blizzard stranded their scenery. Inspired by that tradition, handed to us by Bert, we gave the audience in the high school that night a whale of a good time.

Each year during the Easter vacation Ed took a dozen of his students to New York for nine days of theatergoing. We went by train and dozed all night in the cheap seats. We stayed at the Hotel Bristol on Forty-eighth Street just off Times Square in discounted rooms, two to a room, and sat in the cheapest balcony seats for less than two dollars. We saw plays and performances that year and the next that I have never forgotten. John Gielgud in *The Importance of Being Earnest*; *Oklahoma!*; *Brigadoon*; Helen Hayes in *Happy Birthday*; Fredric March and Florence Eldridge in *Years Ago*. *All My Sons*, by a new playwright named Arthur Miller; Bert Lahr in *Burlesque*; Jessica Tandy and Marlon Brando in *A Streetcar Named Desire*; *O Mistress Mine*, with Alfred Lunt and Lynn Fontanne. And that names just a few. This galaxy of theatrical magicians seems like a distant heaven now. Each year we saw eleven plays and the show at Radio City Music Hall in nine days, and the whole trip cost about $100.

It was a different breed of actors then. There were stars. Not the "movie stars" we idealize today, created by the enormous cinema screen and advertising. Those leading actors of yesteryear were stars because when they stepped on a stage, something happened. A presence arrived. Stakes rose and the ante went up. They did not alter or distort the reality taking place on the stage—they increased it. This happened because suddenly a confidence born of professional stage-craft had appeared. Mary Martin was riveting to watch in *South Pacific* because she was in total delicious control of the audience and happily aware of who she was the minute she stepped out in front of us. You *heard* her and you *saw* her and she was *there*!

Helen Hayes had the same effect in a smaller bundle of power. Her acting was absolutely real, but she took such joy in it—the *acting*—that we caught the spirit of her joy and loved it. In *The Importance of Being Earnest*, John Gielgud's entrance through the French doors upstage was greeted with rising laughter because, clad in a solemn black mourning costume, he silently began removing his gloves, which were also black, finger by finger. This is called a "star turn." You can't achieve it if you're shy.

Fredric March was an actor whose presence in his characterizations was so powerful in *Long Day's Journey into Night* and *Years Ago* that his conviction inhabited everything he did, and we reached out to him with our feelings, because he was reaching out to us.

And the Lunts. You almost have to capitalize "The" because they were a play in themselves. Here the ordinary reality of life was set aside by the personal joy they took in one another's presence and *craft*. They were a magic act onstage, a partnership of sleight-of-hand, two actors sparring with one another with the tools of a star performer's superb technique and loving every minute of it. Watching them, I felt that royalty had arrived on the stage. At the end of the second act in *O Mistress Mine*, when Lynn Fontanne's stage son, Dickie Van Patten, forced the lordly Lunt into taking the public bus and the tube across London to the opera instead of his limousine, Lunt stood downstage right, reciting in tones of anguished frustration the identity of each vehicle they would have to suffer and the route to be taken, and all the while his right hand (toward the audience, of course) was clenching and unclenching in a minute ballet of utter hatred as the curtain came down. I was laughing so hard, I nearly fell out of the balcony.

I could hear them, too, without amplification—all the actors. In the second balcony.

And then came Marlon Brando in *A Streetcar Named Desire*. He was a star because he was born one. He brought the shock of a new acting style to the stage, a shock not only because it was as true as life itself, but because when he stepped on that platform, all the cards were swept off the table and a new game had begun. His was the danger of near-animal presence, the power in a human figure smoking and ready to explode, and it was stardom because the message was "Look at me." When I first saw him in *I Remember Mama*, just the brief scenes he had, I saw this stardom in a deeply subdued manner as he begged his mother not to get on her knees to clean the floor. I thought: Who is this young man? The next year, I found out in *Streetcar*.

The saddest thought I have about the theater today is the loss of Marlon Brando's Hamlet. He was born for it. If he had stayed in the theater and given us his Hamlet, it would have been like nothing we had ever seen. Painful, painful to watch; a soul so tortured in that Brando visceral style, the wild heart of a caged animal searching for Hamlet's eternal question: "Where is the truth?" Poised in thought like a jungle cat only a twitch away from the kill—he would have torn the stage apart looking for answers. Maybe the fear of that experience drove him to Hollywood.

It was time for the summer theater. Ed bought a circus tent. He had worked in his early days as the Boy Impersonator in Chautauqua tents all over the Midwest and now he solved the absence of an air-conditioned theater by building a stage at one end of the college green downtown and putting a big circus tent over it that would hold an audience of several hundred people in shirtsleeves and cotton dresses. It was a six-week season of six plays, a new one every week. A reprise of *Thank You, Stranger*, *The Cat and the Canary*, *Three Men on a Horse*, *Our Town*, *One Sunday Afternoon*, *You Can't Take It with You*. For young actors looking for a chance to act and learn something, it was higher education, and we got six hours of college credit for it. This required rehearsing and acting in the plays, help-ing to build the scenery and run the box office, and dashing out in a rainstorm in the middle of the night to dump the big bulges of water out of the tent's roof so it wouldn't split open.

Thank You, Stranger, Gordon's play, had received such a strong response in its earlier showing at the Opera House that it opened the first summer tent season. It was favorably reviewed by Norman Nadel of *The Columbus Dispatch* (he later became drama critic of the *New York World-Telegram*). This is what he said about Ruby:

> But—and with no implication that the rest of the cast is inadequate— the star of *Thank You, Stranger* is Ruby Holbrook. Miss Holbrook is an actress. She is eloquent when she speaks, and just as eloquent when she is silent. Her face, hands, eyes and posture are a mirror that reflects all speech and action on the stage. The exquisite detail-ing of her performance is a rare thing in a midwest summer theatre— and it is almost as rare on Broadway.

Ruby had the gift of inner silence that I had seen in Newfoundland, the quality which draws an audience toward an actor and makes her a star. I doubt she knew what effect she was having, but the gift was hers.

The role I was looking forward to was Patsy in *Three Men on a Horse*. It was farce, and farce was endless fun. It spun around on timing and melodic beats and ensemble teamwork, like jazz. If you stopped to think beyond a split second in farce, you blew a hole in the scene and crippled it. Self-indulgent acting crippled it, too. Ed Wright had a special fluency for farce and he told us to listen to Bob Hope's radio show: "Turn it on and then go into the next room where you can only hear his voice and the laughs but not what he's saying. You'll know when the laugh is coming without hearing the words, because you'll feel the beat. You will sense it. That's how you play farce." It became the most enjoyable style of acting for me.

In *One Sunday Afternoon* Ruby and I were given our first chance to play leading roles opposite each other as the young lovers, Amy and Biff. The play was a sweet-hearted period piece with some music and dancing, and Ruby and I had lovely scenes together. The way we connected in them made an impression on the theatergoers that would become a factor in the next few years. When he picked the play, Ed must have known that this could be the start of something for us. He was too canny not to see that.

14

"Ed, have you got any kids at that college who can do drayma?" It was Harry Byrd Kline, the school assembly booker out of Dallas, Texas, talking. Ed had met him at the International Platform Association convention at Lakeside, Ohio.

"Oh yes," said Ed. "I have a young couple who will be the next Lunts."

"Well. Do they have a show?"

"Oh yes," said Ed, and waited.

"Well. What kind of a show? It has to be educational for me to book it in the schools."

"Oh, it's educational. They do Shakespeare, you know, Hamlet, and they do Queen Victoria and Prince Albert and those poets the Brownings. And Mark Twain."

"How long is the show? I need fifty minutes."

"That's just how long it is. It can be longer or shorter."

"Well, I can offer them thirty weeks in the schools in Texas and Oklahoma and I'll pay them two hundred ten dollars a week plus fifteen dollars for gas and oil. Do you think they might be interested?"

"I think they might be."

"What are their names?"

"The Holbrooks. Hal and Ruby."

When Ed finished performing this conversation for us, he said,

Harold

"If you and Ruby are interested, you can use it as Hal's senior honors project and have a show ready by next fall."

Ruby and I talked it over and then we dove at it. We would get paid for acting? A miracle. We figured Ruby could make the costumes. Growing up in Newfoundland, you learned to use a sewing machine because you made your own dresses. The closet scene between Hamlet and his mother, the one I had done in Cleveland, would fit in, along with scenes Ed had suggested: the shaving scene from *Victoria Regina* in which Helen Hayes had scored brilliantly in the mid-1930s; the ring scene from Maxwell Anderson's *Elizabeth the Queen*, which had provided another triumph for the Lunts in 1930; a scene between Robert and Elizabeth Barrett Browning, which I would attempt to write; and a sketch Ed gave us by Mark Twain called "An Encounter with an Interviewer." "This will give Hal a chance to play old in one scene."

Meanwhile, I'd signed up for the directing course, and my production of *Hedda Gabler* was to come first. The way you got a passing grade in the directing class was droll and unique. Ed gave you $100. With that you had to cast the play, design and build the scenery, light the show, advertise it, and print and sell tickets as well as direct it. You ran two nights in Denison's "off-Broadway" Studio Theatre and to get a passing credit you had to give Ed back the $100. I went for the best actors I could get—Dick Welsbacher for Judge Brack; Henry Sutton for Tesman; Martha Prater, a rather plain but spirited girl, for Thea; diminutive Pat Cessna as Aunt Juliana; and Ken Telford, the Adonis of *Much Ado*, for Eilert Lovborg. There remained Hedda. Martha Harter was tall and willowy, with a mane of hair flowing back from a nearly classic face with high cheekbones. I didn't know if she could pull the role off, because she simply hadn't had a chance to show that kind of speed yet. I cast her and prayed. I knew only one thing for sure: she would wear red.

The 1890 translation by Edmund Gosse was so stiff and formal that I did some doctoring and wound up retranslating some of his translation of Henrik Ibsen. I knew the scenery had to be cheap so I went into a celestial séance with Robert Edmond Jones and came up with the idea of a "semi-realistic space stage." It maybe cost $25. Three old repainted flats with furniture set in front of them, surrounded by black drapes. There were no doors. The actors just disappeared into darkness between the flats, praying they wouldn't be crippled by the stage braces. I don't recall much about my directorial technique, since I had to make it up as I went along. I found out pretty quick that good casting did 90 percent of the job for you, and I was lucky there with nearly everyone. Martha Harter as Hedda was the only one I had to work on because she had the highest bar to clear from the lowest standing start and it was a tough leap for a socially corseted young woman; but she was a courageous person who saw her opportunity and pushed herself into a good performance, flashing those pistols around to keep the audience at attention.

May I say that my advertising brain wave was a masterstroke? I told the printer to make two hundred small flyers on the cheapest brown paper he had, with the following message in red:

HEDDA IS COMING!
October 16 & 17

I plastered them on every pole and tree around the campus and the village. Nobody knew who in the name of Houdini this Hedda person was, if it *was* a person, or where he, she, or it was coming from, but they were damn sure they were not going to miss it and they didn't. We had standing room only. The most embarrassing part of the whole adventure was that my literature teacher, Eleanor Shannon, whom I vastly admired, could not get a seat.

When Ruby and I began rehearsing our little show that had no name yet, I assumed the role of director and Ruby graciously held her peace. We sought out vacant classrooms for our rehearsals and started with the *Hamlet* scene. I pounded and pummeled it while Ruby dodged her way into the character of Gertrude, queen mother of the seamy bed. I believe her method was to find out what the character was doing first and then do it, while my approach was the reverse: do it and then discover what I was doing wrong. It must have worn severely upon Ruby's patience. For a comedy number we took the two forest scenes from *As You Like It* and spliced them together around a soliloquy to make one continuous twelve-minute scene. Since one of the empty classrooms we stole into for rehearsals had a piano bench, that became our only prop, and I ended up making a breakdown bench in white for the tour. It was the only scenery we trouped for thirty thousand miles when *As You Like It* turned into our opening number. We consulted costume books for the period styles and Ruby made two brown tunics and off-white shirts with billowy sleeves for Rosalind and Orlando, but we didn't know where we'd get the money for the fancy fabrics needed for Queen Elizabeth, Essex, Hamlet, Victoria and Albert, and the Brownings. And we would need a car.

The Mark Twain sketch was a problem. I thought it was the corniest thing I'd ever read. I didn't want to tell Ed that because it might hurt his feelings, since some of the stuff he did in his solo show was so far out in the cornfield that it would have been embarrassing if he weren't so brilliant at it. Finally I had to say it: "Ed, I think this Mark Twain thing is pretty corny. I don't think it's funny."

"Why don't you and Ruby work on it and let me see it?"

So we worked on it, with Ruby playing the Interviewer, who asks the usual questions but is baffled by Twain's moronic responses. "How old are you?" "Nineteen in June." "Whom do you consider the most remarkable man you ever met?" "George Washington." "But how could you have ever met George Washington if you're only nineteen years old?" "If you know more about me than I do, what do you ask me for?" In a disenchanted mood we showed it to Ed.

"I see why you don't think this is funny. You're not getting the point, Hal. This is a man with a sense of humor who's dealing with a person with no sense of humor. Why don't you keep working on it."

An opportunity came along to join up with Dick and Betty Welsbacher for a performance in the suicide ward of the Chillicothe Veterans Hospital. They would sing and act and we would do the Mark Twain sketch. We were led into a large room with windows too high to climb out of and a lot of bewildered-looking guys shifting around making grunting sounds and turning away, an alarming-looking crowd for a theatrical debut. We moved two chairs and a table into position, set an ashtray on the table and lit the cigar, and waited for our introduction by an attendant with big biceps. There was no applause. At first we held their attention because they didn't know who these people were, what they were doing in the room, or why we were talking to each other instead of them. This unnerved them and they started looking up at the windows, muttering to themselves as if planning an escape. Some of them stopped and looked back at us as if we were dangerous. There were others who continued to stare at us, rooted to the spot and clearly afraid to move. One of them made what I thought was a laughing sound, but without the merriment in it, and then another guy looked at him and did the laughing sound, too. He looked at another fellow, as if to pass it along, and the laughing sound moved around the room until it collected the attention of the guys who wanted to get out through the windows, and they chimed in. The only trouble was, no one was looking at us. They were looking at each other or empty space and laughing. We didn't know whether to wait for these laughs or just keep going. Could this be an audience response? In the car on the way home I tried to snatch some useful critique of our work from this tryout performance. "Some of that growling and snorting could have been laughs. In the Twain scene, remember that part about George Washington? Where I said, 'I attended his funeral'? Wasn't that a laugh, that big sound there?" There was a rueful silence from Ruby and the Welsbachers, but a few weeks later we got our answer when we played the Rotary Club in nearby Newark. They laughed at the same places where the people in the suicide ward had made grunting sounds, so either the Rotarians were crazy or the guys in the ward were saner than they looked.

For the scene about the Brownings we got the idea to create an imaginary encounter in which Elizabeth presented Robert with a poem she had written for him: "How Do I Love Thee?" I researched the Brownings and gave it my best literary shot (I had won the poetry prize in my freshman year) and it served us pretty well, depending a great deal on Ruby's classically romantic Mrs. Browning, a strong-minded, spirited woman caged by the physical boundaries of her infirmity. This scene would be a chancy one in the schools but a knockout in the women's clubs we would play in the future. Robert Browning was a stretch for me because even though I was considered handsome, I never *felt* handsome, and that is its own infirmity.

The costume changes were going to be the big hurdle. How to change from Hamlet and Gertrude to Mark Twain and the Interviewer in—what—fifty seconds? We planned to use music and would troupe a tape recorder, but how long could the musical interludes hold the audience between scenes? Thirty seconds tops. A device was needed. An introduction to each scene from in front of the curtain would serve multiple purposes. One, it would allow us to plunge right into each scene without a lot of exposition to bog down the action. Two, it would allow the actor who needed to start the next scene to get into makeup and costume during the introduction and then be onstage doing something for thirty seconds while the actor who made the introduction was slapping on a wig or beard and the new costume. And three, it would allow each of us to come before the curtain in a dressing gown and be seen as our own sweet self.

The inspiration for this simple device came from a couple of seasoned troupers who had played the school assembly circuits for years, Jack Rank and Jay Johnson. This exotic pair were friends of Ed's from the old Chautauqua days. He sent us over to Newark to watch them put on their astonishing production of *Macbeth*. Jack Rank played all the parts while Jay changed costumes on him as he passed behind a screen upstage. Jack would be in the midst of a speech as Macbeth and disappear behind the screen for maybe seven or eight seconds—still emoting in a voice ripened by years of projection in school auditoriums across America—and then pop out on the other side as Lady Macbeth: "But screw your courage to the sticking place and we'll not fail!" With variations of pitch and timbre in that aged-in-gravel voice commanding the stage, no one in that high school audience dared move. Lady Macbeth and Macbeth both had the balls of an angry elephant. It was a marvelous theatrical experience and these two troupers gave us advice and warned us of the pitfalls to come, the truest professionals in the finest tradition of the theater.

With the startling memory of Jack's changes of voice and character, we worked on the roles we would play with an ear for variety, and Ruby devised costumes that could be underdressed or overdressed as required, with snaps or a hook and eye in strategic places. These were the days before Velcro, so steady hands were required. Off with Orlando's tunic, shoes, and green tights, Hamlet's black tights underdressed. On with his shoes and the introduction bathrobe. Dash to the opening in the curtain, dousing the music en route, step through it calmly, and introduce the closet scene while Ruby gets out of green tights and tunic, redoes her hair, slips on Gertrude's nightgown and robe, and gets into place onstage. I finish the introduction and cue the curtain puller on the way to our improvised dressing area just offstage. Ruby starts the scene in pantomime while I throw off the bathrobe, slip into the black Hamlet tunic, zip it up, buckle on a sword, and enter. Precision and practice. Precision and practice.

Just in time something wonderful happened. Enter the Reese family. Gay had been the behind-the-scenes force in getting the tent theater season off the ground because she and her husband, Everett Reese, loved the theater and had a strong sense of community service. Ev was the president of the Park National Bank in nearby Newark. He knew we had to buy a station wagon for the tour and fabric for the costumes, and he knew we needed the fabric now because the final test of the honors project was going to be the performance of our little show. He offered us a $3,000 loan. We could have the money now and would not have to start paying it off until next September when the tour began. The Reeses were the kind of people who helped you believe it could be done simply because they believed in you.

Ev steered us to his friend who owned the Ford agency. The 1948 station wagon with varnished wood sides took its place behind our Enchanted Cottage. We drove it into Columbus to shop for fabrics: brocades in the drapery department for Prince Albert's maroon dressing gown and Queen Elizabeth's corseted green top and voluminous outer skirt. Silk in powder blue for Victoria's peignoir and red satin and grays for Gertrude's night attire. The black velvet for Hamlet was the hardest to find because we wanted the finest velvet. When Ruby got it home she was afraid to cut it up, unsure of how to form a pattern for my upper body. She would lay it on the floor, folded once upon itself, and circle it for an hour at a time. I couldn't stand it any longer. I handed her the scissors, lay down on top of the velvet with arms outstretched, and cried out, "Cut around me!" She did, and the Hamlet costume got under way.

It was now time for my senior play, where you get to do a big role. *Years Ago* by Ruth Gordon. I'd seen Fredric March and his wife, the wonderful Florence Eldridge, in this memoir of Ruth Gordon's fledgling years. I was much affected by March's character study of Gordon's father, an old ship's captain who disapproves of Ruth's passion to become an actress but finally gives her his most prized possession, his spyglass, to pawn and "grease the ways" as she sets off for New York. Patricia Cessna played Ruth, and Ruby was her mother. That retired New England sea captain was as tough and grouchy and authoritative as a man should be who had fought through storms and calms to come to rest in a landlocked job for a bare subsistence. I loved this man. He reminded me of my grandfather, or someone whom life had abandoned. His mother had killed herself when he was two years old and he was put in the hands of relatives. "They were awful people!" He'd run away when he was eight and gone to sea as a cabin boy. He had known the rough edge of poverty all his life, and the final scene, when he makes the decision to give up the symbol of his pride, that spyglass, to launch his daughter's own life story, was very moving to me.

By the time the groundhog had checked the weather out in Ohio that year I had three more roles to do in diverse plays: *Fancy Free*, *Androcles and the Lion*, and the Greek classic by Euripides, the *Alcestis*. Ruby played the title role of the young queen who offers to die in her husband's place to satisfy the gods, while I was grappling with the role of Alcestis's father-in-law. Greek drama was another challenge in voice projection on the outdoor stage and required a great deal of classic stagecraft for an actor to feel comfortable delivering language designed for an amphitheater. It became a lesson for me in how difficult the craft of acting can be when you leave the safe harbor of naturalism.

Fancy Free was a one-act curtain-raiser for George Bernard Shaw's *Androcles and the Lion*. I am having trouble recalling our roles in this play. That we were both in it is proven by a photograph in which Ruby is seated gorgeously gowned and relaxed while I am holding myself in a defensive grip, looking like someone balancing on an I beam one hundred feet aloft in patent leather shoes.

I couldn't wait to shed the tails and worm my way into the rather scant costume for Caesar in Shaw's satiric burlesque of Rome in all its rotten political splendor. I did a bit of research on the Caesars. Who was this guy, really? It turns out he wasn't so much of a guy, not in the heroic sense, because he rather admired boys. Homosexuality was not an open closet door back in 1948, but it appears to have been good sport among the dandies of ancient Rome. So here was a tempting opportunity to plow new ground and stun the Granville audience. Should I do it? I thought of the Belvoir lieutenant and said: Oh hell, yes. My attire was a tunic that ended in a skirt well above the knees, high booties on my feet, and a little gold wreath to crown this cute-looking emperor of the Roman Empire. The wreath would hold the bangs in place. My exposed knees and thighs could work wonders, and of course all those rings, resplendent on fluttering fingers, would be a bewitching touch. Ultra-red lipstick raised the ante on this dazzling portrait before a word escaped my rosy mouth.

It was a chancy business and could easily go off the deep end in one top-heavy beat, so I had to monitor every impulse. In rehearsal

Harold

I found my moment of extreme danger when the huge soldier Ferrovius with the bulging muscles appeared behind my back just as I was turning in his direction. "Oooo!" It just popped out. There was a general breakdown of discipline in the rehearsal hall, so I kept it in. It remained to be seen what the reaction would be on opening night. The moment came and so did the "Oooo!" There was a crash of astonished laughter and Caesar's historic character was nailed in place for central Ohio. This was another lesson for the future. There was gold in researching a character.

Often on Sunday nights we were invited to the Reeses' home for dinner and on one such occasion I mentioned that Twain often wore white, calling himself "a whited sepulchre" when he strolled past the lower Fifth Avenue churches while congregations robed in black poured out on Sunday morning. Ev Reese said, "I have something for you," and disappeared upstairs. He came back with a white Palm Beach suit on a hanger. "Can you use this?"

"My gosh! Yes." I never knew what years of service that gift would come to see.

With graduation in sight, there rose up a mastiff in my path—the final geology exam. I was going to fail. We all knew it, and so did Professor Mahard, a great fan of the theater. His voice was getting softer when he spoke to me. I was on my deathbed and he was bidding me goodbye. He was sorry, and so was I because I had grown fond of him. If I didn't pass I couldn't graduate. I prayed, "O Lord, lift me up to a C. Please."

At this critical junction Ruby got hold of Hartley Ferguson, who had nailed geology the year before. "We're going to drill you all night. You'll be exhausted but it's your only chance." Hour after hour through the long night I tried to get the Paleozoic period sorted out with the Mesozoic and Trapozoic, memorizing which ones had the most crustaceous shells and snails to pass on down to us and which one dug up the Great Lakes so Buffalo could be safely settled later on. Always there was the Old Red Sandstone strata lurking around with all those brontosaurus bones, and what about the Finger Lakes, what about terminal moraines? It was like memorizing lines for next week's play in summer stock. You threw the lines for the next play back and forth until you dropped.

I arrived at the battlefield at 8:00 a.m., tanked up with coffee and geological facts. When Dick Mahard laid the sheaf of questions on my desk he said, "Good hunting, Hal." If I could pass this test just for him, it would be a reward. He had never quite given up on me. I ran through the questions. They were not as forbidding as I thought. With a little luck . . . "1. Where is the Old Red Sandstone deposit located?" Hey, hey, hey! Look out, Buffalo.

Professor Mahard called me the next day. "Holbrook, I thought you'd like to know. You got a B on the exam. And you almost gave me heart failure. Please don't go into geology as a profession. Try acting."

There remained the honors project to complete. I had written a large tome, a thesis, as the honors committee required. It explored the purpose of our show and how it was developed, its historical and dramatic framework, and its costuming and staging. But the real test was going to be our performance. As an honors project it would be one of a kind. We were rehearsing the "ring scene" from Elizabeth and Essex, that final, agonizing confrontation between the rebellious warrior Lord Essex, accused of treason and too principled and proud to beg for mercy, and his lover, the aged queen. Elizabeth pleads with him to save himself from the headsman's ax by returning her gift to him, the ring, which will signal her forgiveness. He refuses. He warns her that if he lives he will take the crown from her.

"Are you ready to give
your crown up to me?"

At that moment Ruby rose up in that magnificent wide-skirted costume, her stricken face made pale by the fiery red hair and her voice rippling with scorn:

"Why, who am I
To stand here paltering with a rebel noble!

I am Elizabeth, daughter of a king,
The Queen of England, and you are my subject!"

It was a breathtaking moment. Until then I never knew she had that power in her.

Queen Victoria was an entirely different creation, an uncertain young girl coming into Prince Albert's dressing quarters the morning after their wedding to watch a man shave for the first time. Albert's reserve and wisdom give a clear sign of the support she will have from him in the years of their abiding love. We were finding real changes from character to character and startling contrasts from scene to scene, enhanced by a variety of rich-looking costumes, which we hoped would help keep the show surprising. Our dedication to the enormous task had so concentrated our minds on its creation that we nearly forgot we were going to be paid for performing it. When we were handed a check for $15 after playing for a local women's club we discussed giving it back.

The night of our performance at the Opera House arrived and Ruby and I were as nervous as racehorses, but just as ready for the test. Luke Utter had volunteered to pull the curtain for us, so when the moment came to step forward into our new life, it was by his hand that we were offered up to our friends and neighbors, the people of Shangri-la, for their approval. What could they do but be kind and loving? And they were.

Ed had arranged for us to give a special performance in Lakeside, Ohio, at the International Platform Association convention before heading out on tour, but first we were driving to New York to see some agents like Chamberlain Brown and maybe audition for them. Then we would drive up to Holyoke, Massachusetts, and pay a visit to Bertram Tanswell, who was with the Valley Players summer stock company. We'd let them take a look at us. Just in case.

At Pittsburgh we hooked up with the Pennsylvania Turnpike, the proud forerunner of a hundred interstates, and in Manhattan the Hotel Bristol took us in. We kept moving the car from block to block to save garage fees, and we hit the pavements. The New York agents wouldn't see us, but we had saved Chamberlain Brown's office in the West Forties for last. We climbed the stairs and opened the door to an album of American theater history. On the walls were faded posters heralding Minnie Maddern Fiske, Sothern and Marlowe, Maude Adams, Richard Mansfield, Ethel and John Barrymore—names to knock your eye out. It was an aging cell of theater antiquity. Not a dustrag had passed over an item in it for decades and the rug was exhausted, past the boundaries of descriptive hyperbole. The walls were reasonably perpendicular, but the glue on a long-extinct pattern of wallpaper was releasing its grip on its old mate.

And now we come to Chamberlain. He was tall and full in the waist, with a kindly face, somewhat cherubic, but it had the presence of a long career to give it strength. His pale blue shirt became the focal point of his appearance because it was not fresh. It is doubtful that he exchanged it for a nightshirt, because it had the exhausted appearance of double duty. The sleeves had been cut off just above the elbows and one wondered if this was a personal style choice or if they had simply rotted off along the forearms so that Chamberlain had to cut them away and was waiting for the rest of the shirt to follow suit. And yet he did not smell bad. There was a smell, indeed there was, but it was not the smell of body odor. He smelled like the walls.

We had taken the precaution to write Chamberlain and his brother Lyman and had given them a brief description of our show and the looming tour. It caught their interest, these two pioneers in the profession, and they invited us into their office. Lyman even stood up and shook our hands. They wanted to know about the tour and our choices of dramatic material "for the cowboy lands." They pointed out that even Edwin Booth, as a boy, had accompanied his father, Junius Brutus Booth, on a tour of the far western goldfields, a kind note to throw our way. We wondered if they had booked it. They said they would like to see one of our pieces if we would do it for them.

"Now?" I said.

"Just pull the chairs away. Can you do one of your scenes there?"

"I guess so. Ruby, what do you think?"

"Victoria and Albert?"

"Not much movement, good. This is the shaving scene from *Victoria Regina*."

"Oh yes," Chamberlain said. "Helen Hayes and Vincent Price were quite fine in that."

"We've had to shorten it. So . . ."

We did the scene for them, and Chamberlain said, "Quite fine, don't you think, Lyman?"

"Quite fine."

"It's important that we see his understanding that he must never lead, but only gently inform his queen. Yes, I think you have the idea of the scene."

"You have a quality, Ruby," said Lyman. "Good for the role."

"Yes, we must do something for you fine young people. We will organize something. We'll keep an eye on possibilities for you. Perhaps when you complete your tour you will return here and Lyman and I will present you in a small performance for the benefit of producers and other influential persons in the theater."

"That would be wonderful!" we chimed in together.

"You must keep in touch. Write us from Texas and let us know how the western lands are responding to your presentations."

We stumbled downstairs in a trance, filled with dreams of a glorious future, filled with the confidence that we could make it because Chamberlain and Lyman Brown had paid attention to us! Whoopee!

Off to Holyoke. We were nervous about this trip because we did not want to seem pushy or to embarrass Bertram. On the way we passed the boarding school where the Headmaster had taken such pleasure in whipping me, igniting an anger that still burned in the regions of my gut. Maybe someday I would rise above the memory and put it to some good use. We drove along the handsome Connecticut River past Springfield, where I had boarded the train with Grandpa for those overnight rides to Cleveland, snug in the upper berth. My past was beginning to connect to my future. I was in New England again.

We arrived in Holyoke just in time to see the play that night, *You Can't Take It with You*. It's an irresistible farce, and in the hands of a company of professionals who could project their characters into the cavernous space of the Mountain Park Casino it was hugely enjoyable. Jean and Carlton Guild ran this theater, and after the show everyone came together at the Guilds' home to drink beer and run lines for the next week's play. We were made welcome, but it was like dropping in on a family preparing for a wedding or the imminent birth of a baby. It wouldn't do to hang around, so we left on Monday for the drive back to Granville.

Ed had persuaded the people at the convention in Lakeside to put the Holbrooks on the evening program with artists like Leadbelly and John Jacob Niles. I believe it may have been the first time the convention had featured a new act like ours on the big stage at night, a remarkable fact we may have only dimly understood at the time, but it was enough to raise our anxiety level. We would be seen by booking managers from all around the country and we wanted to score for Ed's sake as well as our own. In Columbus we purchased two 500-watt spotlights for the tour and an amplifier for the little musical themes between scenes, and rehearsed what we would do at Lakeside: Rosalind and Orlando, Victoria and Albert, Hamlet and Gertrude, and Mark Twain and the Interviewer.

I began to think about my sisters for the first time in ages. Maybe we could drive to California at Christmas and see June. When she was living in an apartment in Cleveland with Bill Meyer right after the war, Gion Fenwick had written Grandma to say he'd always liked June and how was she. Grandma read the letter to June, and she left Bill two days later and went to Los Angeles with her daughter, Cheryl, and married Gion two days after her arrival. I hope she divorced Bill. Sometimes the people in my family sound like characters in a comic farce, except it really wasn't very funny living through it. Sad things happened. Ruby and I had seen Alberta, who was now called Bee for short, a few times when we were able to get to Cleveland, and we would drive there to see her after Lakeside. She and I had practically lost touch during the war. She had married a young man from Cincinnati named David Drazil and had lived there until the marriage broke up. Then she'd taken her small daughter, Diane, to Cleveland, where she'd met Howard Holton. Howie fell in love with her and they were now married and living on the east side of Cleveland in a dreary walk-up apartment. You drove your car through an alley between sooty brick buildings into a dark parking area and entered the apartment building from this unpromising aspect. The stairs were dimly lit.

Ruby and I were nomads now. Our home was the station wagon. We stored in boxes what little we couldn't carry; we owned scant furniture and had no ties to bind us except the one that kept us together. We knew there were miles and miles of unknown territory ahead and experiences we would have to meet firsthand. But we didn't know the realities. We were in a lifeboat with four wheels, made by Ford. Our compass was our show and our hope of survival was our belief in it.

The theater at Lakeside was huge and sat twenty-nine hundred people. That scared us. Could our show go over in such a huge hall? Ed was already there to reassure us and to guide us in our preparations. We needed furniture for the show: a table and two chairs, and we had the bench that served us for the *As You Like It* scenes as well as Hamlet and Queen Gertrude. Soon after we arrived, two young men sought us out, Richard Corson and Mitchell Erickson. They had heard about us from Ed and wanted to hunt up the stage props for us and do anything else we needed. Dick was a makeup artist and Mitch was an actor and sometime stage manager. They were from New York and they opened their arms to us and took us on faith.

In the evening we went to the big theater where we would be performing and saw Leadbelly. God Almighty! Inside his ordinary suit of clothes was a sweating giant in ball and chain, and the torture of his raw life exploded out of him in a voice smoking with brimstone, the living sculpture of a black convict swinging his giant guitar like a sledge in John Henry's hands. "Take this hammer! Whoomp!!! Take it to the Captain! Whoomp!!!" God! It lifted me out of my seat. I had never seen or heard such controlled violence so viscerally employed onstage.

How were we supposed to follow that? The next night we came second on the program. I'd given the stagehands instructions about pulling the curtain, and the huge audience gave us a polite and even friendly welcome. Our first two scenes were received with a good round of applause. We were rolling along in control, but when I strapped on the sword for Hamlet, a sudden wild anger clenched at me and the unleashed energy that pulls an actor out of tune with his role got loose as I entered my mother's chamber.

"Hamlet, thou hast thy father much offended." That line always goaded me.

"Mother, you have my father much offended!" The scene spewed out in emotional bursts too raw and personal for me to control. When it ended and I strode offstage, a stagehand pulled the curtain too soon, cutting off Ruby's pantomime, which gave me the extra time needed to change into Mark Twain. "No!" I shouted, and drew my sword in a fury and flung it past the frightened stagehand, nearly spearing him to the wall. He lunged into a broken field run to get away from this maniac kid actor who'd lost control. We were all shook up and sweating hard, but Ruby comforted the stagehand and went out to introduce Mark Twain while I raced through the big costume and makeup change. My hands shook so bad putting on the mustache that I almost glued it to my nose. Somehow we got through the scene and took our bows and as we came off, the stagehand gave me the sword and said, "You missed me. Better luck next time."

We were told Del Suplee wanted to see us. Who's that? "He's a big school assembly booker from Philadelphia. Books Jack Rank and lots of others." Mr. Suplee looked to me like a man who knew he was important and was going to offer us our big chance at a career. He certainly was offering something big: a guarantee of five years at twenty shows a week playing school assemblies in the northeastern part of the country. Security and sure death all in the same package. We were still whirling this around in our heads the next day when a small lady with the loveliest wrinkles around her eyes approached us in front of the theater.

"Children, you don't know me, but I am your fairy godmother. My name is Ricklie Boasberg."

She was around forty and had large blue-gray eyes in a soft, full face with all those little wrinkles. She spoke to us as if she were our favorite aunt and hadn't seen us for months.

"You have done very well here. Your performance was well received and you will be receiving many offers. Cliff Menz is here and I'm sure he will be talking to you. Now, children, I want you to listen to me very carefully. I know that Del Suplee has given you an offer of five years in school assemblies. You must say no to him. You are going out for a year now for Harry Byrd Kline and it will be very hard work and you will learn a great deal. But then you must never do it again. Listen to me now . . . You must come to me because you children are artists." (She spoke it so gently.) "You must come to me and I will place you in women's clubs and colleges, where your audience will appreciate you." She smiled the most winning conspiratorial smile. "Will you do that?"

"Yes, Miss Boasberg."

"You must call me Ricklie. We are friends now."

It wasn't long before we heard from Mr. Suplee. He caught us on the big flight of steps in front of the theater.

"I hear you've been talking to Ricklie Boasberg. What about my offer?"

"Mr. Suplee, we want to think it over."

"What's there to think about? I've offered you five years of work."

"Yes, sir. And we appreciate it."

"So what's to think about?"

"Well, we might not want to stay in school assemblies for five years."

"Then make it three years."

"Well. Maybe we'll just want to do this year with Harry Byrd Kline . . ."

"So after that you'll be unemployed?"

"We might want to try for the colleges and maybe the women's clubs . . ."

"So Boasberg's been giving you some big ideas. You think you're something, don't you?"

"No, sir. We just want to try for something better—"

"Better! It didn't take you long to get a big head, did it? Just because the audience gave you an easy time of it here, don't take that to mean you've already made it. You need five years on the circuits before you'll be ready."

"We'll think it over, Mr. Suplee."

"Don't think too long. My offer can be withdrawn at any time."

We were young and scared, but not scared enough to take up slavery as an occupation. We hunted up Ricklie and told her what Del Suplee had said to us.

"I will talk to Mr. Suplee. You are coming with me next year. I think Cliff Menz and Phil Pryor will give you some dates, too."

Cliff Menz and his friend Marv Foster did look us up. Cliff said he and his partner out of Council Bluffs, Iowa, Phil Pryor, would get in touch with us. That evening when Cliff and Marv and I started drinking, Ruby escaped to our room, and after I'd taken on enough whiskey to inspire myself, I led them out on the docks of the marina and climbed into the pilothouse of a fifty-foot cruiser, telling them to climb aboard, we were going for a spin on Lake Erie. The owner had, accidentally I hope, left the key in the ignition and when I turned it on, the motor roared into life. Foster jumped on board and restrained me, thank God, from the rash and idiot act I was about to commit. I knew nothing about boats and would probably have driven it overland into dry dock. Why I chose to go nuts that night I do not know, but these wild, suicidal impulses got hold of me sometimes, even when sober. They were in my genes. I hadn't much experience with the stealthy grape and we couldn't afford it, but showing off could be a disturbing flaw in me when it got loose, especially if it was fired up by liquor and I thought I was being funny or daring. This was a warning: the bottle could become an ugly companion.

15

Oklahoma City. THE CHOCTAW COURTS $3.00 A NIGHT. Keep going. Red clay and oil wells pumping. The varnished wooden body of our new station wagon was airbrushed with red dust. It had spread around inside on the seats and window sashes, and on the three trunks wedged behind us on the pulled-down loading platform. PALM COURTS $1.50 STOP HERE. That was the price we were looking for. A loudspeaker was bawling "Let's say goodbye like we said hello, in a friendly kind of way . . ." Inside the office a yellow-haired woman with a bandanna around her head and a throaty voice sang out, "Howdy there. Where are you two from?" We discussed Ohio and a room for one night.

"That's going to be two dollars for the night."

"But it says one fifty on the sign."

"That's for one person."

"Well. I don't know. We're trying to keep our rent down. Maybe we better—"

"Whaddayou kids doing?"

"We're heading for Amarillo. We're doing a show in the schools down here."

"Show folks, huh? Well, I guess I can let you have the room for one fifty. If you're looking for a place to eat that's cheap and won't kill you, Sandy's Café is a half mile down the road."

Harold

We unlocked the door to our room and a cloud of dust blew us inside. There was a bed, not quite a double one, but except for the mashed-up cockroach between the sheets it was okay. Welcome to the "cowboy lands."

We got to Amarillo High School at 6:45 a.m. just after the janitor. He helped us get our trunks in and showed us a room near the stage where we could set up shop. We had two shows here, our first at 8:00 for the senior high school students and then one at 10:00 for the junior high. There was a table where we could sit side by side making up and a few hooks to hang the costumes on. We got everything hung in sequence where we could grab it fast between scenes. I pulled on the black tights for Hamlet and the green ones over them for Orlando. The tights made me feel strong. Then came the blouse and tunic and over them the robe in which I'd introduce the show. Ruby was getting into her Rosalind costume, the mate of mine in green and brown because Rosalind was pretending to be a boy. Then we waited, pretty dry in the mouth. We could hear them coming into the hall, about a thousand of them, young cowboys and cowgirls ready to give us a ride.

The superintendent found us huddled in the little room. He was polite, with a reassuring smile. He must have known this was our first time in the bullring. When he stepped in front of the curtain, the audience quieted down, which was an encouraging sign. His introduction was brief but nice, and then I stepped out. I tried to keep my voice calm while delivering the introduction, which was received with only a few small yelps and a hi-eeee or two, and then I disappeared and told the janitor to pull the curtain while I threw off my robe, grabbed Orlando's poems, and came onstage at a run waving the poems around. The place lit up with catcalls and explosive laughter when they saw a grown man in green stockings and not much else jumping around, pretending to pin poems on imaginary trees.

"'Hang there, my verse, in witness of my love.'" There was a sudden stunned silence while they tried to sort that out.

"And thou, thrice-crowned Queen of Night, survey
With thy chaste eye, from thy pale sphere above, . . ."

Now a spreading moan came from the audience.

"O Rosalind! these trees shall be my books,
And in their barks my thoughts I'll character . . ."

The moan became approaching thunder.

"Run, run, Orlando! Carve on every tree . . ."

All hell broke loose. I began to wonder if we'd picked the right scene to start off with. I finally got offstage, trembling a lot, and Ruby came bounding on to a round of cheers. The cheers were for her well-turned legs and every other attractive section above them, this being a long and happy stride past what a lady drama reader had been able to offer them the year before. The audience had been told in the introduction that Rosalind is pretending to be a boy, but you couldn't fool this audience. They knew a girl when they saw one. The key to getting this scene off the ground with this crowd was going to be the word "lover." I'd cut through Shakespeare's blank verse to pursue it.

ROS: "There is a man haunts the forest, that abuses our young plants with carving 'Rosalind' on their barks; hangs odes upon hawthorns; all deifying the name of Rosalind. If I could meet that fancy-monger, I would give him some good counsel, for he seems to have the quotidian of love upon him." [*A burp and a low raspberry there.*]
ORL: "I am he that is so love-shaked: I pray you tell me your remedy."
ROS: "There is none of my uncle's marks upon you. He taught me how to know a man in love."

ORL: "What were his marks?"

ROS: "A lean cheek, which you have not." [*Now Ruby begins to circle me and paw around.*] "A blue eye and sunken, which you have not; a beard neglected, which you have not. Your hose should be ungartered [*a loud yell of approval from the boys when she flicks a finger across my thigh*], your sleeve unbuttoned, your shoe untied. And everything about you demonstrating a careless desolation. But you are no such man."

ORL: "Fair youth, I would I could make thee believe I love."

ROS: "Me believe it? You may as soon make her that you love believe it, which, I warrant, she is apter to do than to confess she does. But in good sooth, are you he that hangs the verses on the trees, wherein Rosalind is so admired?"

ORL: "I swear to thee, youth, by the white hand of Rosalind [*she whisks the hand out of sight; small chuckle there*], I am that he, that unfortunate he."

ROS: "But are you so much in love as your rhymes speak?" [*Ruby nudges up against me to inspect my face better. Growl from the audience. They are waiting for something past suggestive.*]

ORL: "Neither rhyme nor reason can express how much." [*A big overdone sigh from the football team down front: "O Romeo, Romeo, wherefore art thou, Romeo?"*]

ROS: "Love is merely a madness, and deserves a dark house and a whip as madmen do. Yet I profess curing it by counsel."

ORL: "Did you ever cure any so?"

ROS: "Yes, one, and in this manner." [*She sits beside me on our white bench.*] "He was to imagine me his love, his mistress." [*"Mistress" gets a laugh. We'll take it. Now she performs feats of come-hither pantomime, which the crowd is taking as a cue for its own performance.*] "And thus I cured him."

ORL: "I would not be cured, youth."

ROS: (*seductively*) "I would cure you [*yay!! big laugh.*], if you would but call me Rosalind and come every day to my cote and woo me." [*"Wooo her! Wooo her!! O Romeo!"*]

ORL: "Now, by the faith of my love, I will!" ["*Yay!! Whooo!! Ride 'em, cowboy!!*"] "Tell me where it is."
ROS: "Go with me to it, and I'll show it to you."

And off we went together. It seemed to go pretty well, better than we'd feared it would go, and the second half of the number went over even better because the audience had got hold of the joke. The mock love play that Rosalind practices was in a familiar alley for them. Shakespeare was not going to be such a hurdle for these schoolkids after all, as long as we didn't take ourselves too seriously and let them have their fun. Their participation did not hurt this number as long as it didn't get out of control, which it shortly did with the younger kids of the junior school. They were a hopelessly un-disciplined mob.

The shows had to start on time and be fifty minutes long, but not a second over. When the class bells rang, the audience avalanched out of the hall. If you were still onstage acting, you could be left with a feeling of vast impotence. We had a third show to do at 2:00 p.m. in Claude, twenty-eight miles away; when the janitor didn't show up we hauled our trunks by hand down corridors and out to the station wagon, heaved them in, and went to the superintendent's office to collect the check—$70 for the two shows. We would get 60 percent of it, $42, when Harry Byrd Kline paid us at the end of the week. Meanwhile, we'd mail the checks to him that night when we got the one from Claude. That was the system.

But right now we were in a hurry. It was 11:30 a.m. and we had to drive the twenty-eight miles to Claude, eat something on the way, and set up for the 2:00 p.m. show. We were pretty frazzled by then and the audience in Claude was eager to go out and play football, so the show was shaky. We had to learn to calm down and pace our-selves. In the late afternoon we drove north on a farm road to a tiny place called Panhandle just off Route 66 and found a crumbling tourist court for the night. The only café in town played "Let's say goodbye like we said hello, in a friendly kind of way . . ." four or five times while we wolfed down chili and beans.

Harold

The next day, Tuesday, we had three shows: Panhandle, Borger, and Pampa, each one twenty-five to thirty miles apart. We were driving fast through the big Texas oil boom after the war. Interstate highways were way in the future, even Route 66 was a two-lane all the way to California, so we had to learn passing tactics that got us around slow-moving trucks and cars on these narrow roads. Hug their left rear wheel, scallop out to check the road ahead, judge the space between you and the oncoming car, then hit the gas pedal hard and dodge around a semi just in time to miss the car aiming dead at you. Depth perception and timing were the key, and sometimes it was pretty breathtaking, but we had to travel at eighty miles an hour to make our dates. That was simply a grim fact of life.

After our second morning show on Tuesday we were paid the $35 fee in quarters, dimes, nickels, and pennies. Admission had been nine cents. The principal insisted we count them.

"But we're glad to take your word for it."

"I'd feel better if you'd count it."

"We don't have much time, sir, and I'm afraid—"

"Well, we surely appreciate your performance here and I want to make sure you get paid the right amount."

"We're happy to take your word for it—"

"I may have counted wrong. I want to be fair with you fine young people . . ."

He was being cordial and Ruby was cordial and I was on fire. I wanted to knife him, but his sincere concern for our financial welfare, not to mention Harry Byrd's, was overwhelming my desire to see him die right there in his office, so I started counting. There wasn't much room on the edge of his desk, so I had to pick up a lot of coins that dropped on the floor and some that rolled under it, and this made me lose count. Ruby was trying to keep a nice social conversation going with the principal, who was beginning to see the dawn of an idea rising above the horizon of his desk when my face came up for air.

"I guess you folks have got to be going."

"Well yes, we do. Yes we do. We've got a show at two o'clock thirty-two miles away and we were hoping to get something to eat."

"Perhaps we can make up some sandwiches for you while you're counting?"

"No. No, please, let me just start over again, I've lost my place, and then we'll be going."

"Hal is a very fast driver," Ruby said.

"We'll need to pour it on this time."

"Thirty-two miles. You know, the best way to get over to Pampa is on that little farm road—"

"I think . . . Wait a minute, wait a minute, I've got to start counting again."

"I think Hal can make it on the highway."

"We'll have to average about sixty-one miles an hour, so if we keep the speedometer—oh, heck . . . !"

"Did you drop another one?"

"There's a quarter over there near your foot. What time is it, Ruby?"

He handed me the quarter. "Why don't you folks just go along and count this later, after your show?"

"Good idea. Hold your bag open, Ruby, I'm going to scoop them off the desk."

"It's been real nice talking with you young people."

As each day rose up to face us, the bitter truth unfolded: we were not playing high schools. Ninety percent of our audiences were "district schools" in tiny towns that collected kids from ranches and other two–gas pump settlements miles away and bused them into the only school in the county. So the audience started at the first grade and rose up slowly to the football team, and some of them were repeating a year or two because football hadn't left much time for book learning.

Now we were racing north for the Oklahoma Panhandle, looking forward to our first evening show in Boise City at the far end of that sliver of Oklahoma that slides over the top of the Texas Panhandle. This would be our reward for a week of initiation: our first adult audience.

The stage was at one end of a gym floor that had a small balcony at the far end. The "orchestra seats" were folding chairs set up on the gym floor quite a distance from the stage, a formal gap between us and the audience we would see a lot of in days to come. We had maybe 150 people out there, all kinds of people, some in their mothers' arms trying to suck up culture along with their evening meal; teenagers who had hidden themselves away in the balcony, where they could paw one another if the show got dull, and they knew it would. Then there was the tag team in that no-man's-land between the front row of seats and the stage, healthy young four-, five-, and six-year-olds already in training for the Olympic relays. Somewhere in this mob were the adults, for whom extended conversations were the rule, loud and without apparent consciousness that such exchanges could rattle the actors. We breathed in and out to calm our nerves over the weekend, listening to the oil wells thumping day and night and staring defeat in the face.

We had a couple of big problems. The district schools in these little towns were putting the first to the sixth graders down front and the older students behind them. It was like shouting over a playground to reach your audience. No amount of supplication could move the principals to seat the little ones in the rear, because it was the system to bring the lower grades in first and seat them up front. Maybe so they wouldn't be trampled to death. Too bad.

The other hurdle was the odd configuration of the theatrical playing fields. Many schools built a stage on one side of the basketball court to get double duty out of the building, but the seats were on the other side. Trying to shout the show across a basketball court was not working, so we brought the show down to the gym floor. I tied our two 500-watt Fresnels on the window ledges to warm up the space and it improved things right away.

Our fourth week on the road we had thirteen shows and finally struck gold. At the Oklahoma College for Women in Chickasha we played before an intelligent and culture-minded audience that left us nearly breathless with surprise. It was our first college on the tour and we had hoped for confirmation of our faith in the show we had put together, and they certainly gave it to us. The Brownings, Elizabeth and Essex, and Mark Twain went as we might have imagined in a dream. The schools would rarely let us do the Brownings, they laughed it off the stage. Sissy stuff. Yet we kept trying it, and I see now that's the real point. We kept trying to be a quality act. At the larger city schools we scored better and when we performed in real theaters, but at the Oklahoma College for Women in Chickasha we were given our passing grade. We just had to be tough now and hang on through the rough country ahead.

The fifth week we did fifteen performances in five days and drove more than 700 miles, some of it on dirt roads in Arkansas. Monday, October 11, Okmulgee, Oklahoma, at 9:00 and 10:00 a.m. and then Henryetta 13 miles away at 2:00 p.m. That afternoon we drove 88 miles to Midwest City and started off Tuesday with a 9:30 a.m. show there, then drove 116 miles on country roads to McAlester across the Canadian River for a show at 2:30 p.m. and 31 miles more on backcountry roads to Wilburton, Oklahoma, for an 8:00 p.m. show. On Wednesday the thirteenth we played Wilburton again at 9:00 in the morning, drove 87 miles across the border to Mena, Arkansas, for a 2:00 p.m. performance, drove 79 miles to Fort Smith for a show the next morning at 9:00 a.m. and then 17 miles to Alma for two shows at 2:00 and 7:30. We drove on to Clarksville that night, 42 miles, for two morning shows Friday at 9:45 and 10:45, then 45 miles to Booneville, Arkansas, in the boondocks for a 2:30 show and drove 28 miles for our fourth show that day, an 8:00 evening show at Ozark, Arkansas. On Saturday we drove 81 miles to Springdale in the northwest corner of Arkansas, our Monday morning town. On those country roads you didn't go straight from point to point, you cut back and forth like a broken field runner from farm to farm and you met cattle, redneck cows, and steers with horns and balls and it was *their* road you were traveling on, buddy, so you didn't shout "Out of the way, Bossie." You put the car in reverse with the clutch down and waited: if one of those four-legged steak dinners took off in your direction, you hit the gas pedal and wove backward down that country road like a mouse caught in the middle of a room who'd forgot where the hole was. And when a mean-looking Oklahoma steer wanted to freshen up the road with the remains of his lunch, you gave him as much respect as you would give Laurence Olivier in a performance of *Coriolanus*.

The fifth week of the tour was a crucible of good and bad. In the little town of Alma, at the foot of the Ozark Mountains east of Fort Smith, we had afternoon and evening shows on Thursday. Many of the students were from up in the hollers and most had never seen plays or anything like what we were putting on their stage, yet quite a number came back again to see the evening show. What a feeling this gave us, what a gift of warm, sheer confidence that little town of Alma gave to us. We would not forget it for years and years to come.

On Friday the third show that day was in Booneville, Arkansas, a poor little place and a poor little school, but after five weeks on the road we'd been toughened up. There was a hint of warning in the heavily scarred gym floor, but we unpacked the trunks, set up the stage and dressing room, dressed up, and waited for them. The bell rang and here they came—a full stampede, little grade school kids in high tenor voices rampaging into the gym, bursting with freed-up energy. We pleaded with the superintendent to seat the youngest ones at the sides and the back, but he was unwilling to consider it. So we breathed deep and dove at them with Rosalind and Orlando. It was a zoo, with little kids leaning over the stage, screaming at us, and others perched high on the windowsills like monkeys set free. We couldn't be heard, no discipline, no teachers to rein in this mob. We were out of place here and the school didn't care. When it was over we were told to report to the superintendent's office.

There were two men in the room and they weren't smiling. One was a heavily built figure who might have been the football coach.

"That was a bad show," said the superintendent. "You don't deserve to be paid."

"What was bad about it?"

"I didn't see it, but the coach here said you weren't trying."

"We were trying as hard as we could. They wouldn't listen."

"It is your job to make them listen," said the coach.

"That's true, but we can't do it alone. You had kids from the first grade to the twelfth out there and no teachers to keep them under control."

"We're too busy to have teachers at assemblies. We had a magician here last week and they listened to him."

"Our show is about words. Literature. It requires some attention . . ."

"It was that Shakespeare stuff. You should have left that out."

"That's part of our show. Other schools have enjoyed it."

"We don't. You aren't worth thirty-five dollars." The coach nodded. "That's right. Not worth it."

"Then don't pay us."

"We should write your booking manager about you."

"Please do. He knows our show. Write him."

"No, we wouldn't do that . . ."

"We want you to. We don't want him to book us in these grade schools. Write him."

"Don't worry. We'll pay you."

"Don't pay us. Write Mr. Kline. We want you to write him."

"We don't do things like that around here. We won't tell on you."

We loaded the trunks in the station wagon and started driving. The wall of codified ignorance and complacency was too high to scale this time and we pulled over to the side of the road and cried our guts out. Five weeks of frustration, driving at breakneck speed, the tumbling hope and defeat, and then this cool brush-off, it slugged us and we cried it out of our system. Then we hugged each other and drove to the little town of Ozark for our evening show. That was number fifteen in five days.

At Lakeside we had turned down ten other offers from booking managers around the country, most of them for school assembly tours like the one from Del Suplee. Now we knew we'd been right. But in our hearts we also knew this tour was right, that Ricklie was right. We would learn. We'd get toughened up for the life ahead. No one was going to hand us a free pass anywhere and that is why we were in Arkansas: to learn that.

We were determined to make an assault on acting jobs in New York. Our continuing postal contacts with Chamberlain Brown and his brother Lyman had paid off with a promise from Chamberlain that he would organize an audition for us at the Hotel Astor in May and invite "producers and directors" to see our work. We weren't as entirely naive as Leo the playwright from Oswego in *Room Service* and we took this prospect in with a small dune of salt, but we had to hope.

We weren't even members of Actors' Equity yet and you couldn't get a job in New York City or eastern summer stock without an Equity card and you couldn't get an Equity card without a job in an Equity company. How anyone ever moved up in this profession was a feat of magic in itself. We had one fairy godfather to help us besides Ed, and that was the director of *Much Ado About Nothing*, Bertram Tanswell. He was a real New York actor and he lived with his friend, the actor James Monk, in an elegant-looking town house apartment on East Fifty-third Street. He had that steady summer job with the Valley Players in Holyoke, and we bombarded Bert with news of our travails and small successes on the road. We had a dream, a wonderful dream, baby, to inspire Bert to inspire Carlton and Jean Guild of the Valley Players to let us in and give us Equity cards. By such devious means are careers launched, but the odds are maniacal. We did not beg Bertram to help us, we just knew our dedication would mean something to him. Some of the best friends Ruby and I would find in those hopeful days of struggle were members of that vast and once silent battalion of homosexual men who give life and love to the theater. They stepped forward; they extended a hand and pulled us into the family of actors. They hugged us and made us feel we belonged in the theater. They were not like the lieutenant. They were our friends, perhaps because they needed friends themselves.

I still had a lot to learn about Mark Twain. I was just doing an old man with a drawl. The depths of the man's mind were still unknown to me. I hadn't read up on him much and had very few specifics in my head, but I had read somewhere that his walk was funny or strange. It was described as a "duck waddle" or "shuffling gait" and I wondered if he might have exaggerated it for effect on the lecturing platform to the point where people thought he'd had a bourbon or two. When he visited the Boston home of his longtime friend William Dean Howells, Mrs. Howells thought Twain was drunk. So when our seventh week ended in Helena, Arkansas, on the Mississippi, I found myself looking at a steamboat.

"Ruby, let's go for a ride."

"Where?"

"This thing goes back and forth across the river here, it's kind of a ferry to Mississippi over there on the other side. I've never been on one of these things. Look, it has a paddle wheel. Maybe they'd let me stand in the pilothouse."

"Please don't turn into Mark Twain."

"I won't. I just want to smell what it's like."

It was unexpectedly elegant in a solid, old-fashioned way and it took to the river like a duck. I went up to the top deck and watched the helmsman for a while. Then I started walking along the side decks and said to myself, "Twain walked on decks like this for four years. Get the feel of it. Relax and see what it does to your gait." I did and I noticed my outboard foot sort of flung off a bit sideways because the deck was slanted to let the water run overboard. I'll be darned, I thought. That might be the drunk part. A couple of years later when I went to Hannibal and saw the old five-minute Edison film of Twain walking around his Connecticut house in Redding, I would see him throwing a foot out a bit, and the old-time speeded-up film made his walk look like Charlie Chaplin's.

On November 4 we played Central High School in Little Rock. Nine years later rioting would break out there over the admission of nine black students and it would become a tinderbox of the civil rights movement. We were heading into the South now, where we had never been before. In Arkansas the signs were appearing: COL-ORED ONLY. From El Dorado, Arkansas, we moved down into Louisiana, to Alexandria and farther south to Breaux Bridge in the high arch that shapes the foot of Louisiana. Then Gueydan and we were in Creole country. The slices of American life being served up to us were changing every day, changing faces, the ways of walking and talking, and the ways of thinking. There were black faces everywhere, more than we'd ever seen before, worn faces seamed with the indignities of life. They walked as if carrying a burden, but often they smiled beautifully. We saw them along the sides of the roads and in the fields, bent over their work under the merciless sun, dragging the long bags of cotton. Nearly always they wore a hat. We saw the weathered shacks, the almost improbable homesites where they lived apart, and we saw the fine houses with long driveways and lawns. Everyone understood the rules down here and as long as they were obeyed quietly, life would go on in a cordial manner. But once the rules were broken, when the unchalked line was crossed, the massed anger and fear that lay waiting like a wolf in the night would come howling out of the darkness and claim center stage in the struggle to come.

Each Monday when we sent the check to Ev Reese in payment of our loan, our $225 a week ($210 plus $15 for gas and oil) shrank to $125. We would pay $3,000 in thirty weeks, neat arithmetic but tough. At the headlong speeds we had to maintain over rough road surfaces we got a lot of rim-cut tubes and that ate into our bankroll. We stayed in the cheapest places we could find, a $2 room was our top, and ate our meals in fly-bashed country cafés with Ernest Tubb singing "Let's say goodbye like we said hello, in a friendly kind of way." We were trying to save $15 a week for the Christmas trip to California to see June, but bad luck could wipe us out in a flash. Still, we were hopeful of having one great dinner at the Court of Two Sisters in New Orleans, so we looked for the cheapest tourist court in sight and walked the town. It was Friday night and there was music pouring out of one frenzied place after another. We felt like strangers because we had to hold ourselves in check; if we threw away any significant part of the nearly $100 we'd saved for the Christmas trip to California, it would be a dark day for us. In that frame of mind we went to the Court of Two Sisters and took one look at the prices on the menu and stopped breathing.

"Too much, isn't it, Hal?"

"Yeah. Here's pompano Papillon. That's fish. It's only three dollars."

"We could order soup. You see here where it says crawfish bisque, sixty cents? And they would give us bread or at least crackers."

"Yeah. How about Key lime pie for dessert?"

"We could order one and we'll share it. At least we could say we have eaten at the Court of Two Sisters."

"Okay. But don't let's describe the food, all right?"

"We'll just say it was delicious."

It was. Delicious. A soupçon for gods and children. Maybe someday we'd come back with more money in our jeans.

Monday. Hahnville and Houma down in the bayous, ancient cypress and white plantation houses, the faces of people long gone from Arcadia, great gnarled oaks with Spanish moss clinging to them like decaying curtains. In a week it would be Thanksgiving and we were going to Dallas. We would go to the Margo Jones Theatre and see whatever was playing there.

Dallas looked upon Margo's baby as a gemstone. These were the infant days of the regional theater explosion in America, and Texas was leading the way. It was one giant boomtown after the war. Oil gushed up out of so many holes in the state it was getting to look like a sieve. Oil was money and the people of Texas started doing a remarkable thing with it: they invested in culture. The arts. Starting pretty much from scratch, Texans paused long enough between football games to put their money into the germination of cultural pursuits: museums, symphony halls, and theaters.

In that big-biceps oil town Houston, which had split the seams of its swaddling clothes and was flexing its muscles to give Dallas a run for its money, a woman name Nina Vance had founded a tiny theater in an alley and called it the Alley Theatre. You should see it now. It's planted in the center of town. The Lone Star State should have an extra star on its flag to honor a pioneering spirit that didn't stop short.

Margo Jones had just returned from directing *Summer and Smoke* in New York. A few years before, she had produced *The Glass Menagerie* and launched an unknown playwright, Tennessee Williams. On Thanksgiving Day we got two of the last seats to the play that night: Molière's *Les Femmes savantes*. By the strangest coincidence we had only last weekend tentatively chosen our new scene, the one we intended to work on over Christmas, a scene from—guess what? Molière's *L'École des femmes*. Now we could observe that style of acting and the costumes firsthand.

Sometimes I can't believe what we did out there. Developing a new number on the hurry-up school circuit, rehearsing around the bed in tourist courts, finding a Singer sewing machine center on Saturdays where Ruby could work on sewing the costumes. For Molière—with all that satin and lace? And then *doing* it! Molière in Oklahoma? Stand back, Loretta!

In the next three weeks the road to California would lead us west across Oklahoma into Texas and New Mexico before it set us down in Amarillo again for our last show on the evening of December 17. The next day we rolled onto Route 66 for the wonders of Hollywood and the San Fernando Valley, where the sun always shines. In New Mexico the road dropped down into Albuquerque on a slow glide. This same trail had carried the dust bowl Okies west, their grimed faces fixed with stubborn hope, into Arizona through the Petrified Forest and the Painted Desert, where the Navajo and Apache lands stretched north and south. It was an ancient land, haunted by mystical spirits, and we felt like strangers there. In our hearts we knew it was stolen.

In those slower days you could take the side road to the Grand Canyon and stand on its awesome precipice above the cratered deeps, and there in the presence of mystical gods we pondered the brief length of our life span. We rode over the last stretch of Route 66, which had been paved just that year—it was dirt until after the war—and turned up to Las Vegas, a western cow town then with a hungry look, one or two casinos, and some dusty signs. Then the Mojave Desert, that long, long hot ride on the edge of hell. You first checked the tires and your spare and prayed that nothing would stop you now because the Promised Land was across that desert, the magical land of orange trees and movie stars, and maybe somewhere in that magic kingdom your mother would come walking up to you.

16

There it was again. The Garden of Eden. They were beginning to call it the Valley now for short, because things were starting to get shorter, such as patience and civility, stuff you hardly noticed unless you hadn't been there for seven years. There'd been a war, and young soldiers had come west to train in the desert and on the ocean for Africa and the South Sea Islands, and now some of them were pouring back here to work and live a frost-free life in the happy lap of California. So there were two new odors in the air: exhaust fumes and the smell of money. The orange groves were receding west along Ventura Boulevard, the Adohr Milk Farm had given way to tract houses, and a Ralphs supermarket had been planted on the corner of Coldwater Canyon. But it was still beautiful, still fresh, and so very, very green.

We looked up June. Seven years before this I had driven down Ventura Boulevard with my father and a black widow spider and now his daughter and his son were walking down the same street with his six-year-old granddaughter, Cheryl, a little red-haired beauty whom he had never seen. Where was he? Close by? Subconsciously we kept looking for him because you never knew when he might come back from Juneau or Phoenix or Kansas City and unwind himself from behind the wheel of the Austin and raise his bullet-hole hat. And then there was our mother. She was here. Right here somewhere, and my sister was always on the lookout for her. I'd given up that search. Strange how she'd hidden herself away. Maybe if one of us got famous, she'd give us a call.

One thing about Los Angeles, you were always looking around for a movie star. June was practically on speaking terms with Clark Gable because she'd seen him once at a bus stop on Ventura standing beside a motorcycle. She was getting off the bus with a bunch of people who went into fan trauma when they spied Clark and rushed him for autographs. June didn't. She was always special, that sister of mine with the great legs and all, so she was poised on the steps of the bus as she watched Clark, who was watching her and signing blind with his right hand. He smiled at my sister and she smiled back and then she turned and sat back down where Clark could see her in the window and they looked at each other until the bus and June went away. She said Clark's hair was graying a lot but she always liked older men.

Gion was about fifteen years older than June, also with a mustache and a good face. He was a civilized guy whom you would not find hopping freight cars across the country. What he did was push big movie cameras around at Republic Studios down on Ventura, where Roy Rogers made his movies. Gion said he was "a cameraman," but everyone had a story in Hollywood. And since June had come west with Cheryl to marry him he had set about putting a life together for them. Gion was a likable man and decent company except when he pulled up his sleeve to display the wristwatches on his arm to a prospective buyer. He had great bursts of enthusiasm that suddenly tattered the sartorial gentleman's image, such as when he blew through the door after a drive past the orange groves on Ventura Boulevard and shouted, "If I only had a truck! If I only had a truck!" Then he'd roll a few oranges out of his pocket onto the kitchen table. A good-hearted man, and he wanted to give Cheryl and June a good life.

Christmas was going to be an embarrassment because Ruby needed a new dress and we simply had no money for presents. At one point we got down to $3.52 because there were no checks coming in over the twenty-four-day vacation. It must have been that $100 check from Grandpa's insurance policy that saved us. A couple of days before Christmas Eve, Ruby and I were walking down Ventura Boulevard and we saw a dress in a store window, a lovely blue dress. We stopped to admire it. A placard at one side said XMAS CLEARANCE SALE. All I could think of was how perfect the dress would be for Ruby.

"Let's go in."

"What?"

"Let's go in and look at the dress."

"We can look at it here."

"Maybe you could try it on."

"We can't afford it."

"How do we know without asking?"

"I can see it's too expensive."

"Come on. Let's go in."

So we went inside and talked to the salesman, who was so eager to get the dress out of the window and onto Ruby that we never had a chance to tell him we couldn't afford to buy it. We'd become so excited about it ourselves that our imaginations lofted toward miracles and fancies. We knew the dress was meant for Ruby. Boy! When she walked out of that dressing room there was no doubt. It was hers. It clung perfectly to her contours and the blue was her blue. The salesman was beaming.

"Now, that is a perfect match!" he said. We were silent while Ruby turned in the mirror. Then she turned again.

"May I ask how much it is?" I murmured.

"Oh, this is a true Christmas price. Twenty dollars."

"Twenty dollars?"

"And it's yours. It's meant for your lovely wife, don't you think?"

"Yeah. Yes, it sure is."

"Hal, we can't afford this dress. I shouldn't have put it on."

"It's pretty expensive. It looks so great on you, Ruby."

"Yes, it does, but we just can't afford it and we must face it. I'm going to take it off."

The salesman was embarrassed and so was I. "I'm so sorry. We just couldn't resist it. Christmas and all. I'm sorry."

"Oh, please, I understand. Oh my."

We left the store in the speechless grip of humiliation and impotence. There were too many things to pay for and too few dollars. True. Very true. But it was Christmas.

"I'm going back."

"What?"

"I'm going back. I'm going to bargain with him."

"How?"

"I'm going to tell him he has to give it to us for less."

"Gosh, I don't think you should do that . . ."

"Why not? I want you to have the dress."

So the well-brought-up boy from South Weymouth, Cleveland, and Culver Military Academy went back and told the salesman he had to have that dress for his wife for Christmas and would the salesman please lower the price and he knocked off two dollars and a half and the Culver boy walked out with the dress and put it under the tree at his sister's house. On Christmas morning his wife put it on again.

When 1949 arrived in California, we were full of hope. In the few days before we headed east across the desert for the wilds of southern Texas we saw Laurence Olivier's *Hamlet*. We sat in the movie palace in breathless wonder at the power the great actor-director had brought to the story of Hamlet. We could not speak when it was over. When words began to flow again they expressed our amazement at the clarity with which the story had moved through its dark tunnel of tragedy. We saw it a second time and then climbed into our station wagon and headed for the Rio Grande valley of Texas, filled with gratitude to Laurence Olivier for inspiring us to try harder and to love our profession.

Eight hundred miles to El Paso, but only halfway there. Then down, down, down the brooding sole of the Texas boot across cold, lonely mesas and black hills, two-lane asphalt snaking through miles and miles of gray-black loneliness. If the car broke down in that moonscape you could freeze to death. Alpine and Judge Roy Bean's place on the hump of the Big Bend, then along the Mexican border to Del Rio. Was there no end to Texas? Finally Laredo and McAllen in the Rio Grande valley, 760 miles of Texas, and it was warm again. Our first town, LaFeria, was barely on the map; then Donna and Weslaco. Those were the three towns that pulled us back into the school assembly circus on January 10. But not for long. In ten days we drove right back up to the Big Bend country again, to Alpine and Marfa, where few travelers ventured. It was so cold in January, the defroster on the windshield gave out and the little gas heaters in the barren rooms we found could barely take off the chill. When a dry norther came through, the little gas heaters gave out. We piled everything on the bed but our shoes and hung on to each other's body warmth.

The dreary winter wore on. The trail led us up into Carlsbad, New Mexico, and onto the open plains of West Texas, during which we were snowed out of two shows when a blizzard roared across the Texas flatlands. The girl quartet on our circuit was wiped out by a butane truck on the ice in New Mexico. All dead. When we opened our costume trunks we sometimes found frost on our costumes. If there was no heat we waved the Zippo lighter over them. Standing half naked in those cheerless schoolrooms tested the inspiration Olivier gave us and our resolve to maintain some level of artistry.

Keeping our morale afloat was like dragging a drowning swimmer through choppy water. Indifference to intellectual stimulation in those isolated towns muted discussions or the enjoyment of a challenging idea. The engine of curiosity was stalled. A fear of intellectual curiosity erected a silent defensive wall that shut down every impulse that didn't move along the track of daily remarks like "Been purty cold hereabouts" or "How do you like Texas?" There was only one answer to that, unless you wanted to die. So after a while most everything becomes dull. You have to lift your morale up like a dead weight and ignite it all by yourself. We searched for inspiration onstage, but if the audience refuses to rise to the level of challenging thought, what becomes of the performance? What if the whole country we live in should slowly descend to a level of tasteless mediocrity?

There were times when a kindness surprised us so suddenly that we came close to tears. In Cisco, west of Fort Worth, while we were taking our curtain call, the principal came on the stage and took each of us by the hand and said, "We've had many performances at our school and I think everyone here will agree that this is the finest of them all. We want to thank you young artists for coming to our school." Tears welled up in our eyes. He had called us "artists." Our weariness lifted and we drove away from that school on a cloud of hope, believing that we had not let Laurence Olivier down after all.

Just to add spice to our life we were working on another new number for the show: *Macbeth*. Our youthful ambitions had sprung a leak and driven us to prepare a twenty-five-minute editing job of scenes between Macbeth and Lady Macbeth in which we had clearly been inspired by Jack Rank's riveting solo performance at the Newark high school when he tore through the play at speed, playing both Mr. and Mrs. Our biggest problem was money for the rich materials to make the costumes.

On March 11, in Beaumont, Texas, we heard a voice in the darkness backstage. "Can I help you? Let me carry those trunks for you, Mr. and Mrs. Holbrook." It came from a tall young man with dark eyes who'd been lurking in the shadows. A magical young man. "We've cleaned out a dressing room for you. Would you like some coffee or maybe a coke? My name is Jack Yianitsas and I'm here to help you." Aladdin might have conjured him. During the show he watched intently from the wings, missing nothing. Afterward he invited us to his family's home for a Greek dinner. We made a date for the next night.

The Yianitsas family was all assembled when we arrived. Mama Yianitsas, Papa, sisters Anna, Helen, and Marie. They adopted us without ceremony; I believe they would have made room for us if we wanted to stay a week. And the food! *Ah-h-h*. I thought the Italians had a lock on spaghetti, but they have to make way for Mama Yianitsas.

The family was full of questions: What was it like on the road? Where was our family? ("Oh, you come down to Beaumont and we'll take you in!") We talked about Ed Wright and Denison, and the family grew silent.

"Jack, you're a senior?"

"Yes, sir, I am."

"And are you going on to college this fall?"

"Well, sir, I hope to do that." There was a stretch of more silence.

"What about applying to Denison?" Looks were exchanged around the table.

"Do you think I could? It's kind of late."

"I'm sure you could. Don't you think so, Ruby?"

"I do, Hal."

"We'll write Ed about you." Breath was exhaled and in the young man's eager face those dark eyes glistened. In the fall he went north to Granville.

On the twenty-third of March we made it to the big town. Houston. Reagan Senior High School, where we would have a more mature student audience. That was Broadway for us. We'd been looking forward to it for weeks, but when the superintendent came backstage to introduce us, a flag went up. He looked nervous. Then he forgot our names and had to ask for them twice. When he stepped in front of the curtain to introduce us, the place erupted. Ruby shot me a look that said "Good luck, Hal" and moved off stage right to get ready for her entrance as Rosalind. When the hooting died down we heard the superintendent say, "Personality Portraits from Literature and Life with Hol and Ruby Halbrook." Then he backed through the split in the curtain and hurried offstage like a man trying to get out of the range of gunfire. I stepped out in front of the curtain to introduce Rosalind and Orlando, and the place blew up. One thousand partially grown Texans in full voice and untethered passion were going to spread an acre of hell over the next forty-five minutes. They jeered, they honked and hooted, they farted, they made every sound they could come up with as long as it was loud and continuous. I waited. When the barrage began to slow down I made a start.

"William Shakespeare wrote . . ."

Boom! The place went into stampede frenzy again. It was like the whole rear end of Texas venting itself. I thought, Boy, you're in trouble; big, mean trouble. Hold your temper or you're a goner. I waited. Just stood and waited. The roar rolled over me, it came in overlapping waves like a performance they had rehearsed. When it slowed down I tried to speak again, but that was the cue to launch another breaker at me. I waited, I tried to speak, they roared again, I waited. Minutes were going by, five, six, seven. I was finding it hard to believe we were doing this. Now they were waiting for me to speak, pausing for it, and when I made the first syllable of sound they ran over me with another eruption. They were playing a game now: you start and we'll slap you down. Don't get mad, I said to myself. If you get mad you will lose this contest. Keep calm.

The pauses they opened up for me to start speaking got a little longer. I had an idea. When the roar died down again I said, "This show stinks."

They laughed and applauded and roared some more. Another pause came.

"You'll hate it. It's lousy!"

They went wild again. But they were laughing more than jeering now.

"No, really. It's a boring show! Shakespeare! Boooring!"

Hoots and hollers and laughter, but it was slimming down.

"Look, we don't want to do this show. They're paying us a lousy thirty-five bucks for it, but we can't get the money unless we do one number for you."

More laughs and shouts of "Boring! Shakespeare! Boooring!"

"Yeah. But we need the thirty-five bucks, so we're going to go ahead and do one number, but don't listen to it. Don't listen! Keep shouting!" I ducked back behind the curtain and ran offstage yelling, "Go get 'em, Ruby! Pull the curtain. Pull!"

She pranced onstage in green tights and the place went wild with a combination of derision and approval. No one heard a word while she read the poems Orlando had stuck on the imaginary trees and when I ran onstage in green tights the place went into vocal Vesuvius. We just played the scene and grinned at each other. What the hell. They started to calm down and listen in snatches. By the end of the scene there was some sense of a performance being partially acknowledged and even a pallid scattering of applause at the end, so we cut the Victoria and Albert scene for time and went straight to Mark Twain. He got their attention, some laughs started coming in, they gave us a round of applause and whistles for sportsmanship, and it was all over. We had survived Reagan Senior High School.

We put the *Macbeth* number in the show and it scared the hell out of the little kids. That was okay with us. When I waved the bloody dagger at them they crouched behind the seats and shut up. It was a strong, fast-moving splicing of scenes and soliloquies, twenty-five minutes long, and it gave us the boost we needed for the homestretch. The costumes Ruby created were gorgeous and the rich tones of her voice were wonderfully suited for Lady Macbeth. My dagger had a small swastika on the hilt because we got it in an army surplus store in Austin, but the Nazi emblem could not be seen from the audience. How I loved doing the "Tomorrow and tomorrow" soliloquy, that great, wrenching, soul-weary sigh of utter defeat, one of the most perfectly crafted ten lines in Shakespeare.

Two weeks after Easter we would head north from below Corpus Christi to Arkansas, a distance of nearly a thousand miles, to finish our tour on April 29 in Pocahontas on the northeastern flank of the Ozarks, but getting out of Texas was not so easy. We were marooned at Alice in a flood, the show was canceled, and we couldn't get out of town. When the water subsided we raced on to the next dry town and filled the date, doubled back to fill two more at Freer and Falfurrias, but we lost Alice, which took $21.60 from our last week's pay.

As we sped north toward Arkansas, our plans for the next year began changing. We were giving up on moving to New York. We were so broke that if we didn't get out on the road and earn a lot of money in the coming year we'd never be able to go anywhere. Our fairy godmother, Ricklie Boasberg, wanted more time to book us, so we would add that to the twelve weeks already booked with various managers from coast to coast. We'd totted up our budget for next year again and it came up grim, the same big, grim hole we'd worked our way into this season: no clothes, no peace of mind, no money in the bank, and the same big zero question mark at the end of the road. We paid off our $3,000 loan, but we had to get another station wagon to burn up the highways with come September, keep it fueled as well as ourselves, and find a small pad in Granville to call home. Reality had taken over.

For the moment our big hope was Chamberlain Brown and the audition he was arranging for us in seven days at the Hotel Astor in New York. We crossed the Mississippi at Cape Girardeau and kept pouring on the coal all the way across Illinois and Indiana to Ohio and Granville, and by Saturday afternoon we were home with Ed and Louise, the only home we had, and what an enormous feeling it was to see that gentle town again and enter the cheering inner sanctum of our special family on Mulberry Street.

But it was only for Saturday and Sunday. We had to head for New York and the Chamberlain Brown audition. Dick Corson offered to put us up at his tiny cold-water flat on Prince Street, which had a bathtub in the kitchen. Driving east on the Pennsylvania Turnpike, we ran over the program we would do for Chamberlain and the agents and producers he and Lyman were going to assemble for us. We would start with Rosalind and Orlando to show us "straight"; then Victoria and Albert, Elizabeth and Essex, and Mark Twain, a rangy program. This was going to be a big deal for us. Mr. Pond of *Program* magazine would be there. Ricklie had been talking us up to him all year and he had written two articles about us in the magazine after Ricklie advised us to take an ad in it. That softened him up. As a boy he had known Mark Twain. His father, Major Pond, was Twain's booking manager and handled all his tours, including the one around the world. If he liked our show and was not put off by my Twain characterization, it could bring us the attention we needed to book the better dates. *Program* magazine was the booking bible of the Artist Series field.

But the Hotel Astor was out. We were to do the show on a small stage in a studio above the Jack Dempsey restaurant on Broadway at Fifty-first Street. Chamberlain assured us that a more intimate setting would show us off better to the agents and producers he was gathering together to see us. We had to double-park in front of the entrance to the building and some people started swearing at us for blocking traffic. The police arrived, and while Ruby kept him talking I rassled the costume trunks and lights and sound and the white bench out of the station wagon and piled them up inside by the elevator. The operator came back down and saw all our equipment and was not happy.

"Hey, you can't leave this stuff here, buddy!"

"I know. I know. I'm just going to park the car. The cop is gonna write us a ticket."

"You can't leave it here."

"Okay. Hold it."

I was sweating heavily by now. The cop had his pad out and was writing. "Ruby, Ruby, drive the car around the block. I gotta put this stuff upstairs."

"How many times?"

"Just keep driving. I'll get down as fast as I can and we'll park." The cop slapped a ticket onto the windshield and walked away. Sweet little town, New York.

The studio was small, with a tiny stage that would squeeze our movements. There were only six rows of seats, so maybe we would not have a crowd. That would be tough on the laughs. We were pretty winded dragging the trunks upstairs, but we unloaded our costumes and lights and set up a dressing area in a tiny corner backstage. We'd have to use the windowsill for a makeup table, but first we had to clean the black soot off it with toilet paper from the ladies' room. We hadn't been able to stop anywhere for food, but if we had hunger pangs, we couldn't feel them. Way too nervous.

Half hour. It was quiet out there. Where was everybody? I peeked out through the drapes, nobody there. Then I heard voices in the hall and it was Chamberlain Brown with a great, tall woman who looked familiar. What was her name? Oh! Yurka. Blanche Yurka. She was a famous actress from the twenties and thirties. "Hey, Ruby, Blanche Yurka is out there. Didn't she do Lady Macbeth?"

"I think she did. Quite a while ago."

"Chamberlain's brought her. And Dick Corson just walked in with Mitch. Nobody else yet."

We waited. About five minutes before five o'clock James "Bim" Pond walked in, looking very sober. Nobody was laughing or chatting it up. They sat quietly and waited. Only Mitch was talking, whispering to Dick. Then a voice boomed out, Miss Yurka saying, "Chamberlain, go back and tell these young people they may commence the performance." He got a little wrapped up in the drapes trying to get to us in our tiny alcove, and he appeared to have the same blue shirt on with a sweater over it.

"I think you may begin now, if you are ready. I was hoping Leo Bulgakov would show up, but we must move along."

He fought his way back through the drapes and we looked at each other. "Hal, it looks like nobody's coming."

"Yeah. Maybe they'll show up in a minute or two."

"Who is Leo Bulgakov?"

"I think he directed *One Sunday Afternoon*. But isn't he dead?"

"Shhh. Don't tell Chamberlain."

She switched the amplifier on and our little overture theme broke into the stillness out there. Then I stepped out to introduce our school assembly show to the producers and agents and influential theater people of New York. I could see the faces of all five of them clearly. It made my mouth dry. My eyes darted away from the hung jury expressions fixed on their faces and fastened on a light fixture against the wall while I heard myself saying the familiar words of the introduction as though my voice had gone on ahead and left me behind. What a relief it was to finally get back to safety behind the drapes and see Ruby's determined face; and then she was out there and the confident lines of Shakespeare's verse took charge. Suddenly there was life in the tiny room. But even that was scary because there was too much of it. We'd been playing for unruly audiences of a thousand and more, and now here in this bare closet with five immobilized bodies staring back at us our energy seemed to put their nerves on edge. Draw back, draw back. Listen to Ruby. Focus. Listen.

Somehow in the flirtatious dialogue toward the end of the *As You Like It* scenes Ruby's natural charisma began reaching out to them. You could feel it. By the time we were into the first tentative moments of the Victoria and Albert shaving scene the wild sense of plunging through no-man's-land had subsided and our senses were under control. This scene was always a reassuring one for us, gentle and real and heartfelt. It caught them up and the applause had a note of earnestness in it. Good. Now the big one. Elizabeth and Essex, a dramatic shift of roles for Ruby. Clad in that sweeping period skirt, supported side to side by the iron framework underneath, with her pale face, red wig, and dark, brooding eyes fraught with a lover's anxiety, Ruby paced the small space until Essex stepped into the light, black clad and stoic.

"You sent for me, or so they said?"

The scene is a flameout of fury and proud confrontation, nobody yielding for more than an instant, and Ruby flew into it with a passion and our five New York judges sat up straighter. She had got their whole attention now. There was a silence at the end before the applause. And then it was time for Mark Twain and the spirit gum on the lip getting tacky while I slipped on the padding and shirt and pants, then set the mustache in place with trembling hands, praying the glue would hold; then on with the wig, the vest, the coat, the watch, the cigar, the match, the cloud of smoke, and Ruby was running back from her introduction just before the old man strolled on.

The reactions to the show were pleasant and friendly, but in the afterglow of our big effort it was hard to know how much of a real impression we had made on these seasoned hands. Dick and Mitch were effusive and very encouraging. Bim Pond was hard to figure, but he said he'd like to see us if we'd come to his office. They left and Blanche Yurka remained behind with Chamberlain. She had questions: How had we come up with the idea for the show? How had we chosen the material? Who directed it? She seemed reluctant to leave. She had reminiscences of Lynn Fontanne as Elizabeth. As a young girl she had seen Mark Twain one day on lower Fifth Avenue.

"You are a talented and adventurous young couple," she said. Okay. We could go home happy on that. Producers and agents would have to wait.

17

On Summit Street in Granville we found a little garage apartment up for rent, $30 a month. The owners had sliced the garage into three sections. The front door put you right in the kitchen, about five feet front to back and maybe six feet long to the right of the door. To the left of the door was the smallest bathroom in America. A tiny sink, which served also as the kitchen sink but a plate would not fit into it, a toilet, and an upright coffin called "the shower." You had to inhale to raise your arms. The second slice was the living room, a more commodious twelve feet long, paneled in pine and stained nut-brown. The third slice was the bedroom, exactly six feet deep with a bunk of that length on either side. I had to crook my knees to lie down in it. There were a few tiny windows up high in each of the rooms. It was our first real home and we grew to love it.

Ed had a play waiting for us in the summer theater schedule, *The Constant Wife* by Somerset Maugham. Our hopes for an Actors' Equity job in eastern stock having drained away, this was a plum prospect. Meanwhile, we had to make a home and buy a new station wagon. Our old chariot was going downhill—forty-five thousand miles, bad brakes, repair bills—not a good set for the Mojave Desert. So with help from Ev Reese we got $1,500 on the old car with a $1,000 loan on a new Ford station wagon. Ruby wrote Bert: "The new car rides like a dream—has a steel top [good in case we rolled over] and well constructed body. Hal is treating it like a new born babe—won't drive over 40–45 mph." I was breaking it in for the racetrack later.

What a wonderful life! A home, a new car, two months to prepare *The Constant Wife*, and twenty weeks being booked on the road next season. I pounded away at the typewriter, editing the new scene from *School for Wives*. In my uncle George's costume trunk I had found a gorgeous bright red satin late-seventeenth-century outfit with ruffled lace shirtfront and more lace hanging from the sleeves of the cutaway coat. Think of the hand movements I could devise with that lace! In this delicious scene between Arnolphe and Agnes we would explore a whole new style of acting—new movements of body and posture, a new style of speaking. We were going into fresh theatrical territory and we felt more sure of ourselves now.

The Constant Wife played the week of July 12 and broke the summer theater attendance record. Ed had publicized us as a team, but from start to finish it was Ruby's play. I don't believe I understood at the time that Ruby was a better actor than I. She was subtle. Where I looked for changes of voice and mannerism, Ruby looked into herself. She had all the equipment required to fill starring roles— large eyes, the voice with its lower range, and a manner that bespoke breeding and dignity and womanliness. She lured the audience to her. I, on the other hand, strove for effect. I wanted my true self to be hidden from view because I was unimpressed with it.

We had been deeply affected by the plays and the actors we had just seen in New York. The tightly controlled furies of Wendy Hiller and Basil Rathbone in *The Heiress*; Joe Wiseman and Michael Strong, who seemed to come right off the streets in *Detective Story*; and *Death of a Salesman*, that was the killer. Lee Cobb stunned us. Those two performances in *Salesman*, his and Mildred Dunnock's, swept through the theater and sucked the breath out of us. The forging of naturalism and brutal daring went beyond other experiences of dramatic plays. These actors, along with Brando in *Streetcar* the year before, blazed a path of new beginnings in the theater that we hoped and dreamed would take us in someday. But acting was no longer going to be easy.

Harold

Once the summer theater was over, Ruby and I would drive our new chariot very carefully up to Hamilton, north of Niagara Falls, and spend a week with her sister, Beryl, her husband, Stewart Mathison, and their children, and on the return we'd stop in Cleveland to see my sister Alberta and Grandma. We were drifting further away from them all now. An instinct of survival had distanced me from the overripe embraces of my grandmother. Our contacts were rarer. But I had seen too little of Alberta, my dear, lonely younger sister who was off in a kind of far country of her own on the east side of crumbling Cleveland, the once proud city whose steel mills were closing down, leaving the thousands of black migrants from the South stranded in decaying old houses and apartment buildings. Alberta was stranded on the second story of one like that, at the top of that dark, steep staircase, with four-year-old Diane and baby Howie and her husband, Howard, who worked for the city. Down in the sooty darkness of the apartment courtyard there was no clear and beautiful sky above them for her hopes and dreams to fly up into. Just parked cars under blackened trees.

It was almost time to head for the open road. We had more than eighty dates booked for the new season. Our little two-person road show would travel from Great Neck, Long Island, to the land of Hollywood three thousand miles away, starting with eight shows in schools around the New York City area, booked by a renegade school assembly booker without our permission. They just happened to plug in to our open September time before the start of the Midwest tour in Oshkosh, and we were not in the business of backing away from work. There was a plain gray toughness in those city kids, a challenging attitude, and it took some of the fun out of it. We began to wonder if the best audiences in America were really back east.

Our focus was shifting. We wrote to Bert: "When we come east in late April some agents and summer theatre managers casting in town might be induced to cross the river and see our show!" This illusion had a mote in its eye. The school shows were at eight-thirty in the morning and no agent or summer stock manager was going to cross the Hudson at that hour, drunk or sober, to see two kids from the Midwest play for schoolchildren, but we *had* to keep our dreams aloft. We were now pushing for an entry into the eastern theater mecca, first summer stock, and then somewhere down the road we hoped we would make it to Broadway. Movies never entered our mind.

We had a few days in Granville to clean up and repack the new 1949 Ford station wagon, climb into the front seat with a full platform of trunks behind us, and head for Oshkosh and the new playing field: small colleges and women's clubs. For the foreseeable future we would travel the roads from September to May and four to six weeks in the summer, seeing a big slice of America.

Pryor-Menz out of Council Bluffs had put together those college dates for us in Wisconsin, Minnesota, and Iowa, places like Eau Claire, Bemidji, Grinnell, and Mount Pleasant and a couple as far out as Scottsbluff in western Nebraska. We followed them with women's clubs for Ricklie around the Chicago suburbs in Wilmette and Oak Park and a few small colleges. And we had our new Molière number to spice up the shows. The scene from *L'École des femmes* is inspired by sexual innuendo when Arnolphe grills his luscious young ward, Agnes, about her encounter with a handsome young passerby. Is she as innocent as he has trained her to be, in spite of the provocative suggestiveness in her description of the young man's advances? Ruby's eyes were alight with a hormone rush as she described the young lover's overtures, and it brought Arnolphe to the edge of apoplexy. Could it be that his campaign to groom Agnes to be his obedient and devoted wife has been laid waste by the passions of youth? The college audiences laughed more loudly than the ladies in the clubs, but it was fun all around.

We were learning a new style of performing, linking the actor to the audience, developed in the days when Molière gave his performances in court on the same level with the audience, in their laps, so to speak. Thus the crafted aside, by word or look, that made the audience a partner in the scene. We had no director. We read the books about the acting style of the period and then tried to do it in front of an audience. It was risky and fraught with failure as well as some success. The Davenport, Iowa, Women's Club wrote, "They are wonderful beyond any adjectives used in their brochure . . . we simply loved them." But the ladies in the clubs were always appreciative, if restrained by politeness, and they collectively adored our youthful good looks and the stamp of propriety our marriage gave to whatever we did up there on the stage.

The colleges were another experience, a different arena, alive with combustible responses and rapid thought connections. You could send a good line out there and they caught it with the swiftness of Joe DiMaggio or Lou Boudreau, be it a fly ball or grounder, and the laugh or the thoughtful silence it got resounded cleanly when it hit the glove. This was a game. Clarity of speech and timing were the qualifications required to play it. The audience *listened* to us. We did not have to fight them. We were what they came to see, and all we had to do was deliver the goods. You can imagine the relief and pleasure we began to feel when we saw our little show being embraced by audiences wherever we went. Our battle-scarred egos began to mend and these audiences would teach us to be better actors. They would teach us the craft of timing. We began to see this as the magic key to freeing a performance on the stage, that spontaneous sense of partnership with an audience. Most of all we were learning to respect silence, the gift we could never trust in Texas, and hold it like that magic stick in the conductor's hand at Culver.

That fall of 1949 we went from the Chicago area dates for Ricklie down into Texas to play some small college dates for Harry Byrd Kline and then west to California in the second half of November for the women's clubs in Los Angeles and San Diego before heading up to Utah for some early December shows Fred C. Graham's office in Salt Lake had put together in the Rocky Mountains. It was quite a stretch of America we crossed that fall and it laid its beautiful hand on us. Sometimes we drove through the night after our show and saw America by moonlight. We rarely talked then. If the night was warm, the car windows could be left open and the smell of the country rushed in. In this vast space between oceans the character of our people was clarified. Different opinions. The people in Wyoming would not be adjusting their vision of America to satisfy New York. Someday Mark Twain would adjust mine.

We made it to California just in time for Thanksgiving with June and Gion and Cheryl. Along with his job moving the camera around at Republic, plus those wristwatches for sale up his forearm, Gion was a master chef, so he would cook the turkey. I was sent out to Ralphs for some exotic spices and assorted bottles of wine. That Thanksgiving eve was set aside for the preparation of the feast, the washing of potatoes and carrots and asparagus and the enormous plucked bird, the mysterious blending of condiments, old bread crumbs, and other unmentionables in a big bowl to create the interior dressing for the fowl that would be "like nothing you have ever tasted! Give me that bottle of Paul Masson Burgundy, Harold." He sloshed it over the mound of dressing in the bowl until it was nearly afloat.

"You don't measure anything, Gion?"

"Never. If you have the instinct for it, Harold, measuring is not necessary. Hand me the Krug Chablis."

After it was hosed down with Chablis, the mound of dressing, which by now had congealed, bobbed around in the bowl as if it were adrift in the English Channel.

"So . . . does that all blend together?"

"Slowly. It has to permeate the dressing very slowly in order to bring out the flavor."

"Which flavor? The wine or the dressing?"

"Both, Harold. It takes time."

"When do you put all that inside the bird?"

"About nine-thirty tonight I'll sew it up to keep the flavor in and then our good friend Mr. Turkey goes in the oven."

"All night?"

"All night, but on a low heat. We want the aroma to permeate the bird very slowly."

Even before I went to bed that night I knew it was permeating, because I could smell it in the bedroom. I didn't know if the Paul Masson was overcoming the Krug, or the other way around, but clearly there was a contest for supremacy going on in the bird and it was beginning to affect my intestines. By morning I had worn a path in the rug between our room and the bathroom. Ruby was maintaining a desperate cheerfulness in the high hope that all would be well when we sat down to dinner that early afternoon. Dinner. The thought of it made me want to throw up. So I started doing that. Why was no one else sick like me? It was as if I had caught a disease the others had been immunized against. The dinner hour got closer and I tried to pull myself together in a determined burst of concern for the rest of the family who would sit down for the carving of this massive roasted vineyard. I did make it to the table. And I saw the turkey. Gion brought it in and set it down near me. It was red. Red. Paul Masson had won out and when the aroma swept up my nostrils and made a dive for my stomach I launched myself down the hallway for a season of solace and a fervent pledge of temperance. They laid me to rest in bed.

Maybe part of my stomach disorder was a sensitivity to what was happening between June and Gion. There was a tension darting in and out of their conversation. June was getting restless. My conviction that she had finally found a secure harbor began to waver. Cheryl was enrolled in a dancing school on Hollywood Boulevard and Ruby and I went with them because it would give me a chance to ask June some questions. Was she happy with Gion?

"He wants me to stay home all the time. I can't even go for a walk. I have to *get out*! I feel trapped like I'm in a cage or something."

"He seems like a really decent man to me."

"He doesn't even want me to visit the neighbors."

"Why does he want you to stay home all the time?"

"So I'm there when he gets home. Like a servant or something. He can get out, he has his work. I have nothing."

"You have Cheryl. And a good home."

"I always take Cheryl with me. We go out together."

"What about the home?"

"Oh well."

A claw began to spread out and tighten down in the pit of my stomach. All of a sudden I felt that I was the one who couldn't get out. I had imagined that June's life was now a safe, traditional one with a house and a husband, all tucked in and cared for by an older and wiser head. I'd forgotten who June really was: a springing deer, a creature always on the edge of flight.

We went south to San Diego and played the San Diego Woman's Club. It was a sailor's town then, early California buildings in white wood or stucco fading in the sun, bars and more bars, and side streets you didn't wish to go down. Up in the hills elegance took over. We had one more date to fill in Los Angeles and my mind went back eight years to that New Year's Eve at the Coconut Grove on a blind date with the movie director's daughter. Ruby and I were going to perform for the Los Angeles Women's Breakfast Club right on that dance floor in the Coconut Grove where I had made a fool of myself. That was breathtaking to me. I had been sixteen years old then. My father had met us in the magnificent lobby of this hotel, a wild-looking character with a bullet hole in his hat and no front teeth, an angular misfit lounging in the gilt and silken trappings of the aristocratic Ambassador Hotel. That memory of my father made me feel like a pretender. I had to push it away. This was one show we had to nail down because it would mean a flock of new California dates next season. It wasn't Artie Shaw playing the Grove this time, it was Ruby and me. We worked for an audience arranged on three sides of the floor and survived long entrances and exits from the kitchen, but this was cake compared with basketball courts in Arkansas.

"Appearing at the Coconut Grove of the Ambassador Hotel with only a chair and a table as props, they gave the most magnificent performance it has been my good fortune to see. They are great artists." Great artists we were not and far from it, but we scored, and fortunately for us a booker named Edna Stewart was there to judge our work. Mrs. Francis Boyle Workman, that elegant pioneer lady who had crossed the continent in a covered wagon, had booked us, but she was retiring at the end of that season and we hoped Stewart might take us on. She did.

The night before we left Los Angeles, June walked out on Gion. When we got there he told us she'd quarreled with him and taken Cheryl with her. We jumped back in the car and cruised the neighborhood streets over toward Ventura Boulevard and then started down toward Laurel Canyon. We saw them standing near a motel on the valley side and waved at them. Seven-year-old Cheryl was holding her mother's hand. It took a while, but we persuaded June to come home. She said she was worried about her sister and was thinking of going back east. I knew there was no point in arguing. If June had made up her mind to go, she'd go. When we left the next day, a big gray hopeless cloud of worry rode with us and I pressed down on the pedal to get away from it, as far away as I could, because there was no end to this family sadness. Farther up the valley, my father was probably wandering around swatting black widow spiders, and somewhere in this sprawling stray dog kennel of a city our mysterious mother was hiding out. Jesus. Give me the open road.

We played a women's club in Sacramento and headed north into the Sierras through an alpine wonderland of peaks and precipices called Feather River Canyon. This was the wildest piece of real estate we'd ever seen, railroad tracks snaking along a rock shelf like some drawing in a children's book. A train had jackknifed up there and part of it was hanging over the side. We were a mile up, the snow like a tattered blanket where the black bones of the mountain's volcanic flanks showed through. This was a place for eagles. Then we started down, down from the pass where people one hundred years before had starved to death in the blizzards, until the long, coasting glide flattened out and pitched us into Reno, home of marital car wrecks. Lost seventy-five cents there. Four hundred miles later we crossed the Great Salt Lake. I tried testing out the speedometer to see if it really would go up to 120 miles per hour, but the Ford began vibrating at 107 and Ruby suggested we slow down. We rolled into Salt Lake City and I drove past the Mormon Tabernacle to show

Ruby where I had walked that moonlit night eight years before when the train stopped on my way back to Culver. We played Salt Lake and a few other towns before making the long trek back to Granville for Christmas.

Sometime early in the new year we saw Alberta again. She was still there in that sooty brick building, but she had brightened up her apartment with airy white curtains and fresh slipcovers on the sofa and easy chair, and her spirits seemed higher. Diane was a dear little girl at five years, winning and pretty, and Howie was scrambling about now on expeditions around the apartment. Alberta seemed happier. This was good to see. She and Howard were excited about an outing they'd just had with the children down to Hudson, about twenty miles south of Cleveland.

"It's a beautiful little town, Hal. Right out of New England. White churches with spires and a village green. And the most beautiful cemetery called Crown Hill, with lovely trees shading the graves. I want to be buried there. I've already picked the spot." She and Howard dreamed of finding a small house and fixing it up and living in the clean perfection of that village. My hopes for her began to rise.

Grandma was showing her age now, high in the eighties, but defiantly refusing to give the actual number. When the city of Lakewood declined to renew her license she had walked out of city hall, climbed into the Buick, and driven away, scaring hell out of the citizens whenever she got behind the wheel. And she'd heard from our father. He had been to Alaska and was now in Seattle washing dishes at the Salvation Army in return for food and lodging. I wondered if I'd have to support him someday.

By March we were in the Chicago area again and at Laurel School in Cleveland, where June and Alberta had once been thrown out. The shows were piling in for the next season of 1950–51. Howard Higgins out of Rochester had taken us on for the northeastern territory—New England, New York, and Pennsylvania. Bookings for these colleges and clubs were made nearly a year in advance so our fate seemed to be sealing itself whether we liked it or not. It was a strange feeling to know that a year from now we would play Bryn Mawr College and then some club in Seattle. How could you resist making a living when the openings were there and you were working on the stage? But what if a job in New York came along? Or a baby?

In February I had turned twenty-five. What had I accomplished in life? Not much. There were people my age whose careers were in third gear on Broadway, yet here I was logging road mileage around the country, playing women's clubs and colleges. Ruby and I were creating a team that could sustain itself financially, but what if separate jobs came along? What if we had a child? Were we going to have children? When? Or would we imitate the Lunts and be childless? There were some wide-open questions lying in wait for us.

Ricklie maintained close contact with Bim Pond of *Program* magazine and she urged us to do the same because Pond could help promote our career. So we kept the ads coming to feed his appetite. With Pond it was special because as a boy he had known Mark Twain. He told me stories about him, pulled out of the wealth of experience his father had lived through with Twain, booking his lecture appearances in this country and the great tour around the world. When we visited Bim's office the day after the Chamberlain Brown audition I asked him if he would give me an idea how Twain sounded, and he drawled, "Pond, when I enga-a-ged you to send me out on the public hi-i-ghway with all the other ba-a-andits, there was nothing in our contract sta-a-ting that I would have to sta-a-and on cold railway pla-a-tforms in the middle of the night wa-a-iting for tra-a-ins that never ca-a-ame!"

James B. Pond took over the concert and lecture business when his father died and for a while was preeminent in the field. He booked the top names, like Admiral Byrd and Cornelia Otis Skinner, and developed Ruth Draper's remarkable solo career. Other managers entered the business and one by one his artists deserted him. He went to his office one day, read his mail, locked the door, and never went back. There was a dangerous strain of bitterness in him. He was a mesmerizing speaker and storyteller himself, but his wit was cutting. I believed he was a lonely man. He scared some people, but I didn't let him scare me, because I wanted to be his friend. I think it was he who first suggested I do a solo performance and I stole some of Bim back then and put him into my vision of Mark Twain.

No call came for eastern stock that summer of 1950, but Ed Wright was waiting with a challenging proposal in hand—Ferenc Molnár's *The Guardsman*, which had brought Alfred Lunt and Lynn Fontanne together in 1924, establishing an acting team that would make history. Never one to hide a light under any bushel no matter how small the glow, Ed saw possibilities for promotion if he teamed Hal and Ruby Holbrook in *The Guardsman*, the less than scanty implication being that we were about to pursue and hound the Lunts until they gave up the title. Sometimes Ed went over the edge of the edge, but I have to hand it to him, we broke the attendance record the first night.

Ed had chosen a different breed of theater professor for the Theater Department, young and interested in the newer, experimental plays, and I don't think *The Guardsman* fit into Bill Brasmer's galaxy of theatrical stardust. He may have found himself a bit nonplussed directing the Holbrooks, since we'd been directing ourselves now for more than two years. There were moments when he could have helped me if I'd let him. The challenge for the Actor in *The Guardsman* is enormous: How are you going to convince the audience, yourself, and your wife, with makeup and characterization, that you are another man, especially while you are making love to her? Try pulling that off with a wig and a mustache and a Hungarian accent while you are holding your real and stage wife in your arms and wondering whether the look in her eyes is veiled hilarity or romantic interest. It was a dreadful feat of acting and I could have been only barely successful, but Ruby kept the audience amused and delighted by the way she played upon the ego of her disguised husband. It didn't hurt that the stage furniture, on loan from the Fort Hayes Hotel, had once belonged to Sarah Bernhardt.

Memory. I'm reaching back into hiding places for the clues that whispered warnings, tugging at the mind, weeping in the dark unanswered. When September came the heat in the valley rose and drifted away in the night when I went out to stretch my legs and smell the cool scent of autumn edging in. We were going south this year for Ralph Bridges, a booker in Atlanta. We'd be giving nearly eighty performances in thirty-five states. First we drove up to Cleveland to see the family, especially Alberta. June was there. She had left Gion and come east because her sister had written her to come. When she asked Gion to go with her he replied that he didn't like cold weather. She told him she was going to take Cheryl and go anyway and he said, "If you go, you go for good."

Alberta was pregnant again and there was tension in her face. She told us she did not want another child. Then we got into an argument because she was insisting that Ruby and I must have children.

"You shouldn't delay it."

"Well, we will, but we can't right now."

"Yes, you can."

"How? We have to make a living."

"That's no excuse, you have to start a family."

"We will. We will."

"Stop putting it off."

"Okay. We'll think about it."

"Stop thinking about it! Do it!"

She became so agitated it put me off balance and I didn't know what to say. Later she asked me to come into the bedroom, she had something to give me. It was a letter, a heavy one.

"If anything should happen to me, I want you to give this to Diane on her eighteenth birthday."

"If anything should happen to you? What's that mean?"

"Just keep it until she's eighteen."

We went down the steep staircase and got into the car. I looked up and she was leaning out the window, her beautiful pale face framed by the shadowy grimness all around, and she was smiling.

"You take good care of each other."

We were leaving for a show in western Pennsylvania on September 26. At four in the morning the phone rang.

"Harold, are you sitting down?"

"Who is this?"

"Howie."

"Yeah."

"Are you sitting down?"

"No. What's the matter?"

"You'd better sit down." A long pause.

"What's wrong, Howie?"

"Alberta died tonight."

I put the phone on the table and sat down. I could hear Howard's voice through the mouthpiece. "Harold. Harold." He was crying. I picked the phone up again.

"God, Howie . . . How did she die?"

"Harold, she fell down the stairs. I couldn't stop her."

"She fell . . . On those stairs?"

"Yes. In the dark . . . she fell. I tried to . . . She started bleeding so I carried her up here and she went in the bathroom and sat down . . . because she was bleeding . . . and the baby was, it was all . . . I tried to get her to the hospital but it was too late."

"God . . . dear God."

"She died on the way. I'm sorry, Harold."

"Hal." It was Ruby. She was standing in the doorway to the bedroom, white as a sheet.

We were driving through the night to Cleveland. That morning we had put ourselves back together, loaded the trunks into the station wagon, and driven into Pennsylvania to do our show. Now we were heading for that dark staircase to find out why my sister had died. I had been on the phone with Uncle Al and Aunt Merce and Grandma, trying to uncover some facts that would explain this horrible accident, and already a chorus of private opinions was rising around the cause of her death. Did he push her? Did she fall on purpose? Why didn't he get an ambulance right away? It was not going to be easy. No death was easy in this family.

Through the blur of this event, while I was breathless with horror, my sympathy kept tending toward Howard. Whatever troubles they may have been having, he was her husband. I found myself defending him, trying to balance the family's emotional reactions into a reasonable scenario. Howard said they had come back to the apartment that night and she had started bleeding. Near the top of the stairs she fell. Where had they been? I asked him. To Lorain. What for? To go up in an airplane. There was an airport in Lorain where you could go for a ride in a small plane and Alberta loved doing that, even though she'd been warned by her doctor not to fly with the pregnancy. She and Howard had gone anyway.

June's story was revealing. She had seen Alberta the day before when she'd come to the apartment with her friend Nicky. The doctor was in the bedroom with Alberta. After he left she called out for June to come in. Nicky stayed in the kitchen with Howie while June and Alberta talked for two hours. Alberta had papers spread out all over the bed, papers she'd saved about her life and ours.

"My papers are all in order now," she said. She was very depressed. "I don't want to have this baby."

When June was leaving with Nicky, after they had gone down the staircase and were getting into his car, Alberta leaned out the window and said to him, "You take care of my sister for me."

Had Alberta and Howard gone to Lorain? Had they gone flying? There were so many whispered questions that could only come from shocked emotions, it was hard to get anything straight. I wanted it all to stop so we could just think about Alberta and be sad. Howard looked lost. The children had been taken away by his mother and now he was alone in that apartment at the top of the stairs. It seemed cruel to question him any more about the details of Alberta's death. The only question that clearly called out for an answer was why had he waited so long to call for help. One version being circulated was that he had called an ambulance too late. Another was that he had waited to see if she would recover.

The funeral home had an unreal quality—my sister, so white and still in the coffin, Howard's lost face, the families striving in awkward ways to bridge a wound that lay open like a sword cut. Words could not be found to close it up. We moved in slow motion. Stunned. My sister June had a locket she wanted to put in the casket with Alberta. Grandma objected. So she waited until they had all drifted away and laid it in Bee's hands. Finally there was nothing to do but move on, and the long drive to Hudson began, a silent ride filled with questions no one wished to hear. I did not see my sister laid in the ground. Ruby and I stayed at the cemetery until the last moment of time left to us and then climbed into the station wagon and drove to our next performance with tears blinding us. Sadness was going to be our companion for a long, long time.

At Crown Hill Cemetery, where a small band of mourners assembled at the grave, a woman appeared and joined them. No one knew how she had come or who had informed her. It was our old nurse, Nettie Wigton. Later June told me that she had driven down to Zanesville, Ohio, with Alberta and Howie one time to visit Nettie Wigton because Bee had been sent to live with her when she was having so much trouble in Cleveland, and Bee wanted to see her again. Nettie told them to go down to the ice-cream store and get some ice cream. They were sitting at a table when Alberta leaned over and said to June, "I am not your whole sister. I am your half sister." June got an awful sinking feeling in the pit of her stomach and just looked at Alberta and said nothing. Why she didn't ask for an explanation is another twisted link in the lifeline of broken dreams hounding this family. The wall of secrets silenced us. It made June feel so strange she said nothing.

It wasn't only June who fell silent when slugged with a revelation that shattered the patched-up family portrait we had to carry in our head. I fell silent, too. Why? Because when I asked questions I never got answers. I got evasions. Why did our mother leave? "Well . . . I don't know, Harold." But why? There must be a reason. "Well. I guess she just wanted to run away." Why is our father in the insane asylum? "Well, he's not really crazy, you know. He's just disturbed."

But why is he in the asylum? "Well, they take good care of him there." But who put him there? "Well. The doctors." What doctors? "I can't remember now, but Daddy is safer there, Harold."

When you live in a fortress of lies, you lose confidence in the people who tell them, so their stories become meaningless and you just walk away. Quietly you leave the family and go hunting for a real life somewhere. But by then reality has become a stranger to you and you have trouble recognizing it when it shows up. You live in an uncertain solitude.

"Harold, do you remember that shoeshine man in Uncle Al's store, I think his name was Charlie? He was black. He'd been there since Grandpa had the store and he always shined our shoes for us. Well, I went in there after Alberta died and Charlie came over to me and said, 'Sit down, June, I'll give you a shine. C'mon, sit down, I want to talk to you.'" June sat down in the chair and Charlie told her how long he had known us, since we were born, just little kids coming into the store. "And I've shined your shoes. I've watched you children grow up, through everything, everything, all kinds of times, and I've loved each one of you children. Now, June, girl, your sister was unhappy in her life for a long, long time. What has happened here is, that child committed suicide."

No, Charlie. I know now what happened to my little sister. She did not go to Lorain to ride in an airplane. She went there to have an abortion and the abortion went bad. She started to bleed and they couldn't stop it. Her doctor in Cleveland, who was with her when June and Nicky came to see her the day before, was quiet and distant about the whole event. It turns out that Howard called him that night in desperation while my sister was bleeding to death. Why didn't the doctor call for an ambulance? Why didn't Howard? Because it was an abortion and it was illegal. There was a police investigation and it was all hushed up. The truth was hidden away and it took me years to hear what happened because the specter of family silence descended. The truth was buried with my sister.

Sadness was going to be my companion. It was a disease the family had caught and it never goes away. I see that now. I see it in

June's face, in her worn blue eyes. I saw it tracing its pattern of resignation on my uncle Al's face. I see it in the faces of Alberta's children, Diane and Howie. It has taken years for these marks to trace their story in my own face, but I can see them now. They have crept past my facade and settled there. This sadness is not a showy passenger, it rides with you mostly out of sight and quietly. It's just there and travels around somewhere inside of you, near your heart I guess. I think it probably formed my character, because escape became an engine. I was going to survive. If other lives were crashing I would steer a course along the edge of trouble and break free somehow, slip by into the open, the distance runner pressing his luck.

My sister longed to break free, too. She knew that God's mysteries get closer in the country, and she wanted to be buried there. In the cities the tall buildings shut them out. Once you get in the open, people hear that voice in the sky and in the mountains and the plains, and I think they hear it in stillness and in thunder because there's nothing to shut the mystery out. It's naked out there. That's why Alberta longed to get to Hudson, to get there alive or in spirit, to rest in peace.

18

We needed a new show for return engagements. Something different. Modern. It should have a varied grab bag of scenes and character changes to keep the audience on their toes. I began reading through plays that reflected our own world and the one freshly past, plays like *Winterset*, *One Sunday Afternoon*, *Waiting for Lefty*, *Dulcy*, *Private Lives*. I tried writing a couple of scenes based on some of the ideas the plays raised, with characters like the twenties flapper, the soldier returning from World War I, the disillusioned youths of the Depression, as well as modern-day sophisticates. We'd call it *Twentieth Century Show* and have it ready for the middle of the next season.

Until then we would run the guts out of our new station wagon. Up in Seattle we played the Washington Athletic Club. I'm trying to figure out why. They must have had some kind of stage as well as a swimming pool and exercise mats. Whatever the reason, they liked us. "Both Mr. and Mrs. Holbrook have great futures ahead of them. It has been a long, long time since we have had as talented young people in the club." Could these people have been snowed in for a year or two? Maybe we were better than I remember. I don't know. We'd come up the long coast of California and Oregon after a brace of sterling bookings from Edna Stewart in L.A. at the Friday Morning Club downtown and the Ebell Club on Wilshire in Hancock Park, where all the moneyed people built those beautiful homes years before the movie crowd planted themselves westward toward the sea. We were startled to discover that these two women's clubs had full-scale theaters the size and feel of Broadway houses. The theater in the Friday Morning Club downtown was paneled in wood and looked like the Booth on Shubert Alley.

On the way back east we picked up engagements in places like the College of the Ozarks and the University of Minnesota, and when the trail took us through Council Bluffs we stayed with Phil Pryor at the old house built by his father. Lucius Pryor had been the preeminent concert manager in the far Midwest and you felt the artistic life had been working its way into the woodwork of that house for years without pretension. But the surprise was that all that beautiful classical music should be flooding a house on the east bank of the Missouri River across from Omaha. Phil's partner, Cliff Menz, whom we'd met at Lakeside, came over with his wife, Suzanne, for dinner and the conversation was rich with stories about people in the world of theater and music, the kind of talk you hungered for when you were down in Waycross, Georgia, or out in Ogden. On one of these prized evenings we had dinner with Leadbelly and his wife. In those days it had not become fashionable to show off your black friends in society and the ease with which Phil hosted the evening left an impression on me. A year or so later we were chosen to fill the last two dates he'd booked for Leadbelly when the great folksinger with the big guitar passed away.

Once the snow started melting we drove south for Ralph Bridges's Alkahest Celebrity Bureau. "Alkahest covers the South like the dew" was their slogan, so we started sprinkling ourselves through the Virginias and down into the Carolinas and Georgia and over into Alabama and Tennessee. This was still the Old South, with the formulas of behavior still in place. COLORED ONLY. COLORED. COLORED. You tried not to look at the sign above a drinking fountain because it was embarrassing. The anger this public humiliation must have been breeding in the black population, especially the World War II veterans and their families, seemed contained and out of sight then. People were polite to one another. They followed the rules and got along, but for us it felt unnatural because no voices were raised in protest. The slow, measured cordiality and kindness in the people we met was disarming, but to our northern-trained sensibilities it seemed unreal, like watching a period play. And then there were the rednecks. The pale, blue-eyed crowd. When you ran into them in gas stations or diners and slovenly eating joints, a warning buzz ran through your body. The sensation of lurking violence crouching in those places was foul and ugly and when the pale blue eyes locked on yours, you learned to look away.

Before the season ended we had two performances with special significance: Culver Military Academy and the Brooklyn Academy of Music. It was a compliment to be asked back to Culver and I wanted to do well for my old teacher Major Mather, a colonel now; but my track coach, Mike Carpenter, was there and I had failed him. What would he think of me doing this sissy acting stuff? He didn't come and that was just as well because it might have baffled him. But Colonel Mather took personal pleasure in his novice student who had loved listening to those recordings of John Barrymore's *Hamlet*. "The Holbrooks held the cadet corps spellbound for an hour of outstanding acting. Their scene from Hamlet beautifully portrayed the tragic conflict between Hamlet and his mother. By an overwhelming majority their program is rated tops for the year." Ah, that was lovely to read. We did the *Hamlet* scene for my teacher. The year before, he had asked me to come back to Culver and take over his job teaching drama. I had turned him down and now I hoped he'd think I made the right decision.

The Brooklyn Academy date was the most important one we'd ever had up to that time. The place was run by a man of such superior breeding and self-importance, it was hard to feel higher than twelve inches in his presence. His name was Julius Bloom. It was pretty clear that this engagement was a grudging favor to Bim Pond, because we felt we were being received like a couple of backcountry actors. Maybe it was our nervousness; the place was awesome and big, right across the river from Times Square, but when we got to the stage and tried to find the stage crew no one was there. I raced through the maze of hallways to find Big Chief Mr. Bloom and said, "It's getting late. May we get some help now to set up our show?" He let me feel I had interrupted him doing something important.

The stage crew finally showed up. Now we were about to meet a version of the New York stagehand two generations ago. Dose guys don't move fast. Dey move at dere own pace and that was the pace the boys were moving at on the stage of the Brooklyn Academy.

"Youse doan like dis chair? So whadisdamadder widit?"

"It wobbles when I sit in it and it's supposed to look elegant."

"Youse wan elegunt?"

"Yeah. You know Mark Twain didn't spit in spittoons."

"Youse wan uh spittoon?"

"No, no, forget that. It's late. Could we just get started on the lights?"

"Lights?"

"Yeah. So people can see the show."

"I know nuttin' 'bout lights. Dat's Larry."

"Where is Larry?"

"I tink his mudder died."

They finally sent me upstairs to find Charlie, who had a left-handed monkey wrench. He just shrugged. I was nearly in tears and went back to the dressing room to tell Ruby what a bunch of bastards I was trying to cope with and how I'd looked all over the building for a left-handed . . .

"Oh, my God."

"Hal, dear, sit down for a while."

"Left-handed. I'm stupid! Stupid!"

I forget whether the show was good or bad, but I was learning not to trust people. On the road your expectations get chopped to pieces too often by people who don't care about the job they're supposed to do or the promise they made.

Harold

Holyoke came through! We were hired for the summer. We would each be in six to eight of the twelve plays and get our Actors' Equity card. We were going to step across the big threshold. There is no doubt that Bert Tanswell's hand was on the throttle to pull this off and I'm sure Ed had somehow got himself into the mix of influence that persuaded Carlton and Jean Guild to hire on two young unknown actors from the Midwest to join their company of professionals from New York. It was a leap of faith for them.

We had to prove ourselves. We stepped into the arena as youngsters, surrounded by a company of men and women from twenty to seventy years old and playing their own ages, not a band of college actors playing ages way beyond their own. Standing on the rehearsal stage with John O'Connor and Jacqueline Paige at Holyoke was a different experience. They had matured to near the half-century mark and if this does not sound intimidating, think about it again. Yet they were kind. In the dearest tradition of the theater, they were going to give us our chance. We were family now.

Holyoke, Massachusetts, is an old mill town that started putting itself together down on the banks of the Connecticut River about two centuries ago. Route 5 runs through it right on up to Smith College in Northampton, and a few miles downriver is Springfield, where Grandpa's train stopped to rescue me at vacation time from the moist clutches of the Headmaster. That weird little man would have been hard put to dream that sixteen years later young Harold, whose bare ass he loved to whip, would be working on a stage a few miles to the north, assuming a new character each week in his endless search for a disguise that would free him from the haunting memory of that boy-who-got-whacked.

The audience in Holyoke's Mountain Park Casino loved their actors, but you had to win their respect first, and the reviewers from the four newspapers covering the plays would be judging our worth to the company on this first shot out of the box. The play was *The Firebrand*. We were beyond Shakespeare now and into the mill run of modern drama, moving at speed week after week. Since each of us was going to play roles in six to eight plays in breathless succession, the ability to knock out a wide range of characterizations might increase an actor's value in the pressure-cooker arena of a new play every week for the twelve-week season. Not only would the producers feel they were getting two actors for the price of one, the audience was kept wondering, "What's he going to do next?"

The Firebrand was a pseudo period piece about the Italian Renaissance poet, sculptor, and lover Benvenuto Cellini, creaking amidships despite an acrobatic performance by Phil Arthur. But Ruby, playing his artist model Angela, cleaned up in the reviews. "The play is made more enjoyable by the performance of newcomer Ruby Holbrook" (*Springfield Daily News*); and "Hal and Ruby Holbrook, in their first appearance of the year at The Casino, impressed us very much." While *The Firebrand* was playing eight performances, Monday through Saturday, we were also rehearsing *Goodbye, My Fancy* to open the following Monday. While *Fancy* played its eight-performance schedule we'd rehearse the next play, and so on down the twelve-week summer season. We rehearsed five hours a day, but only two hours on matinee days, Wednesdays and Saturdays, and we learned the lines at night after the evening's performance. Jean and Carlton's rambling old home became our clubhouse, where there was close companionship and plenty of beer on ice. We cued each other over and over until we had nailed those pages of lines into our brains. Sleep was the only thing that was rationed.

In Fay Kanin's *Goodbye, My Fancy*, young Joyce Van Patten was in the cast and Jackson Perkins guest starred as the congresswoman who upsets the university's conservative applecart. "Ruby Holbrook's Professor Birdshaw is a gem" (*Holyoke Transcript-Telegram*). In the next play, *Because Their Hearts Were Pure*, an old-time melodrama with vaudevillian turns, I was given my only scheduled featured role of the summer, Sebastian Hardacre, described in the *Springfield Union* as "a cape-sweeping figure," which faintly rings the bells of a memory. I think I swept the cape so it effectively cut off the view of the other actors, distracting the audience from the dialogue that had tired them out by the time I came on. Bertram Tanswell joined the company that week as Little William and kept us turning upstage in stitches.

Two Blind Mice, authored by Sam Spewack, who with his wife cowrote the libretto for Cole Porter's *Kiss Me Kate* that same Broadway season, was a farcical take on Washington bureaucracy. Jean Guild and dear Louie Mudgett played the two elderly ladies who run a Department of Medicinal Herbs, abolished years before but never officially terminated. My role, Brenner, was a small character part, but Ruby had the choice feminine role of Karen Norwood, opposite Gaylord Mason, the company's young leading man. In *The Joyous Season* by Philip Barry, Jean Guild lifted the role of Mother Superior Christina into a favorite with our audience and Ruby was praised as the emotionally troubled Sister Theresa. I was once again noted in the "fine supporting roles" category as her husband, Francis.

Of the two of us, Ruby was turning out to be the more useful to the company and was playing a range of more interesting roles. I think the Guilds were in a bind with me, needing Ruby but rather checkmated as far as my position in the company was concerned. Gaylord Mason was the expert hand in the young leading male department and his longevity with the company influenced the roles he was given. I was grateful to have the job, for the time being, but I was going to have to learn how to play "straight"—play myself— before I could move on. Jean Guild urged me to stop characterizing: "Just be yourself, Hal," she'd say. I had trouble with that because I wasn't sure who I was and it sometimes gave me a feeling of inadequacy in this company of professionals.

See How They Run gave me the chance to do some farcical acting—"this play turns out to be the only one this season that really comes close to laying them in the aisles"—and Bert Tanswell directed the tenth play of the season, *Come Back, Little Sheba* by William Inge, one of Major Mather's students at Culver. Ruby's season of plays was over now, but I had the role of Nancy Wells's boyfriend and was listed among the "good supporting roles" once again. Not a great end to the season.

Then I got lucky. Archie Smith was to play a leading role in *Candlelight*, but a television job caused him to leave and they gave his role to me. Here was my chance to prove myself, and I knew the performance I gave would determine my future with the company. While Ruby went to Hamilton to see her sister, I got to work on Prince Rudolf Haseldorf-Schlobitten, an Austrian nobleman who exchanges identities with his valet, Josef (Gaylord Mason), in a masquerade in which a parlor maid is deliciously wooed. Miriam Stovall, pert, pretty, and gifted, made this game a pleasure. Louise Mace in the *Springfield Union* cited Miriam's "sparkling performance" and then went on to say, "Hal Holbrook has the distinctive bearing to fit his princely character, and he plays with a nice sense of humor and forbearance, being at all times the controlling factor in the charade." The local critic loosened up a bit more with "wonderfully convincing as the real prince, an elegant rogue whose tastes run to cigarettes, vintage wine and titled women," and for the Northampton critic I was "inimitable, impeccable and downright excellent as the high-spirited Prince Rudolf." So the season ended with maybe a last-minute three-bagger for me and a smooth, continuous home run for Ruby. But in *Candlelight* the important step taken for our dual careers was that I had measured up as a leading man.

The Ford station wagon took us home to our paneled garage in Granville and then we kissed it goodbye, thirty-five thousand miles, dents, grime, and all, for a shiny new chariot. Still a Ford and still a station wagon, but a fresh and eager model ready for the deserts and mountain passes. Just before we left for Fort Smith, Arkansas, and the southern and western territories, Ed called: "Would you kids like to pick up Ruth Draper at the Granville Inn and escort her uphill to Swasey Chapel?" She was giving her program of monologues that night and we had to hit the road, but Ed was giving us a chance to meet her. This dark-eyed lady was the supreme artist in the solo field, an international name, housing in her small frame a cast of characters that ranged across society's spectrum from elegant matrons to a French teacher to the lady on the Maine porch. We had seen her perform at the Forty-eighth Street Theatre in New York and took the honor of escorting her uphill with studied seriousness. But on the way, we let her in on the big news: we were in the business, too! Modestly, we thought, we gave her a brief biography of our touring experience, which she bore stoically. Later she would say to Ed, "How can that young man hope to succeed in the theater with that awful midwestern accent?"

We watched her show from a vantage point backstage until we could wait no longer. Then we jumped into the Ford and headed west, driving all night and most of the next day and a half. The following morning on the Fort Smith stage Ruby fell down in a faint in the middle of Elizabeth and Essex. I ran off and pulled the curtain. We thought it was exhaustion, but it turned out to be something else. Alberta's wish had come true.

Nature had taken its course and we were going to have to change ours now. The new Lunt-Fontanne act was going to break up before it got into third gear. The prospect of finally having a child was exciting, but it hung a big question mark over the road ahead. How were we going to earn a living? We felt suddenly foolish that we had come so blindly upon this change of fortune. All our plans began to fade.

We'd have to replace Ruby. She could work until Christmas, no more. In the new year I would have to find a new partner to fill the dates. A bleak prospect. I began to secretly worry about the strain on Ruby, especially when the queasiness in the morning began to cause her discomfort. It scared me. If we could just get through until Christmas . . . and then the offer came to tour the show across Newfoundland in early December, Ruby the champion returning to stun her folks at home. Five months pregnant. Ruby said, "Let's do it."

We went south for Ralph Bridges into Tennessee and Alabama and over to Philadelphia, Mississippi, where two young civil rights workers from New York would be buried in an earthen dam thirteen years hence. We had done the show there the previous winter, and as we drove north through the rural countryside, the trip became a nervous one when a heavily armed pickup truck with a beef-shouldered redneck at the wheel pulled alongside and looked us over. Then he fell in behind and stayed there, his pale blue eyes on our Ohio license plate. On the outskirts of West Point, Mississippi, we pulled into a tourist court and he moved away. We checked into the bug-infested place and wondered if he'd be back. It was hard to settle our nerves down. Ruby went into the bathroom. She was in there a long time and I began to worry about her. She had been quiet and edgy lately; was the strain of touring too much for her? I knocked on the door and heard a sob.

"Ruby?"

Another sob and then another, a deep, choking sob, spinning my nerves up tight.

"Ruby? . . . Ruby, are you all right?" The sobs poured out of her now in a sudden lava of anguish. I tried the door and it was locked.

"Ruby, let me in, please!" The shocking cries of pain continued. Why was the door locked?

"Ruby, for God's sake, let me in, please! Please, are you sick? Please!"

"Go away!"

Jesus! She'd never locked me out like that. My imagination went wild. Was she trying to kill herself? Had the brutal grind of the road broken her? "Let me in. Please!! Goddamn it, let me in. Don't do this. Let me in!" I was pounding on the door. She would not unlock it. I threw myself against it and it wouldn't budge. Crazy thoughts of insane asylums and Alberta ran wild in my head. I was trembling, the fear sweat pouring off me, picturing a terrible scene unfolding beyond the door. Razor blades. The sounds ceased.

"Ruby? Ruby? Please. Please let me in."

The lock clicked. I pushed open the door and she was sitting on the edge of the dirty, stained bathtub, leaning over the toilet bowl, quietly sobbing.

"I can't do this anymore."

Life stopped there. An awful silence grew in the cold, dirty room. I put my arms around her. The miles, the torture of miles and miles

Harold

had got to her. Our trail through the wild heart of America would have to end. Maybe now, maybe soon, but it would end. One can stand just so much and then the clock stops and it's over. The team of Hal and Ruby Holbrook was dead-ending, and I didn't know what would become of us now.

19

Ruby was not about to give up the triumphant return to her homeland. It was a risky move after that breakdown in the Mississippi motel, but after seven years, almost to the day, I was headed back to Newfoundland with my nearly five months pregnant wife. In December 1944, in the foul bowels of a troopship, I had read *The Grapes of Wrath* to fend off seasickness. Now I was arriving by plane, married to a Newfoundlander who had become an actress sure to grab your attention, which was what she was about to do across the whole rugged island of England's oldest colony. The St. John's *Evening Telegram* greeted us as enthusiastically as their restrained English style would allow, but the glow on the faces of Ruby's friends was more personal and welcoming. Mr. Johnston's pride in his suddenly famous daughter was hard for him to hide, but it must have been an awkward adjustment for him, his quiet and often neglected daughter returning to outshine him. The excitement among the members of the St. John's Players was especially disarming and kind. Our performance took place on the same stage where we had first acted together in *Lady Precious Stream*, an evening laced with nostalgia for us and the audience.

There was no road across the island then. We had to cross the 425-mile interior of this raw green wilderness on the narrow gauge railroad, to Grand Falls in the interior and Corner Brook on the west coast. The speed of this train echoed Mark Twain's description of the railroads in New Zealand: "One of the passengers advised the conductor to take the cowcatcher off the front end and put it on the rear because at the rate we were going we were not going to catch any cows. But there wasn't anything to prevent them from climbing aboard on the rear end and biting one of the passengers."

Our train was attired in the English style, clean and starched and formal despite its humble narrow tracks and hesitant progress. Moose came out of the woods and watched us roll by. Several passengers got out and walked awhile to exercise their limbs, and if the train managed to pull ahead of them, it obligingly paused to allow them to climb back on board. I tried walking myself, but only after a careful search of the tree line for moose and an assurance from the conductor that he would not leave me behind to perish. In all fairness to the engine pulling us along, the incline it had to conquer was an exhausting climb toward the summit of the Tops'l's, that lofty mountain range which slices the island from north to south. The Tops'l's. What a beautiful, salty name.

This rugged country is peopled by an enduring race of Scotch and Irish and English. Their quality is staying power. They draw it from the sea surrounding them, or the sea may have harshly bred it into them; they are strong, resilient, reserved. Near the center of this mammoth wedge of rock and pine rising from the sea is the logging town of Grand Falls and here we gave a performance. Even in this most remote settlement the English character had taken hold and from it comes that civility and dignity which can astonish the traveler to territories England has colonized. Life is meant to be lived in a certain way. Period. It was this tradition, which allows culture to survive and grow, that gave us such an appreciative audience in the heart of the giant forests of Newfoundland.

We flew to New York to cast Ruby's replacement, an awkward and unfamiliar role for us. In a rented studio we assumed the guise of producer-director and auditioned the actresses who had answered our notice in the casting sheets and on the Equity bulletin board.

We were surprised at the response. They were quite good and it made the choice difficult. I had not expected to find so many serious young New York actresses wanting to go out on tour in our little road show. The hunger for work was raw and unsettling and my mind leapt ahead to what our own chances might be when we moved to this tough city.

One girl did a scene from *The Country Wife* by Wycherley. She was good. Funny and in control. She'd studied under Alvina Krause at Northwestern and had summer stock experience with Krause at Eagles Mere in Pennsylvania. Her name was Lee and she had an easy control of the period style and was attractive in face and form. I could not see her as Queen Elizabeth, but she'd make a fine Ophelia if we worked up the nunnery scene, and a fine Rosalind, and she could certainly do the Interviewer with Twain. We discussed adding her audition piece, the letter-writing scene from *The Country Wife*. It would fit well into the show and give her a familiar start in the rehearsals. We chose her. Then we drove back to the little village of Granville, aglow in tiny Christmas lights.

Dearest Wife:
Tomorrow will be our last Christmas together. Next year and for years afterwards it will be a family day for us. Another threshold in our life. Every time we cross over one I hear the sound of a door closing like a great dull ache in my heart and I realize that another stretch of time has gone by and I let it slip too fast. I know my imperfections. I can only ask you humbly to forgive me. Thank you for all your gifts to me, your understanding and sympathy, your courage and diplomacy, your wisdom that sustains us when my own fails, and for trusting in me.

This was the first of many letters I would write to Ruby in our four months of separation, and I sound worried. I had not allowed myself to think of the strain this would place upon our marriage, because we had to make a living, but now the lurking possibilities of four months alone with another woman rose up to haunt me. Early in January my new partner and I left Granville and rode south in the moonlight. I felt like a boy, tongue-tied on a bizarre date. I had always felt vulnerable around attractive girls and here was one of them sharing the front seat of the Ford with me as we plunged into the nocturnal wilderness of West Virginia's spooky mountains. I may have been twenty-six years old, married, and an expectant father, but the grip of that reality was being threatened by the willowy female sitting beside me in the station wagon. It was no use pretending. This was not going to be easy.

I forget where we had our first date. Excuse me. Performance. Somewhere in the rumpled lap of West Virginia. These ancient mountains with spectral vapors snaking through them like possessive ghosts had been scrambled together in a geological nightmare. After the show we got into the car and started blindly toward Bluefield or some such place on the way to Tennessee. I thought the driving might calm me down, because conditions in our shared dressing room when we changed costumes had been pretty close. Too close and too intimate. The damn moon was out and it cast a bewitching light across the hollows and knotted hilltops we were blazing a trail through. If only Lee would chat it up, but she was quiet, very quiet, and it made the silence feel unfinished, as if something were hanging in the air. What could it be? What was she thinking?

Anyone who says you can set off across the country in a station wagon with a blonde and feel like a good boy has never been in a station wagon in the moonlight with a blonde. The eons of silence continued until we rolled into Bluefield in the dead gut of the night and hunted for the hotel. There would be only one, and we found it by the railroad tracks. When the night clerk got his body warmed up he gave us a room. I mean, we each got a room for ourselves, separate from the other person. On opposite ends of the hall. We had to make this clear to the clerk because he seemed to have something else in mind, the foul-minded fiend, and I had to clarify our requirements for him, which caused another chasm of silence to open up. I panted good night and closed the door to my room and bolted it against invasion and finally I was safe. Caged. I wondered what Lee was thinking.

ROYAL YORK HOTEL, CLARKSVILLE, TENN.
JANUARY 13TH, 1952

My Darling, I miss you tonight so very much. Got myself stowed away in another hotel and have finished my <u>washing</u>. I never knew what I was getting into until I came to those awful white stockings I wear in the Country Wife *number. Had to use the nail brush and they still look bad. A man's gotta have a woman! [Hold it! What in hell have I just said?] 475 miles today through the mountains. Took us only ten hours and fifteen minutes, and we did 110 miles more after the show last night. Lee is as glum as me, driving. I find myself trying to make conversation because you always felt I was too quiet. Now I wish for someone to chatter at me! It sure is different. It makes me almost afraid to think how desperately I need you. No one could ever take your place in my heart. The trouble with this life and our show is that it is so very personal. You have to be together in all ways to keep it from being lonely. The special magic is gone. The show, as you forewarned me, "is no longer ours." Nor the life.*

Amen, brother.

My discomfort was aggravated by Lee's independent nature. No holding doors or coats for her, which was the way I'd been brought up. She always beat me to it and left me stranded. I would have loved to shower some attention on her—on anyone who would let me—but I was having to learn a new form of behavior, self-sufficiency without warmth.

By the nineteenth of January we were in Atlanta at an old boardinghouse on Peachtree and my feelings had dropped down an octave.

How lonely can it be when you are alone? How quiet it seems at night when the room is empty and you can listen to your heart and almost hear it sigh. Why must one always turn the radio dial to the saddest music and increase the emptiness and yearning? This is an old house and it hasn't many sounds at 1:00 a.m. except the consumptive woman in the next room coughing and the cars rushing by on the dark street outside my window. In between these sounds there are long silences. I've got into the habit of coming into my room at night without turning on the lights and closing the door and standing there a while in the dark. I haven't felt so alone since I married you. It's a throwback to my childhood when I fought battles in my mind and felt things so keenly. My inner hurts are rising up again. What's coming over me? The desire to like myself has ebbed a lot. The next thing you know I'll start writing poetry again and the cycle will be complete.

My only outlet was these letters, written in the dead silence of the night. I was afraid to voice my attraction to Lee, but wouldn't Ruby have guessed it? How could she not? This separation cut me loose from my emotional bonds with her and I was drifting. I'd always needed to be tied to someone in order to feel safe and I'd had few people to tie onto before Ruby. Now I had lost my partner. Once our child arrived I would lose the show sooner or later, and I was going to be a father and the child would want to tie onto me and, frankly, the prospect scared me.

Stage facilities in some of the schools we played were slim or none and the smell in the locker rooms we dressed in could knock you down. In the morning we left for Normal, Alabama, a college date, and then Huntsville, where "our show was at a handsome, clean Negro college and one of the best audiences we have had thus far." In Atlanta, where we had dinner with Ralph and Cindy Bridges, who were booking us through the South, we were surprised by their attitude toward the Negro. "If anything they are more liberal minded than I am about it. Both their families had the typical southern outlook and both grew up under it, yet they have a completely different view and think the Negro is an equal." I wondered how many other southerners had this feeling.

"We could find nothing in this town of Huntsville after an hour of hunting and had to settle for a 'share the bath' suite in a motel. We are being eminently decent, however. She disappeared into her section two hours ago and I have not heard from her since." Why did I write Ruby about that? Was I trying to convince myself that I was out of danger? The truth is that I did hear from Lee again. She wanted to take a bath and knocked on our adjoining bathroom door to tell me there was something wrong with the drain. She was in her robe, obviously ready to step out of it and into the water, and my hormones began to whirl, especially when we knelt over the tub to inspect the drain and discuss its mechanics. What if her robe fell open? I watched the tub fill up with water, so there wasn't anything wrong with the drain after all.

"I guess it's all right," she said.

In the silence that followed, my hormones whirled even faster and I had to back out of the bathroom in a state of nervous confusion. I grabbed the portable Royal typewriter and started writing Ruby in a desperate effort to shut out the watery sounds of the blonde in the tub on the other side of the door and to assure myself that we were a couple of innocents, that the exquisite torture I felt was all in my own imagination.

On Saturday night we played the tiny town of Mathiston, Mississippi. Dumas was nearly nine hundred miles away on the Texas Panhandle and we had a day and a half to make the show. On Sunday morning it was raining. I had always been afraid of wet roads. We moved fast along Route 82 across the state of Mississippi to Greenville and crossed the big river into Arkansas, heading for El Dorado and Texarkana and then straight west across the top of Texas. It was still raining. I figured if we kept the speedometer at eighty miles an hour we could do it with a short night's sleep. We slowed down for a sharp left turn and then accelerated up to the top of a railroad viaduct. I checked the speed to make sure we were at eighty again and we started down. Lee was asleep on the seat beside me. Ahead of us a new blacktop road stretched straight as an arrow through the piney woods. Not a soul in sight.

Coming off the viaduct I saw gravel glistening on the wet tar below, thrown off by a farm vehicle. A warning, but too late. We hit it, the steering wheel went dead, and the car began to glide. It was on its own and moving to the left, ghosting toward the shoulder, which looked about four feet wide and well below the surface of the new blacktop—a big drop-off of five or six inches, and the shoulder was red clay drenched with rain. It would be like hitting glue. Beyond the shoulder was a deep ravine seven or eight feet down. If we hit that thick mud, it would grab the front wheel and flip us over. Near the edge of the blacktop I tapped the brake pedal lightly, ever so lightly, and the station wagon reversed direction like a small electric toy and headed for the right side of the road.

I had a few seconds to make a decision. Lee was still asleep, slumped sideways on the seat beside me. Engine drag would slow us down. If the car stayed straight and the two right wheels dropped off the pavement and hit the mud at the same time, maybe I could use the brakes and slow us down enough for survival. I thought it was our best chance. If we began to spin, we'd have no chance with those deep ravines on each side. We'd roll. I put my right hand on Lee and got a death grip on the steering wheel with my left hand. The front wheel must not turn. Bang! We were off the tar, into the mud; the steering wheel shuddered in my hand as if a giant animal were shaking me in its jaws, and I came down on the brake slowly.

The wheel wrenched out of my hand and we started over in a big arc; the right front wheel was the fulcrum, caught sideways in the wet clay. I kept my hand on Lee as long as I could and then turned off the ignition to keep us from burning up. We were in the air, turning upside down, and when we landed roof down in the soft ravine it was like doing the crash in a nightmare. I didn't actually feel much. Silence. Then my head felt funny. I heard the wheels spinning and the rain falling and that was all I heard. I was sitting upside down behind the wheel, but my brain wasn't working good, it wouldn't calculate, it wouldn't tell me up from down and it wouldn't tell my arms what to do. I think I had my fingers on the ignition key but I wasn't sure. Then I thought of Lee.

"Lee."

Silence. Jesus.

"Lee?"

Silence. The wheels were whirring. Was she in the car? Was she, please God—not dead! Silence.

"Hal?" She was alive! "Are you all right?"

"I don't know. Are you all right?"

"I think so. Can you open your door?"

"Let me see." I couldn't find the handle. Upside down, the wheels whirring, the rain falling, nothing was real and there was no direction.

"I can't seem to . . . I don't know where it is." My left hand was groping but the compass in my head was upside down and it wouldn't guide my hand. "Can you find your window?" I heard her moving and pulling something and then I felt a puff of wet air.

"I got it."

"Can you get out?"

"Yes. Where's the *Life* magazine? Oh, here." She laid it on the mud and climbed out. "Can you get out of there, Hal?"

"I don't know. Lemme see."

"Is anything broken?"

"I don't know. I can't . . . I'm having trouble figuring out which way is down. I mean up. I mean—"

"Just try to come this way." She reached her hand in and I got hold of it and pried myself from under the wheel. The *Life* magazine was all muddy now. I crawled over it and stood up. We looked at each other. We looked at the car, upside down, the wheels still going. She took my hand and we climbed up the ravine to the blacktop road and looked down it in one direction and then looked down it in the other direction and there was no one in sight. Just the long black road going straight through the piney woods. The wheels of the car were gently turning, the steam was rising. The rain was gently falling. We looked at each other and reached out our arms and held each other for a while.

Then I thought of the show in Dumas. How would we get there? I looked back at the upended Ford, its axles and pipes and gas tank strangely exposed, steam rising off the hot metal, and wondered if it could be put in good enough shape to drive to the Texas Panhandle. We had to get help, whether we made Texas or not, but there was nobody on the road this Sunday morning. We went down and looked inside. What a mess. The show trunks, suitcases, the sound equipment, the white bench that had been jammed together behind the front seat were all tumbled in a weird heap. My old Royal portable typewriter had scraped its own path around the loading platform and ended up against one of the cracked windows. They were all cracked in crazy patterns. We heard a car coming over the viaduct and ran up to flag it, but it was already slowing down. A pickup truck with a man and a woman inside.

"Had a little trouble here?"

"Yeah. We hit some gravel on the road back there."

"That'll do it. You folks all right?"

We guessed we were and asked him, if they were going to El Dorado, could they send a wrecker back to pull us out?

"I know a fella. Doesn't work on Sunday but maybe he'll be able to do something. He ought to be back from church. We'll have you pulled out of there anyway." It was decided Lee would go with them and ride back in the wrecking truck. She climbed in and I stood on the road and waited. The rain had soaked us through and my shoes were covered with a heavy layer of viscous red clay from our dive into the ravine. It seemed a miracle that I was walking around. Staring at our upside-down chariot, knowing we had ridden it through that arc and the upside-down crash landing, yet walked out alive, it was surreal. The top of my head hurt, I was sore, and there were cuts and bruises we'd discover later on, but my mind was now on Dumas. We had to get there somehow. We had covered about 180 miles that morning and still had 700 left to go. El Dorado was about 40 miles away, so Lee would be a few hours getting back with the wrecker.

I was taking it for granted that we had survived the acrobatic somersault in the Ford and had to be on our way. Only five days before, I had taken out a combined life insurance/endowment policy that would pay $1,000 if I died now and $10,000 in thirty-nine years, or a monthly income of $68 when I got to be sixty-five. It didn't seem like much money now. The $250 I was hoping to save from this Alkahest southern tour would be wiped out by repairs on the Ford, so we had to make that payday in Dumas.

In the two and a half hours I waited on the road, some drivers slowed down or stopped to ask if anyone was dead and then looked disappointed and left. When our savior arrived in the wrecker with Lee he ran some heavy chain and a hook down to the Ford and rolled it right side up. It was a mess. The roof was punched down and all the windows were heavily cracked but not broken out. Only the windshield was still clear. Our friend hooked the chain under the rear axle and slowly we saw our cruising home crawl out of the ravine and up to the road where it had begun its maiden flight. We piled into the cab of the wrecker, and he towed the car into El Dorado. He thought he could get a friend to work on it that afternoon and maybe get it running again. Lee and I went off to a café for some food and coffee and then stood around and watched while our savior and his disciple pulled the front fenders away from the wheels so they would turn, pulled the radiator forward into its designed position, and managed to pry the roof up enough to get the right front passenger door open. It closed, but not completely, so we'd have to add a piece of rope for security. The driver's door was jammed tight and they didn't have time to punch the roof up again, because our main concern was to get the engine working and hit the road. By six o'clock we climbed into our bandaged home with her one working door roped shut and headed for Dumas.

We drove all night in shifts. At Wichita Falls we stopped for two hours of real sleep in a motel. We each took our bag in and that's when we found out that the mud had got inside our suitcases. How it had entered we did not know, but Lee's dresses were soiled with it. We wondered what it had done to the costumes but were too tired to pry them out of the car. We'd find out in Dumas. Earlier that night I had telegraphed ahead to the chairman in charge of the show in Dumas and explained our condition and how little time we'd have on arrival to set up the show. "Please make sure the stage is all ready for us when we arrive." It was about 4:30 p.m. Monday when we drove up to the high school in Dumas. Locked up and no one in sight, and it cost us precious time to find the chairman to get the place open. No preparation had been done on the stage. Nothing. We lugged our trunks inside and were mad, mad as hell and mad at the audience we hadn't even seen. It was a small town but there must have been eight hundred to nine hundred people crowding into the hall, and their response was wonderful. We began to thaw out. Afterward the chairman and his committee fed us a fine dinner and by then our resentment had melted away.

The Ford agency in Dumas found that the gears in our transmission were burned out. The oil had leaked out when we were upside down. The bill was a shocker: $75. Almost as much as we got for doing a show. We rode Route 66 all the way up to Oklahoma City and on the way a squeak developed in the left front wheel. At the speeds we traveled it was a warning. The next day we had a 210-mile drive for a college date at Miami in Oklahoma's northeast corner, but first the Ford agency found that the spindle in the wheel was bent, so $33 for a new spindle and wheel balancing and alignment. I was getting worried about money and so was Ruby back home. She knew nothing of the accident, but she saw our bank account draining down and had to wire me for money.

In Miami, Lee insisted on another share-the-bath arrangement to save money herself. More water splashing and visions of the girl in the tub. I got out the Royal to work on the comedy scene for the new *Twentieth Century Show* we were preparing, but first I wrote Ruby.

How I miss you, you will never, never know. I have never been so terribly lonely in my whole life, nor more in need of your wise

*ways and your reassurances of love and faith in me. I want you to
know that I have never loved you more than I have in these last
three weeks and that my life's tie with you has become more
important than ever before. I thought I was a mountain of self
control and self sufficiency and now I feel like a great coward and
I hate myself for that. I am alternating these days from being mad
at myself, to feeling lost, to being cheerful and kind—and back
again to being mad.*

I can see the guilty turning of my mind here, the anger at my
predicament, how my imagination had become an adversary testing
my honor and faithfulness, my helpless feelings, all adrift. I felt neutered. The need to do something about it was bewitching me, but
half the moral choice was in Lee's hands and I didn't know what she
was thinking.

I needed to talk to someone about Lee. I didn't know how to
take her. When I got moody she became cheerful and when I got
cheerful she became moody and silent again. What did it mean? I
suppose her hormones could have been racing around, too, but the
thought of broaching the subject was fraught with signal fires of
danger for me. I was too susceptible and what a mess that could
have been. In Oklahoma City there had been a famous band playing
and when she appeared in a smoky dress she had bought in Atlanta
for the California market and suggested we go dancing, the jailer in
my mind shouted, "Holbrook! The fire is warm enough! To embrace it is nuts!" I persuaded her to go to a movie with me. That was
fire enough.

My only escape was to pound away on the Royal to let her know
my mind was on show business while she splashed around in the
tub. The clatter would help drown it out. I got only four hours' sleep
before our show at the college in Miami the next morning, but we
had the best response in ages. It seemed such easy work. Might it
have had something to do with getting north again? Afterward we
drove four hundred miles farther north to Council Bluffs, Iowa,

where we would be spending time that weekend with Phil Pryor and Cliff and Suzanne Menz and there would be music and wine and good conversation. We'd found a station that was playing Louis Armstrong on our car radio and some other blues people with strange-sounding names and I liked their music, it stirred something in me way down. I think it got Lee and me talking. We talked of our feelings of isolation and discomfort with each other. She professed to have none, which I found hard to believe. We skirted the man-woman topic but it was there in the silences. She talked a lot about Ruby and how much she admired her and felt she was the salt and savor of the earth and I agreed with her on that and wondered if she was sending me a signal. It was not a frank discussion emotionally, but it did me a world of good to get some of the tension out and I think it made her feel good, too. No grounds for divorce.

COUNCIL BLUFFS, IOWA

FEBRUARY 2, 1952

Darlin':

I am dead drunk! It's a wonderful feeling. I have knocked off half a bottle and spent the swellest evening of the tour at Phil Pryor's. We've listened to records for 8 hours—all the way from folk songs (with Leadbelly) to Bartok and Hindemith. Phil played the banjo for a few hours while Lee sang folk songs and honest to God we were all enchanted by her feeling for them. She amazed us. We sat around the big coffee table and drained off two fifths, straight. No water. We turned off all the lights around midnight and listened by candlelight and Phil was in his element with Lee. She does Barb'ry Allen in a different tune—more minor and sad than I have heard it.

There in that old house, steeped in the voices and moonlight memories of artists who had come this way and left their ghosts behind, I found a ticket to the land of forgetfulness. The bottle. Forget your troubles and let's get happy.

The fear of loneliness never left me for very long—and the hunger for love. It was lurking around inside, waiting to come again and again like a poison that could alter me, and it frightened me to think how my confidence could so easily be washed away when I felt abandoned.

20

Webster City, Iowa. We drove after the show. It helped control my emotions and I could think. Clear and cold and dark blue all around. Fields lit with silver starlight disappeared into haze. The road was straight and narrow, a lonely road that went on and on, vague and endless and shrouded. The night seemed beautifully desolate and everything was silent, inside the car and out. Deadly silent, motionless almost. Living is like that sometimes when you lock your feelings up, your thoughts, your dreams and they dwindle more and more as the years pass and you get lonely and afraid. I think it must be horrible to have no one to love you. Why did I feel trapped with my emotions? I didn't want to show them unless the black hole of the theater was out there. The spotlights protected me and the pinpoint of quiet and the holding of many breaths persuaded me I could open up and reach for something true, fragile as a feather in flight—until someone coughed and it vanished. Gone, and maybe no one saw it.

A depressing letter had reached me from the chairman of the concert series in Baxley, Georgia, saying the *Hamlet* scene was "time wasted because the scenes from *Hamlet* did not seem to fit in so well." *Hamlet* was important to me because the emotions I felt burst out of me. I could not hold them back. I was speaking for myself, his isolation and violated feelings were mine. Barrymore's voice had never left my head and I wanted to be good!

We started into the play's dark regions with the closet scene and then the "To be or not to be" soliloquy and then into the anguished nunnery scene with Ophelia. In Dumas at the dinner party after our show one poor fellow who had seen John Barrymore told Lee my Hamlet was "brilliant." So I had the Baxley, Georgia, and Dumas, Texas, opinions to guide me. Most of all, I wanted to be *understood.* But I wrote to Ruby, "I am not the type for Hamlet—let us face it, Ruby, I should not be doing it seriously, only as an exercise in acting. It is far beyond me and I know it. I am a character man and sound like one." But did I look like one? Or did I feel like one? Or did I look and feel like Hamlet?

I find the letters from which I have culled these memories astonishing in many ways. The revelations of feelings more than a half century old are too fresh to have been forgotten. I am writing much closer to the grave now, but these cries of solitary desperation are like echoes for me. I hear them and have heard them all my life as I reached for a life raft and a home. The energy, the punishing race he ran, this young man.

We got up early and headed for Kirksville, Missouri, 248 miles south, for the show that night. From Kirksville we would play Peru, Nebraska, on Wednesday, a flyspeck on the map 220 miles due west; Thursday we'd drive south 116 miles to Topeka, Kansas, for a 2:00 p.m. show and then jump into the car and drive like mad 107 miles back north for our show that night in Auburn, Nebraska, which is 9 miles from Peru, where we started. Then it was 1,200 miles to Billings, but we had three days to make it. Forget looking it up in the Rand McNally. Take an aspirin. Keith Herrington, our English actor friend, was seeing the show in Topeka. What would he think of our *Hamlet* number?

I couldn't get a laugh in Peru. Lee got two and that burned me up, but somehow it mutated to a what-the-hell attitude and we left the theater in high cynical spirits, joshing each other with more ease than we'd had in several weeks. She couldn't get the drain stopper on her bathtub to work (there we go again!) and asked if I could come in and make the damn thing close up so she could get a bath. I checked first to see that she was not in the tub and somehow the whole episode had such a wholesome ring to it that we arrived at some happy point of relaxation. And she wanted to go skiing with me when we got west, keen as a knife for it.

AUBURN, NEBRASKA
FEBRUARY 7, 1952
My Darling:
In the words of Will Faithful "I am myself again!" I have felt that way for nearly two days now and I am sure my horrible malady of the last six weeks is over. It's as if something just quietly slipped into place one fine moment and here I am—cheerful, buoyant, tasting life again, and finding pleasure in being at ease and jovial with everyone. It is one of the most puzzling and happy events of my life. Lee has reacted to the change. We are kidding around like old pals. I feel quite foolish; the things that bothered me before seem far less important now and it gives me final proof that most of the blame on this trip must have been on me all along.

Please. If a willowy woman slides around naked under a terry-cloth robe and invites you to fix the plumbing, shouldn't any red-blooded American male want to rip the robe off and jump on her? Get real. I was neutering myself.

One hundred miles to Topeka before breakfast to get our mail so we could read it before the show. They had a huge turnout and the show wasn't bad, considering the fact that Keith Herrington sat in the audience and watched us. We were both petrified, doing *Hamlet* for an English actor who had acted at Stratford with John Gielgud and other greats, although he was the most likable fellow you could meet. He was complimentary about our show and when we probed him for criticism he was very mild about it. *Hamlet* was "most engrossing" and his strongest criticism was that I seemed to give everything at climactic moments; he got the feeling "that I must have been exhausted when I left the stage." I was, because I was so scared and trying so hard. That damn trying too hard business was my downfall.

He looked at me rather strangely once and said, "How old are you, Hal?" I said nearly twenty-seven. He wondered how much longer I intended to keep on with this show.

It made me reflect on this in my letter to Ruby.

After reading Carlton's letter today about my work last summer at Holyoke I realize again that this show we are doing has served its useful purpose for me as an actor. And no doubt for you. [Was I refusing to believe that Ruby could not return to the show?] Doing a new show next year with modern instead of classic characters should be a great advance and a help. But essentially what we both need—and me especially—is a slower and more normal approach to acting. I have been forced for so long to create quickly and on my own that I am a bag of technical tricks and these tricks have not given me the real confidence I should have in myself. Until I can play a straight character with ease and conviction and depth, I will not be a very good actor or a well rounded one. I must learn to stop trying so hard. I must learn to develop a role from my own self outward, instead of merely clothing myself in the eccentric trappings of a "character."

We start for Billings tomorrow morning. Further and further away from you. Oh, Ruby, I wish I could see you while you are growing into a beautiful, full pregnant woman. I'll bet you are so lovely, with your clear face and deep, warm eyes, and the look of a real woman coming out of them. I love to think of you being a mother. My, you will be the best one that ever was. So compassionate and practical and such a pal for our son or daughter. How will I ever match your understanding? I miss you and love you every moment.

Does this ring true? I was *trying* to love the idea of Ruby being a mother, but I was scared of the whole prospect and could not erase my secret feelings that I was being set adrift again. I wonder if she could read this between the lines. The life we had dreamed up and toiled over for six years was being taken away. I had to become a father. Everything would change. It was going to be my job now, but how would I play that role? What was a father?

It was February 7, 1952. Ace Morgan died on this day seven years ago. I was alive, I had a future, a loving wife, and a child waiting in the wings to make its appearance. But I was scared.

Heading west for Billings, looking for something inspiring on the radio: "Send right now for that life-sized portrait of Jesus. That's *Jesus*—J-E-S-U-S, Waco, Texas. Send no money; just pay the postman one dollar when he delivers it to you. But act now! That's *Jesus*—J-E-S-U-S, Waco, Texas." No help from that quarter. How can these people turn religion into a sales pitch?

The God I found in nature was more real to me.

The sun beat down on my left cheek with such fierceness as we drove along today, 490 miles up the river Platte into the vastness of Wyoming. The most thrilling moment came at sunset. A burnt orange flame left by the sun paused on the western rim just after its disappearance below the horizon. Fanning the top of the sky above it were gray-lavender clouds, hanging in wisps and odd shapes before the cyclorama of blue-green sky beyond. The primal land around us was shadowed in patches of coal black and gray, notched crazily by irregular hillocks and bluffs and spotted with the silvered reflection of ice-covered ponds which had been put there by some recent rain. The hand of evening in pastel velvet reached over everything and gave a transition to all it touched. It was a vista filled with joy and thrill and grimness and the waiting destiny of life.

There was someone inside me trying to come out—the boy who wrote poetry by flashlight after lights-out at Culver. Why did I go into hiding? Why was I trying so hard to control my life, to patch the artist stirring in me onto the practical man straining to be—what? A faithful husband. A good wage earner and soon a father. But it wasn't working. I didn't know what fire was in me, but it was desperate to get out.

From Billings we drove south through the Wind River Canyon along the Bighorn to Shoshone and crossed the eight-thousand-foot snow-fields of the Continental Divide, looking for a way into Colorado. At Craig we'd covered eighteen hundred miles in the last five days. Back home Ruby was doing her best to save everything she could by making her own clothing. The generosity of the Reeses was endless; she had moved in with them and they were taking good care of her. Gay had given Ruby a jacket and she was now sewing up the clothing to go with it on her sewing machine. She was also studying French and applying for her citizenship papers. She had taken control of her new life. If she shared my fear of the future, she did not talk to me about it.

OGDEN, UTAH

FEBRUARY 14TH, 1952

Sweetheart:

Happy Valentines Day!! How nice and comforting it is to be back at my typewriter again where I am alone with you. These nightly sessions with you have been the greatest joy of the last five weeks and your letters are such a genuine gift to me, Ruby. And thank you for my lovely, lovely shirt and the scrumptious fudge!! You are such a busy gal, knitting that sweater set for our child and making yourself that maternity outfit, plus writing all those letters.

I got a new book today, Dos Passos' U.S.A. Once I finish Fitzgerald I'll start it. Gives an account and an analysis of the twenties and before that a shorter Tolstoian look at this country and it may provide the background for working on some of our scenes. Lee suggested it. Maybe I can write some good scripts for

My grandfather, our Rock of Gibraltar

My father, Harold R. Holbrook, in his twenties

My mother, Aileen Davenport, posing behind the Palace Theatre in Cleveland, Ohio, 1931

Mother, dancing her way to eternity

We three kids—on the steps of the Cleveland house, about 1931

Me, June, Spot, Aunt Ruby, Paul, Alberta—and the twenty-five-dollar Buick

Grandma and her "blue-eyed baby boy" at Culver Military Academy

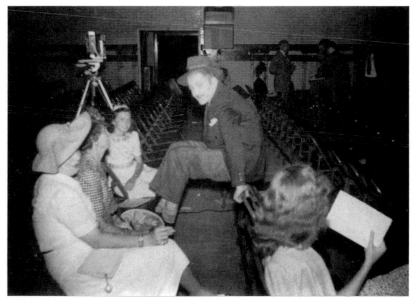

My family—Aunt Merce, Grandma, Cousin Jeanne, me, and a stray someone—after the performance of *Room Service,* all stunned that another Holbrook might become an actor

On maneuvers in the
Smoky Mountains, at
war with the U.S. Army

Me, Blackburn, and Boyd at Fort Pepperell, Newfoundland

Ruby on our honeymoon, waiting to go fishing in the Canadian woods

Me on our honeymoon, dragging a worm around a Canadian lake

Androcles and the Lion, with me as Caesar, Dick Welsbacher as Androcles, and [??] as the Lion at Denison University in 1948

The Butter and Egg Man, with me, Dick Welsbacher, and Luke Utter at the Denison Summer Theatre in 1948

The Constant Wife with Ruby at the Denison Summer Theatre. We were now an acting team.

Considering the future

The station wagon, ready for the road

As You Like It, with Ruby as Rosalind and me as Orlando, from our two-person show *Theatre of Great Personalities*

In our two-person show, as Robert and Elizabeth Barrett Browning

Mark Twain and
the Interviewer

In *Room Service*, at
the Holyoke Summer
Theatre, 1952, with
Bert Tanswell, Ted
Tiller, Mitch Erickson,
and Nancy Wells

*Bell, Book and
Candle*, at the
Holyoke Summer
Theatre, 1953, with
Miriam Stovall

Vicki and her dad in the pool at
Holyoke, 1953

Victoria, about two years old

Daddy with corncob pipe and covered up with David and Vicki at our
cottage hideaway

On Mount Shasta, 10,000 feet. This self-portrait was taken by holding the camera at arm's length.

On the glacier. The peak—14,162 feet—is obscured in clouds.

Upstairs at the Duplex with Bruce Morton and Lovey Powell, 1956

As Mark Twain at the Lambs Club performance, 1957

As Mark Twain, 1959

Ed Wright, my teacher

us, the kind that will let us find outlets for ourselves which we cannot find in our present show.

I was hoping Ruby would be able to continue our partnership, but how? With a baby. That was the silent question mark.

We have a big decision to make: Holyoke versus Bemidji, Minnesota, this summer. Bob Gaus has written again about our taking over the summer theatre there. It's a challenge and we could play some great roles. And yes, I felt Carlton's letter might have been the gentle preparation to me for a letdown, but I am inclined to the second fiddle position there, dear, rather than the major roles in Minnesota. Holyoke offers convenience to New York and the promise of advancement if I play my cards right. I'm convinced you are set there and will get lovely parts as soon as you are able to take them. Meanwhile, I have a lot of learning to do.

I certainly did. I was in for a shock. So was Ruby if she thought Mom and Dad would carry on as before. Desperation was churning its way through my gut, but we were silent about it. Why? Our life was going to change and we were walking blindly toward it.

From Las Vegas, Lee and I flew across the Mojave Desert on the magic carpet of Franck's Symphony in D Minor, Ruby's favorite, the "Angelicus." When the faint lights of Barstow rose up to say hello, it was early dawn of my twenty-seventh birthday. We staggered reluctantly to life again at noon and set off across more desert to seek out that Pump Room Paradise called Los Angeles. The Mexicanos who named it for the angels must have been in shock. True, it was a thrilling sight to cross the San Gabriel Mountains and dive down into the watered greenery of the San Fernando Valley, alive with self-conscious palm trees and hardware stores in pink and pale green stucco, but you wondered if the stuff inside could actually be real. The newness and artifice all around inspired a form of awe: you were amazed that you'd arrived there before the buildings had begun to rot at the foundations and the hard green lawns had run out of water. Beneath all this was the same desert you just passed over. Yet here it was fresh and in glowing Technicolor, stretching north, south, east, and west in widening ripples of invasion all the way up into those ancient unfertile hills where the live oak tree brooded in the sun, waiting for the morning dew.

Lee and I had been offered shelter by Stuart and Virginia Blashill at their home in Pacific Palisades. Their son John had been with us at Denison and Lee was occupying a room in the house while I was secluded away in a garret apartment behind the garage, a perfect peaceful refuge where I could write.

PACIFIC PALISADES
FEBRUARY 17TH, 1952
Dear Ruby:
Gee, honey, I miss you tonight. I wish I had never left you. How we do need each other to cling to in this wide old world. Home will always be where my darling's heart is. Keep well and strong and God bless you always. My love is in your kind hands.

Finally Ruby hinted at her private feelings. "Some of us are born lonely," she wrote. Her admission was a surprise. She had been quiet about her feelings so much of the time it was hard to know what she was thinking. Her silence had been one of the qualities that attracted me to her, but now I saw I had not been attentive enough. Ninety percent of the time, I was working on something. I should have asked questions. She could be dwelling on her fears now, with the baby coming and the emotional roller coaster of motherhood about to begin its ride. And there was a chance that Ruby would have to deliver by Cesarean section. If she did, that would make her recovery less certain before she entered the brutal racetrack of summer stock. It was a warning, and it lodged in my mind.

My twenty-seventh birthday. The cocoon we had woven around ourselves was unwinding day by day. A life was waiting up ahead to join us. A stranger. This was not what we had planned. Our plan was dissolving like a dream and we would need another one soon. And I had no plan.

On Wednesday morning at 7:30 Lee and I rose early and snaked up the surf-torn Pacific coastline to Santa Barbara for our matinee in the Santa Barbara Women's Club's beautiful clubhouse. At 5:00 we were back in the car, driving fast for Reno and our show the next afternoon. We covered the 490 miles to Sacramento by 3:00 a.m. and stumbled into a motel, desperate for sleep. The motel manager delivered the grim news that a blizzard had just closed down the Donner Pass over the high Sierras, where a hundred years before, the Donner party had turned to cannibalism to survive. We'd have to change course and drive north to the Feather River Canyon, seventy miles long on a twisting road cut like a shelf into volcanic rock, and try to make it across that sky-high place where three Union Pacific streamliner cars were still hanging down the side of its deep, deep gorge. The Feather River route would add another 140 miles to the original 110 to Reno, so our night's slumber was cut short at four hours. We wolfed down breakfast and left at 8:30 in the morning, drove the 250 miles over the top of the world, arrived in Reno at 1:30, and went up at 2:45. Gave a good show, very successful, and the only explanation I can give you is a short one. Youth.

Reno. February 22, 1952. Skiing! Finally. The top of the world. I was alone up there, breathing air with the gods. The snow was untouched, not a mark on it. I poised on the summit of a ski slope at Squaw Valley, waiting to take off straight down. I hadn't skied since my Culver days, but the technique came back pretty quick. I found myself slipping into small jump turns on the second run and using my knees to absorb shock and steady my balance. There was such freedom in it. I think my chief fault was in being too eager or reckless with my unconditioned strength, and the lack of oxygen up there had me coughing incessantly. These so-called slopes out west were close to perpendicular. You accelerated fast to tremendous speed. Lee took one god-awful fall and ripped to shreds a number of useful muscles in her left foot and knee. She had a large pail of water in her room and wintergreen liniment and was working over the sore spots. Hardly anything could keep us out of Squaw Valley the next day!

But the fall Lee had taken was more serious than we'd thought. In the morning she could not move her foot or her knee. Walking was almost impossible for her, and I carried her to the doctor. For once, she was trapped into needing my help. We sweated out the X-rays, but no bones were broken. The ligaments in both knee and foot were badly sprained and would not heal for at least three weeks, but the doctor felt she might be able to walk enough on Monday to fake it through the show. Then there was only the show on Tuesday, followed rather neatly by a thirteen-day layoff. With luck our shows would be salvaged. But all her dreams of spending a week flying down the slopes were crushed.

Lee insisted that I go skiing, and it did not take much effort to win me over. We went to Mount Rose, where she could watch the ski meet taking place from the lodge, and I helped her up on the porch and took off. The big T-bar lift intrigued me, so I took it—up, up, up—more than a quarter of a mile to the top. The ski run was just about straight down. If you charged it without braking you'd reach a speed of seventy miles per hour, and a spill at that velocity could kill you. I started down, crossing sharply to the other side of the bowl, and was amazed at how fast I was going before covering twenty feet. Stopped myself, turned and took another run, and got to the bottom, finishing up with a long, winding run to the lodge that had quite a flourish to it and fell right in front of everybody. Great sport. You feel like a bird and then there's a nice Scotch and soda when it's all over.

I drove us the 470 miles from Reno to Bishop with Lee propped up in the corner of the front seat, supporting her leg across my cane from *The Country Wife*. She felt she could let go a bit the next day to do the show in Redlands. All down the eastern spine of the Sierras just east of Yosemite we saw people skiing, sweeping like birds across the snow.

Harold

Ruby had found out about the accidents. Both of them—the other one that I had kept secret.

My dear Girl, I read your letter demanding the facts and simply roared over it. The first accident occurred on that night ride through West Virginia after our first show. Lee was sleeping, the road was narrow and dark, butane trucks kept passing and their lights were blinding. A truck went by and I heard a loud report like a rifle shot and felt the car lift up an inch or two to the right and then continue. The truck sheared away most of the two door posts on my side and plucked the lock neatly from its socket. That was all. We went on. The ladies at the Santa Barbara Women's Club were quite put out when we drove our scarred and mud splattered land cruiser into their pretty driveway.

Now, my dear wife, please forget about it. The somersault in Arkansas sounds ghastly and it was, but I learned that no date is ever worth that effort or risk and will not allow it to happen again. I would have canceled the Reno jump last week, except we needed the money so much.

I wouldn't allow it to happen again? Only on the Reno jump? Bull! For years I would be taking risks, loading up schedules because I couldn't afford to say no to a paycheck. Pushing my luck, the distance runner going for another lap. Survival and suicide impulses working in tandem. This is the young man who stood in the rain watching the wheels of his upside-down car going around and figuring how he could make it to Dumas seven hundred miles away.

The lack of money was a storm cloud hanging over us. We needed it to rain dollars, and Ricklie was our big hope now. She came through with a date in Fort Wayne on March 27 for $200. But it was a return engagement and we needed one new scene, a modern one without costume, to play the date.

Darling—I'm way the hell out on the road. Could you possibly find us a ten-minute comedy scene, modern dress, among any of

*the plays there? We need an opener. Ask Ed. There's only a
month left to get it ready.*

Good news from Fred Graham. He now had a big week for us in
Utah, more than $500 income. With Fred and Pryor-Menz we'd
bring in over $1,000 on our way home. And there were decisions to
make. There was Bob Gaus, the booker for Pryor-Menz, a young
man whose optimistic energy appealed to us greatly. He wanted us
to join him in a new theater company he was forming in Bemidji,
Minnesota, and now another letter had come from him. "Bob's letter brings up a feeling that has troubled me of late," I wrote to Ruby.

*That we are at a parting of the ways in our climb up the ladder.
One direction leads off into the hinterland to the theatre-that-
might-be, that idealistic young theatre we saw so eloquently
expressed by Margo Jones in Dallas and dreamed of joining. The
other road leads straight up. Cliff-like. It requires a hand over hand
motion. This is New York. While the obvious choice is between
Holyoke and Bemidji, there is a more subtle one, the choice
between the big time and the theatre of the idealist. It has to be
made now and there will be no retreat once we make the choice.*

Then we got a shot in the arm from Howard Higgins. He told me
of three new bookings and his merger with Redpath, which put him
in a bigger class in the eastern territory. Howard had chosen us to
grow with him and that gave me a feeling of security. I told him to go
ahead. If he got those three dates on a weekend this fall in Albany,
only ninety miles from Manhattan at $200 apiece, it would be a real
break. We could leave the baby with a friend in New York who might
well be able to use the money we could pay her for that. I dearly
wanted our new show to be a knockout, but could Ruby do it?

There was one straw in the wind.

I had an idea today. I was leafing through Life *magazine and read
the article on Emlyn Williams doing Dickens recitals in makeup.*

*Tremendous New York hit as you know. It suddenly struck me
that I could, if I wished, do the same thing with Twain someday.
Make up as Twain and read his stuff. Remember, I had this idea
before? Since it seems to have gone so well for Dickens, might it
not for Twain?*

Back with the Blashills. I was restless. Nervous. Lee was off with
friends most days and the prospect of going up to the mountains to
ski alone was losing its joy. I walked into the village of Pacific Palisades and then walked down to the cliffs and looked out to sea. The
Pacific Ocean was gray, an endless, friendless gray under cloud
cover. The surf launched itself onshore and one lonely figure moved
along the sand, his pants rolled up. That could be me or my father
down there, walking his solitary journey through life. The moment
felt like the end of a worn-out dream.

The thought of the long trip back east, the lonely days on the
road driving in silence, had sapped some of the heart for adventure
out of me. I'd really done nothing in Los Angeles and had spent
most of my evenings writing Ruby.

THE GARRET

MARCH 3RD, 1952

Dear Ruby:

*The letter from Carlton Guild has speared my dreams in flight.
I see the logic of your counsel that we return to Holyoke this
summer instead of taking the more challenging job in Minnesota,
but in all three respects—salary, roles, length of time I'm
wanted—I feel set down. My talent, whatever it is, just doesn't
fit the type required at Holyoke. Hackwork is what they want
from me, the K.P. detail I did last summer, acting without heart
and soul, and without desire which is so terribly important
to me.*

Thank you for sending along the Life with Father *scene.
Yes, it would be a wise choice for Ft. Wayne and we'll get to work
on it for the repeat dates. All I need is the black frock coat I used*

for Disraeli and the brocaded vest and shirtfront. I can attach the Browning collar to that and turn the collar tabs down.

At some point in the last year I had written a scene between Disraeli and old Queen Victoria.

"I will *not* throw away your letters, old girl. They are all I have of you right now." (But somewhere in the labyrinth of packing boxes that moved with us through life's changing crises, most of her letters are gone now.) Ruby had sent some pictures of herself featuring her pregnancy in silhouette, but the evidence was not apparent. "Are you really pregnant or has it all been an impish mistake?" There was pride in the way Ruby was handling her pregnancy and the approach of motherhood and I knew I was supposed to feel that great thrill of anticipation—but it was a thrill acted out. The image of my father with his bullet-hole hat and casual drawl came strolling into the pictures I saw of myself with a child. "Hey. How's it going, Harold? Got a kid, huh?" Was I going to get beyond that?

I had to. I had to. I had to go past my father and my mother and be responsible and love the responsibility, love it and love my baby, and love being a father and playing with my child who would love me and want to do what I wanted it to do. Wait. They didn't do what you wanted them to do and they made all kinds of messes and you would not know why they were crying, but you would have to be patient and take the time to find that out. Patience. That's what I'd need. Time and patience. And love. Love I didn't recall ever getting from the tall stranger or that young woman tap-dancing with him under the archway. Where was she, anyway? This blessed event had a dark, nervous side, waiting for fatherhood to open its sudden mysteries. What if Ruby couldn't work? How could I earn a living alone? What if I couldn't get an acting job in New York, where would the money come from to feed us all? The main emotion rising in me was desperation.

Desperation seemed to hound us. On April 5 we would play Western Reserve Academy in Hudson, where my sister was buried. The small village where desperation had driven Alberta to dream of finding a new home and a new life. And where was June? Well, she was in Cleveland. She had been courted by a Mr. Nyles, who lived in a house on Lake Avenue east of ours and had watched her walk by years before on her way home from St. Augustine Academy. Walking by seemed to be June's starring turn; she could capture the attention of any American male by walking by. She had caught the attention of Bill Meyer and Gion and reeled them in and now she'd landed another one back home on Lake Avenue. But this guy was strange. He was a collector. An old yellow automobile rusted in the backyard, visible from the street. Inside he collected boxes and labels from canned goods, and newspapers. These he stacked up indoors and as the years went by they had reached higher toward the ceiling until they nearly touched it. The rooms had disappeared into narrow passageways, say from the front door to the kitchen, through what used to be the parlor and then the dining room. You could sit on the front porch in good weather and watch the neighbors shooting pained glances at the only unpainted house on that mile-long avenue of affluent homes, but when the nip of October forced you to go inside, it was the kitchen for all-purpose living. To give Nyles his due, he had arranged his stacks to allow access to the stairway going up to the bedrooms. That was in his favor. The second bedroom up there was Cheryl's hideaway in this eccentric asylum, but she would soon have a roommate. Baby Kathy was on the way. One further touch: Nyles's first name was Nile.

There seemed to be no way to straighten the course of my sister's life. She had become a fugitive on the run, stopping here and there to hide awhile and then moving on. Her independent spirit made it impossible for her to remain caged for long and that was how she seemed to feel about marriage. A cage. She kept locking herself up, but sooner or later she would escape like our father, the fugitive. I was praying the disease would not be catching. At least June took her children with her.

At income tax time our total income for 1951 was close to $12,700, nearly $4,000 more than in 1950. Wonderful, but we'd have to pay more tax. "Ruby, your salary at Holyoke was $75. I think the total for six weeks plus rehearsal pay was about $480 for you. If you can collect any unemployment insurance, do so and put it in the bank, huh? I will try to do the same over May and early June before we leave Granville." A letter from Howard Higgins kept me smiling—"a date in Athens, Ohio on the 28th of April for $275! Fantastic! Our largest fee this season and a morning date at that!" This final week for Howard from April 28 to May 2 had grown to a full week of five dates with an income of $583, strong medicine for our bank account, and I knew I had to go get the money. Stuart Blashill, our host in the Palisades, pointed out that this would do a lot toward paying Ruby's hospital bills, but the timing was so close to B-day it was making me nervous, and the devils of guilt were gathering for a howling festival in my gut. Our baby was expected on April 21. "Listen to Dad, boy. Don't miss your entrance cue!"

Only six or seven more weeks and I would be a father, and I was expecting a boy. I wonder why? Image of myself from top to bottom? Or did I think a male child would be easier for me to handle? Visions of building him a complete electric train set, laid out on an elevated table with mountains and tunnels and switch-off tracks, were racing around in my head because I could enjoy that, too. It would be fun for me and it would rival the one in Pete Pillsbury's basement and I wouldn't have to be invited over to play with it. Me and the kid would have it to ourselves. We could have fun together.

But there was something evasive about this cartoon version of fatherhood. Throughout this period at the Blashills I'd been observing their late-in-life child, young Stuart, and trying to feel easy with him, and it wasn't working very well. That evening around dinnertime he had been as difficult as a donkey—screaming and bawling and having to be put in his room and then taken out again and cuddled. There seemed to be so many things that upset a child, and flying off at him would do no good, I saw that, but I was baffled by such displays. I couldn't help noticing how he peeked through his fingers every time he rubbed his teary eyes, looking to see what effect it was having on us. It reduced my sympathy. I could see I was in for a beginner's course in tolerance. I had served for eight years on the battlefields of two boys' schools and for this kind of behavior they would dump you. At young Stuart's age, when I threw fits in the backseat of Grandpa's car while Henry was driving us to Aunt Anna's or Longfellow's Wayside Inn on Sunday, Grandpa let me play it out. I held my breath and kicked my feet, hoping to break down the bar of discipline my grandfather had raised. He would not lower it. My face got redder and redder while I stared defiantly back at him, not breathing, bug-eyed and crimson. The bar never came down. I had to breathe or die. So I breathed.

I have been reading Spock's baby book. No nonsense about him. According to Dr. Spock, Momma needs a lot of help those first few weeks or she might turn into some kind of depressed psycho and we don't want that. If anyone is going to go psycho let it be me. I feel so ignorant about all this baby care business. My God!—what if I give him a dose of Four Roses in his formula while I'm sipping it to keep my strength up? Keep strong and healthy so you can get back on your feet quickly and help Papa. I'll be helping you with the housekeeping and baby keeping and getting the stuff you need, bottle warmer and such. Where will we put the stuff? Hey, honey, we'll have fun with our kid, won't we?

I sound dangerously like my father, the boy who didn't grow up. "Hey, Ma, how's it going? How you fixed for cash?" Was I going to be able to do what had to be done? Ruby was beginning to see through the strain of my cheerfulness as I approached fatherhood. And the weeks of separation were eating away at her own morale, too. "Everybody is a stranger when you are truly lonely," she had written. The words leapt out of the page at me, they reminded me how selfish I had been, always harping on my own feelings of loneliness when I should have been concentrating on hers. Ruby had been the strong one and I the weak one, seeking help in a barrage of letters. It was a sour portrait of myself and it caused me to stuff my feelings back in the black hole of my gut and try to act like a man who was going to be a father, with a wife who might be in shaky condition.

I read what you said about fearing that I am not looking forward to being a father with very much zeal. Dear little wife, I am. I am looking forward to it and I'm extremely happy about it, but I know how you got that impression. I am a bit worried. What I've been reading and common sense tells me that expectant fathers have mental fears and doubts assailing them, and you know how susceptible I am to doubt when something new and strange enters my life and alters my routine. But once I'm in the woods the trees won't loom so large. I shall be proud to be a father with a mother like you beside me and a dear baby to love, yours and mine alone. I'm sure this fatherhood deal is not so difficult. Once it becomes familiar I shall no doubt feel I am rare among fathers. You know me—the best or it's no good. That applies here.

Uh-huh. Sometimes I had the sensation that the tall man with the bullet-hole hat was reading over my shoulder. Under his dark eyebrows the blue-gray eyes were veiled and secretive. What was he thinking? And the little dancing girl, the blond one in the archway who never spoke a word so she had no voice, what was she thinking? No sound came from the dancing girl. Just sad smiles. "The best time to start being a good father is when the baby is born," Dr. Spock wrote. Okay. Okay. But I have to go to work, don't I? How do I manage it all? I couldn't get answers from the traditional sources. Uncle Al and Aunt Merce would give me platitudes, Ruby's ma and pa lived on an island in the North Atlantic, Ed and Louise had never had children. The Reeses were our second-best hope, since we wouldn't be hearing from Fred and Ginger in the archway. What was the tall man thinking? Why did he keep appearing just beyond my shoulder? "You built yourself a box, kid. You're married and comfy, this stage play thing pays the bills and now that's all gone to bird shit. What do you want to bother with a kid for? They're no fun."

21

Bob Gaus was waiting for us when we rode into Council Bluffs. He was pulling new balloons out of every pocket, the most likable guy of my age I had ever met. His plan was to run not one, but two theaters in the Bemidji area, the Pine Beach Playhouse on Gull Lake near Brainerd, which he'd started two years before, and the Paul Bunyan Playhouse on Minnesota's Lake Bemidji. His promotional flyer announced this two-theater operation as a festival that had "risen from obscure beginnings to a prominent position among the foremost summer theatres in the nation." He was not expecting to be challenged on that claim up there in Bemidji.

If his enthusiasm for this roundhouse flyer was real all the way to his gut or covered just half the distance, it didn't matter, because his pitch was mesmerizing. The announcement he'd prepared listed thirty-six plays, out of which we'd choose twenty, ten for each theater, and run each one for a week of seven performances. Such as:

Harvey	*The Little Foxes*
Mister Roberts	*Death of a Salesman*
Arsenic and Old Lace	*Room Service*
All My Sons	*I Remember Mama*
Our Town	*Born Yesterday*
You Can't Take It with You	*The Hasty Heart*
The Winslow Boy	*The Philadelphia Story*

Hal Holbrook

Three Men on a Horse	*Life with Father*
Angel Street	*Rain*
The Drunkard	*The Corn Is Green*

An actor whose eyes did not glisten in the reflection of this starry galaxy was a deceased actor. And the boldness of Bob's plan never lost altitude. He was going to entice twenty-four production assistants—"selected from the leading college and Community Theatre groups in the United States"—to join the staff of each theater and "live and work with professional company members," and they "would often find themselves playing leads or assuming positions on production crews." They would be charged no tuition for the summer's employment and "will be responsible for paying their complete transportation and living expenses." Work for nothing but experience and the wild thrill of being in a theater with "real actors." It was called knocking at the gate.

I was to take over the three-hundred-seat Paul Bunyan Playhouse in Bemidji and he would continue to run the smaller playhouse at Gull Lake. I would organize the town's support for the Bemidji operation, staff it, run it, direct some of the plays, and act in some of them. When the debts were paid off he wanted us to have the Paul Bunyan Playhouse as our own.

Holyoke began to feel like the easier choice that summer because this adventure in the north woods was fraught with pitfalls. The choice Ruby and I were going to make had to be considered on practical issues. With the baby to worry about, there was too much riding on it. Bob admitted that it might turn out to be a twenty-four-hour-a-day job. But then I thought, maybe I could get John Sweet and his wife, Deana, to come and direct as well as act; and maybe Hank Sutton from Denison would take on the job of business manager as well as act in the plays. Three good actors, a second director, and a business manager. I had to stay calm and think clearly now. I needed to talk to Ruby.

Lee and I left for St. Jo, Missouri, on March 17 in Cliff Menz's Chevrolet station wagon. Our banged-up Old Faithful was getting a new roof, glass in its windows, and some inner organs replaced while we cranked the Chevy around Iowa and Missouri. When we set off I was pepped up and eager to work on our *Life with Father* scene that night, and for a while the hum of the road increased my excitement for it. But along the way, bitterness moved in. Silence in the car with Lee had become an enemy. Being alone like that with another person was sly torture.

But after the show and dinner we rehearsed the new *Life with Father* scene in my room, hoping it would get enough laughs to alternate with Mark Twain. Meanwhile, something disquieting had begun to occur to me about Bemidji. How to cast the plays? With me or John Sweet directing, we would have only four professional actors, and the apprentices would have to act the remaining roles. An amateur would stand out like a sore thumb. But the real question standing in the road was: Where do we want to go this summer? Do I play a variety of character roles or learn to keep my head down and play straight? Tagging along with this choice was another question: In what months to place the bookings by Ricklie and Howard next season and have enough time left to search for work in New York? We had to make a living. If Ruby couldn't tour, I'd have to do the shows with someone else, like Lee. I was cornered.

It had begun to snow. By the end of the show in Chariton the snowfall had turned steady. The following morning we had to backtrack 150 miles to Council Bluffs to pick up our newly repaired station wagon. The snow had heaped up on the road in some places to the hubcaps. Under the snow was ice. Tornadoes to the south had whipped up a powerful wind, and when I climbed out to put on the chains I had to work in stages because my hands went numb so fast. The most dangerous obstacles were the huge trailer trucks on the hills, which slid back down and jackknifed. If you got behind one of them and couldn't twist out of the way, you'd get crushed. So you waited at the bottom for a clear stretch and then accelerated through the snow to a speed that you hoped would get you to the top before losing traction. If the car in front of you lost momentum and began sliding back down, you ground your teeth and tried to dodge around it. One cannot imagine how fierce and terrible fifty-to-sixty-mile-an-hour wind gusts can be with ice particles in them. When I got out to check the chains, the wind bit so savagely at my skin I climbed back in the car.

Next morning the hotel clerk warned us not to leave for Chicago. "I've called the highway patrol and every road out of town is blocked." We said we'd give it a try. For fifteen miles on Route 6 we bounced and twisted around snowdrifts and then had to stop where two huge trailer trucks had made a wall across the road, one of them dangling over the edge of the embankment. Four hours out of Council Bluffs we struck a dry highway and raced 350 miles across the state of Iowa to the glorious accompaniment of Kirsten Flagstad's farewell concert with the New York Symphony Orchestra. She got the greatest ovation I had ever heard and we joined in, the two of us applauding her in our eager Ford station wagon, a tiny speck racing across America.

Chicago. Sandburg's big blue-collar town, rough and roaring. The Croydon seemed like coming home to me; even its cheerless clerk managed a twisted smile. Lee took off to Evanston to join her friends at Northwestern, so I was free and footless. My spirits bounded up and then the phone rang. It was my Jewish mother.

"Ricklie, you darling thing, you're in Chicago?"

"I stayed in town to catch you."

"Let's have dinner!"

"I can't. I have a four o'clock train to Terre Haute."

She told me she had a lot of Chicago dates lined up for next season, but since she still didn't understand what our new show was all about, it was hard to book it. "Something about 'Great Actors,'" she said.

"No, no, no." I explained it to her all over again, all the while knowing that she would lose the information somewhere in the recesses of her mysterious bag. It was fun to talk to her again, our dear friend, and she was wise.

"Hal, dear, how did you like your trip?"

"Oh, it was okay. But, gal, all I'm thinking about is getting home and staying there for good."

She laughed long at that and then said, "Hal, Ruby is awfully good for you."

"Woman, don't I know it?"

"But let me tell you now, you need her . . ."

"I know—"

"Hal, I know what it's like with you handsome young actors! You have to tour all over and meet these pretty young girls and work with them, and I know what that means, what you have to go through. But let me tell you, none of them will be as good for you as Ruby. Do you know why? Because she knows how to handle you!"

"Ricklie, you said it! Don't I know—"

"Now listen to me. She knows that your particular type has to be made to feel he's looked up to and that he's a wonderful guy, and he has to be flattered quite a lot. She *knows* you, Hal!"

"Ricklie, God, you're so right!"

"Ruby is a wise little woman, Hal. She knows what the score is and don't you think she doesn't."

"I know, I know—"

"And she knows how to handle you better than anyone. Harlowe and I were talking about you the other day. He thinks you can go a long way in your chosen profession if you stick together and *help* one another . . ."

"Yeah—"

". . . and don't forget that the little woman likes a pat on the shoulder once in a while."

"I won't, Ricklie. I got you. And you're a pretty smart gal, you are."

This was unexpected, even from Ricklie, and it set me wondering; did she and Ruby think I'd been fooling around? I had thought about it. Hell, yes. But even if I had tried, I don't think Lee would have gone for it. She was on her own trip, not looking for company. But pretending to be indifferent during the fast changes in those cramped, makeshift dressing rooms we had to share, where we stripped down to our underwear, trying to look the other way and not notice the curves on a female body, was a form of Puritan torture and an unnatural test of behavior for a man who was all those months away from his wife. At times I was wild with desire, but the specter of dishonor hung like a spider in the air. I had maintained the rigid pose of my Puritan forefathers, never straying from the path that was straight and narrow, but it was a bitter style of godliness.

Tonight I was on the town. What should I do? I could be a good boy and stay in the room and try to finish writing the opening scene for the new show, but I was stirred up and restless and wanted to *do* something. I dressed myself in a white shirt and bow tie and my blue suit and looked myself over in the mirror. In California I'd been gaunt and drawn but since then, eating more to get a leading man look for the summer, I was changed. I'd tipped the hotel scales at 170 pounds with my coat on; that was 165 stripped, the most I'd ever weighed, and at an even six feet it had filled out the hollow places on my frame and made me look . . . Should I say handsome? People said I was, but I didn't care for my looks. Too boyish. I was twenty-seven years old, for God's sake, why did I still look like a boy? I wanted to get old, get lines in my face; that would make me feel safer. So what about tonight? I was in Chicago, twelve thousand miles and twelve weeks down the road, and this boomtown was ringing in my ears. "Do something!" it said. "Move!"

I'd start by taking the typewriter to get fixed. The string had broken. That'd be a good thing, a fine thing, a useful thing. So I hit the street with the Royal. After that I went to a music store and rooted around until I found four long-play Leadbelly albums. I bought them for Ruby, a gift for her when I got home in four days. Then I picked up the typewriter and went back to the hotel and started a letter to Ruby. Between paragraphs I washed my clothes and spread my blue sweater on two towels on the floor to dry. I could exercise by jumping over it. What else? The paper said *Guys and Dolls* was in town. I could try to get a ticket—it would get me out of the room and onto the street—and *The African Queen* was playing here, too, and they said that was a good movie, or maybe I could just walk around and get rid of the frantic feeling; or maybe I ought to eat dinner at the Town House across the street for old times' sake. Yeah, good idea. I'd take the newspaper along to keep me company. Then I didn't know what I'd do. I'd think of something.

No, forget that. I called the Shubert Theatre and there were a few singles left so I hailed a taxi and said, "Shubert Theatre."

"I got three singles behind poles," said the guy in the ticket booth. I thought he said it in a tone used for people in the theater, not just someone off the street.

"No," I said. "I'll catch it in New York."

On the curb I studied the night and its music and the options open to me and thought, "I should treat myself to dinner at a classy eatery in the Loop." Then I remembered that I was an actor, poor, so I went into Thompson's Cafeteria instead. The waitress looked me over with a lingering, suggestive eye and she was worth a suggestive eye herself. We joked a bit and my blood got warmer. She asked how long I was in town and where was I staying. Whoa. "Just two nights. I'm at the Croydon on Rush Street."

"I know where that is."

Big pause. "Your cue," I thought, and backed off. "Yeah. It's the theatrical hotel." She gave me such a hot look before she swiveled away it almost frightened me. This was deep water for me. I was married.

By the time I hit State Street I was kicking myself. Most men on the road would not pass up an opportunity like that. What was the matter with me? Be a man, Holbrook! Jesus. All these months on the road, living like a monk, and more months ahead, maybe. How many? Grandma's blue-eyed baby boy, morals in check, slinking down State Street like a whipped dog with old man Satan nipping at his heels and grinning a devilish smile. "I'll get you yet, baby boy!"

There was always *The African Queen*. The hell with that. Uh-oh, there it was. The Silver Frolics! The time had come at last. We'd passed that place so many times, clucking in disapproval at the nearly nude posters. Now was the time to find out what went on in there. I walked inside and two beautiful blondes tore the coat off me and shoved a stub in my hand before I could protest that I was only going to have a drink and leave. They rubbed against me and breathed heavily. In the bar I got a seat and a beer and allowed my eyes to swing over to the scene onstage. There was so much flesh exposed up there I was embarrassed to be caught looking at it. I thought of my relatives, dead and alive, and wondered if the dead ones were watching me. The women did not have more than three and a half square inches of clothing on and the men had knives and pistols. I nearly spilled my beer trying to pour it into the glass without missing anything onstage. It was a Frankie and Johnny sort of thing with a good deal of leg fluttering and bending over, an orgy of sexual dramatics that went beyond anything I had seen before or ever wanted to see again.

Then came the stripper, far superior to anything at the Old Howard in Boston. She had flaming red hair and was built exactly the way any man would build her if he were putting her together piece by piece. She took an agonizing stretch of time getting to the stripping part, undulating around on high heels, fingering her limited wardrobe, which looked as if it might pop open here and there, maybe on the next bounce, as she strutted back and forth twitching and swirling and smiling at me—oh, it was me all right! Then she got down to business.

One thing after another flew off her like shingles in a hurricane and I can't describe any more because describing it wouldn't do the trick. I had switched to Scotch by then, so I can say with authority that she had the talents to fit the role. I gave her a round of applause and was surprised to find myself the only one clapping. Most of the men just sat there, hardly paying attention to her. What in hell has happened to the male population of the human race since I've been out west? This girl deserves a standing ovation. I ordered another Scotch and wondered how such a firmly put together young woman got into this sort of work. Most strippers I'd seen sagged in crucial areas. But then the next act came on, eight girls stumbling around in Hawaiian ragpicker costumes and a man in a black cape and pointed ears who seemed to be the Devil. He started to sing into a microphone about his being the Devil and how he was going to be purged from Evil by the Goodness of the Beautiful Creature. Then the Beautiful Creature came on and I got up and left. One look at her face was enough for me.

Out in the hall the two hat- and coat-check girls rubbed up against me again while I was carefully looking at my stub and trying not to appear drunk or undignified, looking very hard at my stub and reading the number over and over to myself. One of the blondes took it from me and said in a husky voice, "Would you like to see what's on the other side?" I said, "No, one side is enough, thank you." I should have been more clever, but I was concentrating on my balance. So she slipped me into my coat and breathed a cloud of perfume on me as I veered out the door. I walked off toward the Croydon and began talking to myself and roaring with laughter, telling myself that I really ought to take a night sometime and just be as wicked as hell because everyone was being so sexy and nice to me. A man passed, looking at me queerly, so I stopped laughing for fear he would try to pick me up or call the police or maybe knock me down. I retired to the Croydon with my morals still secure. The blue-eyed baby boy.

Two days and I'd be home. What would it be like? I wondered. Would I still be attractive to her? Sex would be out for a while—right? I mean, things would have to heal up, especially if she had a Cesarean delivery. That recovery would really take time and I'd go on living like a monk. Hell. Maybe I could talk to someone about that. But who?

Ruby had written that my letters had helped her understand me. How?

Now I feel needed, which I truly did not before. I felt all my talents were completely dwarfed by yours, whereas now I feel I

*have an important role to fill, loving you and being your WIFE
with all its implications. To make you happy and bolster your
morale and help develop your talents to their full capacities—that
is my job and I can think of nothing I love doing more.*

I found this hard to believe. Ruby was an achiever. The picture
of her playing the good little wife was okay for the stage, but as a
portrait of reality it shrank to the size of a joke. And yet I encouraged it in my response:

My dear Ruby,
*I can't tell you what a sensation of happiness you gave me. I'm
old-fashioned. I couldn't live happily with a woman who did not
want to be my wife more than anything else and the fountainhead
of our home. To have such a companion in you, actress and wife,
gives me more courage than I could have alone. My drive would
melt away without you.*

We were playing hide-and-seek. Hiding from the wave of reality
rolling toward us and seeking shelter in a fantasy that our life would
not be rudely altered. Our real-life roles from the beginning had
been joined by a life on the stage. That's what kept us together and
motivated us. Now it would not be Hal and Ruby Holbrook, the
actors in a play. It would be a version of real life with us playing
Mom and Dad.

The road back from California had been endless. In Chicago I
found that Lee was still a part of her college environment. In the
morning her college friend, Patty Preble, met us at the hotel for
breakfast. I would have much preferred to eat alone and might as
well have done so. Not being able to express rapture over the list of
Northwestern names and events that excited them, I realized that
my inability to do that was characterizing me as a social queer in the
eyes of Patty Preble. Then she made the decision to accompany us
to Joliet to see our show. Oh God! I thought, Give me shelter. Knowing glances fluttered back and forth throughout the drive down, like

hummingbirds in a feeding frenzy. I was an object of amusement. It came over me that I was being relegated to a chapter in the college psych book.

I knew that our Catholic college audience of girls would be putty in my hands, so I handled myself with confidence and properly bewitched them, all the time aware that my performance, as well as Lee's, was being subjected to a rigid and authoritative inspection by no less than a student of the School of Speech at Northwestern. I had made up my mind it would be a good one and we did *Hamlet*— the closet scene, the soliloquy, and the nunnery scene, the whole shebang at my command simply because I like committing suicide. The fact that "Jim Olsen did Hamlet brilliantly at Northwestern" did not weaken my resolve. I didn't care how brilliant the son of a bitch was.

Jim Olsen had put the role to rest for her. This was made clear. While I was out of the dressing room she may have whispered some hurried critical pearl into Lee's ear, but as far as allowing me any indication of whether she felt the show measured up to her standards, there was only a long pall of silence while we dressed. In the car I finally got her reaction. "Hal, I was telling Lee that you look really quite handsome onstage." This shot of complimentary shrapnel fell short.

Let's face it. Good show or bad, if you must see a performer afterward you have got to express enthusiasm. One does not ignore an actor. Good or bad, the job requires such an exposure of vulnerability that even Al Capone would drop his gun at such a time.

In her letter of March 20 Ruby had cautioned that I must "learn tolerance and humility," and in this she was right. I'd be struggling with the angels of Tolerance and Humility for years and years because the three of us never got along too well. Ruby had cast her vote for Bemidji but I was bending toward Holyoke. I did not feel ready yet for the apprentices. Ruby's argument for Bemidji touched upon the idea of "reaching for personal glory in a small place rather than a larger one."

"I don't think it's really personal glory we're after," I wrote. "I

have to succeed by my own standards and I need professional stimulation and a tougher arena for that. The personal glory melts away once
you've achieved it." Meanwhile, personal glory expired in Chicago.

It was ironic that I should feel lonely that last night in Chicago.
The appropriate ending to a journey of emotional deprivation. I had
begun to hold loneliness in awe. To respect it and to know that it
was in me like a stain. My goals were too far away. The success I was
dreaming of would never come, because no sooner had one achievement been reached than it would be diminished by the achieving
and I would look for more. So success was a dream, a drifting cloud
in a summer sky.

On Thursday, Lee and I would be in Fort Wayne trying out our new
Life with Father scene and then she would go home to Canton for
two days and I'd drive on to our little home on Summit Street where
my wife was waiting for me. The timetable was getting tighter. Our
baby's arrival was maybe a month away, and a show date in Olean,
New York, had been moved forward to April 24, dangerously close
to the baby's expected date of arrival. This was a blow. But it was a
$200 engagement and we needed the money. At the end of the week
I'd have that day-and-a-half reunion with Ruby in Granville before
Springfield, Ohio, on Saturday, and an extra day at home after that
because a Chicago date the following week was changed from Monday
to Tuesday. This chessboard maneuvering was making me nervous.
What if the baby didn't come when he was supposed to? Or she?

22

I drove into Granville in the evening with the lights twinkling, past the Presbyterian and Methodist and Baptist churches and the Opera House and the Aladdin Restaurant and Peoples State Bank, Rollie Thompson's photography studio and the grocery store and post office, turned left for two blocks and right on Summit Street to the middle of the block and left into the driveway leading right up to the door of our little home. By the time I got out of the car Ruby was holding the screen door open, rounder than I had ever seen her before and smiling at me. It was such a relief. I had never seen another pregnant woman who looked so lovely. She looked happy and composed. Thank God.

That first night was strange and new. Here was a person growing into two persons and moving too confidently, causing me to fear she'd bump into something and knock against the baby's little unborn head in such a way as to endanger the tiny brain. I was in a state of anxiety until Ruby explained that our child was safe in water, inside a sac, and then I worried how it breathed. Ruby had worked out in surprising detail the organization of our midget home. I never knew she was such a qualified commander in chief. And the whole town was her battalion. Ed and Louise, the Mahards, Doc and Alma Utter, the grocery man, the bank clerks, and over in Newark, Gay and Ev Reese and probably the mayor and the police department.

Opinions on the child's gender circulated through the town. This was going to be an arrival of royalty. I was nervous, but proud.

A letter from Carlton plunged us into a discussion of Bemidji-Holyoke soon after we had embraced the realities of being home together. Carlton had come through with some good roles. We agreed that to leave Holyoke before it had taught us all it had to offer would be a step back, and this goal had been far from reached. Ruby gave up her preference for Bemidji quicker than I had expected. A large factor had to be the choice of environment for the baby. Our relationship was going to undergo a crucial test and I'd be less distracted at Holyoke. We would be among friends there, and suddenly a house with a yard was being offered to us, not far from the theater. The tide had clearly turned. We heard from Dixie Campbell that her mother wanted to come east with us to help Ruby out with the baby, an astounding offer of friendship and concern that suddenly made me pause under the shadow of a warning: Would Ruby recover soon enough to handle the tensions we were about to encounter?

I would play a few good straight parts and Ruby was all for that. She was impressed with the improvement the extra weight had made in my appearance and she felt that something in me had matured, that I was more relaxed and less eager to impress. My most intriguing role was Uncle Desmonde, the woman-chasing French Canadian in *The Happy Time*, a play of lovable characters and emotional crises set in Ottawa in the 1920s. And in *Room Service*, that great farce, it looked as if the leading role of the zany producer, Gordon Miller, would go to me. So a letter I'd dared to write Carlton, telling him we were seriously considering an offer from Bemidji, had paid off. Ruby and I were to star in *Season in the Sun* and in *Gramercy Ghost* with Bert Tanswell. It was going to be Holyoke, but when I realized that I had replaced their young leading man, Gaylord Mason, I felt a sour mixture of shame and pride.

After the show in Springfield, Lee drove back to Granville with me for a day before she and I left for Chicago. Ed and Louise put her up. In the hours she spent visiting with us, talking mostly with Ruby, I was pretty silent. It felt strangely like having "the other woman"

present. A curtain of separation had drawn itself between Lee and me, and Ruby took note of my reticence. I tried to explain to her that its source was a change in me, that I no longer felt an eagerness to please everyone. That something in me had grown silent, and I hoped she would believe me. I think she suspected more.

Our drive for the Chicago show was an eight-hour session of meditation. Lee left to see friends on the North Shore and I walked along Michigan Avenue on an aristocratic spring evening, topcoat open and fluttering, enjoying the bright displays in the store windows and telling myself I was going to like being a New Yorker. At a music store I came up with an old recording of Bix Beiderbecke that would work well in the twenties scene in our new show.

On April 5 we played Western Reserve Academy in Hudson, Ohio. I went to my sister's grave at Crown Hill Cemetery under the tree that protected her, and I was astonished to find that there was no plaque, only a little number. Why had Howie not provided a memorial? Why? What a lonely sight, that little number buried in the grass on the quiet hillside of the dead. I wanted to spend a day beside her, but the next show was waiting to be played in Cincinnati, where she had lived in the brief term of her first marriage. I had to put my sister's grave behind me. I would put the plaque there myself.

When I arrived home we got sobering news. Ruby could not deliver the baby in the natural way. It was going to be a Cesarean section, an operation to remove our child because its head was not going to get through her pelvic area safely. Ruby appeared to absorb all this with calm detachment, so I did my best to copy her and believe the reassurances from her doctor that it was "an easy way to deliver." Yeah. Inside I was holding my guts together because the whole idea of an operation scared the wits out of me. I'd never had one, nor had anyone in my family except Alberta and it killed her, so they could assure us until the moon turned purple and it would not steady my nervous system. How Ruby could handle all this so benignly was beyond me. Was she aware that this would shrink the time for her recovery before rehearsals began in Holyoke? It would surely postpone our lovemaking for a long time. In a week I would

receive the following letter from her, one of a very few existing now, written the day after I left her for the East Coast.

APRIL 15TH, TUESDAY
NEWARK, OHIO

Hello my darling—
One whole day and a half has passed without anything terribly eventful having developed, my sweet, dear, hunk o' man. Mama is feeling great and getting awfully used to this C section business . . .

Dorothy tells me I'm to report at the hospital between 3 and 3:30 p.m. on Sunday. I will stay there overnight and the operation will be Monday morning. Now dear, there's no need for you to rush home in order to drive me over there. I think I shall make arrangements with Doc Utter—just to have someone with me. However, even going by taxi would be all right. When you arrive home you may come visit me and probably stay until it's time for me to sleep. Call Dorothy or Dr. Avery and they will tell you what room I'll be in, etc. And there will be a surgeon in attendance, Dr. Roland Jones. Gay says he's a fine surgeon. Guess our bill will be a little steeper, my sweet. But probably the total may not be any more than what we had anticipated before Dr. Avery amazed us with his quotation of $90.

She goes on to ask me to paint the bassinet that Gay has come up with. White, and with non-toxic paint. She hasn't left anything out, like a regimental commander getting ready for battle.

Got a wonderful long sleep last night—perfectly relaxed. S'long, my sweet. Hope the shows are going well. Drive carefully and come home to your family. We'll expect you around seven p.m. Sunday.
My dearest love—Ruby

The confidence she had—was it real? I felt as if I were the one walking along the edge of a precipice and had to be careful, careful,

careful all the time. I *had* to keep standing and I was going to do that, damn right I was . . . it's just that . . . if anything happened to Ruby . . . God, please . . . not that!

Early Monday morning I had left Granville to pick up Lee at her home in Canton, and the Pennsylvania Turnpike shot us eastward at seventy miles per hour to Lansdowne on the fringe of Philadelphia for another women's club. Lee and I must have wormed a lot of rot out of our systems at home because we were at ease again on the drive up the New Jersey Turnpike, now open all the way to the George Washington Bridge. As we drove through the biotic smells of Elizabeth and Newark along the necklace of new roadways, sparkling through the night like glittering lanterns and rising high over factories and streets and rivers and sweeping low into the marshes, the approaching skyline of the great city was something to see at seventy miles per hour. The marvelous, challenging city full of dreams and aspirations greeted us with a roar of sound as we rose up out of the Lincoln Tunnel.

Somewhere in this jungle I had to find a home. An apartment, far from the tradition of Granville. Cheap, but a safe little nest for a family of three fresh from the Welsh Hills with a stop for the summer in Holyoke. I dropped Lee off at Lovey Powell's apartment on West Fifty-third Street. Lovey had acted at the summer theater in Granville two years before, and I left the two Northwestern graduates to gab about things. I called Dick Corson and Mitch Erickson and took the subway downtown to Prince Street and spent the rest of the evening getting them up-to-date on Ruby and the imminent debut of our baby. They had saved their copy of the apartment section in the Sunday *Times* to give me a picture of what was available. Rents were so much higher than in Granville. There was the possibility of an apartment on West 108th Street in the building where Leah Ashbrook's friends Ruth and Robert Williams lived. I left the tiny cold-water flat on Prince Street ($29 a month) and walked the forty-seven blocks uptown to the Bristol Hotel to get my head clear.

In the morning, April 16, Lee and I played the high school in Summit, New Jersey. Dull audience. Utah was smarter. Thursday

morning the seventeenth, only five days from our baby's arrival, after the show at Albright College in Reading, Pennsylvania, we drove to Gordon Condit's house in Maplewood and took the train into New York, where Gordon and I had dinner with Leah, who was as enchanting as ever. We went our separate ways for the theater. I saw *The Fourposter* with Hume Cronyn and Jessica Tandy. Just two in the cast, a captivating play with endearing moments between the Cronyns, but I felt it was being played too hard for laughs. This was a play Ruby and I could do.

On Friday I was back in New York to see Audrey Hepburn in *Gigi.* Her starlight seemed to shine brighter in film than onstage. Saturday I checked on some apartments uptown with Ruth and Robert before leaving for an evening show in a steel mill town in eastern Pennsylvania. Bethlehem. The last show before the baby came, and a star was in the sky. I was an excited wreck. On Sunday the twentieth I tore across Pennsylvania on the turnpike, dropped Lee off in Canton, and tore down the state through New Philadelphia and Coshocton to the Newark Hospital. There was a one-day delay for some more tests. On Tuesday morning our baby was born, all eight pounds and six ounces. Rollie Thompson put a sign in his window at noon: IT'S A GIRL.

Granville could stop holding its breath. Late that night I sat down and wrote out my feelings to our friends.

APRIL 22ND, 1952

Dear Bertie and Jean and Carlton:

Well, by George, this is really something! Here I am a father and I don't really feel much different, except that I want to work and succeed more. Never been so frightened in all my life as I was from the time they wheeled Ruby into the operating room until she came out and I saw her washed out little face. I could have cracked up for sure, she'd looked so chipper going in. The first thing she said was: "It's really a girl and she's alive and everything?"

Harold

That little tyke is not a day old and she's already a human being.
It knocks me out. She's got puffy cheeks and blue eyes and looks
kind of like she's going to sneeze and once she did when we had her
in the room. It scared me silly. I remembered reading somewhere
that your heart stops beating every time you sneeze, but she kept
breathing okay. So I did, too. She sure is healthy looking. You
should see some of the others. If I was their father they'd scare the
hell out of me! I can hardly wait to wheel her around in a buggy.

Her name was Victoria. We thought that was special, too. It came
from the affection we and our audiences always felt for the Victoria
and Albert scene in our show, the scene in which the young queen
sees a man shave for the first time. Our daughter's middle name was
mine and my father's, and it was the surname of my great-uncle,
George H. Rowe, the actor who had left me his costume trunk in a
gesture of respect when he was dying. It was a returning gesture of
respect and perhaps a hopeful connection to an older generation in
a family broken apart. Victoria Rowe Holbrook was her name. She
was born on the day before Shakespeare's birthday.

Two days after our daughter made her debut I was on the road
again for that date in Olean for $200, which had been moved for-
ward to the twenty-fourth of April, and Victoria had timed her entrance perfectly. But leaving her and her mother felt like a kind of
desertion. The next day I raced home, a six-hundred-mile round-trip,
and wrote again to Bertie:

We figured on a girl all along. I knew Ruby kind of wished for a
girl—"they're more familiar to me." A boy would have been sort
of like I'd got what you're supposed to get, but having a girl gives
me the feeling that I've got something extra.

Ruby started walking last night. She gets to hold the baby and
feed her, but she won't even let me breathe on the kid. Wait until
we get that little thing home—boy, I'd like to see them stop me
from poking it then.

A day later I wedged myself behind the wheel of the Ford again in pursuit of money, driving through angry sheets of rain along that tortured landscape the ancient glaciers had wrenched into the Appalachian Mountains of West Virginia. It was a Halloween landscape again, the two-lane road a crippled ribbon of slippery blacktop with not more than one three-hundred-yard straightaway on the whole trip. The same route where Lee and I had begun our uneasy partnership one moonlit night nearly four months before and been nudged aside by the butane truck, a land of spectral magic then, grim and dark on this ghoulish night of rain, and the wet road slowed me down. It would take nine and a half hours to drive the three hundred roller-coaster miles to our destination down near the Cumberland Gap.

I've been very cautious today, too anxious to get back to Mummy and my baby to be daring. Honey, you looked so pretty this morning. I'm looking forward to having you back with me all flat and gorgeous again. I must admit I'm a little on the starved side—but I can hold out for the required time remaining, don't worry! My dear, I don't think you should leave the hospital until you really feel rested and strong. I know I seemed to urge you the other way, but that was only to get your mind set on moving around a lot which is the way to get well fast now.

I was worrying about our return to the marriage bed—would it be a successful reunion? Could it match the dreamworld of longing this trip had planted in my head? And I was thinking ahead to Holyoke and our rehearsals. Seven weeks away and a hushed circuit inside my brain was tapping out worry signals.

The next day Lee and I did the show in the afternoon and headed back up the roller-coaster trail to Granville. The day after that we drove northeast to Warren, Pennsylvania and the next day, May 1, we sped eastward to the terminus of our twenty-one-thousand-mile journey to every crotch, armpit, and breastbone of America, driving four hundred miles with a stop for a matinee in Rochester and com-

pleting the journey that night in Manhattan. I checked in at the Bristol. Just one more show to go.

On April 30 Ruby had left the hospital and was staying with the Reeses. She wrote her last letter to me:

My dearest—Father of our little girl—a little calmer today, this new mother, but still elated over the miracle of becoming a parent. Every fiber in my body is tuned to a fine song and I am deeply happy.

Your letter received at the hospital yesterday was beautiful, my darling. Tears of happiness sprang to my eyes as I read it. I am so proud to be the mother of your little girl. I could hunt the whole world over and never find a man who suits me more—a man so keenly aware of life; a man very sensitive to each moment, else how could he record the beautiful and sad notes with such depth, perception and understanding. My darling, the beautiful words you put on paper are ours to have always. I am determined now to keep a scrapbook of every letter, beginning with Christmas Eve through to this last beautiful one.

I think Ruby felt those emotions truly at that time, as I tried to feel the emotions I expressed, but could we have been composing letters to each other to sustain the pageant of a storybook life together that blossomed mainly in our imaginations? This is not how we talked in person.

I weighed in this morning at exactly 119 lbs. I can't believe it—from 137 to 119 in one week! Gee, it's fun to be flat again— feel real sexy, too—something I haven't felt for some time. Now my body is awakening to the old urges. How wonderful it will be to have you close to me again, my very own. I'm afraid I shall tremble like a bride.

I couldn't escape the feeling that we were going to be performing roles in a play, and I may have been getting stage fright.

And so, my sweet, to our reunion on Saturday Eve. Our baby
sends her deepest contentment to you—how she will love being
held by her Daddy and have her lambs wool head caressed by
Daddy's cheeks. She's getting impatient so hurry gently home.
Your Wife And Mistress Ruby.

The wanderer was home. And so were his baby and his wife. I joined Ruby's battalion as an obedient and eager soldier packed full of dedication. I learned how to hold Victoria and feed her the bottle and help her burp and before that prepare the formula and wash and sterilize the bottle and the nipple afterward. I washed all the dishes. I learned to change the little helpless child and to remove the discharge and clean her little bottom and accept the fact that it was all right for me to be looking at a naked female. I gave up my bunk bed for Victoria Rex in her bassinet and slept on the pullout sofa. All Ruby had was her own three-foot-wide bunk bed built into the other side of our eleven-by-six-foot bedroom closet with bureau in between. Because of the operation, it would be a while before we could share a bed together.

When Ruby was gone to the grocery store or post office and our tiny permanent visitor cried, and cried mightily I may say, I took command. I felt the diaper for wetness and looked inside for stuff there; I looked for an unlatched pin; I held my little daughter and patted her gently and wondered if she could be hungry after drinking lunch an hour before. I wished Ruby would come home and tell me what to do. I paced up and down the living room of our garage— four paces, about-face and four paces, about-face and four more. It only seemed to ramp up the vocal crescendo. When the howling rose toward King Lear on the heath I felt panic and a dreadful sense of failure. I grabbed up Dr. Spock and clawed through the pages for help. "Don't worry. Is she hungry?" No, Doctor. "Is she wet?" Nope. "Maybe she has colic." Rub the stomach? A burp would clear out the colic, but she won't burp when she's howling. Oh, disgrace. Disgrace and failure and a feeling of being cornered.

Harold

The worst was when she stopped breathing at night. I rarely slept, I only listened to her breathing, and when it stopped I launched out of bed in a fit of terror and groped around the bedroom door to bend over the bassinet with my ear close to my little daughter's nose and mouth. Then she started breathing.

"Hal?"

"Yes, Ruby?"

"Are you all right?"

"She's breathing."

"I know, dear. You can go back to bed."

"Thank you."

Being a father took more training than I had ever imagined. And time. It took time. Lots of it. Lots and lots of it. You couldn't call it a part-time job. This was the first revelation of fatherhood. Any idea I had of pursuing other activities, like writing our new show, was sliding away.

I did get to go on errands sometimes. The first item I purchased was an electric heater because the gas one that had warmed up the place for years might asphyxiate Victoria, and when that possibility arose I spent our second night at home sniffing for gas as well as checking on Victoria's breathing. The next day we had an electric heater, which kept Victoria and her mother warm, but not me on the sofa. But that was nothing. Spring was in bloom and it was warming up in the daytime and high time to get our baby out in a carriage and wheel her around town. First we had to buy the carriage, an awesome expense. I was midway through adding up our gold deposits at the Peoples State Bank when Ruby reminded me of a resource I had overlooked: unemployment insurance. If I applied right away the check would start coming in two weeks—$25 a week plus $2 dependency benefit for Victoria. So she was already earning us money and barely two weeks old! Then I thought, what about Ruby? She was unemployed, too. (Whadya mean she couldn't work yet? She could walk, couldn't she?) We were going to be rich—$54 a week and we didn't have to go to the office. Then my conscience began to roll over.

"Ruby, don't you think there's something wrong about taking money for not doing anything?"

"Not if it's going to feed the baby."

"Yeah, but . . . last week I earned four hundred and fifty dollars."

"And how much of that is yours?"

"Uh . . . after expenses and Lee's share . . . about two hundred and twenty dollars."

"There, you see."

"What?"

"The government owes you money. You lost two hundred and thirty dollars."

"How—"

"When you gave it to Lee and the hotels and gas stations. They all pay taxes. Some of that money is supposed to come back to you when you're not working."

"Right."

"You see?"

"Yeah. It still feels wrong."

"Why?"

"I'll feel ashamed standing in line at the unemployment office in Newark. People will think I can't support my family."

"They'll be standing in line, too."

I saw that I had to do it, so I drove the Ford over to Newark with my pride tossing insults at me for nine miles and got in line at the unemployment office.

"Occupation?"

"I'm an actor."

"No, I mean when you work."

"Ah. I work at acting."

"Oh."

"I've been working since January but now I'm unemployed."

"Can you do anything else? Besides the movies?"

"Well. I've painted stuff."

"Good. I'll put you down as a housepainter. Maybe something will come in and you can work."

"Good."

"Okay."

"So . . . do I get the unemployment money?"

"Until a house-painting job comes in, you get it."

We got the baby buggy and a couple of warm blankets and dressed Victoria up in her knitted booties and hat set from Beryl and Stew and a pretty dress from Louise and Ed, checked the temperature, and rolled down the sidewalk. Getting past the corner where the football coach lived was a challenge because Woody Hayes sat on his porch and never smiled at anything, especially actors and their offspring. Once past this grim lookout, we had smooth sailing for two blocks to the corner of Broadway, never missed a smile, and the march from there a block and a half into town was triumphant. It was a royal presentation and was short only on banners, bugles, and drums. But it was pretty taxing for Ruby, so Rollie Thompson drove her home with Victoria in her arms and I wheeled the carriage back empty, the long way around so Woody Hayes wouldn't see me and think I'd gotten rid of the kid because she couldn't make the team.

Leaving Granville was not going to be easy. We were going to be cutting ourselves loose and I was damn well going to have to measure up. I could try to imagine what living in a house would be like, but acting in plays, staying up late at night learning lines week after week, and taking care of our baby had a nightmare feeling to it. Uncertainty set in when I needed confidence.

Ruby must have been shadowed by the same uncertainty. And I was worried about our sexual reunion, fearful of harming her after the operation. But we were silent about these feelings. We hid them from each other. We were afraid to confront them.

A lot of our possessions would go into storage and be sent to New York later when we found a home. We had less than $600 in the bank for the big leap into the future. I got pretty desperate about working on our new *Twentieth Century Show*. The interruptions

stopped my creative impulses just when they wanted to fly and that was a frustration I found hard to accommodate. I knew I would have to get used to this in our new life, but I resented it. I hid the feeling, but I didn't know where to put it.

In the second week of June, Dixie Campbell's mother, who was also named Dixie, had finished her teaching job in Dayton early enough to join our departure caravan. She would live with us and be our sainted godmother through thick and thin. Jean and Carlton had maneuvered the schedule to let me out of the first play, *O Mistress Mine*, and Ruby would not be in the second play, *Second Threshold*, which I'd begin rehearsing on June 16. With the operation slowing Ruby's recovery, this schedule gave us an extra seven days to get set for the summer racetrack.

Early in the morning of a Wednesday in June, with the coolness still hugging the ground, we were ready to go. I had loaded the station wagon up so high it was necessary to open a chasm in the mountain of luggage so I could see through the rearview mirror. Dixie's mother would sit in back with the bassinet, and Ruby would hold Victoria up front with me. Our first stop would be the local gas station, where I would force more air into the tires. They looked depressed from the load and possibly from having overheard me issue the discouraging news that we would drive the seven hundred miles to Holyoke in one day.

We'd said goodbye to everyone the day before—all our friends. But saying goodbye to our little home, the rustic white garage surrounded by green things and the sweet new colors of spring flowers reaching up, cheerful to the last, was an awful wrench. We stood together and looked and looked until our eyes blurred with tears and then we climbed into our chariot with Victoria in her mother's arms and Dixie Campbell's mother riding shotgun behind us, and drew away from the safety of Granville.

23

It was going to take a while to get our heads straight. The house was someone else's. We did not shoot the family and cement them over in the cellar, and they weren't going to kick us out in the middle of the night, so calm down. Calm down. Nice house. Big. Nice yard. Nice street. The trees were nice. It was okay for us to be here. The family had gone to Ogunquit for the summer. We were damn lucky to have such a roomy place to camp down in, strange or not. Victoria didn't mind at all. "Great spot, Mom and Dad," she was trying to tell us by blowing bubbles and smiling. "We'll be fine here. Relax."

Ruby seemed unusually focused. She and Dixie Campbell's mother jerked the place into shape in short order and liberated the supermarket of a large part of its inventory while I worried about the physical toll on my wife. We had a big job on our hands. We began to eat real meals at a dining table, with Gorham silverware. Sitting at the head of the table with Ruby and Dixie's mother and our baby, surrounded by framed pictures on polished walnut tables and multi-colored rugs all over the floors, I commenced to feel like a banker. This was living on a higher social scale. The house went on upstairs, too. Three bedrooms. I had to force myself to belong to this house and the more I felt like a banker the more I felt a secret distrust for myself. Actors were not reliable people like the ones who lived in this house. It was going to take an effort to go play silly games with them in that dusty rehearsal room.

When I walked into rehearsal they were all there. John O'Connor, Bert Tanswell, Nancy Wells, Mac Gress, and someone new, Gloria Hoye. Immediately I did not feel like a banker. She was slim and finely banked from shoulder to toe, curved like a ski slope; she had a movie star face, big dark eyes, and lips that drew my attention because in the play I was going to kiss them. I was a leading man now. The father in me fled in a panic and there I was, all alone, an actor with insecurities at home and in the rehearsal room.

The play, *Second Threshold* by Philip Barry, read less self-consciously clever than those other plays of his I'd struggled through, like *You and I* at Denison. The characters were emotional and the dramatic crisis pulled you in—the decision of an estranged daughter to save her disillusioned father from destroying himself. I was in love with the daughter, Gloria—I mean Miranda—and this was my big test because Carlton and Jean had thrown me into the center ring as a romantic young leading man in my first play out of the box and I'd had barely enough time to recover my balance from the ego-smashing captivity of four months on the road with a silent and willowy blonde. My feelings had been a shock to me. I had been so rigidly faithful to Ruby in thought and action, never allowing my imagination to stray into sexual clover with another woman. I had slammed the door shut on those feelings until life put me in the front seat of a station wagon with this sexy-looking girl. That's when my Puritan ancestors lost their grip on my imagination.

An actor's little gold mine is his secret nest of feelings, born of the way life has treated him and how he has chosen to respond to it. When he reaches in there for help in playing a scene, the emotion he wants may have gone into hiding because it's scared. That was my case. I had been safe when I could hide behind a character, but now I had to let those private feelings out to play Toby, who was going to stop Miranda from throwing herself away on an older suitor by making her fall in love with him. I mean me. It's very personal and you can't shut down your sexual yearnings and pull it off. Mine had been scorched by the experience with Lee and confused by my temporary status as a monastic father, and out of this emotional imprisonment

something had happened to me and it was soul shaking and scary. I was going to be attracted to other women.

The desperate season of self-denial on the road had released a devil in me that had been hiding in captivity for seven years. Now I had to bring the devil out of hiding. Right now, in one week. Somehow I managed to pull it off well enough to fool the critics, but not me. "The resourceful Hal Holbrook makes the role of the observer and family friend to whom the girl eventually turns, a pillar of strength. He is humorous, easy and frank." Okay. To help assure the Guilds they had done well to give me this chance, the Holyoke paper backed up Miss Mace's review by saying I was "especially good, bringing warmth and understanding to the confused intellectuals." So a confused actor pretending he understood himself and other confused people was making progress in a confusing profession.

Then it was our turn, Ruby and me, working together in *Gramercy Ghost*. We rehearsed in the daytime and I performed in *Second Threshold* at night while Dixie's mother took over the care of our baby. I could see this worried Ruby and plucked at her confidence. She couldn't hide that. Our baby was barely ten weeks old and it worried me. On Sunday, the day off, while the whole cast cavorted around a swimming pool made available by a sainted supporter of the theater, Victoria visited us in her mother's arms and was the center of oohs and aahs and gentle touches from our tenderhearted comrades. I remember watching Ruby showing her off and knowing what a clash of emotions must be surging through her, because motherhood was a role touching deep, deep emotions and now she was taking on another one of much less consequence.

As we began rehearsing *Gramercy Ghost* the actors were quiet witnesses, too—the younger ones like Mac Gress spreading cheer and concern; John O'Connor and his wife, Jackie Paige, polite and kind, a wealth of understanding etched in the creases life had worn into their faces; Ed Fuller, new this week and watching carefully; and Jean Guild and our director, Dorothy Crane, a little edgy about moving things along. And then Bert Tanswell, our friend playing the charming ghost of the title, the actor doing his job, working for

laughs, and carefully observing us. There was something ironically sweet about the sly efforts of his ghost to bring our characters in this play together—Ruby and me. It was like an unplanned vote of confidence the play had asked him to deliver.

Gramercy Ghost required from the actors a spirit of fun and the craft to deliver it, which Bert and Ed Fuller took care of. This was the kind of pure theatrical fun that taught actors how to regale audiences with laughter in those long-ago days before people got into the tense habit of worrying about when the next war would break out. Ruby played the heiress with "complete ease" and the Holyoke paper said we were "an attractive team." So far so good.

We had delightful character roles in *The Silver Whistle*, which Joe Ferrer had carried to victory in New York; and before Ruby and I took on our biggest challenge for the summer, the lead roles in *Season in the Sun*, I did a bit part in *A Streetcar Named Desire* with Miriam Stovall as Blanche, Si Oakland as Stanley, Nancy Wells and Ed Fuller as Stella and Mitch. To do this eloquent play with one week of rehearsal was a quixotic challenge and yet such challenges were undertaken in summer stock and sometimes the results were surprising. Even riveting, if you had a play like *Streetcar* and gifted actors who fit the roles. A production could catch fire from its own insecurity and achieve a spontaneous life that mesmerized an audience. I felt it onstage playing Pablo Gonzalez in the poker game, mustache, accent, trying to keep my head down while the crushing wave of this great play was building up behind me. I would find in the acting classes of New York a mountain of scorn for actors in summer stock. I thought those drama savants were fools. The daring and the talent and the fun that broke loose while sweating out a new performance week after week could teach you a lot if you didn't think you were above it all.

Ruby and I had passed up the post-performance happy hours at Jean and Carlton's house because we were anxious to get home to our baby and relieve our greathearted nanny, Dixie's mother. Instead of sipping beer and learning lines with the help of a company of comrades, we worked to absorb our words for *Season in the Sun*

in the quiet house we were trying to call home, with no prop of convivial fun to sustain us. Our preparation was done in isolation. Maybe that's what misled us. Sometimes actors don't foresee the emotional forces that will assail them in a play. Wolcott Gibbs had written a disturbing play, amusing and funny at times, but sour; and the sourness grew until it poisoned the marriage of the couple we were playing. The sourest note of all was a blonde. I don't think it ever occurred to me that there might be a trap for us in this play.

In *Season in the Sun*, George and Emily Crane have come to a beach cottage on Fire Island for the summer. He's a writer on the staff of *The New Yorker* magazine and wants to start a new life. He has quit drinking, quit the magazine, and is writing a book railing against the rootless excesses of the New York intellectual tribe, the drinking and sleeping around. His wife thinks he's deceiving himself and wryly tells him so; she can no longer humor his irrational switch to a comfort zone inhabited by straitlaced people who keep dropping in and spreading a pall of uptown mendacity. And then a blonde in shorts and halter waltzes in on the prowl with George's old drinking buddy from their wild days in Paris. The friction between Ruby's character and mine becomes more abrasive and deadly as the evening ratchets along. Finally she takes our two kids and goes into town to a hotel. The blonde stays and I start drinking again.

Rehearsals are a sweatbox of conceiving a character until you feel reality taking over. The emotional reality of the play is now fighting with the emotional reality of real life, and the runaway forces in the character can subdue your feelings about who you are, where you are, and to whom you're truly committed. If the actor playing your antagonist is in fact your wife, it will unscramble feelings you may have folded up and hidden away, and if there's a blonde in the picture it can tap into dangerous fantasies. The cutting edge of scorn with which Emily finally slashes George in the play wasn't fun. The subliminal wounds had come out of hiding.

Ruby entered the arena of our biggest test that summer just three months after delivering a baby by Cesarean section. A normal birth is enough to unsettle the hormonal balance of any woman. The phys-

ical changes she has fought through for nine months can bring on a term of depression and silent suffering while her body comes back to its remembered shape and her confidence in herself is slowly repaired. An operation to remove the child is an invasive trauma, and if she is a sensitive woman, she will be frightened and reluctant to discuss her feelings, and few men have a grain of understanding about them. I was not among the few. Even if Ruby had wanted to talk to me about it, that may not have pulled my attention back from its intense focus on the play and trying to score with a strong performance. I think Ruby held her feelings in and did the play.

It was not a big winner with the audience. We had been such a success as a stage team at the Springfield Women's Club the year before, we'd already been rebooked for next season. Sour grapes was not what the Mountain Park audience expected from us. The fact that the acting challenge in *Season in the Sun* was worthy of attention did not cut the mustard. "*Season in the Sun* is not a play for the kiddies," Louise Mace wrote in the *Springfield Union*.

Daytimes, while I rehearsed for the next play, Ruby took care of Victoria and tried to rest up for the buzz saw of our evening performance. The final two shows were on Saturday, a matinee and evening. We came home from the matinee and suddenly something went wrong. Dixie's mother had greeted us at the door with Victoria in her arms and we kissed our child. Ruby said, "Please take her upstairs." I waved bye-bye to the baby and turned around. Ruby had gone into the kitchen and was pacing back and forth. "I can't go on."

"What?"

She was sobbing. Then she shouted, "I can't do it! I can't go on! I can't! I can't! I can't!" It all broke open, the coiled-up feelings she'd been hiding, they just unwound and crashed out of her in a rush and then she ran upstairs to the bedroom. The shock of what was happening rooted me to the floor. She'd told me she couldn't go on. The final performance . . . Saturday night . . . a full house . . . eighteen hundred people. No understudy. To cancel a performance . . . it was unthinkable to me. We had gone onstage in every corner of America under the whole range of emotional tensions and

now all I could think was, How do we get through this night? We have to. I should have followed her, but my mind was fixated on survival, as it had been on the road in Arkansas with the station wagon upside down in the ravine. How do we get to Dumas?

I tried to make my brain work. Should I call Jean and Carlton? Oh God, our goose would be cooked for sure. I must wait and think, maybe Ruby would change her mind. But what kind of a show could she give? Would she break down on the stage and would that terrible cry "I can't go on!" erupt out of her again?

Dixie's mother came back down the stairs.

"Where is Ruby?"

"She's lying down, Hal."

"God. How is Victoria?"

"Ruby is holding her. They're lying down."

"Oh God."

"You've both been working very hard."

"Yes . . . oh God."

"I think she's just worn out, Hal. She'll be all right in a while. Let her rest."

"It's . . . five-fifty. Half hour is seven-thirty. I don't know what . . . I have to call Carlton and Jean and tell them—"

"Wait a while. Let her rest."

"Don't call?"

"Not now."

"Okay."

She started putting some dinner on. How could we eat it? The minutes were ticking away. I had to go upstairs. I could lie down with Ruby and maybe that would comfort her. She was on her back on the bed with Victoria's little hand feeling around her face. I lay down beside them.

"Did you call anyone?" she said.

"No. Not yet."

"I'll get ready in a minute. Just let me stay here for a while."

"Sure, Ruby." The baby was making little sounds. "I'm sorry, Ruby. It's too much."

"No. I'll do my duty. I won't let us down."

And of course she didn't. She went through the show as if nothing had happened, while I watched her closely. Less than a year before, she had broken down in our motel room in Mississippi and declared "I can't go on." Locked herself in the bathroom. I was frightened again, about us and our life together. Could our precious team go on? Would it end? I tried to shut my mind against these thoughts and think of Ruby, but they stormed me for answers. I reassured myself that Ruby had always been the calm one, the strong and stable one, and that she would pull through and be fine again, but now I knew I should never have let her go back to work so soon. A terrible guilt was rising in me. The following week was a godsend because she was free to be with Victoria. No play and no rehearsals. I had a role in *The Luck of Caesar*, but my mind wandered toward our future in New York. What was it going to be like?

Then I had to turn to Uncle Desmonde in *The Happy Time*. "This should be one of the biggest weeks ever at the Mountain Park Casino," wrote the *Holyoke Transcript*. "The Valley Players are putting on *The Happy Time* . . . a wonderful show . . . a hilarious comedy of fond memories of a French-Canadian family. Last night's audience loved them and it is hard to see how anyone could fail to do the same." The young son Bibi is led down the grand path of approaching French manhood by his older brethren, tutored in the ways of women, wine, and morality. Grandpa explains to him that achieving manhood is a matter of the glands. Uncle Desmonde, the traveling wine salesman who has laid waste the female population of Canada, displays a succession of garters as treasured trophies of each conquest and gives Bibi his copy of *La Vie Parisienne*. And Papa, in a memorable scene late in the play, explains to his young son the meaning of true love, and that desire for a woman is not evil, but natural. It is only evil when the reason for the desire is evil.

"Our own favorite in the lavish outlay of comic parts here is Hal Holbrook's utterly engaging Uncle Desmonde, dapper, flirtatious and French to the fingertips." It was to Nancy Wells as Mignonette that Desmonde addressed his amorous attentions. Like a handsome

bull following the graceful turns of the toreador flicking her dust cloth around the room, he uses his bewitching talents in the art of wooing to entrap her. Until that summer of 1952 I had rarely ever been cast as the romantic lover. I had played character roles unless I was playing opposite Ruby. She was always the object of my desire. Then Lee came along and took her place, onstage and off in the close companionship of the dressing room, and something I had not planned for began to emerge. Desire. The natural desire to touch another woman that Grandpa talked to Bibi about. It was a shock and it became a torture for me because I denied it. A battle began, the male animal struggling against the vows I had promised to keep. In *The Happy Time* I had to act out the desire as Desmonde, and the question haunted me: Was it evil? The zone of safety that had bound me to Ruby was beginning to come apart while the disordered emotions we were experiencing kept us physically isolated.

During the daytime I had been rehearsing the lead role of Gordon Miller in *Room Service*, that gorgeous farce with a cast of Damon Runyon characters trying to get a theatrical production on. At Fort Belvoir I'd played the playwright, Leo, which Mitch Erickson was now taking on (what a good actor!), and Bert was funny as Faker, the role I'd played at Culver. I was overconfident going into the rehearsal week, but pretty soon I didn't feel so swell. I was in a shark tank. The cast around me were daring and funny. It took some of the wind out of me, but I recovered. "One of the best performances of the season." (Mace) "It would be difficult to single out any individual as being outstanding." (Northampton *Gazette*) So it was a home run for everyone, an ensemble piece, and I was part of the ensemble. Finally fitting in and learning pretty fast.

I had the days free that week and so did Ruby because we had not been cast in the next play, so the week became an oasis in which we got to know ourselves again and could spend time together as the parents of a tiny child. I got to hold Victoria and tickle her, push her down the street in the buggy and enjoy her welcome smile, and marvel at how such a little human being could maintain her confident manner in the presence of a mother and father so tensely wound up

about each other and the road ahead, that big, intimidating battle-field called New York. Our surface behavior seemed calm, no more emotional crises, but I know that my entire body was wired for trouble and I was trying that week to send it messages of hope. Our four-month-old child accepted that and smiled at me. What feelings Ruby may have been hiding I hoped would go away.

In that week a plan was formulated for Ruby to leave Holyoke early and take Victoria to Canada and stay at her sister Beryl's home while I did the final play of the season and then drove into New York to prepare the apartment Ruth and Bob had found for us in their building at the corner of West 108th Street and Amsterdam Avenue. It was a sensible plan and a relief to know I'd be free to get that crucial task done before they moved down to New York. I wanted it to be clean and perfect. But I felt discarded. We had always done things together.

Two plays left, *The High Ground* and *I Like It Here*, and our summer employment ended. But we had been made a part of the theatrical family. Ruby and Victoria boarded the bus for Hamilton, Ontario, and our greathearted friend and support, Dixie Campbell's mother, left for Ohio. She had pulled us through. When the final curtain came down I packed up the station wagon and turned south for New York, praying that our life together would not go up in flames.

24

Mainly I remember the dirt, a fine black dirt like miniature sand, that spread over the window ledges and moved down over the metal radiator cover to the floor. It crept everywhere like a black plague, and my first battle in New York City was to get rid of it. Wipe it away, this ugly scum of dirt that covered the floors and walls and windowsills of our new home and filled me with disgust and insecurity.

At the end of the block on Broadway was a hardware store with a Jewish name that looked as if it sold everything but submarines. First I had to buy a metal bucket and a scrub brush and detergent soap and some rags and a broom and dustpan—this was getting expensive! When I got the stuff home I looked at the walls and ceiling and realized I'd have to have a ladder. Cripes! I hadn't figured on all these expenses. Ruth said there was a Puerto Rican hardware store on Amsterdam. He had a six-foot stepladder for $8.58. I was thinking of checking that price out with the Jewish guy's store, but I didn't want to make an enemy, so I got the Puerto Rican's ladder.

Our apartment was on the seventh floor of a brick building and it cost $79.25 a month. The money from Grandpa's life insurance was still coming in, $100 a month, so that would cover the rent and phone and maybe some other stuff before taxes; this money from my grandfather was a gift from heaven. We had some bookings for the two-person show that fall, but for now the bucket and toilet-bowl brush would start to drain our savings.

The apartment was surprisingly fine. A 1920s- or '30s-style place, well constructed, with a tiny entrance foyer, then a living room that ran straight ahead for about twenty feet, with a double set of windows at the far end looking into a big air shaft maybe fifteen feet wide. Some light came in. On the right side of the living room was a small kitchen in a kind of shallow open closet without doors, wide enough for a small stove, a sink, a narrow refrigerator, and maybe two feet of counter space. Right away I saw the possibility of building an L-shaped partition that would provide counter and cabinet space and be open at one end. In the wall just before that kitchen space was a short hallway with a pretty small bathroom on the left and a bedroom at the end. It had a closet and a window to the air shaft. There was room for a double bed, a bureau, and a chair, and somehow we'd have to get Victoria's bassinet rig in there, too. Maybe. Or maybe in the living room. But first—first clean this place up!

I was meticulous. So many layers of chipped paint had built ridges and grooves where the black stuff had settled in for years. The kitchen and bathroom were spirit-killing. More soap and another pail were needed so I could work with clean water in one pail and dirty soapy water in the other. There were bugs, too. Cockroaches hunting for old crumbs or God knows what, and when I got to the stove it nearly broke my heart. I had to go out for a walk.

The cleanup took several days. I didn't want to see anyone, I just wanted to get the place clean so I could buy a bed and receive our furniture, which was on its way by truck from the storage place in Ohio. The green sofa bed, my desk, an armchair, two side tables, two lamps, and a bureau for the bedroom. I did not want anything to be put into the apartment until it was clean and freshly painted and *ours*, not a place where anyone else had lived. I worked late into the night, scrubbing down the walls and finally the floor, slowly bringing back the oak pattern, which made the place look elegant to me. It was, in fact, a handsome place and properly designed with good wood molding and baseboards. I was proud of it. Now I had to paint.

One night while I was balanced on the ladder, painting the ceiling and leaning back to cover as much area as I could, I heard a loud

crack in the stillness and a sharp pain shot up my back. I had to get off the ladder because the pain did not stop. I wanted to get the painting done that night so I climbed back on the ladder and finished the job. My back hurt bad but I kept going. The pain stayed with me for several days and then it slowly went away. I didn't know it then, but my impregnable body had just been breached for the first time.

I started walking. Checking out the neighborhood. There were a lot of stores on Broadway, neighborhood places like the hardware store, grocery, dry cleaners, liquor store, and the subway stop at 110th Street. Columbia University was a few blocks north, where Bob Williams worked, teaching English literature. Sixty-six blocks south was Times Square—the mecca of the world—and I was supposed to conquer it. I'd have to start looking for a job, but not yet. Not yet. First get the apartment ready, everything perfect for Ruby and our baby before I moved on to the next task. The furniture arrived and one of the sofa legs was bent so I had to fix that right away. I moved the furniture around to see where it looked the most comfortable and when night fell I turned on the lamps and just stared at our new home. It was beautiful, beautiful and clean and cozy, and even the smell of fresh paint had an attraction. Bob and Ruth came down for coffee and a look-see and Ruth brought a big hunk of cake. I was moved in.

I called Ruby in Hamilton and she sounded a little distant and unsure about when she and Victoria would come down to our new home. Not the eagerness I had wished for, so I told her how nice it was and that I had found a really good mattress and box spring and iron frame to set it up on and we could get a headboard that would make the bedroom cozy. She said she'd like to pick it out when she came. Great! When? Maybe in a few days. Great.

This was not the way I imagined it. We were supposed to be together. We were a team and it was hard to feel confident on my own. I called Mitch Erickson and Dick Corson and went downtown on the subway to Prince Street for dinner in their tiny little home, and their reassurances gave me a boost. "Ruby is just nervous about coming into New York, Hal. As soon as she sees what you've done

to make the apartment warm and cheerful she'll love it!" When I left their place I walked around awhile trying to feel comfortable in this enormous people jungle and remember how it was during the war when I was stationed down there at the Broadway Central Hotel, so I walked over toward Mercer Street and looked at it and thought how strange it was that life took you to where you were and how you got there. When I was that little boy, Harold, did I ever dream I'd be standing here someday?

I'd been in New York a week now without looking for work. I had to start. But how? Mitch had said I could get a list of theater agents at Actors' Equity, our union, so I would start there in the morning. I knew where some of them were located, from the bold forays I'd made on trips to New York back in the Denison days when we came in to see the plays. And there was always Chamberlain Brown. Hey! I'd start with him.

He had on the same blue shirt with the arms cut off, only they looked shorter, so he must have trimmed off the worn edges. The walls had aged a bit, but eight years on top of fifty doesn't really show up sharp. Nor did they on Chamberlain, but his watery blue eyes lit up a bit when he saw me, and he called out to his brother in the back reaches of their inner cave: "Lyman, Lyman dear, it's Hal Holbrook." Lyman came diffidently out of the shadows and shook my hand and mouthed a mute whisper. Chamberlain was the talkative one.

"And how is your dear wife?" he said. "Such beauty, such charm."

"She's in Canada with her sister. We have a baby. A girl."

"Ahh. A baby."

"Yes, and we've moved to New York. I just finished painting the place."

"Ahhh. Yes. A child." I thought the light in his blue eyes dimmed a little. "And I suppose you would like to have work? Did you hear that, Lyman? Hal wants work and we have got to get busy." An undistinguishable mumble from Lyman, who turned away and melted into the gloom.

"Ruby and I were at Holyoke this summer . . ."

"Oh, yes. I'm aware of that. I believe you were in a play with Ed Fuller. Ah—"

"*The Silver Whistle?*"

"No . . . Ah . . ."

"*Season in the Sun?*"

"I think that must have been it."

"I did ten roles up there, Chamberlain, and Ruby did four, because of the baby."

"Yes. Ah, yes. Will she be continuing in the theater?"

"Oh, yes. Sure. We just have to get settled, you know. Once the baby—"

"When she's a little older, yes. Well, we must find you something right away, right away, to welcome you and feed the child, I'm sure. I will keep you in mind."

"Thank you, Chamberlain. And thank Lyman."

"We will see you again."

When I got down the dim stairway and onto the street I felt terribly lonely. That was it. Chamberlain felt like a dead end. Who else could I count on? I didn't know anybody. Not really. There was the Max Richards office up in the Fifties, but you had to lean over and speak through a hole in the glass to announce yourself to the receptionist and she was not friendly. No one was friendly like Chamberlain. The world passed by, cars and trucks, taxis and people, while I stood wondering in which direction I should go. Move, Holbrook. Move. You won't make it rooted to the spot.

So I went up to Max Richards and leaned over and the woman glanced up and said, "Nothing." There was a fellow in the waiting room reading something thin, like a script for a commercial, maybe, or something like that. He looked up and smiled and I smiled back. A phony smile. I should have said hello or "Are you reading for something?" but I was too embarrassed to ask. So I left and another young guy, a tall, handsome guy, passed me in the hall. I looked down and then turned and watched him go into the Max Richards office. I waited by the elevator to see if he would be sent away. I

didn't push the button, so when the elevator doors suddenly opened I felt trapped. A saucy young woman smiled and said, "Going my way?" I grinned at her and shook my head. "Bye," she said, and the doors closed. Probably an actress. I waited some more. The good-looking guy never came out, so I pushed the Down button.

What the hell was the matter with me? Afraid to be turned away, afraid to say hello to another actor, afraid to be just an actor looking for a job? You're not special, Holbrook, get it? You're no different from all these other guys beating the pavements in this damn town. Afraid to say hello, for Pete's sake! Grow up! You're a goddamn actor, just another goddamn actor! Got it? I walked up Broadway fifty blocks, but I didn't know where I wanted to go. I didn't want to go home.

"Hi, Ruby."

"Oh, hello, Hal."

"Well . . . I'm all ready for you."

"Dennis . . . Dennis!" She was off the phone for a minute. "Dennis is playing with Victoria. You should see them. So cute together."

"Yeah. I wish I could."

"Dennis just loves our little baby."

"I'll bet he does. I'm sure looking forward to laying eyes on her again."

"Beryl and Stew have such a lovely backyard."

"Yeah. When do you think you'll come down?"

"Well . . . it's so nice here . . ."

"I'm all ready for you. The apartment looks real nice. No backyard but it's clean and fresh-looking. I painted every bit of it."

"Is the neighborhood nice?"

"Yeah. Well, you know, it's New York, but there are no gunfights or anything like that."

"My goodness, I hope not! Gunfights?"

"No. No, I'm just kidding. It's really okay."

"It is?"

"Yes, Ruby. It's okay. Fine. You'll like it. Ruth and Bob like it here and they have Liza . . ."

"Oh, yes. That's right, Liza. Well . . . I suppose we'll take the bus down in a few days. Or maybe the train. The bus is so crowded."

"Take the train. Ruby, you know we have our first show date on October first in Wellesley Hills, Massachusetts."

"Oh, my. So soon?"

"That's only two weeks away now. Do you think you want to do it?"

"Oh, dear."

"Or should I ask Lee?"

"Ask Lee. That's a little too soon for me."

"Yeah, I thought it might be. I mean, we'd have to rehearse."

"It's been so long . . ."

"But Ruby, it will be wonderful to have you doing the show again."

"You really think so?"

"Yes. Wonderful! So wonderful." I felt a burst of emotion. It hit me so hard I couldn't speak. We were both silent.

"Well . . . goodbye for now."

"Goodbye, Ruby."

I felt motionless. In critical suspense. Was something strange going on or was it my imagination? Everything felt surreal all of a sudden. The enthusiasm she'd always had for being with me was not in the tone of her voice. I didn't know what to think. Could the bottom be dropping out of our partnership? A chasm had suddenly opened up between us, it was nameless and frightening, and I had done something to cause it. Something this summer that had caused that explosion—"I can't go on!" It had changed her feelings for me, and to be honest, a thought had been slow-dancing around my head for weeks, but I didn't want to stop and face it. We had made love very seldom this summer. Was that it? The work and the tensions—and that operation to deliver the baby—they had got in the way. I hoped that wasn't it.

I had to call Lee. First I sat down and counted up the shows we had booked for the rest of 1952 and there were only three. Three? I thought there were more. Wellesley, Mass., Sewickley, Pa. and Lancaster, Pa.—$675 less about 60 percent in expenses, salary, and commissions. My mind had been so occupied with the Holyoke season and moving to New York, I'd forgotten about the fall show dates. I was only concerned with the grim image of the New York scaling wall and how to get a job in show business. I had to call Alkahest and see if they could get any fall dates to bail us out.

Lee was staying with Lovey, and they invited me over for dinner. Lee said right away that she was free to do the three dates in the fall, so that gave me a big relief and I was able to relax and talk about my feelings. These people were, after all, my friends. They knew me. I told them about my weird conversation with Ruby and how it was scaring me, and they were sympathetic and understanding. They both assured me it would pass, that Ruby would be okay once she got here, and that I must be strong and confident. That would mean a lot to her. It would be the key. Confidence. I was glad when they changed the subject.

After a silence Lee asked me if I knew anything about the Herbert Berghof Studio.

"What's that?"

"It's an acting studio."

"You mean acting classes?"

"Uta Hagen teaches there," said Lee.

"Yeah. I saw her in *Othello* with Joe Ferrer."

"They're divorced."

"They were arguing when I saw them in Columbus. I was sitting in the theater after the play was over, waiting to go backstage and congratulate Paul Robeson for a great performance, and Iago and Desdemona came striding across the stage from right to left, cussing each other out. It was Ferrer and Hagen in street clothes, and they weren't acting."

"Uta teaches classes down there—"

"Acting classes?"

"Yes," said Lee. "It's in the Village. She's really good. I audited one of them."

Okay. Here we go. Lee had been dropping hints to me about the Method and interior motivations, hating your parents and sisters and brothers, from way back in Idaho and here it was again, and there were two of them staring at me now.

"Acting classes. Cripes. You mean like the Marlon Brando mumble method, right? Lee Strasberg, the Studio, all that stuff?"

"Yes. Sort of. Uta has her own methods."

"Method, shmethod, and God have mercy on us, Tiny Tim. You learn to act by acting."

There was a deep silence. Deep and meaningful. Deep as a canyon and meaningful as a holy Easter sunrise. These two women looked at me, actresses I'd worked with, and I swear that a glint of pity lit their eyes. All four of them. Lovey spoke first.

"You know, Hal, you are always looking to improve yourself. Even back at the summer theater in Granville, I watched you work hard at it, and you've been doing these same roles on the road for several years, and maybe, well, you could have run out of ideas. It would be natural."

Hah, I thought, they've been talking.

"So working with Uta Hagen could be exciting for you."

"She's taking people now for this next session," said Lee. "Sixteen weeks. It starts October third, right after our Wellesley show." Another pregnant silence.

"You're conspiring against me, right?"

They laughed. "No, Hal, we are not conspiring," said Lovey. "We just think it's a smart move, coming into New York, to try it out. You'll meet actors there, hear about jobs, maybe—all kinds of stuff."

"How much does it cost?" I looked at Lee.

"Something like ten dollars a lesson," she said.

"Ten bucks. For what? I didn't have any parents to hate, so how am I going to learn the Method?"

"You don't have to," Lee said. "You'll just find out about it."

I said I'd think it over.

Grand Central Station was where lovers met in the movies. Or where lovers said goodbye. That was in my mind as I broke through the gate and walked down the dirty gray platform with the plain smell of iron in my nostrils, searching for my wife and child. They weren't there. God, what had happened! Wait. Was that them? They looked so humble. They were walking slowly behind a porter carrying the bags. I stood still and watched them coming closer and then reached out and put my arms around them both, trying not to squeeze too hard because Victoria was nestled against her mother's breast.

"Hi, Hal."

"Ruby."

"I thought you'd be right there when we got off the train, waving at us."

"I was trying to do that, but they don't let you through the—"

"Well, it's good to be here, I guess. What a trip!"

"Awful, isn't it."

"Trains are dirty now. The Canadian ones are nicer."

I got us into a cab and while it took us uptown I was allowed to hold Victoria. She studied me seriously and then tried to pry my nose off my face. When we arrived and I opened the door to our apartment, I held my breath while Ruby looked at the living room and over toward the kitchen alcove. "My, I can smell the new paint."

"You should have seen it before I worked on it."

"It's nice. Nice. Quite spacious, too. This is the kitchen?"

"Yeah. Kind of a kitchen."

"It's better than what we had in Granville. More room."

"Yes, and I want to build a partition here; see, right around here to sort of shut off the kitchen and give us some counter space and more cabinets."

"You should have been a carpenter."

"Yeah."

"Maybe you were in another life. Maybe you were Jesus."

"I don't think so."

Harold

She went down the hall and surveyed the bathroom and bed-room. "It's cramped, but you've done a good job of freshening it up for us. I'm so glad."

"Thanks."

We were safe now for the moment. Her voice lacked enthusiasm, but a crisis had been met and had retreated. We got some dinner together and put Victoria in her bassinet and talked about where we were and what our life would mean to us here in Manhattan. We counted up our friends and found we had a small platoon of them on this strange island, so we needn't feel lonely. We were stalling for time. Finally we went to bed.

It had been a long time since we had made love. A long, long time. If I had been possessed of a shred of maturity and restraint, I could have helped us pass this fragile intersection of feelings and fear, but I was out of control and it was a disaster. Something close to rape. It couldn't have been worse or come at a worse time.

When I look back at this humiliating blow to each of us, I know that this was my moment of failure as Ruby's husband. She needed comfort and understanding, not the unleashed emotions of a starved man unable to think past himself. My feelings were unimportant here and the shame this crisis laid on me was going to hound me for years. It would set in motion events that poisoned the fragile partnership we were trying to embrace. It put us at a distance from each other and we didn't know how to shut out the hurt and resentment and the abandoned feelings. All we knew how to do was shut them in.

There were times when I wondered if we would ever feel easy again, and Ruby must have felt the same way. A whole string of things had happened to pry apart the dependency we had felt for each other in the seven years since we exchanged our vows at the Little Church Around the Corner. That had been a cool, impersonal place to pledge ourselves for life, and the union there had felt but partially joined. Granville had closed that gap and brought us together and we believed the hard years on the road had seasoned and toughened us. But not enough. The runaway pace we'd hitched ourselves to broke down in that lonely Mississippi motel room a year before and

the heart of our dependency began to come apart. It was more fragile than we thought. Looming over us now was the question "How do we fix it?" We had a child.

In a bewildered state, I knew only how to move forward. Crush feelings with movement. So I piled it on. I signed up with Uta Hagen and rehearsed with Lee. At home I concentrated on completing the writing of the new show, the *Twentieth Century Show*, which seemed quixotic, a ridiculous project now. Where would we do it? Ruby and me? I didn't want to write it for someone else. But it was a form of action that made me feel partly safe, so I worked on it and slowly the work became an instrument of removal from the uncomfortable union existing in our new home. We had become strangers, but we could act out our roles as a married couple with a baby in an apartment in New York. And I made the rounds, looking for work at the agents' offices, hours of rejection that slowly deflated the balloon of hope I had to pump up in the early morning of a new day. There had to be a better way. But what?

The Berghof Studio was downtown on the West Side in a lone and decrepit section of the city's meatpacking district near the Hudson River. One frigid night later that winter I would come upon a man fallen to the pavement and frozen to death. His pale, rigid body was silent in the desolation of the Manhattan night. I touched him and the cold specter of death frightened away my humane impulse to call for help. I left him there.

Uta Hagen's classroom was up a flight of stairs. I was very nervous. A girl took my name and pointed to the rows of chairs in one half of the room, and if I remember correctly they were student chairs, the kind with a small desk attached on one side so you slid under the desk part in front of you and were trapped in your seat. Trapped is the memory of emotion that gathers itself together in my mind as I try to recall how it felt to go to acting class in the meatpacking underworld of New York. I was overdressed, I saw that right away. I had foolishly ironed my shirt. The young men and women who had got there earlier had not ironed anything before

they put it on and may have been wearing their shirts as long as Chamberlain Brown's. This was a subculture crowd and I had been brought up by people who sold shoes.

There was a guy named Charlie who looked as out of place in that crowd as I was feeling. He said hello right away. The others had a set look of depression on their faces. Except the girls. They looked relaxed. Maybe Uta Hagen would take care of that.

I didn't even see her come in. When I pulled my attention away from the girls, there she was, surrounded by two or three rumpled young people. She was tall. Her face looked a bit puffy and textured, as if the wind had been opposing it and backed away. I was not looking at Desdemona. This was a mature woman, businesslike and in charge. When she began talking she made it clear to us that anyone who was late or missed a class would be garroted and left to bleed to death. The few students who laughed at her witticisms identified themselves as "old students," ones who were continuing in classes with her. I began to get the picture of the place, some old hands, some new ones like me pretending to be confident but rather damp in our underclothes and hoping we would not be called upon to perform.

Uta talked carefully about her approach to acting a role, her discovery of her own superficiality in such plays as *Othello* (that was a shock; I thought she was terrific), and her admiration for actors who could find their own version of the truth. She made a reference to Stanislavski and the Method, but gave the impression that her own path to character development was not ruled by these schools. I was getting a message that she might not be as big a fan of Laurence Olivier as I was, which dampened my desire to become part of her family. I waited a long time for someone to get up and act, and when she finally called on a couple of older students, a scrawny guy named Bill Hickey and another one, she spent the rest of the class tearing them apart and demolishing what they had done, until I left the place with a dread of having to be butchered by her in front of everyone. But not before she'd assigned me a scene from *The Country Girl* with a student named Alice. We made a date to get together and work on it.

Hal Holbrook

As I searched for a route that would take me to a more cheerful part of town, one with a few lights here and there, I thought, was the assignment of *The Country Girl* meant to terrorize us, or did it just feel that way? Two years before, Uta had knocked everyone dead (including me) as Georgie in Clifford Odets's searing exposure of an alcoholic actor and his wife, and now she had plucked me out to do the role of Bernie Dodd, the director, who has to get a performance out of him. The scene she saddled us with was the one at the beginning of act two, which erupts in a violent standoff between Georgie and the director. Alice had been nailed with Georgie, Uta's role. Nailed to the cross right on top of Jesus, I may say. She should have quit right there. One thing was clear—Uta was as tough as she looked. Any pretense at being a sport or a temporary pal was an act. Was there something about me she hated? I thought. My face, my clothes, my name? I left the place feeling I'd never belong to her crowd. What Alice felt I couldn't guess, because she had a mask of composure on her face, as if she got hit with thunderbolts every day.

We met at a friend's apartment, Alice's friend, who left us alone to thrash our way through the jungle of emotional possibilities between Bernie and Georgie. Right away I saw that Bernie was a foreigner to me—an urban street fighter on a high-stakes catwalk across the bodies of the fallen, a killer with shrewd intelligence. He was trying to tame big game but the intruding female would not lie down. Georgie sees him as "a machine without manners or style—self-driven, curt, wary, and worried—pretending to a humanity you never practice!" When I read those lines a half century ago I could have known next to nothing about such people, so the danger in them did not go deep with me. I didn't know how to search for it in myself, so I had to fake it. I acted out the lines and that was red meat for Uta. I couldn't tell what Alice was up to, because in my game plan she was just feeding me the cues. She was not the kind of passionate performer who could force me into an engagement, but I'm sure she had the same reaction to me. We had set the perfect trap for Uta's scorn.

The day of our execution we sat through the dismemberment of

two other couples. Charlie was half of one of them. I wanted to call for the ambulance and have Charlie and myself carried out.

"Okay. Alice and . . . Hal. Up!" I was hiding behind a pretty good-sized guy, so Uta had trouble finding me. She had a half-amused expression on her face. I was sure this meant she was licking her lips, and my legs began shaking as I made my way forward, resisting the will to advance to the platform. I tripped mounting it and performed an impromptu balletic maneuver that was unsuitable for the character of Bernie Dodd. Unfortunately, it got a laugh. Before launching into the scene, I had to do "the Wall." This was a preparation trance that I had observed the other actors doing before they commenced acting. You went over to the wall and placed your head in your hands and leaned against the wall. The idea was to stay there until you got "into yourself" and had made contact with a "memory of emotion" that prepared you for the scene. I laid my head against the wall and tried to contact a memory, any memory that would rescue me and help prepare me for the grave, but the only thought racing around my mind was, What are you doing with your head against the wall? I felt like a nut. Was this the way those other people felt? Even Charlie? Like a nut? Or were they really getting "into themselves"? I didn't even know where myself was, nor had I ever known it, but wherever that self was hiding, it knew it was going to be slaughtered and had run as far away from me as it could get.

I was afraid to turn around, because it would be like saying "Okay, shoot!" So mine was the longest preparation of the day and did not end until I became conscious that Alice was waiting for me in the center of the stage. I had to go to the bathroom, that's what I got out of my preparation.

Playing in a high school gym was softball compared with Uta's class. Bodies in the audience moved in the gym. On the second floor in the meatpacking district of Manhattan there was a solid wall of dark gray silence in the room and every desperate syllable we uttered bounced off the wall right back at us. It was like being hit on the head with a soundless sledge. By the time it was over I hated

myself for signing up for this bleak ordeal. I wanted to sit down, but Uta started asking questions while I was still checking out my sense of direction.

"Hal, what do you think of her?"

"Who?"

"Georgie."

"Oh." Jeez. She's played the part! What should I say? "Ah— what do I think of her? Well, she's protecting her husband . . ."

"Yes."

"So . . . I know that."

"What else do you know?"

"Well . . . could you—"

"How does it make you feel?"

"Feel? You mean, about her?"

"Yes. What are your feelings about her?"

"I think she's covering up. You know . . . hiding something."

"You do?"

"Yeah."

"How does that make you feel?"

"So . . . it makes me angry. You know. Before this she brought up about Frank should have a dresser and the salary stuff. She's a pushy dame."

"A pushy dame?" I wondered for a still moment if Uta might think I was referring to her. She was really Georgie. "Is that all, Hal?"

"All?"

"Yes . . . All, Hal."

"All what? I don't know what you—"

"She's a pushy dame. What else is she, Hal?"

"Well, I mean she's tough and she's pretending to be a big pal of her husband's, but she's telling me he's a lush and going on a bender, and—"

"And what?"

"She's a phony."

"You're sure of that?"

"Yeah. I gotta get the show on. But she's out for what she can get. Actually she's a killer."

"A killer?"

"Yeah. I know. I was married to one."

"You were?"

"Yeah. It says so in the script."

"Okay."

Did she think I meant *her*? Christ, I'm digging myself a hole here. And I don't know what I'm doing in the scene and she knows it.

"Alice, do you think you're a killer? He thinks you are."

"He's the killer."

"Really?"

"He's only interested in my husband for what he can get out of him."

"Like what?"

"Well, the performance. Once he gets what he wants . . . I mean, he has no idea what an alcoholic mess he's dealing with."

"And you do?"

"Sure. Sure. You're darn right. I'm living with it. He's not."

"But . . ."

"But he will. He'll find out."

"So how do you feel about Bernie?"

"I don't trust him."

"Yet you find him attractive?"

"Who?"

"Bernie."

"Attractive? No. I mean . . . no."

"Okay. I want you both to work on the scene and bring it back in two weeks. Work on how you feel about each other. Work on what's going on between the two of you."

Hell. No compliments in this place, I thought on my way back to the school desk. "How do you feel about each other?" Another hill to climb. I thought we'd do the scene and move on to something else, didn't think we'd be married to it. Thrashing out all these emo-

tions, plowing up all that stuff. It was easier to just *act*, for Pete's sake! I mean, yeah, I'd had personal feelings in plays and scenes, lots of times, with Ruby and others, too. At Holyoke, but mostly with Ruby. There was something too damn highlighted about all this talk about emotions. I didn't like that. You could overdo this sort of thing.

These unfriendly thoughts carried me out into the streets and pursued me all the way uptown on the IRT subway. I felt I'd bitten off more than I could chew. And something was wrong at home. I knew something was brewing and had been for a long time because Ruby had become more and more silent. I was reluctant to open the door and face another problem, but it was too late. When I came in she told me she was going back to Canada. Just like that. She was more comfortable there, she said, and she'd have Beryl's help with the baby and her companionship. It caught me off balance and shocked me. I thought we were doing okay, getting along, maybe not perfect, not fine in every way, but . . . to leave? Why?

She said she did not feel good in New York. "And you get angry all the time."

"I get angry?"

"Yes. You get frightened about something and then you get angry and I don't like that. I don't like being around that."

"I guess I am frightened. I mean, the whole thing is frightening, making a living here, trying to pay this high rent—seventy-nine bucks—all the expenses here, it's scary. But I'm not angry."

"Well, you get very unpleasant and angry and it frightens me. I don't feel like eating. And you spend all your time on the typewriter. I'm lying in bed feeling sexy and dying for affection, and—"

"Feeling sexy? When?"

"All the time."

"Jesus. How am I supposed to know that?"

"Well, you're always on the typewriter, typing a letter to Ed Wright."

"I'm working on the new show. It's for us."

"I don't want to do it."

"Well . . . I don't know. I have to work on it. Maybe you will later—"

"I don't think so."

"But our bookings. People want a new show. They don't want us back in the old show. They want new stuff."

"Do it with Lee. I don't want any part of it."

Was that what was bothering her, me working with another actress? Or was it the other thing? Sex. Or both? For a split second I had an impulse to beg her to stay, to ask her what she meant about feeling sexy and how she felt about Lee and me, but I didn't want to get into that. It would be like asking a judge for parole. Our apartment had become a kind of courtroom where we scored points in silence. I had felt such a fool and a failure since that night she'd come home and I had thrown her down on the bed. I didn't want to talk about it, I wanted to avoid the subject of my own feelings. I had repressed them so long it was getting to be a habit. "You really think you have to go? Back to Beryl's? For how long?"

"I don't know. I just have to go. It's no fun being with you. You don't make me feel loved and cared for and you're working all the time."

She had exposed me and now the bitter pill made me angry. She was feeling sexy? When? How? She had never been a ball of fire in that area, but how was I going to hit her with that? I retreated and tried to hide the bitterness in the deeper layers of consciousness where it wouldn't hurt so much, but it had already reached the pit of my stomach and grabbed at my emotions. For several weeks I had been asking myself why this slow degeneration was happening, knowing why, but afraid to stop and talk about it with Ruby. It was too threatening and the attraction we felt for each other had shorted out.

We had miscalculated. Ruby had gone back to work too soon and I was not ready for fatherhood, and it had unwound everything. A hell of a year. The separation, the intrusion of my feelings about traveling with Lee, the anguish of each other's loneliness, Ruby's careful preparation for motherhood extinguished by the shock of having them cut down the middle of her belly to deliver the baby.

She'd been worn out by that ordeal, and frightened. Seven weeks later she faced the fear and tension of going into rehearsals and performances, and this disorientation from the role of motherhood created a dreamlike world where our baby was out of place. A source of awkwardness and inconvenience for both of us because summer stock is a twenty-five-hour day and everything else is a distraction. We'd fooled ourselves into thinking we had planned it well. No, we had not planned it well, and now we were going to pay for the mistakes. I felt the blame for planning so unwisely because I had taken the initiative and steered us into the summer commitment. We were two people who had spun our private cocoon in the absence of a larger one that should have included a family that could have advised and assisted us when help was needed, and now we needed it. So Ruby was heading for Canada to seek help from her sister and I was staying in New York, the mecca of our dreams.

25

That long-ago day when I was hit in the face with the cleats of a football shoe and dismissed in disgrace by the coach for crying about it, a piece of my character was laid in place. I walked over to the running track and ran the mile. That would become the way I responded to shame and the persecutions of my conscience—accomplish something to defeat the feeling of failure. I would run a mile or climb a mountain or sail across an ocean, or go to work at my desk to avoid facing the truth with Ruby. I didn't analyze my reaction then, or on that hollow day when Ruby went back to Canada with our child, but the habit was going to stick with me.

Nor did I understand my inability to get down on my knees and ask forgiveness for the failure. That was out. Intuitively. It was shut out by the humiliation and the rush of anger that took possession of my emotions when failure overwhelmed me. Anger was the warrior that kept the shame at bay and it became the fuel for action.

Sometime early in life I'd become convinced that once love had suffered a wounding, the total sum of love was reduced ever after. Love could start at 100 percent, but when someone who loved me became angry it meant that person's love would diminish on a percentage scale and the lost portion could never be replaced; and my love went down with it. Eventually, only a crippled portion of love could ever remain between us. So if anger had become my defender,

it was also my enemy, and with this uneasy partnership I began my New York experience alone.

After Ruby left I kept to myself and did not seek out companionship; nor did I seek condolence. I was too ashamed to call friends, I'd have to tell them what happened. I worked on writing the new show, cooked and cleaned up the place, rehearsed the damn scene for Uta, and walked and walked around town. Fifty blocks at a time. Walking was action. And while I walked I ran my life through my head. Over and over I chased life around in my imagination, constructing scenarios of a bitter personal world I lived in but did not share with anyone. I was haunted by the possibility that I would lose Ruby. She was my best friend. Losing her would be like stepping off a cliff. The stunning thought that I would be alone again pulled the breath right out of me, so divorce was out of the question. But I could not find a way through our minefield of crippled love to do the one thing that might save us: go to her and change my ways.

Lee and I had done the show at Wellesley Hills, and I began to write a brief report of every show we did in a small red loose-leaf notebook. I had not yet gone in to see Bim Pond. He and his assistant, Agnes McTernan, had been a source of sustained support with articles about the show in their magazine, *Program*, which reached all the buyers. Now the fear of losing the show hung in my mind. How would Ruby and I make a living? The idea had never entered my head that we would not be joined together. I walked the streets at night, working off the apprehensive feelings, trying to imagine how we'd survive, but they wouldn't go away. I wanted to know what Bim felt about the chances that our show could be booked with another actress. He'd been in the business all his life. He had helped me visualize Mark Twain because he'd known him as a boy. Bim would have an opinion. It might be gruff and blunt, but I'd get one.

"Have you thought of doing a solo?"

"What?"

"He did lectures, you know. Twain. My father booked them."

"You mean . . . alone on the stage? Go out alone? God, I can't imagine—"

"I think you could do it. I think you could get bookings. Have you read his books?"

"Not really. I read *Tom* once, I think. And *Huck*."

"Read 'em again."

He hadn't responded to my query about booking the show with another actress. Bim was not a pleaser. He didn't sympathize. He looked at you and then he said something and it wasn't often what you expected. He hadn't asked about Ruby. On my way out, Agnes did and I tried to explain her visit to Canada in a simple, evasive way—that she was tired from the baby and the work this summer. Agnes gave me a little hug and a kiss on the cheek. In his office, Bim was watching me.

I kept walking. On my rounds from agent to agent the only response was rejection. When Alice and I did our scene again for Uta, there wasn't much encouragement. I was angrier in it, but the interior emotional shape of the encounter was lost to me. I had no real technique to find it and blasting away didn't work. I watched the other actors do scenes and when I admired what they were doing Uta took them apart. Bill Hickey and another guy did a scene from Synge's *Playboy of the Western World* that I thought was dazzling. Boom. Uta shot it down. I couldn't understand why. She seemed to be opposed to theatricality and that's what I admired. When I went to the theater, the plays and the people in them seemed to live in a world I had nothing to do with, so how could I get into it? More and more I felt like an outsider.

My trailblazing around town sometimes took me in the direction of Bloomingdale's, where I could admire the easy chairs and bureaus we couldn't afford. On Fifty-ninth Street I passed the Argosy Book Store. It was old and worn-out looking, a pit stop for used books. I paused and looked in the windows—there were two, one on each side of the door. Hmm. I didn't go in the first time or the second, but finally I ventured into the stained interior and asked a clerk, "Where would Mark Twain be?" He pointed to a disorderly corner. Here there were a lot of Twain's books and books about him, too. Strange names: *A Tramp Abroad, Roughing It, What Is Man? And Other Essays, Pudd'nhead Wilson, Mark Twain in Eruption*, and, of course, *Tom*

 319

Sawyer and *Huckleberry Finn*. Had I read those? I couldn't remember, though I did remember the word "nigger" in *Huckleberry Finn*. It had made me feel uncomfortable. I didn't like to see it in print. Too many people had used it where I came from and I always wished they would stop, because there was something unkind about it. It made me think of Charlie, the elderly black man who shined shoes in Grandpa's store on Sixth Street; he was always glad to see us and talk to us, my sisters and me, and he had a deep, throaty voice that rumbled with warmth and a kind smile. I didn't like that word. "Nigger." So I bought *Tom Sawyer* and left.

I had to force myself to call Ruby, because I felt angry at her for leaving me and taking our newborn child away. It was unfair of me to feel that way, I knew it, but the feelings were there. I felt deserted. They should have stayed. We could have worked it out if she had stayed with me, that's what I told myself, but this rupture had started bleeding when she deserted me and I could feel ancient emotions boiling up through my bloodstream. I tried to control them. They could get out of hand so easily. I made the call.

"Hello."

"Ruby?"

"No. It's Beryl. Hal?"

"Yeah. Hi, Beryl. How are ya?"

"Pretty good."

"Good to talk to you."

"You, too."

"How is Ruby doing?"

"She's at the psychiatrist."

"What? . . . She's at what?"

"She's seeing a psychiatrist."

"Whaddya mean? A psychiatrist?"

"That's right, Hal."

"Well. Is she all right?"

"Her spirits are pretty far down, you know."

"Yeah."

"So she's going to a psychiatrist."

"My God."

"You should come up."

"I should? Whaddya mean?"

"It would be good for Ruby."

"Oh. Okay. Is she—let me think—"

"We'd like to see you, too. Me and Stewart."

"Yeah. It would be great to see you."

"She should be home by four-thirty if you want to call back, Hal."

"I will. Yeah. Four-thirty. Okay."

"Until then, Hal."

Jesus. A psychiatrist! What was happening to us? Some kind of panic spun around in my head. Here we go. Here we go. Ruby was having mental problems. Where was our beautiful marriage? Our love affair? This couldn't be happening. My father all over again, for Christ's sake. Now my wife? What about our child? This is nuts. Nuts. These thoughts raced in my head until its interior became a zone of silence, the strange silence after a bomb has exploded and the sound track of a film goes silent while the fragments of still life rain down and settle on the ground and lie there, mute. In 1952 no one mentioned psychiatry out loud. No one talked about it, it was only whispered. Crazy people went to psychiatrists and they all wound up in the insane asylum. Like my father. Maybe Tennessee Williams hinted at it in his plays, but not Bob Hope and Jack Benny. They did not joke about it on that new thing called television.

What a lonely thought. Going to a psychiatrist. Far away in Canada. Alone. I had to talk to her.

"Ruby."

"Yes."

"Ruby, are you okay, darling?"

"I don't know."

"Are you—how is Victoria?"

"She's playing with Dennis."

"Do you want me to come up there?"

"I don't know if you should."

"Well—Beryl said you're going to a psychiatrist."

"Yes. I found her in the Yellow Pages."

"You what? What in the Yellow Pages?"

"A psychiatrist. She's a woman."

"Oh. So . . . what . . ."

"I have to get rid of these feelings."

"Sure."

"She's giving me shock treatment."

"What treatment?"

"Shock. Electric shock treatment."

"What the hell—"

"Don't get angry. I don't want to talk about it . . ."

"I'll come up—"

"No—"

"Ruby, please. Don't you think if you came home it could all straighten out?"

"No. I'm afraid not."

"Please, think about it."

"It's better here. I'm better here. Beryl takes good care of Victoria. I have to get off the phone."

"Please, Ruby, let me talk to Beryl. Please." I waited. Beryl got on the phone.

"Hal."

"Yeah. Beryl, what the hell is going on?"

"What do you mean?"

"Well . . . I mean . . . who is this psychiatrist?"

"She's supposed to be very good."

"She is? Who says so?"

"Ruby likes her."

"But what are these shock treatments? What does that mean?"

"They are supposed to get rid of the things that worry you."

"How?"

"That make you, you know, depressed. It does something to help that."

"Can you check up on this person? No, hell, I'm coming up there myself. The Yellow Pages. God!"

"Maybe you shouldn't. I mean, you don't want to make her feel bad. Right now she's very calm, Hal."

"Okay. I'll think . . . I'll figure it out. Beryl, please, you and Stewart, check out this doctor."

"We will."

"Bye. Love to everyone."

The bomb in my head was exploding again and spreading. It was a firefight, people shooting at each other, soldiers in battle, shooting and throwing grenades and blowing each other up. Ruby was being blown away, she was in fragments, and I had done it.

What in the hell were shock treatments? I didn't want to know, I wanted to go out and walk and walk and get away. I had to talk to someone—who? Ed and Louise? No. The shame of it, to admit that I had caused this? No! Never! Uncle Al and Aunt Merce? Never. Grandma? "Harold, it's your father all over again!" Ruby's mother and father? "If I ever hear you've abandoned my daughter, I'll come down there and kill you!" Who can I talk to? Who? Maybe Bob and Ruth.

Ruth thought that Canada might be advanced in mental doctoring, that they could use techniques that might not be given to patients here. She was from Canada. They were so decent, these two people, sympathetic and intelligent but quietly concerned, and I read in that quiet a message. Get on the road for Hamilton.

Let's see. Uta's class was tomorrow. I could go the day after that. She might be ready to give me a new scene to do, I was tired of this one. The next date with our show was October 27 so I could get back in plenty of time for that. Ruby didn't want me to come, but I had to—I had to. I couldn't leave her up there alone, and who was this psychiatrist? I had to talk to her.

"I'm Ruby's husband."

"Yes. It's good of you to come."

"Well, sure. I just found out about her . . . about the . . . that she was seeing you."

"Yes."

"No one told me. I didn't know—"

"Well, it was good that she found me."

"She said in the Yellow—in the phone book."

"Yes."

"I guess she didn't know anyone who'd, you know, would recommend—"

"Yes. It was good that she found me. I am familiar with her condition."

"Condition?"

"Yes."

"What is it?"

"She has suffered a loss of confidence. Through depression. Her confidence is low. She needs quiet now."

"I want to see her."

"She will be finished with her treatment in a short time."

"Can I see her then?"

"Yes. But you must be . . . well, calm. If you become angry . . ."

"No, I wouldn't . . ."

"Or irritated. She is afraid of that in you now."

"Afraid of me? That's . . . I'm her husband."

"Just now she is unsure of you."

"I love her. I came all the way up—"

"Yes. You must show her that you love her. That is what she will want to know."

This was a nightmare. This thin, sallow-faced woman was a phantom in a nightmare. No, a movie. A movie with Boris Karloff. And the hospital—what a joke! An old house, a plain, old-fashioned clapboard house with a porch. That was the hospital, and inside it women were walking around like zombies in robes and pajamas. No men, only women with faraway expressions, and here was Ruby coming down the hall. She had that same detached look and when she saw me she didn't seem to see me. For a second I thought she would pass me by.

"Oh. Hal."

"Ruby. Hi!"

"How did you get here?"

"I drove up in the car. I wanted to see you, Ruby. I'm so sorry. I love you."

"Yes, well . . ."

I tried to put my arms around her but she went limp. She was lifeless.

"Is this place okay for you? Are you comfortable?"

"Very."

"So . . . you'll be staying here for a while? Ruby? Not at Beryl's."

"What?"

"You're staying here now, not at Stew and Beryl's?"

"Victoria is there. With Beryl. Victoria is happy there."

"Ruby, darling, I'm so glad to see you. How are you feeling?"

"I don't want to talk now. Goodbye, Hal."

"Ruby . . ."

"Say goodbye."

I walked out on the street with an enormous feeling of revulsion. Rejection. Horror and disbelief. The person I knew was not there. I had to talk to Beryl and Stew and see if we could do something to get Ruby out of that place. Stewart was someone I admired. He was a quiet, reflective man and would not offer rash judgment. Beryl was the opposite, impulsive and opinionated, but she loved her younger sister. I was not prepared for them to disagree with me, but they did and it surprised me. They thought that moving her or interfering with the doctor was not advisable. They felt it was a safe environment for Ruby, a quiet place to help her recover, and that this new treatment—this electric shock therapy—was supposed to be very helpful, people were doing it in Canada. Their feeling was that we should wait and see if Ruby improved and they would take care of Victoria.

It was a hard moment for me. I could have taken a tough stand

and insisted on getting her out of there, but what about Victoria? The mysteries of psychiatric healing were a far country, and their opinion sounded reasonable. The task of finding another doctor who would oppose this one and fighting her to force Ruby out of there against her will felt like a choice for disaster. I began to feel that it was no longer my decision to make, like an outsider, but I was enraged to see Ruby in such a place and to have our baby snatched away from me. But how could I raise her alone?

I was impotent in Hamilton. I tried to see Ruby again but she was not pleased to see me. I withdrew and tried to play with Victoria and Dennis but I couldn't control the thoughts churning through my head. My brain was out of control. I had to go. I had to get in the car and drive and get the hell away from all these people, drive until some kind of sanity took over, so I said goodbye and kissed Victoria and headed for New York. I was deserting my child, like my mother and father had deserted us. Miles went by before my heart stopped racing and my grip on the steering wheel relaxed and the images drumming in my head slowed down and stopped repeating, and then one thought hung on and rode with me in the night: You're alone now, pal.

And in that house in Canada, what must Ruby have been feeling? It was beyond my imagining. We were both fogbound in silence and could not find each other for comfort and reassurance and search together for a way home. If things had gone so far wrong, what must Ruby be feeling about us? Our marriage? How long had this been going on? Some disease had penetrated us and she could not explain it to me, wandering in that dreamlike limbo through the hallway of a bizarre prison far from home. The psychiatrist had told me that after the treatments she would weep and weep. What a terrible isolation she had fallen into, this beautiful and accomplished woman I loved.

I detached myself in a spiritual sense from everyone then. I lived in a new world of silence where I could concentrate only on my survival. I'd been cut loose, that's what it felt like, and when I looked around, there was no one who could fill the space that Ruby and

Victoria had vacated. I feared they were going to vanish, so I began to fill the space with myself. The hope that the Ruby Johnston I knew would come back again was dimming out. I would have to take care of this new person, but it would not be the one I married. It would be me.

26

Survival. Whatever devotion Ruby felt for me had taken a radical drop and I was convinced that it could never be renewed. So where was my confidence going to come from to assure her we would survive this blow?

I fought these feelings for possession of my days and nights and plowed them under with work. It was my weapon. I walked the Ping-Pong routes from one agent's office to another, listening to actors discuss their own lives in the offices and hallways, but I kept silent. I forced myself to work on the new two-person show, hoping that Lee or maybe another actress could do it and keep us afloat. But it had no emotional future for me, it had become a survival task. Lee agreed to rehearse with me, and Alkahest came through with five more shows in the first eight days of December, and that was money we needed desperately because after Lee and I played the October 27 date near Pittsburgh, the total income for October was $475, less the 33⅓ percent commission and Lee's salary.

I made out a budget.

HOME EXPENSES	PER MONTH	SHOW EXPENSES
$100—Rent & Utilities		$180—Travel
$100—Food		$ 75—Publicity
$ 65—Clothes		$ 35—Costumes
$ 35—Car		$ 40—Misc.

Harold

$100—Misc. &	$330—Per Month
Entertainment	
$400—Per Month	

$$\$400 + \$330 = \$730$$

That was if Ruby were home. What the Hamilton expense would be I wasn't sure yet. Even with Grandpa's $100-a-month life insurance check we were going to come up short.

I got reports of Ruby's progress from Beryl and Stew and was able to speak to her on the phone once, maybe twice. She sounded a little more in control and Beryl thought she was improving. I hoped she would come home for Christmas. Lee had found a story by James Thurber, which I adapted for the new show, about a strange guy named Mr. Preble who decided to murder his wife, but his plotting is hopelessly inept. We both thought it was very funny. In Uta's acting class I was finally assigned another scene to do, but I don't recall having any greater success with it. I walked the midtown streets and avenues hoping for a break, but I was an outcast there as well.

In the Village I saw an actress named Geraldine Page giving a weird, evanescent performance in *Summer and Smoke* by Tennessee Williams. She was so talented I felt like an amateur watching her. One night on Eighth Street I passed the Bon Soir nightclub. I had never been inside. Felicia Sanders was appearing there so I went downstairs and sat with a Scotch in one hand listening to the lovely sound of her voice. It roused tender feelings in me that I had crushed and put away. A beautiful night. When I walked the streets I saw beautiful girls, fresh-looking and alive and smart, and wondered what it would be like to know them. But I kept walking and closed the door on myself at 200 West 108th Street.

Day and night I worried about where the money would come from to pay our bills. I was too proud to ask for a loan I couldn't repay. One night I started reading *Tom Sawyer*. For a page or two it was a duty, then it started to become fun because there was life in this literature. You heard the voices coming right off the page. This was a surprise and after a while I began to feel pleasant with myself

 329

and that was a surprise, too. Bitterness receded and in its place a boy came crowding in, his friends came in and his family, and it wasn't very long before I did not feel so lonely anymore. Mark Twain had cheered me up. The idea of a solo show entered my thoughts again.

We were not able to get the new show ready by Christmas, and I left for Hamilton. Although Ruby had been out of the hospital for quite some time, she did not want to come home, so it was strange to be there as the odd man out. Beryl and Stew were friendly and that opened up the family to me in a way that Ruby could not, and it was fun to see my alert eight-month-old baby rolling around on the floor with Dennis pursuing her. Victoria was remarkably alive and curious. I thought she resembled both of us, but Ruby thought she looked like me. Ruby seemed almost normal, but distant. I tried to pretend we were okay again and hoped that Victoria would feel we were, but it felt like playacting, repeating a memory of who we were once upon a time. In my heart I felt helpless.

The year 1953 did not burst upon us with banners of hope. I returned to New York alone and was soon back at the Argosy Book Store to purchase more Mark Twain. *Roughing It* looked like a gold mine to me, raucous early adventures out west that might kick a show into gear early on. Laughs were what I started looking for; laughs were legs you could move a performance forward on until your anxious heart slowed down. Twain had a wild sense of humor about himself and that might play well, but the idea of going out there alone was frightening.

Early that January I got the best acting lesson of my life. Uta had assigned Charlie a scene from John Van Druten's lovely play *The Voice of the Turtle* with an attractive young actress playing Sally. It's wartime, 1943, in New York, and a soldier, Bill, gets stranded in Sally's apartment when her roommate dumps him for another guy, and that's when Cupid begins to let fly his magic arrows. Sally has been bruised by love affairs that went bad and is afraid of getting hurt again, and Charlie's natural fineness could be a good match for

a girl like that, but his lack of confidence throws him off track. At their first performance Charlie's portrait of the soldier in love appeared to be a cohabitation of Ronald Colman and Ray Bolger. We held our breath, sure that Miss Hagen would leave his lifeless body on the stage floor, but a surprising compassion greeted Charlie. This kind young man was a prince and we knew it. So did Uta.

"Charlie, how do you see yourself in this scene?"

"Not very well."

"Have you been in love with someone?"

"Well, let me see . . . yes. Maybe."

"Then you know you don't have to be a movie star to fall in love."

"That's a relief."

"You're trying to be a movie star."

"Me? Impossible."

"Ah! But it's not impossible for you to be in love. Charlie, who is this young man?"

"Ah . . . a guy who is . . . falling in love with a girl . . . who's afraid of getting hurt."

"She's afraid to give in to her own feelings. For you. They frighten her."

"I see that."

"It's about you, Charlie. Not someone else. Just you." The room was silent. "Work on this scene and bring it to me again in two weeks."

That was going to be one of the last times I would ever go to Uta Hagen's class, because she was going into a new play. I wish I could recall the name of the young actress who did the scene with Charlie and returned with him to do it one more time for us. My memory of her is of a young woman, vulnerable but hopeful, like Sally. But it was going to be Charlie's hurdle and we all held our breath for him as he unwound his gangly frame from the school chair and approached the stage. Would he trust himself? It was Charlie going up there, and it was Charles Nelson Reilly when he walked on the stage, our classmate, doing what Miss Hagen had told him to do and holding us

breathless with the quiet and genuine man he really was, express-
ing his feelings for Sally and persuading her to believe in her feelings
for him.

Charles showed me something I hadn't learned. Nor was I likely
to learn it behind the wigs, sideburns, and mustaches I was plaster-
ing myself with in the Theater of Great Personalities. Those characters were set in a groove I could not climb out of, and for the moment
it was the only way I could make a living. I was an itinerant actor. I
had been formed in an ancient tradition going back to the road-hungry
actors of the commedia dell'arte and Molière, the young Edmund
Kean, and even Shakespeare's wandering troupes. We went where
they threw us a coin to perform. No doubt that metaphor is too exotic, but it felt real to us who made a living that way. We had to im-
provise a stage, to learn on our feet how to hold the attention of an
audience. Introspection was a cupcake we could rarely savor.

It was a long wait to the first show date of the new year, but then
they came pouring in on top of one another. Back on the road with
Lee again. From my red notebook:

> January 23, 1953, Troy, N.Y. 2:30 p.m. Ilium Club. Stage wide and
> shallow, Ballroom Henry Hudson Hotel.
> January 24. Cohoes, N.Y. 8:00 p.m. Saturday Club. Stage a platform.
> Presbyterian Church House hall.
> January 25. Albany, N.Y. 8:15 p.m. University Club. Stage 6"
> platform, bare, end of living room.
> January 26. Schenectady, N.Y. 2:00 p.m. Schenectady Women's
> Club. Stage platform in YWCA. And Delmar, N.Y. 8:15 p.m.
> Progress Club. Stage, high school.

The Albany area raid brought in 800 wonderful dollars, less
33⅓ percent commission, which took it down to $532.67 and $127
for Lee, who appeared to have been underpaid, giving me a balance
of $405.67 to pay my own salary and pay down some of our bills.

Out of the blue a call came for me to audition for a television
show entitled *Hollywood Screen Test* on ABC. The producers were

looking for someone to do the voice of Abraham Lincoln. I had no idea why they called me, but the two producer-writers, Lester and Mort Lewis, explained that in this television play Lincoln would never be seen, but the actors would speak to the camera as if the camera were Lincoln. What they were looking for was his authentic voice. Lester and Mort Lewis had researched Lincoln thoroughly. Newspaper and personal accounts of his speeches described Lincoln's voice as "high, shrill, nasal, and unpleasant." That voice was the crucial element in their story.

"Can you try for that, Holbrook?"

"I think so."

"We've been told you do a lot of characters on a stage show. That's why we brought you in. We've been looking for this sound for a couple of weeks and no one has come up with it."

"Can I go out in the hall for a minute and work on these speeches?"

"Sure. Take your time."

I walked out into the bare hallway. This was my chance at a job. Away from the elevators there was a window and I went down there to think. For some reason I didn't feel scared about reading for them, maybe because I understood what they were saying about Lincoln, that he was strangely ordinary, that he came from the land of farms and plain people. I tried to remember how those relatives of the Spaldings in Indiana had sounded when Paul drove us out there one summer and we stayed on their farm for a week—farm people and their voices. The producers had stressed that Lincoln's voice had to be high-pitched. I couldn't exactly place the face, but I remembered the Adam's apple of a man's neck, a scrawny neck, and the high, shrill sound of his voice from somewhere in the past on some farm, maybe not even in Indiana. It was just that neck and the rough, unshaven reddish skin and the Adam's apple moving up and down. And the smell of the barn on him. In my mind's eye I saw that tall, outrageously eloquent whipsaw figure of Lincoln and the Christ-like rural face. I watched the elevators in case someone came out, and I made sounds out of the lines on the script and listened to the

sounds until I felt good about a certain high-pitched level and a twanging, diphthong accent. I tried it out on the speech they'd given me and then did it over again and went back into the room and did it for them. It was his farewell speech as Lincoln leaves Springfield to assume the presidency.

> Friends, no one who has never been placed in a like position [posee-shun] can understand my feelings at this hour [kin understan ma fcelin's at this aurr], nor the oppressive sadness I feel at this parting. For more than a quarter of a century I have lived among you [liv'd among ye], and during all that time I have received nothing but kindness at your hands. Here I have lived from my youth until now I am an old man. Here the most sacred ties of earth were assumed; here all my children were born [awl ma childern were borrn]; and here one of them lies buried.

There was a silence when I finished, so I put the speech down and waited. "That's it!" Lester said.

"Holbrook, that's the sound we've been looking for," Mort said. "You've got it."

I was handed a job as if it were all in a day's work. The voice of Lincoln. I had never thought of playing him. I looked nothing like him. Who could even have imagined it? Lincoln was an American hero to me, as he is to most of the world, but I knew little about him beyond the epic boyhood legends of his rise from log cabin to statesman. I went back to the Argosy and hunted around in the passageway where Lincoln occupied the shelves. I needed something personal, authentic descriptions of him by people living in his time, and I found it in Billy Herndon's book. Herndon knew him day after day while they worked together in the law office and as Lincoln entered the local political races. His descriptions of Lincoln's physical manner and speech have the robe of plain authenticity. In newspaper accounts of his speeches and his debates with Douglas it was that "high, shrill, flat, nasal, unpleasant" voice that cast Lincoln as a

prairie hick in the eyes of the eastern establishment. But in the opinion of some who knew him in Illinois he looked like an "intelligent farmer."

This early research on Lincoln was like the research I had begun on Mark Twain, but with Twain I was looking for material I hoped could get laughs in a theater. I had yet to discover who Twain really was. I had found a book about him in the boxes I'd unpacked at 108th Street the year before—*Mark Twain at Your Fingertips* by Caroline Harnsberger—and its sourced quotations led me deeper into his books. I had already edited a speech he gave on his seventieth birthday, an irreverent string of advice on how to reach old age corrupted by bad habits.

On the seventeenth of February, my twenty-eighth birthday, Lee and I gave the first performance of the new *Twentieth Century Show* at the State Teachers College in Bloomsburg, Pennsylvania, at eight o'clock in the evening for $250, with an attendance of six hundred.

In the little red notebook: "Very good show—despite a shaky performance." But when I read the list of scenes I had written for the *Twentieth Century Show*—one about a World War I soldier determined to search for a more adventurous life, another exploring the changes a baby can make in the life of a married couple, and my dramatization of James Thurber's bizarre sketch about the man who tries to persuade his wife to "go down in the cellar" so he can murder her because he's fallen in love with his secretary—I am struck by the fact that in all these scenes the man feels trapped by the way his life is going.

As the snow and ice piled up on the sidewalks of New York, Ruby returned to the frozen city with Victoria curled against her for warmth and tried to find shelter in our two-room prison on the seventh floor. Her stay was brief. It must have felt cheerless, locked in with a husband who was distracted, emotionally confused, and frightened, when what she needed more than anything was a tender and confident friend. I was not that. Ruby felt distant to me, as if she were role-playing, and something deep down in the New England

warping of my character had clamped its cold and unforgiving hand on me. The loving friend had fled in shame and confusion. In its place rose a self-wrought will to survive and serve my term in this marriage, however long it would be. I became a provider. That was the one thing I knew how to do.

Ruby and Victoria left New York in March before the birds came back to sing in Central Park, and my hope that she would return to the show was sparking out. I could get no enthusiasm from her for returning or rehearsing the new show, and it was a measure of the desperation in our predicament that I could have even dreamed that we would get back onstage together. But it was the only dream I had. So Lee and I bore on, doing the new show at the Pennsylvania Military College on February 20 for $200 in the pocket. After that the bookings came hot and heavy because I had sent out an SOS in the fall: "Book more dates!"

February—Lynn and Springfield, Massachusetts, and Amsterdam, New York. The February gross was $1,100, with $593.33 for my share. But these dates had been booked for Ruby and me and there was a measure of disappointment over her absence that hung like a grayish cloud above the performances.

March—Winnetka and Chicago, Illinois, and Creston, Iowa. Sheboygan, Wisconsin, that vaudeville town of song and story. Lima, Columbus, and Wooster, Ohio. Lee and I were getting along better now. I had locked myself into an emotional isolation tomb for the duration of Ruby's depression. March brought in a total of $1,550 less the commissions and Lee's salary. So $738.85 went into the bank at 108th Street, paused briefly, and left. The first three weeks of April the Alkahest office in Atlanta drove us headlong through the South at a set fee of $125 a show for us. Georgia, Mississippi, Alabama, Georgia, South Carolina, Tennessee, South Carolina (Bob Jones University), and Mars Hill, North Carolina, in the gorgeous Smoky Mountains.

Holyoke was waiting up ahead. Carlton had me in mind for some

good roles, but he'd also heard from Bert and Mitch about Ruby's condition. I did not want to betray her in any way, but the idea that she would face a season there, especially with Victoria, scared me, and Ruby ended the speculation by choosing not to go. Should I go? Carlton was offering me nine plays, which was ten weeks' employment and featured roles in *Affairs of State*, *See My Lawyer*, *Sight Unseen*, *Bell, Book and Candle*, and *Gigi*. The last two were especially attractive romantic roles and I would be paired again with Miriam Stovall in one of them. Sitting around on a beach and sipping martinis for the summer was not an option, so I said yes. Ruby was going to make another try at 108th Street in May and maybe this time it would work out. Ruby sounded normal on the phone so I could not suppress waves of resentment wondering why she prolonged her stay in Canada. I had to be the reason for that.

Lee and I hit the road again with shows at Alfred and Hornell, New York, and Lowell, Massachusetts, for a heartwarming total of $1,769.48 for April, less Lee's salary. Nancy Wells had come up to see a show at Middlesex, Massachusetts, with the possibility in mind that she would take over for Lee in the fall. Lee was looking for New York employment and sensed that we were urging a nearly dead horse around the circuit. I knew it was time for me to get on with another life, but where was the horse to get me there? Even Holyoke felt like a too familiar trail, so I had to lecture myself: "Secure the home, secure your small family, book every show you can get for the coming season."

On May 14 I got my second job in New York, one day on a Piels beer commercial for $55, sitting at a table with three other guys, smiling wildly over glasses of foaming beer. The foam was more important than the actors, but who the hell cared? It was a job. It came from Nancy Morrow, a casting director at the ad agency Young and Rubicam. In those days the ad agencies booked most of the shows. I especially wanted to break into radio, where an ability to come up with different voices and accents was something I felt I had to offer.

Lee and I crossed the Hudson River on May 18 and played the Hackensack Women's Club. Until then I thought the name came

from a vaudeville sketch. Nancy and her father, Jimmy Wells, came over to see the show, which made me aware that Nancy's mother and father were going to be crucial in her decision to replace Lee. They were showbiz people. Her mother, Agnes, starred in the radio soap *The Right to Happiness*, and they wanted to have a good look before letting Nancy take part in our little theatrical oddity.

We had two New Jersey shows the next day in Trenton and that evening at the State Teachers College in Glassboro. Jimmy Wells came down to help us set up the show that night, a fine gentleman who was getting interested in the show. Good! At this stop the program chairman, Miss Tohill, said she wanted to book "the solo Twain," so Higgins must have been promoting it. And then—just one more show left in the season, a wonderful performance of the old show in Baltimore at a women's club. This could be Lee's swan song.

Ruby came back in May, and things seemed almost normal. Sometimes it seemed as if nothing had happened to us, that we were just another couple living in New York with our one-year-old child claiming most of our attention, crawling over and up everything her industrious mind could seek out. Sometimes Victoria would pause and study us with large, curious eyes, and I wondered what she could be thinking. Was she aware that a ghostly intrusion had torn away at our life together? A tentative intimacy returned, but the desperate shadows of the past year had not vanished: there was still that untouchable space between Ruby and me. Yet the child had moved us together into a fragile partnership resting on the need to hold on to what we had. She and Victoria would join me in Holyoke for brief stretches and spend the rest of the summer in our home on 108th Street. Bob and Ruth Williams and our neighbors Pablo and Lois Morales had young children, too, and the apartment house had become more friendly. Life began again.

When I arrived in Holyoke alone to begin rehearsals for *Affairs of State*, an upstairs apartment had been found for me that could expand enough to contain Ruby and Victoria when they came to visit. Helen Harrelson had returned after an absence of several years

to star in this play with John O'Connor and myself. It was the first of five "straight roles" I would play in the succeeding productions—*The Velvet Glove*, *The Shop at Sly Corner*, *Sight Unseen*, and *Happy Birthday*—and by midsummer I was losing my enthusiasm for the season, playing these colorless straight guys. It was a relief and a spur to have Ruby and Victoria come up from New York and a god-send to cut loose in the farce *See My Lawyer*, with Ted Tiller and Bert Tanswell featured with Ed Fuller and me. We had broken all attendance records in *Room Service* the previous summer and now we had a chance to raise hell again at a farce pace.

Daytimes I was free to spend with Ruby and Victoria because I was not in the next play. We had time together to mix with some of the company by the pool, to be ourselves again, and to discuss the New York future. Nancy had decided to take over from Lee in the show come fall, the dates were rolling in, and finally there was a feeling of permanence moving into our life.

But when Ruby and Victoria left for New York, I was alone at night to ponder the stark realities of our marriage. It had become a marriage we acted out, a lonely marriage, and our sexual intimacy had gone nearly dry. Daytimes I rehearsed for the role of Dick Tassell in *The Happiest Days of Your Life*, not mine exactly, and at night it was hard to concentrate on the lines I had to learn in this loony play.

Shep Henderson in *Bell, Book and Candle* was a role I'd looked forward to all summer. I was cofeatured with Miriam Stovall, and if ever my mind wandered, it wandered watching her, which put more than a pinch of something into the scenes we played together. Miriam was archly enchanting, a featherweight with turned-up nose and pursed lips. "Miriam Stovall and Hal Holbrook were exceptional, wonderful—all the superlatives in the thesaurus actually—in their characterizations. As the lovers brought together by a spell they kissed—some of the most convincing kissing seen on the Casino stage, by the way—and quarreled charmingly." When the *Springfield Union* said that my "varied roles this year have been admirably handled," this summing up of my summer's work was a suggestion that

I may have learned to play the young leading man without uncertainty and searching for effect. In *Gigi*, the final show of the season, Louise Mace wrote that I was "giving a notable performance, polished and confident." Watching Charlie in Uta's class was beginning to reward me. But New York stood ahead like a colossus.

27

I had to think of something new. A better way to land a job than tramping all over New York, pinballing from one rejection to another. That's when I saw the small mimeograph machine in the store window, the type used to imprint messages on penny postcards. I bought it and started rolling them out.

HAL HOLBROOK
Actors' Equity Association
Young leading man
6 ft   165 lbs.   dark hair
200 West 108th Street   Apartment 7B
Phone: ACademy 2-7221

I showed one of these cards to Dick Corson, and he said, "Why don't you get a photograph of yourself reduced down to a postage-stamp size and stick it on the upper-left corner?" So I did that. Every week I went to the post office on 104th Street and bought two hundred postcards at one cent apiece for a total of $2. Then I ran them through the mimeo machine and sent them out to two hundred casting agents around town. I followed up with a personal appearance until my feet gave out. Chamberlain Brown thought the cards rather humorous. So did some of my friends. Ruby kept the machine away from Victoria, who would mimeograph our new rug.

I'd heard about the American Theatre Wing classes and joined the radio and television class. Some of the leading radio and television directors, like Arthur Hanna, Delbert Mann, and Ralph Nelson—who directed *I Remember Mama* on television—taught there and gave us scenes to do, so we'd be "seen" by them. The Wing was trying to help us out.

Ten days after I got back to town there came a shocker. On September 24 Higgins called from Rochester and asked if we could fill a date the next morning at a high school in New Jersey for an attraction that had canceled. Nancy was not free. Would Ruby do it? The fee was $55. We sat down and stared at each other, the sudden explosion of old familiar images running around our heads. Victoria sensed something and plopped down on the rug to watch.

"What time?"

"Eight thirty-five in the morning. East Orange, the Clifford Scott High School. We'd have to leave early."

"What scenes?"

"I don't know. What do you think? Maybe Victoria and Albert and Twain?"

"Let's see if I know the lines. 'Albert, may I come in?' "

" 'Yes, dearest, if you wish . . .' What about the introduction?"

"Oh. Of course. Let's see . . . 'For our next number . . . Hal and I would like to bring you a scene from the lives of Queen Victoria and Prince Albert. You may remember that Prince Albert, a German, never completely mastered the English language, and in that lies much of the humor of this scene. Unfortunately, the world remembers Queen Victoria as the plump and rather austere little woman for whom the Diamond Jubilee was celebrated in 1898. But Queen Victoria, too, was once upon a time very young.' "

I was struck again by the beautiful quality of Ruby's voice and the aristocratic accents that had isolated her from her Newfoundland family. She was royalty without training for it.

" 'Our scene takes place the morning after the child-queen's marriage to Prince Albert when, for the first time, she sees her husband shaving.

" 'Albert, may I come in?' "

" 'Yes, dearest, if you wish.' "

Ruby paused, so I pantomimed raising the straight razor to my throat.

" 'Albert! What are you doing?' "

" 'Shaving.' "

" 'Oh, how exciting! May I stay and watch you?' "

" 'If it would interest you, *Weibchen*.' "

" 'But of course! To see you shaving is wonderful! Something I never thought of.' "

" 'Did you think one did not have to shave oneself at all?' "

" 'I have never thought about it—till now . . . You see, Albert, I have never seen a man shave himself before.' "

The lines passed back and forth between us. Easily, no faltering. We finished the scene and then did the Interviewer with Twain. She knew them both as if she had never stopped playing them.

"Let's do it, Hal."

"Good. Great. We'll do it."

I was unprepared for what she had done, stunned, and it was time to hug each other, but I didn't move and neither did Ruby. We just sat for a minute and watched Victoria watching us.

"I'll call Ruth and ask her to take Victoria in the morning. What time should we leave?"

"Six-fifteen. Maybe six-thirty. I'll check the mileage."

Dawn was glancing off the Hudson when we drove through the Lincoln Tunnel and past the steaming Jersey meadows to the Clifford Scott High School in East Orange. The eight hundred students gave Ruby and the show a fine response and the principal said it was one of the best shows they'd ever had there. Ruby had made a daring choice and come through like the pro she always was, and she recovered some of the confidence beaten out of her by the yearlong struggle with depression. She was stronger than I had realized and that resilience would toughen in the months ahead. I felt proud of her, but her achievement did not dissolve the restraint we felt toward each other. There was no forgiveness. The rockbound character of

the North Atlantic Newfoundlander could not submit to the granite spine of my New England ancestry.

Two days later Nancy Wells did her first show with me at Greenwich High School for $60, the same program of Victoria and Twain, and Nancy did a good job holding her own with an unruly audience of six hundred sons and daughters of the Connecticut gentry. On October 2 we were at Rye, New York, and the same day at Mamaroneck for $50, where Nancy got her baptism in *The School for Wives* in front of seven hundred kids. The following night at the Stony Brook School on Long Island we did the full show, not helped by the disgraceful fact that I had forgotten to pack the Queen Elizabeth costume, so Nancy had to go on in this awesome role for the first time in her dressing gown. A dreadful spear in the heart, but she was a cool professional and handled my unforgivable memory lapse with the gritty determination of an overboard survivor stroking for shore.

Nancy and I pursued the fall bookings on the road with shows in Rome, New York; Milburn, New Jersey; and Bronxville and Larchmont, New York, where Nancy's parents saw the show and were pleased with it. That was a real gift. I respected them both and their daughter was worth the respect they gave to her. I was relieved that she did not rouse the same feelings that Lee had torched in me, nor did the actresses I worked with at Holyoke, except Miriam Stovall. So it wasn't just women that threw me off course. It was a certain kind of woman.

During all this bouncing around with the show I was pushing myself to work on the Mark Twain solo, looking for selections that would fit together for a program, and I kept after Arthur Hanna in the hope that he would use me on one of his radio shows, so there wasn't much breathing time before Nancy and I headed upstate for Cooperstown to play an evening show at the Knox School on Saturday, October 24. Two days later we were in Vermont at Castleton Teachers College in ski country and had a wonderful evening show interrupted several times by applause. Nancy was turning Molière's *School for Wives* scene into a delicious performance of wide-eyed, mischievous innuendo, which collected laughs and applause. These

two show dates brought in $200 each, and two days later we finished the October bookings with a strong response at Great Neck High School on Long Island. Nancy Wells had hit her stride and was more than holding her own.

There was a feeling in the air that something might happen, and the following week it did. I landed a job in radio, a one-shot on NBC's soap opera *The Right to Happiness* for $33.60. It was directed by Arthur Hanna. This was Agnes Wells's show and I know that quietly she had a lot to do with my being given the opportunity. Then three days later I got a second television job, a bit part on ABC's *Chevrolet Showroom* for $46.70. These were jobs of small consequence in show business, but of real importance to me. They gave me hope that I might be able to make a living as an actor in New York. The Chevy TV show was more stressful than it could have been because on the morning of the show we had a performance at a high school in New Jersey for seven hundred roughhouse kids, and Ruby did the show with me again—Molière and Twain. We got back at about four-thirty and I did my bit that night on live television.

In between these shows I continued doing scenes for the Theatre Wing classes at night, and in one of them I worked with Arthur Seelen, who would open the Drama Book Shop, soon to become a theatrical landmark. Arthur was wise and thoughtful and we became lifelong friends. The bookings on the road kept me out of town, so our life as a family became a series of visitations by me, and this began to codify my role as a husband and a father. The unspoken space between Ruby and me became habitual and a safety zone we didn't enter. We became friends again but not lovers. Our occasional intimacies did not last. Something that was once precious had hidden itself away.

Nancy and I went south for Alkahest, playing seven shows down through the knobs of Appalachia and over to Baltimore, making some mighty mileage runs in the station wagon, and from Hinton I wrote a letter to Ruby. It was about the state of our marriage, dated November 18, 1953.

I would not ever want to separate from you. I have a firm faith that people can always work out their problems and make a better life. I'm not afraid to stick and work for that, and I don't believe you are either. I'm too proud of the fact that I have a wife and a baby to ever want to separate. And I love you, with all our problems. Though I admit that sometimes they seem too overpowering and I get mad at them.

No, I don't think I'll ever get to the point where I will not be a very busy person. I'm a willful, hard-driving person and I have to accomplish work. I wish it were possible for you to encourage me in that and not make me feel I am doing it at the expense of pleasing you. Sometimes I think what our marriage really lacks is a good sense of humor.

I do not want you to be dependent on me at the expense of fulfilling yourself. I always admire you more when you do something on your own. I know you have a turmoil inside you sometimes, bad feelings that must be let out. You should let them out. I have always admired you more than you have admired yourself. I would feel wonderful if some day you could catch up with me. That means standing on your own two feet—doing just what you say in your letter that you want to do.

Got to close now. Don't tell me I look tired when I get home, darling. I will be. I'll have been driving for 12 hours, so it's only natural. Goodnight, my dear. See you soon. All my love.

Always, Hal.

Thanksgiving was a week away. A call came from Nancy Morrow at Young and Rubicam for me to meet the writer and producer of a radio soap opera moving to television; it had the cheerful moniker *The Brighter Day*. I went to 485 Madison in a pretty nervous state because this was a big-time shot for me—maybe a running part on a network TV soap. It wouldn't have the class of a nighttime show, but class my ass, as the saying goes, it would pay the bills. I was scared and I had to pretend I wasn't. That was my acting job and I

was sure I'd botched it until I got a callback the next day to read the part of the son in the family. This was getting serious. My imagination started cartwheeling around the notion that I might get the job. That dream went flat when I got to the waiting room and saw the competition. Three guys who looked like quarterbacks for the Michigan football team; not marked up or crippled like linemen, these guys were handsome.

Inside the room, a big man named Bob was in charge—I guessed he was the producer—and Nancy Morrow was there smiling at me; and there was a middle-aged lady who looked like a maiden aunt and had kind eyes like Ricklie. It turned out she was the writer, Doris Frankel. She asked me a few questions about myself, where I was born and raised, stuff like that, and I gave them a short blast of my crooked family history. In the waiting room they had given us sides to look over so we could prepare ourselves, but the speeches marked for me were for a character named Grayling, and nobody by that name could be the offspring of two human beings, so I asked who Grayling was and Bob said, "He's the son in the family. The head of the family is a minister."

"Grayling's father is a minister?"

"Yep."

Miss Frankel said, "You haven't heard the radio show, I take it."

"No, ma'am, but I will now." She smiled at that and then I read the scene with a woman who couldn't have been an actress, because she was awful. And so was I. It was like reading with a telephone operator. There was a bleak silence; then they smiled and thanked me and I slunk out of the room like a coyote. I walked home, fifty blocks north, to calm my jittery heart. I told Ruby not to expect anything. "Let's just enjoy the Thanksgiving turkey."

On Monday, November 30, I got a callback again. This was making me really nervous, but it was Mark Twain's birthday so maybe that was lucky. I had to report to the CBS Radio building on East Fifty-second Street and wait in the hallway with the competition. I leaned against a wall to support my nerves and help me look nonchalant, and across the hall I saw Jason Robards. Hell, forget it! I

could never make it in this crowd. Every damned one of them looked confident, and they were chatting away as if they were attending a goddamn cocktail party. All except Robards. We had to go in there and read a scene on mike, like on radio, because now the show was going to be on both TV and radio. The actor playing the son on radio was probably nearing fifty years old with a limp, and that wouldn't serve the TV show. I think I did pretty good on the radio audition because I knew what to do when I faced the mike. I had *done* radio! So far so good. Maybe. I went home and waited. Prayed and waited. I had discovered prayer.

It worried me a lot that I was beginning to imagine what it would be like to have the job and all that money. So I began forcing myself to think I *would not get the job*. This turned my mind toward Twain. The Mark Twain solo idea was beginning to look like my next salvation stop because I wouldn't have to count on anyone. I'd do it alone. Everything. Put the material together, learn it, set up the stage with whatever was available, and carry one suitcase with the suit, padding, shoes, shirt and tie, the wig, mustache, a watch, and some cigars. I'd already figured that a cigar could be a good prop because in so many pictures Twain was holding a cigar. And he said funny things about it. Like "I make it a rule never to smoke when asleep. Not that I care for moderation myself, I do it to prove that I am not a slave to the habit. I can give it up whenever I want to. I've done it a thousand times." Actually that was two things he said. I just put them together. I'd have to do that here and there to construct a show. Connect things. Maybe Twain wouldn't mind. So I told Higgins to go ahead and look for Twain dates.

But two days after Mark Twain's birthday I got a call for another audition. Thursday, December 3. My God! I had a show that day with Nancy in Scranton, Pennsylvania, at 2:00 p.m. I couldn't cancel out $200. I called Nancy Morrow to see how late in the day I could audition for them and she consulted with someone for a long moment of no breathing.

"I think five-thirty is the latest, Hal."

"I'll make it."

"You can?"

"The show's at two o'clock. One hour, maybe fifty minutes. I can get a three forty-seven American Airlines flight to La Guardia, it gets in at four twenty-four. I'll get a cab and make it."

"Good luck."

It was one of the best shows in many moons. Jackie and John O'Connor and Jackie's mother were there, and Jimmy Wells to help put on the show and pack up. I made the flight and made the audition just in time. It was not on camera, but in a studio with an older actor, Bill Smith, who was going to play the minister/father. He was good, very natural—he'd been doing the role on radio and they were going with him on TV. I tried to be natural, too, and calm, but I wasn't. I felt as if I were in a trance. I was feeling that way all the time now.

Meanwhile, I'd gotten another job, a bit part in a small film called *Days of Destiny*—$70, for Sam Robbins or Bud Roth, I forget which one was the character's name and which was the agent. By the weekend I hadn't heard back about *The Brighter Day*, nor did I the following week, so that was gone. What a hell of a way to celebrate Christmas. Anyway, we had two dates to fill with the new show at Brunswick, Maryland, and Richmond, Virginia, but my confidence in the future took a beating on the long drive back to New York. That soap opera job would have meant a steady one or two hundred bucks a week and that would have secured the family.

Back to the Mark Twain solo, and now I had to get serious. I read *Huck*, *Tom Sawyer*, *Connecticut Yankee*, and some of the essays. I thought "Captain Stormfield's Visit to Heaven" was funny, but long and chancy if it died on me in front of an audience. I needed laughs. There was a speech in one of the volumes in which he started off kidding himself with funny compliments he'd received, and one idea was to start the show that way, complimenting himself, and then pull out the cigar and do stuff on that. Boy, if the laughs didn't come, what would I do? I'd run across some funny lines in Harnsberger's *Fingertips* and there was a funny story about a poet who wanted to commit suicide—maybe that wouldn't amuse them in the women's

clubs—and I'd heard about the Italian Guide routine from *Innocents Abroad*. That was supposed to be funny. But when I tried out a few anecdotes and laugh lines on Bob and Ruth they looked at me as if they thought there was more to come. They didn't know the joke was over. Disheartening. The whole idea of pushing myself out on-stage to face a firing squad with this material was feeling loonier and loonier. I considered giving it up, but Bim Pond had told me to do it and he was no dope. Twain had done it and he got laughs. But how?

An agent named Milton Goldman heard about our two-person show and wanted to know if I'd give a free performance for the Fountain House in midtown, a kind of halfway house for people recovering from mental illness, and Nancy and I said we'd do it. Hell, the show had worked in the suicide ward of the Chillicothe Veterans Hospital in 1948, so maybe it would be a big hit here. Anyway, it was a good idea to do a favor for an agent.

Bang. A call came from Nancy Morrow. The final audition, two other guys and me, next Monday in front of the cameras at Lieder-kranz Hall. This was going to be my fifth audition for the role. It wound me up like a top. One of us three guys would get it.

The Fountain House performance came first on Saturday night, and even though we worked at one end of a room for fifty people, the quality of the response was surprising. Some of the mental patients we had talked to seemed in a bad way, but afterward they were earnest and sweet about their feelings and what the show had meant to them, and it settled me down. This was real life and real people.

On Monday I got a call to do the radio soap *Right to Happiness* again later that week, and then I hugged Ruby and Victoria and took the subway downtown for my audition. I was so scared I had even stopped shaking. My heart was a big drum that made such a racket it had taken command of my whole body and scared off the shakes. When I got on the subway I tried to connect with God to see if he was too busy to handle me when I got to the studio at Liederkranz Hall, but it must have been tough for him to reach me underground. I could see it was going to be me all alone in front of that camera, and then it occurred to me that I had never been in front of a camera

all alone, only in a group. This time they'd be watching the nervous zit rising on my chin and exploring the fear in my eyes.

In the waiting room I was introduced to the other two guys and they were nervous, too. Nothing could hide it. One guy was tall, dark, and handsome, one of the Michigan quarterbacks, I thought, and the other was a twin of the movie star Robert Walker. A little shy but manly. That seemed to cover it, so I didn't know why I was there. Walker was called in first and then the quarterback. I tried to pull myself together alone in that room. I wanted this job.

It was a big, bright space with a couch and a coffee table and a girl in it to do the audition with me. A beautiful redhead. Her shape was so perfect I had to look away from it, so I tried to concentrate on her eyes. She was scared, too, I saw that, and it calmed me a little because while she was a knockout, she looked like she needed protection here and I stepped right into the role of protector and she sensed it. The smile she gave me was grateful. We were in it together.

They had given me a script to look at and I'd tried to memorize some of the lines before they called me in, but when I entered the studio the lines flew out of my head all the way to Florida. Two enormous cameras rolled into position like General Patton's tanks, and on the other side of a large glass window in one wall, dimly lit, dark figures were watching us. They must be the ones who would decide my fate. I didn't know if the redhead's fate had been decided or if she was just reading with me and the other guys, or just me, and I was too out of body to ask her who she was. In the script it said she was Sandra.

"Grayling, where have you been?"

"Huh?" I hadn't heard them say start. "Oh, downtown."

"Aunt Emily said you'd be here more than an hour ago. So I waited."

"I'm glad you did."

"Are you?"

"Yes."

"Well. Here I am." It was hard to look at her, this beauty, lips parted, without a sensation of real desire.

"Sandra, I've been walking around thinking and talking to my-self, telling myself how crazy in love I am . . ."

"Oh, Grayling . . ."

"Sandra . . . I'm crazy for you."

"Grayling, why have you waited to tell me till now?" She was angry—eyes flashing. "Now that Roger has asked me to be his wife."

"Tell him no. Tell him you love me . . ."

"Oh . . ."

"You do, don't you?"

"Please . . ."

"Tell me you do."

"Yes. Yes." She flew into my arms. We kissed.

The scene we actually did was longer, but this imaginary one will provide its spirit and the temptation. I had to declare love for a stranger I had just met, and the dark crowd of people beyond the glass were giving us marks for how believably we acted it out, and that meant both of us. You couldn't solo in a scene like that. It was like walking blindfolded into someone's private chamber and reach-ing for them as if your life depended on it and taking them. When it was over the girl was trembling and there was a kind of frightened look in her eyes.

"Thank you. I hope that was okay," I said. She dropped her eyes and a voice from the booth said, "Thank you. Thank you both. Stay there for a minute, Hal."

She picked up her script, which had dropped on the floor when we embraced. I was too dazed to reach for it quick enough. Then she took my hand, gave me a kiss on the cheek, and was gone. My ears felt red; something inside me was pounding up into them and exploding. The girl was beautiful.

An amplified voice from behind the dark glass said, "Hal, come on up into the booth." I felt off balance and couldn't decide which way to go to get into the booth, and somebody took my arm and moved me toward a short stairway. Inside, it was dark and crowded—the darkness blinded me coming out of the light—but people were jostling me and smiling and someone put a glass of champagne into

my hand and more people came and smiled, but I couldn't hear them, because I'd gone deaf somehow. It was only my own voice I was hearing inside my head, saying, What's going on? Someone tell me what's going on. Then Doris Frankel was smiling at me and I thought, Should I ask Doris? She said something to me quietly, but I couldn't catch it.

"Doris. Do I have this part?"

"Yes, Hal."

"I do?"

"Yes, Hal."

If I live a hundred years, I won't forget that. I think it was the moment life said yes to me. Nancy Morrow came out of the crowd. "Hal, you know that postcard you send me every week? With the little picture on it? That picture reminded me to call you for this role. Congratulations."

I was having trouble with my emotions. I had to get out of there. When I got down on Fifty-eighth Street I turned blindly and walked to the corner of Park Avenue and then turned left and walked a block, and there on the corner talking to another fellow were the quarterback and Robert Walker. They shook my hand and wished me luck and I thanked them and moved across Park Avenue fast because I had started to cry. The tears wouldn't stop, they ran down my face in a rush and kept coming until I had to turn my back on the street and pretend to look at the display in a store window to hide what was happening to me.

I think Ruby was as stunned and bewildered as I was by this sudden turn of fortune. I had no agent, so it took a couple of days for me to get my courage up and call Nancy Morrow. I was afraid they would change their minds. No, it was the real thing. I would be playing Grayling Dennis in *The Brighter Day*, a fifteen-minute radio show and a fifteen-minute TV show, live, five days a week. I'd get $100 for each day's dual performance I was in, depending on when the script called for me. If I averaged two shows a week, that would amount to $200 a week for fifty-two weeks, which was more than $10,000 a year, and they had an option on more years. We couldn't believe our luck. If I

could fit in some dates with our two-person show, we'd be rich. And that wasn't all. I had started to get a few other jobs—the *Right to Happiness* job again the next day (I wanted to tell Agnes, Nancy's mother, and the show's director, Arthur Hanna, the good news) and I got a call for a TV job on *Rocket Rangers* on the Saturday after Christmas. It was a good year after all, 1953. I'd done sixty-one program dates with the two-person show, nine plays at Holyoke, a few bits on television and radio, and I had a steady job in New York for the coming year. We hadn't been to church for years, but on Christmas Day we went to the Riverside Church and thanked God.

28

The day before the New Year's Eve bells rang in 1954 we did our first radio show and I met my family: Bill Smith, my father the minister; Mona Bruns, my aunt Emily; Lois Nettleton, my sister Patsy; Mary Lin Beller, my younger sister Babby; and Brook Byron, my older sister Althea, who thought she was going insane. I didn't see the redhead and that was a disappointment. Our director, Marvin Silbersher, was a stocky blond guy with a crew cut, a real machine in the workplace who kept us moving right along. No time for small talk. Being part of a "family" was a whole new adventure for me and I was unprepared for it. Having a "father" who preached sermons instead of hopping freights and hanging out in the insane asylum, and "sisters" who were not married to guys who piled the labels of tin cans up to the ceiling, was unfamiliar territory for me. You didn't have to worry about them. They were as capable as I was, maybe more, so it was hard to feel like a son or a brother to them because I felt like the one who didn't belong. Yet Grayling was rather interesting. It would come out before long that I had a drinking problem. I kept waiting for the redhead to appear.

I wouldn't need the Mark Twain solo now. Higgins had booked only two shows so far, at Poughkeepsie and at a college in Pennsylvania. They would have to be canceled, but what about all the other dates he and Ricklie had booked for the two-person show? There were twenty-eight of them between January and May, and twenty-four

of these in the first nine weeks of the year. It was going to be a knock-out blow to Ricklie and Higgins if I canceled, and what if I needed them later? Would they take a chance and book me again? My own show I could count on. *The Brighter Day* could disappear next year.

Hell. I had to bring it up with the producer, and soon. The first Twain solo was ten days away. Bob was a large man and authoritative and I hoped to God he wouldn't fire me. So after the first radio show, when we rehearsed for our Monday television debut, I broke the news to him. He wasn't happy, but he promised to think about it and talk to the writer. That would be Doris Frankel. I said I'd cancel whatever I had to for *The Brighter Day*, but these commitments were made with people I had worked with for four years and I wanted to be square with them. An agent might have handled it better but I just told him the truth and hoped he'd figure something out. Then I told Howard to be prepared for cancellations on our January dates.

Monday, January 4, I found out what live television was like. How can I describe it, even to the actor of fifty years later when shows are done in the safety net of film? Think of the circus clown being shot out of the cannon. Imagine it's your first ride. I don't know what they use to launch the clowns out of cannon barrels, but in live television it is fright. "Five, four, three, two, one!" In those final seconds you are assuring your terrified self that you will re-member a bucketful of lines you learned last night. *And if you don't*, America will be watching you fail!

I tried to seal the lines into my brain over the weekend and get them to feel natural, but I never "owned" them. I spent my energy being natural in rehearsal and this led me nowhere; it isolated me from the life of a scene instead of joining me to it. But the prime lesson to come out of my first day on live television was—depend on your fellow actors! When the dreaded moment came and the next line was nowhere on earth or in heaven, nobody could save you but them. This made you feel part of the family mighty quick. After our bath in a fifteen-minute pit of terror, we collected ourselves and moved to the rehearsal room to read the script for the next day's show. I began to

hope my role would get smaller. On the street and in the subway on the way home I had the script in my hand, trying to stuff the dialogue into my memory. The more I worked on it before sleeping, the better I'd know the lines in the morning. Sleep plowed them under.

I had one more *Brighter Day* show on Friday, that made three out of five the first week, and three more the second week. Now the cancellations began: Rotary Club in Poughkeepsie for the Mark Twain solo and the two-person show in Jersey City. But on Saturday evening the sixteenth, for the Bethlehem, Pennsylvania, Dinner Club, Nancy and I had a wonderful performance of the new show with four calls. The following week I had four *Brighter Day* appearances and two in the next week to round out January, and by this time Ruby had had enough.

"I'm going back to Hamilton. There is no life here for us. You're gone all the time."

"I'm trying to make a living for us."

"But you're not even here when you're home. You're studying lines all the time. And staying up late."

"I know. I feel bad about it, but I have to get them in my head in one night. It's scary."

"It's scary for me. And no fun for me or Victoria. I'm taking her back to Beryl's."

Our wonderful good luck was not so good now. Its shabby side was loneliness for Ruby. The same loneliness she had bequeathed to me when she went to Canada was now the bitter pill the *Brighter Day* job had served up to her. It was a sad exchange. I wondered how all the other actors up and down the West Side were handling this. It might not damage Victoria too much, she was not quite two years old, but it punished our shaky marriage. Living with a machine was no fun for Ruby.

Their departure was followed by weeks of high-flying tension. The word came back to me that the soap would try to keep me out of shows if I gave them a list of the road dates, but I might have to cancel some pretty late in the game, so I gave Ricklie and Howard

the choice of canceling all the road shows or playing roulette with *The Brighter Day*, and that's what we wound up doing. But it was hair-raising. In the first week of February, just before Ruby and Victoria left, I had the soap opera on Monday and Tuesday and a show Tuesday night in Rochester for the Council of Jewish Women for $150. So after the TV show went off the air at Liederkranz Hall I sped to La Guardia and got a 3:40 p.m. one-stop flight to Rochester, arriving at 5:50 p.m. A cab got me to the Hebrew Y in time to help Nancy finish the setup for the show. She'd driven the station wagon up there alone, so the next day we drove it to Niagara Falls for an evening show at the College Club ($175), where Ruby's sister Beryl and some friends came across the border to see us. The next morning before we left, Ruby and Victoria arrived by bus from New York and I had a brief visit with them before they drove off to Hamilton with Beryl. I was unsure when I'd see them again. Nancy and I headed south toward Pittsburgh, where we played the new show at Geneva College in Beaver Falls the next morning. That was Friday. Nancy drove me to the airport and I caught a TWA flight for New York at 4:00 p.m. for rehearsal on the *Rocky King, Detective* show while she headed for our Monday show town.

Rocky rehearsed Saturday and aired Sunday for $76.10, but I had to take the sleeper overnight to Pittsburgh on Sunday at 11:59 p.m. after the show because we had an 11:45 a.m. performance at Mount Lebanon for $200. I felt like I was coining money. On Tuesday afternoon we played the Woman's Club of Cuyahoga Falls, Ohio, for $200. On Wednesday the tenth we had two shows in the Cleveland area, the second in Lakewood at St. Augustine Academy, where Sister Ernestine had said the morning prayer for my grandfather when he died. The Sister was away and I was so sorry I never had the chance to tell her how fondly I remembered her. I flew back to New York on a 6:00 p.m. United flight and rehearsed the next afternoon for Friday's *Brighter Day*, following that, flew back to the Midwest to join up with Nancy for a show Saturday at Terre Haute, Indiana. This was the pace I had to keep.

They had decided to write me out of the soap opera for the rest

of February to allow me to fill all Ricklie's engagements, so we continued to hit the road. Our second show was in Terre Haute two days later, where Nancy nailed Queen Elizabeth good. We had seven more in the next nine days in and around Chicago, and I wrote to Ruby, suggesting that she join me there, but got no response. I didn't really think she'd come, but it was a gesture of friendship. Our seventh show was performed on a marble staircase in the Wedgwood Room at Marshall Field's department store, an Astaire-Rogers exhibition, performing on that staircase in period costumes.

Two days later I had to be in New York rehearsing for *The Brighter Day*, and I knew Nancy's mother and father were very uneasy about their daughter taking that 850-mile drive alone, so as the winter night darkened Chicago we hit the road together and started clicking off the miles. We made it to Fort Wayne late that night and hit Route 30 again in the morning, hell-bent for leather across Ohio toward Pittsburgh and the Pennsylvania Turnpike. My mind was on Ruby. I knew from her letters that she was seeing Dr. Martins, the psychiatrist, again, but all she had given me was a post office address and no phone. I knew Victoria was being taken care of at Beryl and Stew's, but Ruby's failure to give me a better address had meant "Leave me alone." It felt pretty sour, so on Valentine's Day I tried to lighten things between us:

> *I want to send you a Valentine's card but got so fed up searching through those ridiculous verses which fail to express a real emotion that I gave up. Today I went into the telegraph office to send you a greeting and realized after I started it that I didn't have any street address or phone number to send it to, except the post office, which seemed kind of foolish. So—I'll say it in a letter: I am very happy to be married to you. That you care about me and what happens to me as I do about you. That we are both trying to build a good, happy life together and in spite of our many failures along the way we are headed upwards instead of down. This all seems very worthwhile celebrating—so Happy Valentine's Day! (P.S. I love you!)*

I was beginning to feel like a juggler trapped in a performance I could not stop, keeping the career airborne with one hand and trying to retrieve my family life with the other.

I left Nancy at Harrisburg to drive the last leg home and took a plane into New York in time for the Friday rehearsal of Monday's performance of *The Brighter Day* and was relieved to discover they hadn't cut me out of the show. On the contrary, I was in deep. I had four scheduled that week, with one of our shows in Providence spliced between *Brighter Day* performances on Thursday and Friday. By the end of February I had done sixteen shows with Nancy for a total of $2,775. After the 30 percent commission and Nancy's share of $664.50 (she was getting 35 percent) I had a balance of $1,290.50 plus the income from the soap. I began to daydream. Maybe money could pull some of the tension out of our life. Maybe we could get a larger apartment and go out to dinner once in a while.

When I got to the studio, my father the minister was gone. They had replaced him with an actor named Blair Davies, whom I had met on the *Hollywood Screen Test* show. It was a shock. Bill Smith, perfect in the role, had played it on radio for years. I inquired discreetly of Mona Bruns and she whispered, "He was bald." They got rid of him because he was bald. Now my dream job was featuring a nightmare: you could be replaced. I got my own job replacing a radio actor who was too old, one of the hardest-working radio actors in the business before television came along and killed it. This was not a kindly business. Maybe I ought to try out the Mark Twain solo once at that college date in Pennsylvania, just to see if there was anything there worth pursuing. An instinct for caution had kept me from canceling it, so I decided to ask Bob and Doris if I could get out to do just this one show.

The answer was yes. I think Doris may have been bemused by my literary pretensions. When I realized the show was only two weeks away, on March 11, any impulse I had to smile died a quick death. I had to pull it together fast and really learn it, learn it solid; I'd be all alone out there. I'd been working on the material for a while be-

cause I enjoyed fooling with it—it made me laugh out loud some-times—but if I forgot my lines onstage at the State Teachers College in Lock Haven, Pennsylvania, confidence in my solo acting career would collapse.

First I had to settle on an arrangement for a fifty-minute program—what followed what? My plan was to start with the com-pliments routine and the cigar stuff and maybe put the poet story next (the guy who wanted to commit suicide with Twain's help). Then I was uncertain. I knew from Bim Pond that Twain had used the Interviewer and the Italian Guide, but in those two I'd have to play the other roles as well as Twain. I'd read that Twain acted out the different characters, but I was going to have to act *him* acting out the other characters. That would be tricky. How would I act their voices so that I'd sound like Twain impersonating *them*, not me doing it? And I needed another fifteen minutes that would keep the show afloat. I'd been much amused by "Captain Stormfield's Visit to Heaven," but if I used that piece it would be the big key number be-fore the seventy-year-old stuff at the end of the show, and "Stormfield" was a long, high dive off the suicide platform. It didn't have joke lines to drop on the audience, and once I started into it, there would be no way to get out. It could sink the show. But I'd never resisted the suicide impulse onstage, so I took the dive again and began beat-ing "Stormfield" into my memory alongside Grayling Dennis.

Then Ruby wrote that she was coming back to New York the first week of March. That felt like the face of crisis, and I was already in one. She would be carrying a full load of psychological firepower from Dr. Martins and I couldn't handle that now. I asked her to wait until I got Twain out of the way, but she was coming anyway at the end of the week. On *The Brighter Day*, my sister Althea had lost her husband in Korea and thought she was going insane. Most of the story line in February and March dealt with this crisis and also my drinking problem. I can't remember why Grayling drank, maybe because Dad was bald and they fired him, but I was lapping it up pretty good, so when I went back on the show the first day of March,

Aunt Emily gave me a good talking-to about evil in the bottle. Two days later I was on the soap again, still drinking, and also Thursday and Friday, but Nancy and I had a show in Providence on Thursday night. They let me out of Thursday's rehearsal early and I flew to Providence, arrived at 7:07 p.m., and went onstage with Nancy at 8:15 at the Plantations Club. Nancy's father had driven up with her to set up the stage.

At this show I met Madame Charbonnel, who had known Twain and his daughter Clara in Vienna. She talked about Clara's opera ambitions, her courtship with the pianist Gabrilowitsch—all news to me—and Twain's colorful character. She also stressed his seriousness, that he was a deep-thinking man, and I realized I hadn't given any consideration to that. How strange that this friend of Mark Twain's appeared just seven days before I would go out onstage to assume his identity for the first time. Was it a benevolent sign or a warning? Was he testing me from wherever he was in the hereafter? It was hard to tell where, because he'd said, "Heaven for climate, Hell for society."

Over the weekend I set the shape of the Twain program and tried to welcome Ruby and Victoria home again, but I knew she'd been having electric shock treatments in Hamilton and it set me on edge. She'd written that she'd been discussing sex with Dr. Martins, so I didn't know when that bomb was going to fall on me. She didn't drop it right away. She was pretty calm and respectful of the Twain hurdle I had to clear, but I knew the bomb was up there waiting to drop. I tried to be as attentive and kind as I could, but my brain was racing.

I kept the lines for the solo show running through my head on Monday, Tuesday, and Wednesday while doing *The Brighter Day* and when my memorizing became audible the actors thought I was having mental problems; but once I explained that on Thursday I was going to debut the Twain thing they got sympathetic right away. So I tried out a few laugh lines on them, ones I was counting on to carry the show. All I got was a strange look or a weak chuckle. I was

scared—all my life I'd been afraid to get up in front of people and give a speech—but this was a death message. I told Ruby about this bleak response and she said, "Work behind a lectern. Have the 'Stormfield' number all typed out so you won't get lost halfway through if the audience response isn't what you hope for. It doesn't always have to be funny, you know."

I'd make a few notes, too, about what selection came next to guide me through the swampland I was wading into. Half the time I wanted to back out of the date, but I was driven by the instinct that someday I would have to know if this thing worked.

On Wednesday after *The Brighter Day*, Jimmy Wells drove with me across the George Washington Bridge and into Pennsylvania, across the Poconos to where the Susquehanna curves up to Williamsport and Lock Haven. The next morning Mr. Gillam, who was in charge of the assembly program, greeted us at the college auditorium, which was large and well equipped. Jimmy and I positioned the lectern at stage left with a big rug under it that I could wander around on if I felt safe enough to let go of the lectern. That was going to be the life buoy. There were about 350 students and faculty out front and they were paying me $125. At 10:00 a.m. I was ready to go onstage in the white suit and wig, the mustache glued in place, my eyebrows whitened, and a more careful hour-and-fifteen-minute makeup job than I'd ever done before. There was a cigar in my vest pocket and matches in the right pocket of my coat, which I intended to strike on the sole of my shoe. I was in control of myself and pretending to be seventy years old. In the wings I thought of Ed Wright, how he had held that pause as Elmer Wartz for a long time before he grinned and revealed those big buck teeth, which threw the audience into hysterics. Remember to pause for the teeth, I thought, and walked on.

They surprised me. My first line was "I wish to begin this at the beginning lest I forget it altogether." I hoped there would be a laugh at the end of the line, but the laugh came early, on "at the beginning," and then a second one came on "forget it altogether." More

surprises came. Some lines that I didn't know were funny got laughs. I was pretty sure of a laugh on "I was born modest, but it wore off," but didn't expect one on the lawyer's introduction of Twain as "a humorist who is really funny." The cigar stuff was fun for them and I started to enjoy myself. It was wonderful to hear people laughing together. Even the Interviewer, with Twain playing both parts, collected. At the end of a half hour I was gliding along on the pleasure of surprise, and then came "Captain Stormfield's Visit to Heaven." I felt sure they would love it as much as I did and laugh at Captain Stormfield's astonishment when the heavenly clerk couldn't find the captain's home port of San Francisco on the celestial map. Once Stormfield got in, his wings didn't fit and he crash-landed. The halo kept falling off, which drove him to salty exasperation, and he couldn't manage the harp, nor could he endure the endless repetition of harp music. As I got into this story the response began to fade away and finally the audience went silent. I was shocked and it rocked my confidence. The seventy-year-old stuff at the end of the show got them laughing again, but I was puzzled. So I asked Mr. Gillam what he thought was the cause of the poor reaction to Stormfield. I had to pressure him for a response.

"They may have found it somewhat irreverent," he said.

Never thought of it! Never imagined anyone would be set back by the irreverence, because that's what I loved about it. Sixty years earlier, this had been funny. What was happening to our sense of humor? I had a lot to learn.

I had been acutely aware that Ruby felt cut off from the new direction of our life. Now Ruby said she wanted to talk, and I knew what was coming. The disappearance of the habit of sex from our marriage was the subject and she had some questions about that.

"What happened to us, Hal? I mean the tenderness we felt for each other."

"I think it's been knocked out of us by what we've been through."

"Well, I guess you mean what happened after the baby. My depression."

"Yes, partly. And the long recovery from it."

"But that wasn't my fault. I had a Cesarean, they cut me open, and then I went back to work too soon. It was a mistake."

"Yes, it was. I should never have let you do that, it was a terrible mistake."

"Yes, and I had no help."

"We had Dixie's mother."

"I mean no help from you. You were always too busy."

"I had to be busy, I was learning all those lines, rehearsing and stuff."

"You avoided me—it was a way of avoiding me, that work you did."

"Maybe, in a way, but I didn't feel right getting physical with you. I mean, you'd had that operation."

"Well, I couldn't do anything for a while."

"For quite a while, Ruby. And when we tried it when you came to New York, I was a failure."

"A failure?"

"Yeah. I felt like one."

"You didn't talk to me about it."

"It was obvious. I felt embarrassed by the whole thing, the way I attacked you that first night. I was out of control."

"Do you feel sexy about other women?"

"Yeah, sometimes. Yeah."

"Who?"

"Well, I mean, you know it was a terrible trial for me to be out on the road for all that time with another woman. An attractive one. That was rough."

"You mean Lee?"

"Yeah. I'm not made of stone. Going down to our underwear in the dressing room. Nothing happened, but it was in my mind a lot. I mean, God, I'm a man and it was like torture sometimes."

"You mean being true to me?"

"Yes."

"Maybe you shouldn't have been true to me."

"I had to. I would have felt too guilty, and anyway, Lee would not have done something like that. It was out of the question."

"How did you feel about that?"

"Feel? Hell, I felt neutered. Trapped. I felt trapped and it made me angry."

"That's the way I feel now, Hal. Trapped in more ways than one, trapped in this apartment and in my life. I feel trapped by your isolation from me. Work has become your mistress."

"I know that."

"Because you no longer find me attractive?"

"Ruby, it's because you have withdrawn from me. I feel like a failure with you, that's why I don't get passionate. I'm a failure there. It's humiliating."

"Well, I'm waiting."

"I'm sorry. Sorry as hell. I'll try, but I feel very mixed up about it. Our dear feelings are gone. I suppose that's why I work so hard, to wear myself out, because I have urges, lots of times, but I have to suppress them. Even with you, because you don't feel up to it or you're not in the mood. And there was that horrible long time of denial, over a year. It was torture for me, real torture, and it took a big toll on my confidence. And now I don't want to get rejected any more like that night when you came back, when I lost control. I'd rather sidestep that humiliation."

"Well, I certainly don't want to force myself on you."

"If we could just relax with each other again, be happy again, I'll bet the urges would come back."

"I would hope so."

"We used to have some fun together. Everything has become so terribly important and grim."

"Do you love me?"

"Yes. I do. I love you, but I feel defeated by what has happened. If only we could get happy again."

We left it there. The question of separation or even divorce did not come up, although I knew it must have been on our minds, an

unwilling guest for both of us. She had surprised me, suggesting I should have had an affair with Lee. Maybe that would have helped, got rid of the horrible tensions; but Ruby and I needed each other, we truly did. And now I knew we were reaching a terminus because the combination of our genes—New England and Newfoundland, a stubborn heritage to conquer—would not allow us to forgive. My mind was on survival. When the last of the two-person shows were over in mid-May, there would be no more bookings. The producers of *The Brighter Day* had made that clear. I hoped Ruby would want to come back and play out the final performances. I think it would have helped her regain herself if she had, but she did not do it. Nancy was going to fill them and then it would be over. The theatrical offspring Ruby and I had brought into the world and labored over and nurtured as it grew and prospered, the show we had transported thousands of miles across America's vast landscapes, was headed for the grave. In its place we were constructing a vulnerable family fortress in which life with a baby was lived on the edge of chance. That was the road ahead for the team of Hal and Ruby Holbrook. Victoria took the place of our show, an innocent child, eager for life.

After the solo debut at Lock Haven, there was one more show to do on Monday evening in Rochester the following week, on the heels of a performance of *The Brighter Day* that afternoon. Then I'd be locked in the embrace of CBS Radio and Television for the remainder of March.

When I arrived at the studio for rehearsal that Friday a sudden thrill shot through me. The redhead was there. There was something expectant in her face. I had to keep my eyes down because meeting her gaze exposed me. As we read the script and it became clearer where the story line would be going, I had the sensation that life was suddenly extending a dangerous gift to me. The intention of the story was clear. Sandra was a woman of ill-repute whom my father, the minister, was taking under his wing. I believe his intention was to reform her and that was okay, good for him, but any fool could see that reforming a woman as shapely and long legged as this one

was never going to work, not in heaven or on earth, not if seventeen ministers took on the job. Knowing that I was destined to be mated with this forbidden nymph left me scared and uncertain. Could I handle this?

I had the weekend to construct a mental shelter around that question, which I hoped would not collapse when Sandra and I did the show on Monday. My worst moment came just before the performance, when I was pacing around the set, trying to control my nerves. I happened to wander into my bedroom and found her stretched out on the bed with her eyes closed and her long legs propped up against the wall with her skirt tucked between them. I backed out of there as if I'd come upon her naked, because in my mind's eye that was what I had just seen. When we met each other in front of the camera I tried to cover my feelings, but her intent brown eyes bored into me and it was possible to imagine anything I wished.

When two actors press their bodies together, one male and one female, a certain heat is generated. In most cases we keep this warmth impersonal, controlled by the safety valves of the actor's craft—the aesthetic distance between an imagined life and the real one—and the strength of our attachment to our real-life mate as well as our moral sense of right and wrong. If these controls are weakened, if the imagined life becomes more powerful than the real one, then the last restraint holding us in place is the moral choice between right and wrong. Who we thought we were can shift. I would have to mask my feelings because the part of me still in control did not want to lose it. A touch or an unguarded look ignited my imagination, and such contacts were waiting, moment to moment. Sometimes our hands lingered together too long or our bodies brushed each other and brushed again. Was it accidental? When we did our scenes together, building show by show to the time our characters would fall in love, the undertow of emotion between us became a hidden partner and I wondered what would happen when the day came for Sandra and Grayling to fall into each other's arms. I was twenty-nine

years old and all of a sudden I felt like a boy in the spell of infatuation.

I raced out of the studio in a state of confusion to catch the plane for the Rochester show. Our performance that night for the Women of Rotary was out of balance and it was my fault. Higgins saw it—the new show—and didn't like it as well as the old one. I returned to the apartment on 108th Street the next day, haunted by thoughts of infidelity, and felt like a man carrying on a secret affair. That is what my conscience told me I was doing. I did not feel right with Ruby, and my baby daughter began to acquire the image of an angel of purity disappearing in the shadows of her father's indiscretion. The life I had painstakingly put together in my head was dissolving.

On Thursday, Sandra and I were together again and the following week again and by the end of March we were covertly stalking each other on and off the set. But it was still a courtship of the imagination, a waltz of temptation. It was interrupted when Nancy and I got back to our show, our fine, dependable show, at the Masters School in Dobbs Ferry, New York. It was the original show, Victoria and Albert, Molière, Elizabeth and Essex, and Twain, and the purity of Nancy's presence and the professionalism of our relationship was accentuated by her mother's attendance. Having Agnes there made me look into myself and question the secret life my imagination was pursuing. I felt separated from decency.

My father, the minister, entered this double life. I knew he suspected something—hell, who wouldn't?—when he began paying special attention to me. The name Blair Davies had to have more than a seam of Welsh in it and the mystical insights of the Welsh character would put him on the trail of my fancies. One afternoon he invited me to have a drink with him after rehearsal. We had moved to studios at Grand Central Station, so Blair led me to a rather elegant bar in the Roosevelt Hotel on the corner of Forty-fifth Street. When he ordered a Scotch I followed his lead. Our conversation turned cautiously from personal histories to the show and its story line and paused at Sandra. I said she was a remarkable-looking woman

and he agreed. Beautiful, really. Yes. Very distracting to look at her, I said, and he asked me about my family. Did I have children? Oh. Yes, one. Do you think she's southern? Who? Sandra. Maybe. What is her name? Who? Your daughter. Oh. Victoria. And your wife? Ruby. I hope to meet them sometime.

I couldn't get him off the family theme and in a sudden rush of jealousy I wondered if he was interested in Sandra himself. But there was something comfortable about Blair, steady and human, and I went home with the feeling that I had a friend at court if I wanted one. Someone who knew more than he was prepared to discuss and perhaps felt some concern for me.

On the show I worked hard to be convincing. Pouring my feelings into the job of acting had carried me through emotional disturbances before, so this was a rich opportunity to use myself in spite of the sometimes stilted feel of the dialogue and swift dramatic plotting required to grab an audience in fifteen minutes. Daytime soaps were scorned by the people who worked the big evening shows like *Philco-Goodyear Playhouse* and *Studio One*, producing serious writers and directors like Horton Foote, Delbert Mann, and Martin Ritt and actors like Marty Balsam and Paul Newman, who wound up in Hollywood doing films. Before it all migrated west, the serious television work was still done in New York, with actors from the theater and the Actors Studio knocking down the good roles. It was hard to break into that club, so I felt like a loner with the moniker "soap opera actor." On the set of *The Brighter Day* there were times when I felt I had caught a moment of clear reality, usually in a scene with the actors I most admired, like Lois Nettleton, who played my sister Patsy. And with Sandra, but there was danger in pouring out my feelings with her because she was vulnerable. That was the killer touch, the vulnerability inside that perfectly formed body. I don't know how good an actress she was and I didn't care, because what I responded to was the pulse of a hungry emotion hiding out in her.

For the month of April we were on the show together only once or twice a week and I tried to get control of my imaginings and put my mind on my wife and my child and our future, for God's sake.

Harold

That it should be so difficult frightened me. I knew there were men to whom a double life was okay, but to me it was a dishonorable choice and I didn't know how I could live with it.

Then in early May my television dad suggested that he and I take Victoria to the beach at Spring Lake, New Jersey, for the weekend. The weather had turned warm early and it sounded like a good thing for me to be doing. So we took my two-year-old daughter down to the sandy edge of the Atlantic and introduced her to cold ocean water. She was delighted. Flew down the beach in her ruffled swimwear like Roger Bannister did that afternoon of May 6 when he broke the four-minute mile.

On Thursday, May 13, Nancy and I played the Woman's Club of White Plains and I went up twice in Molière. Mind on the long-legged redhead from the Smoky Mountains. Four days later, on May 17, our show gave its farewell performances, two of them, at 8:45 a.m. and 9:45 a.m., at the Mineola High School on Long Island for $80. We did two good shows, in a high school, a fitting resting place. The show ended where it began. Driving home, I had a feeling of helpless loss. The rug had been pulled out from under me, and Ruby and I had no safety net to catch us now.

The next day I was back on *The Brighter Day* and now the intensity of attraction I felt was becoming hard to handle. We were playing love scenes, and the contact between us, the soft contours of her body and the intense tactile warmth racing through us, our blood drumming out voiceless invitations, became unbearable. I couldn't believe what was happening to me. I thought I'd settled on a careful life for myself, emotionally poor, but protected by the boundaries of convention and my own self-discipline, and now that life was slipping off its pedestal. I was speeding down a precarious path, uncertain of who I was and my direction in life. I had spent months on the road with Lee contending in my mind with the nature of temptation, and more than a year since then existing like a novice monk, and now—just when things at home were beginning to feel somehow sustainable, when I felt I could settle for a prosaic but safe existence with Ruby and Victoria as a good provider and more attentive

father—this exploding attraction blew these illusions away. I was on the high board of suicide again, ready for another dive, but this time I was risking the lives of the two people who depended on me. The cage I had entered was not going to hold back passions I'd suppressed for too long. When we closed the door of the hotel room and let those wild emotions loose, it was like nothing I had known before.

29

I felt guilty, so I tried to be a more attentive father and took my two-year-old daughter to Riverside Park, where she could chase the squirrels and observe the mixture of people with her studious gaze. We liked being together. Her eagerness to be with me was winning, and the times I spent with Victoria gave me a better feeling about myself and took my mind to a safer place.

But chasing a ball in the park was as tiresome to Victoria as it was to me. People claimed her attention. And trees. Leaves delighted her, as they had delighted me in the tree house I built in a spreading maple on the farm. While the fashion of the approaching decade, in which Dad would become not only provider but a part-time mom, was insinuating itself into the culture of upper Broadway, its grip did not lay a comfortable hand on me. I longed for a place away from the jungle of stone and people, where I could create a life we would enjoy together. I had been quietly putting Grandpa's $100 a month in a savings account and I was able to tell Ruby we had $600 in there. Maybe we could find a cottage somewhere on a brook or a lake, way outside New York, and go there sometimes, winter and summer, now that I had a steady job.

I spent more time with Blair at the bar in the Roosevelt Hotel. If he knew about my affair, he never spoke of it. We drank our Scotches and talked about Joe McCarthy, the pathological patriot who was on a campaign to search out Communists in America and Communist

sympathizers as well, anyone in whom his bloodshot eyes could discern the shade of pink. Ruby and I had bought our first television set and had begun watching the congressional hearings presided over by this bizarre junior senator from Wisconsin, which sold more early television sets than it ennobled American justice. Bewildered patriots jumped on McCarthy's bandwagon and dragged America backward in a frenzy of cowardice that proved out the ironic title of Sinclair Lewis's study of homegrown fascism, *It Can't Happen Here.* It did.

McCarthy's special target was show business. He saw the gravest danger to America in the ranks of writers, actors, and producers, especially when one of them dared question his shady methods, so the televised hearings in Congress became a political sideshow featuring showbiz folk sure to capture the attention of a whole new audience glued to their television sets. Including me. McCarthy's witch hunts inspired a disgusting publication called *Red Channels*, a compilation of 151 names of people in radio and television designated as Communists or sympathizers by self-appointed watchdogs who published a right-wing newsletter, *Counterattack.* Its staff listed the names of subversives according to its own interpretation of the right to dissent. By their standard, if you were opposed to racial discrimination in the South, you were a subversive.

From this publication sprang the blacklist. It denied employment in Hollywood to actors, writers, and musicians and spread fear through the industry because if you were blacklisted, you did not even know who had named you. Innocent people lost their jobs. To me, the McCarthyites were the true traitors to America.

On *The Brighter Day* we all shared the big makeup room. Interesting discussions took place there and the McCarthy hearings were a favorite topic. Since most people in show business try to stretch their understanding of things, a liberal intelligence seemed to rule these sessions. Opinions were aired freely. One day I walked in from the lunch break with *The New York Times* in hand and said, "Did you read what this idiot McCarthy said today? He's accusing General George C. Marshall."

Harold

Silence fell.

I thought I'd rudely interrupted a story in full play, so I waited for the talking to resume. It finally did. About ten minutes later, unable to contain my impatience with McCarthy, I burst out again. "This damn fool McCarthy says the army is being infiltrated by Communists. I think the guy is a drunk or a retard . . ."

Silence.

It struck me then. *Red Channels.* Fear had invaded our small family of actors because someone we knew had been named, and we had gone silent. I don't remember anything that has happened to our country that gave me a more personal shock. To think that in America, the nation whose founding ideals my grandfather taught me to respect, the nation whose flag he helped us raise every Flag Day, to think that the right to speak your mind was being shut down—it was beyond believing. But it happened and it made me angry. I would find that Mark Twain had plenty to say about this kind of back-alley patriotism.

But the dishonor invading our country put the dishonor in my own life into bleak focus. How could I be doing this to Ruby and my blissful child, who took me on faith? I was their protector and their deceitful friend. While I was hating McCarthy he was teaching me something about my own betrayal. My mind flung accusations at me day and night and turned the life I was leading into a strange unreality. The guilt made me more concerned about Victoria and Ruby, how I was taking care of them, at the same moment I headed toward another hotel for a wildly emotional tryst with the fantasy woman whose attraction I could not resist. If McCarthy was a traitor, what was I?

When the emotional storm in my head overwhelmed me I lit the lamp in the dark corner of our entry hall and searched for new Twain material. It was the one diversion that for a time carried me out of the hellhole I was in. Twain was no pretender. He put my mind to work on subjects larger than myself and he made me see the world

in a challenging light. Human motivations began to fascinate me, too, including my own. He put me in touch with irony.

June was a heavy month for Grayling and Sandra on *The Brighter Day* and I tried harder to grab pieces of the real world and hold on. I drank more with Blair and we talked more intimately and I could swear I was talking to a minister. He was the voice of calmness and reason. When July came in with its heavy heat he suggested we take Vicki to the beach again, so we drove down to Spring Lake with my daughter, who was making a pal out of Blair, and she hopped around in the surf.

There were times I thought about divorce and what it would mean. What life might be like with the beautiful redhead. Was she too exotic? It's amazing how little we spoke of our personal life or of a future for ourselves together. It felt off-limits. The one time a future together was suggested it went nowhere. Ours was not a conversational relationship. We got together for one thing only, the thrill of encounters I had only imagined and knew would not exist with Ruby, so it grew upon me that we were facing a dead end. And then, by strange coincidence, the life we lived in the soap opera began to suggest the one we lived in real life as her character's past became increasingly suggestive and mysterious—"Did she have another affair going in Chicago?" Offstage the real-life Sandra was becoming the character in my mind. Was she playing a role with me? I was not wise to the subtleties of a woman's behavior, so I began to feel cut loose again.

I hid all this from Ruby—did she suspect? I don't think so—and we built the structure of a family life with friends. I was playing a role everywhere now. We went to parties and I drank a lot. When my head was clear and my emotions in some control, I knew I wanted more than this long engagement on a soap opera. I had dreams about a great career as an actor. If I could land a job on one of those big evening dramas, I could see future light, but the door to that possibility was closed solidly. Whenever I thought it might open up a crack, the minute they heard *The Brighter Day* it closed again. I was a soap opera actor. I was overcome with a sensation of being trapped

at all corners of my life. Was divorce an escape? Escape to what? The image of betraying Ruby and Victoria and myself beat the thought out of my mind. So I chose the silent betrayal of a double life.

July continued the uncertainties and the mysteries in the Sandra-Grayling relationship for fourteen shows and kept it up with twelve in August. The story line between us was tilting toward uncertainty, and because it had such a vise grip on me I was increasingly unsure of where the plot of my real life was taking me. This role-playing at all hours of the day and night was against nature and it began to corrode and crumble mine. Then a break appeared. On September 9 I would go off the show for twelve days, and I decided to ask the network for a guest shot on an evening show. I made an appointment with the casting director at CBS.

He had three names. Robert Dale Martin. I walked down Fifty-seventh Street to the CBS Center near Tenth Avenue and received the suspicious approval of the guardian on the ground floor to go up to his office. I waited there and was finally sent in. Robert Dale Martin's face was bland and so was his manner, and it remained that way after I said hello and sat down. Silence. I reminded him that I was on one of his shows.

"The soap."

"Yes."

"So what else have you done?"

"I've been in New York for . . . Well, I've done the voice of Lincoln on the *Hollywood Screen Test* show and a couple of *Rocky Kings*."

"That's it?"

"So far, yes."

"We don't—"

"And I've brought this. It's the show my wife and I have done around the country for five years. The two of us. A two-person show." I handed him the three-color, four-page brochure with the Rolan Thompson photographs of us in costume for Victoria and Albert, Rosalind and Orlando, Arnolphe and Agnes, the Brownings, Disraeli and old Queen Victoria, Elizabeth and Essex, and Mark

Twain and the favorable quotations we'd got from coast to coast. He flipped it open, glanced at it, and flipped it back across the desk.

"Did you get paid for that?"

For a moment I didn't know what to say. This was the enemy. The face that would kill you with cool indifference if you let it knock you down. The wall.

"Yes. We got paid. Thanks for seeing me."

He sat there silently like a serpent and watched me leave. The casting director at CBS. In twelve years, 30 million people would watch me on his network, doing a solo of one of those characters for one hour and a half in evening prime time. It would win the night.

I walked back up the slope of Fifty-seventh Street and knew I would never forget that insult. He had sunk the blade deep and it would stay there. By the time I got up to Eighth Avenue the dismissal had worn down the edges of my anger and my hope. I felt stranded. A loser. I stopped on the corner in front of the Cadillac Agency and stared at a young couple inside the window admiring a big white convertible with lots of chrome. They could afford it, I thought. Drive away in it. Get free. Hell. I've got twelve days off. I've never had a vacation. I can't buy a car, but I've got money in the bank. What do I want to do more than anything?

I kept looking at the people admiring the car.

I want to get into clean air. Go skiing. Just me alone.

I'd never done anything like this before. I walked to a ski shop up Broadway. In September I'd have to fly to the Andes in South America to ski, or Switzerland, and the cost was $750. Out of my range. "Anyplace else?"

"Well, you could ski on the glacier at Rainier or Shasta."

"Where is Shasta?"

"In northern California. You could fly to San Francisco and take a train up there."

I went to a travel agency, bought a round-trip ticket to San Francisco, and then went home and told Ruby I was leaving in the morning for California and Mount Shasta. I didn't ask her permission or counsel. She took in this blunt announcement silently for a while

and said, "You could see Lovey. She's singing at a club in San Francisco."

Going up Shasta would have to take the place of running the mile. In San Francisco, Lovey was singing at the Purple Onion in North Beach. She had got herself a "look," cut her dark hair short and wore a plain black dress. No frills. You concentrated on her high cheekbones and dark, luminous eyes and the voice. She sang stuff like "Lilac Wine" and "Ten Cents a Dance," backed up by Brooks Morton at the piano. He was good. The message Lovey put out was "Watch me, listen to me, but don't touch me" while she told the musical story of a woman who got used badly. I hadn't seen that cool reserve when I directed her in *The Winslow Boy* at the summer theater in Granville and I wondered what had happened to bring it out.

When I told her why I was in northern California she said, "Go over to the hungry i, my cousin George is there waiting tables. I think he climbed mountains up north."

In fact, George told me he'd climbed Shasta and Lassen and Hood and a lot of them with "Papa" Hemingway and his son, and when he heard that I intended to go skiing on Shasta's glacier he began describing it to me. "Starts at ten thousand feet. Get someone to drive you up to Sand Flat at sixty-five hundred and you hike the rest of the way. You can stay in the Sierra Club cabin at timberline. Eight thousand feet." Until then, I didn't know I'd have to climb up the mountain.

"Will there be people up there?"

"There's usually someone going up or down. How long you figure you'll be up there?"

"I've got four days."

"Four days. Okay. You got supplies and stuff? A pack?"

"I was gonna pick that up here or in Shasta City. I've got my skis and ski boots."

"Yeah."

"Yeah."

"Why don't you go over to the army-navy surplus, it's only a few blocks from here, and get some warm stuff. Sterno cans are good, too. And a pot to melt snow."

"Okay. How high is this mountain?"

"Fourteen thousand feet."

"Fourteen?"

"Yeah. It's not too hard to climb if you have that in mind. Have you done any climbing?"

"No."

"Okay. Well. I was in the forest service up there. So I know the head forest ranger. I'll give you his name, you can look him up. But listen, don't tell him you haven't climbed before. You know? I mean, he might not want you to go up alone."

"Right."

"Just pretend you've done it."

"Okay."

"I tell you what. Hemingway's son left me his pack. I'll lend it to you."

That's when I first began to form the idea of going all the way to the top. Ski awhile and then climb. The Hemingway pack. It deserved an extra effort. It scared me that I had never stayed out in the woods overnight alone and I wasn't sure I could start a fire, but that must be easy. I was rather afraid of the dark, but I could stay in the cabin at night. At the army-navy store in the morning I would get a sleeping bag, some heavy shoes for climbing, another pair of warm socks. I had long underwear, a parka, and my sweater. I'd get food in Shasta City. It began to bother me that I might be getting in over my head, but it was too late to turn back. Mustn't forget Sterno cans.

At the surplus store I added a mess kit, a Swiss army knife, sunglasses, gloves, and some clamp-on spikes for the mountain climbing boots I'd picked out. The spikes would dig into the ice and keep me from sliding down the glacier. The store stocked with rugged outdoorsman stuff gave me confidence. All kinds of mountaineering equipment, even a pickax for ice work. It looked damn professional,

but I decided it wouldn't be needed. The Hemingway pack was getting pretty full. I had not yet thought of bears.

Lovey let me stow the stuff at her place while I took in the action on North Beach. It was the new scene, a breeding ground of cabaret performers like Bill Cosby, Shelley Berman, Bob Newhart, Barbra Streisand, Woody Allen. This intellectual comedy frontier would spread onto the late-night television shows on NBC and CBS. Lovey had positioned herself well. Jorie Remus's Purple Onion was the other hot club in San Francisco's version of Greenwich Village, and Lovey was wooing that new audience. While we got something to eat at a café across from her club she told me to go to the hungry i and catch Mort Sahl's first show.

"Mort Sahl?"

"He's cool. You should hear him. You can come over to the Purple Onion afterward and see my second set. Ask for Keith when you come in, he's Jorie's partner."

Mort Sahl was a handful. Angry energy spewing out of him, grabbing the audience and backing it against the wall, shooting 50-caliber liberal tracers to the point of mutual exhaustion. His wit had a dangerous political bite torn off the front page and I heard the opening cannonades of an advancing squad of tough comedians who would move us past Bob Hope and Jack Benny. The times they were a-changin'. I wondered how Twain would show up in a pack like that.

At the Purple Onion, Lovey controlled the room in a different way. With silence and a haunting message carved out of a wounded heart, but in the manner of a goddess. Tall, dark-clad, pale-faced, a survivor going it alone. The subtle cascading of Brooks Morton's piano fingering filled the smoky room, a blue shaft of light cutting through it, the bass thrumming in the dark corner, memories stirred in the soaring sound that lifted you up, up, higher than the world outside the blue haze, and in its center Lovey's pale face, red lips, and dark, dark eyes. And then a smile, a suggesting leer, a pause that hung for a moment in that hushed room while the magic of wonder-

ing what she was thinking held the breath in you for an extra second or two.

The milk train for Shasta left at one in the morning from a rail siding in Oakland. I stood in line in the gravel beside the tracks with three other sleepy people. No platform, just a conductor who put down a metal stool you stepped on to launch yourself up to the train steps. There were iron handles on each side to help you pull your body up, and while I waited I studied those handles and measured the distance I would have to heave myself up into the car to grab the handles, with the weight of the Hemingway pack on my back. It had his name stenciled on it and weighed about sixty pounds. The other passengers looked ordinary, but I was dressed for the wilderness and I was not going to take the pack off to get into the railroad car. The conductor offered to hold it and pass it up to me, but I shook my head, handed him the skis, and in one robust movement stepped on the stool and swung myself up toward those handles—to within inches, but not quite high enough to counter the weight of Hemingway's pack—and I crashed backward onto the gravel at the feet of my fellow passengers. The conductor helped me up and brushed gravel out of my gear and clothing and then he and one of the passengers shoved me up the steps. Hell of a way to start climbing a mountain.

I struggled out of the pack and sank down into a seat to nurse some bruises and a skinned palm. A sailor in the seat across the aisle passed over a bottle of whiskey.

"Pour some of this on your hand, buddy. It'll sterilize the cuts."

"Thanks."

"Saw that fall from the window. Beautiful. Have a drink while you're at it." The harsh glow of whiskey sank swiftly down to my fingertips and I felt revived.

"You going home?"

"Yeah. I'm off a carrier laid up in the upper bay for repairs. You headed for Lassen or Shasta?"

"Shasta."

"Nice mountain. Clean lines. Where you from?"

I had thoughts of catching some sleep on the way to Shasta City,

but he wanted to talk and share his bottle so for a couple of hours that's what we did. He was a southern Oregon youth who loved the outdoors and Jack London's stories, which he retold in his own fashion, spiced by the whiskey.

"Di'ya hear 'bout the guide on the Jon Lindbergh party las' year? Wha' happen to him on Shasta?"

"No. No."

"Son-a-bich. Fell and rolled down the glacier, hit tha' damn big boulder, ya know the one b'low the red cliff up there?"

"No."

"Yeah. You'll see it. Killed the son-a-bich. Slipped, ya know, lost his foot, and slid right down that big basin. Splat. End of line."

"Okay."

"Washa it, kid. Doan' fall."

"Right."

He lapsed into a coma and I got an hour of sleep before the conductor announced breakfast in the dining car. The scent of hot coffee swam into our imagination, and we headed down the swaying aisles to the dining car. The waiter, a cordial colored gentleman, seated us at a table covered with a pristine tablecloth and a place setting of heavy silverware.

"I imagine you gentlemen would enjoy a hot cup of coffee, am I right, gentlemen?"

"Yes. Oh yes."

"Yeah, thanks, yeah, coffee."

It revived us. We ordered scrambled eggs and bacon and the toast came in a silver covered dish. Wonderful. Meanwhile, we looked out the window. A wilderness of green rolled by, trees in numbers beyond anything I had seen since Newfoundland. The iron tracks curving ahead of us cut a lonely gash of civilization through them.

"Where are you gentlemen heading, may I ask?"

"He's going home. I'm going to Mount Shasta."

"Mount Shasta?"

"Yes. I've been looking for it out the window, between all these sharp pointed hills."

"Oh, you'll see her when she comes into view. You can't miss her."

"Does she have snow on her now?"

"I would say so, yes. Very white on top. Are you going camping?"

"Yes. On Shasta. I'm gonna go skiing. I may climb her, too."

"Skiing and climbing. Mm-uh. Well, she'll be around the bend soon."

We dug into the scrambled eggs and bacon and smeared marmalade on the toast. This was living in high style. My sailor pal was sobering up and falling silent. We were sipping coffee when the tracks swung us around a curve and there in a wide cleft between steep ridges stood a dome of white, a pyramid as perfect as one of those over in Egypt, silent and high, a godlike sentinel above the wilderness of green. I was awed by it and frightened. The waiter came up behind me and leaned over my shoulder.

"There she is! You gonna climb her?"

"Yes."

"Man, you're in for some walk."

An hour later I stood on the main street of Shasta City with the forest ranger, studying Shasta, and I beat back the impulse to tell him I had no experience while I tried to understand what he was describing.

"You see the heart-shaped basin between those two ridges? The lip of the glacier is on the low end of that. About ten thousand feet. The ridge above it, below the top? It's kind of red? It's really about two thousand feet down from the summit. I think there's a rope over there on the right side someone left there, it can help you up. Pretty steep."

"Right."

"You know about the crevasse?"

"I'd like to hear it from you."

"You'll have to watch for it. If you fall in, we won't be able to help you."

"So . . . how is the climb above the ridge there—where it's kind of reddish?"

"Yes. Above that it's not too steep. Just a walk up to the summit."

Harold

"The Sierra Club hut is at timberline?"

"There's a kind of path to it from Sand Flat. I've asked our weatherman if he can drive you up there. Just keep walking up and you'll find it. The path is pretty faint."

"Okay."

"You'll be up there four days?"

"That's right."

"Arrange a meeting with the weatherman for Thursday. If you're not there, we have to go looking for you."

"I'll be there. I'll set the time with him."

"One more thing. Don't stay on that mountain after four o'clock. The cloud cover comes in fast then and you won't know how to get down."

The weatherman helped me stow my gear in his station wagon and we headed up the wooded flank of Shasta. I had tried to pick my supplies carefully. Bacon, dried eggs, three cans of beans, three cans of soup, two frozen minute steaks, chocolate bars for energy, Sterno cans, matches (and I had my Zippo lighter), bouillon cubes I could carry in my pockets with a couple of Sterno cans in case I got lost, some oleomargarine, and a couple of long loaves of French bread. The road turned into two tire tracks worn to a trace of dirt by some vehicles that had ventured up here. Above the track rose trees of enormous height, redwoods with trunks the width of the car, an army of giant wooden soldiers defending the approaches to that solitary dome. It was silent. Only the toiling of the car's engine broke it. This was a land of storybooks, moist and dark and mystical, hiding its natural creatures who were watching out of sight. I felt half boy–half man invading a forbidden kingdom.

"This is as far as I can take you. Have to turn around now."

"Okay."

We sat for a moment, looking around. The gigantic trees rose so high the tops of them were out of sight. There was no sound, but the silence was alive. Before he could say "You sure you want to do this?" I got out and started pulling my gear onto the mat of pine needles that covered the clearing.

"Thanks for taking me up here."

"Sure. I'll meet you here at four o'clock Thursday."

"Good."

"Four o'clock."

"Yep. Four o'clock."

"You'll be okay up here?"

"Sure. Fine."

"The path is over there somewhere. It's not much of a path."

"I'll find it okay."

"Okay."

"Thanks for the ride."

"I'll see you Thursday." He was opening the car door. My chance to turn back was disappearing.

"I suppose there are bears up here?"

"Mostly brown ones. Just make a lot of noise as you go along. They probably want to stay out of your way."

"Right. Probably so."

"Just make noise." He looked around again. "Four o'clock Thursday."

He turned the car until his wheels found the two-lane track and slowly disappeared. I was alone. For the first time in my life I was alone as I had never been alone before.

30

I stood in the clearing, waiting for something to come out from behind a burly trunk and challenge me. No, not something. A bear. I had begun looking for one the moment the weatherman's station wagon disappeared and I did not stop looking for one, ever. Suddenly I had to go to the bathroom. The only one available was behind a tree, so making sure a bear was not occupying it, I went behind one of them and urinated. Then I picked up the Hemingway pack and adjusted it on my shoulders and carefully stooped over to grab my ski boots where the laces were tied together and slung them over one shoulder. All the while I was asking myself, "Were you prepared for this, Holbrook? This fright? You're scared, aren't you?" "You're goddamn right I am. You think I'm a nut?" "Yes, you are a nut, but it's too late now, pal. Your nuts are cooked, and if you don't get up this trail to that cabin before a bear makes an evening meal out of you, there will be other animals waiting in line. Cougars, mountain lions, you name it, Mr. New York idiot. Move, idiot. Move it!"

I looked around for the trail. The great redwood trees rose up around me to a height I'd never imagined. They were guardians of an underworld penetrated only by the dim shafts of light that found a tiny opening in their tops. The trail was faint, faint and steep. The straps cut into my shoulders. The damn pack had never seemed so heavy before and the ski boots flopped around on my shoulder trying to slip off. The skis were heavier, too. What in hell were they

made of? Lead? "Couldn't you have waited for winter to do this somewhere safe? Squaw Valley? Kilimanjaro? You want thrills? There's a thrill for you. How about the Matterhorn?" The boles of the trees, eight feet across, stood like the legs of giants and disappeared into the whispering greenery above. Little sounds came out of the damp duskiness around me, unfamiliar little sounds. Animals approaching. Bears. Maybe cougars? They would leap on me and rip me apart. Bears I had checked out, but not cougars. People kept telling me bears were harmless. "Just throw a rock at them." Throw a rock my ass. I was not about to throw any rocks at them. What I planned to do was stare them down. I'd read somewhere you could do that, stand stock-still and stare them in the eye and they would leave. It would depend on who had the biggest balls.

The pack was so heavy I had to stop often and lean it against one of the mastic trees. They were easy enough to find, one every ten steps. Once, I sat on a stump, but that was like offering myself as a sacrifice, so I scrambled up again. Finally there was daylight ahead, at first uncertain, but as the white piece of sky grew I launched myself toward it, straining for the light, on the edge of desperation to escape this wooded cathedral of horrors where devils lurked in the shadows waiting for me.

There it was. One hundred yards away beyond the trees—the cabin. Not a tree nor a bush in sight, just the cabin alone at the foot of the slanting gray incline of broken rock reaching up to where Shasta's white shoulders disappeared into the upper regions. The cabin door was heavy and strong. I closed it. Whew! Thank God, safe at last. There was a hefty hunk of wood that lowered across it and looked as if it would keep out a large animal. Good. I scanned the place for intruders. None evident. A big, serious-looking fireplace was the main item in the cabin, and tiers of double bunks took up most of the space. Plumbing? It was an outside rustic kind. The cabin ceiling was high and its beams ran across the large room. On the wall at the right of the fireplace was a map, a topographical one like the maps we'd worked with in the army engineers. It had con-

tour lines on it. I inspected it long enough to locate the approximate position of the Sierra Club cabin, which I knew was at 8,000 feet. I found the 10,000-foot contour and the 12,000-foot line where the cliff was supposed to be. And the top: 14,162 feet.

I felt hungry. A little lunch would help. Beans or soup? A can opener—hell! I searched the place and found none. Then I remembered the Swiss army knife, and it did, indeed, have an odd blade that might open a can as well as an artery. I'd need a fire to heat the soup or beans. There were a few logs beside the fireplace, but no kindling, and then I noticed the small sign that informed the visiting woodsman to renew the logs beside the fireplace by splitting more at the woodpile outside. Let's see, how far away is the woodpile? I unbarred the door and looked out. Judas Priest, a hundred feet away. I glanced down toward the trees. Timberline. It was a line all right, no kidding about that. A solid, impenetrable line of spruce trees, as if they'd been planted in a perfect row. And inside their dark green deeps? You can pretty well count on six families of bears with cubs to feed. In a footrace could I make it back from the woodpile before the head honcho of the family got to me? It was a close thing to estimate. I'd have cold soup for lunch.

I had to quell this fearfulness. It would ruin the trip. I was on the mountain and I had to put some trust in it. And in myself. I went out again and looked up at the cheerless slope. Rocks, rocks, and more rocks. Hardly a bush in sight above that line of trees behind me. Why would any animal want to leave the comfort of trees and pine needles and bugs for this quarry of igneous till? My misspent years in Professor Mahard's geology class began to accuse me, so I tried to remember the names of formations rising toward the sky in front of me. Those long black ridges to the left and right, spanning down in an open triangle from the white field of Shasta's glacier, what geologic name could make them more awesome? How eerily they resembled the serrated backs of dinosaurs, sharp-pointed silhouettes waiting on either side like the open arms of a prehistoric creature, waiting for me, the puny man, to thrust himself forward into their

embrace. Across the top of the glacial basin a formation of faintly reddish rock cut off the view of Shasta's peak. It was up there somewhere. "Come on up, pal," it said to me. "Come up if you dare."

I felt better now. Why not just walk up there to the glacier and ski a bit this afternoon? I pulled out a small knapsack I'd stowed in the Hemingway pack and put the ski boots in it, a few Sterno cans, bouillon cubes, and chocolate bars in case I got lost, but that eventuality seemed remote. All I had to do was come downhill. How could I get lost? I slung the skis over my shoulder and started off. If I met a bear I'd let him try the skis. Ha. Ha, ha.

For maybe five minutes I was okay. Then I couldn't breathe right. I was gasping for air and stumbling around on the broken rock like a drunk falling out of New York's McSorley's bar. The incline hadn't looked so steep when I started out, but now it was threatening me. When I balanced on one rock and leapt forward to the next one I was done in, and I slid back half a step for every step I took. What air I managed to gulp into my lungs squeezed out on the next step upward and I was gasping, desperately gasping. I didn't know why.

I refused to quit. This was getting personal, like the times I'd been flattened with a left hook behind the ear. I was beginning to see stars up here, too. Blinding sweat and stars in my eyes and the skis kept sliding off my shoulder and clattering against the rocks, an irritating intrusion of sound in this enormous airspace between the mountain and the sky. About five hundred feet below where the glacier's edge curled up like a lid was a cairnlike arrangement of huge boulders, suggesting a shelter against the wind, which had now joined in to challenge me. It came moaning over the crags, but I heard it outside my sphere of consciousness; I couldn't let anything else in there. My goal was to reach that cairn.

I made it, stunned and uncertain of my balance, but I had reached an objective. The space between the boulders was the size of a small room, but these igneous monoliths gave it a magical protection on that shelf of earth in the sky. Fires had been built here. I could bring my sleeping bag up tomorrow and spend the night. Maybe. Give me

a head start on going for the summit. I wedged the skis and ski boots between the rocks and looked up at the lip of the glacier; it didn't seem far away now. I could try for it. Over toward the black dinosaur crags wisps of little clouds were moving. An image of witches dancing on them came into my mind. Maybe I wouldn't spend the night up here. I looked down toward town. Jesus, I was on the moon! There were groups of clouds below me and all I could see of the town was the sun glinting off a tin roof. Would I ever get back there again? I was out of touch with human life, and the loneliness I felt frightened me.

But I couldn't let that take over, so I climbed up onto one of the boulders to snap some pictures and checked my watch. Four-thirty. God! The ranger had warned me not to stay up here after four o'clock. When I looked up I saw a coil of white snaking over the witches' crags. Clouds. They were coming in like fog and moving fast. Get out of here! I jumped down off the rock and grabbed my knapsack and looked down toward the way I had come, and the coil of cloud was there below me, filling up the sky faster than I'd ever imagined clouds could move. I started running, stumbling over rocks and into depressions. In less than fifty yards I couldn't see fifteen feet in front of me. I tried to slow myself and think. "Think, pal. Think!" But I was in a shroud of white, looking at the ground to see which way was down. I began to realize I was on a small ridge, a saddle between two ravines, one to the right and one to the left, but I couldn't see into them, so which way should I go? The ravines would spread at an angle as they ran downhill, and the wrong choice would land me a long way from the cabin. I'd be lost. I tried the left-hand route and it felt wrong so I moved over the saddle to the right. That's when I saw the pumice stone. I had walked over a field of pumice stone on the way up and this could be it. But it had taken me more than two hours to climb up here, how long would it take to get down?

I stumbled along now at a faster pace, heart pounding with the beat of my feet, and suddenly a huge boulder appeared on my right hand with the number 88 painted on it in blue. That I had passed.

Who in the name of crazy Sam had come up here with a paint can to lay down this landmark for me? Who knows, but thank you. I stood in front of its imposing bulk, feeling more confident now, and then I heard the ripping sound. Like fabric ripping. A sudden fine sweat broke out on my back and shoulders. What the hell was that? There it came again, a ripping sound, and it was from beyond the boulder. Okay, it's a bear. I knew it was going to come, so now what do I do? Run or look? If it's a bear and I run, he'll run after me and eat me. If I look, he won't have so far to go. The ripping sound again, louder, like some mass being moved. The suicide impulse took charge. I'd rather know and get it over with, and I stepped around the boulder. Nothing there. A rock flew by my head. Another hit the ground and ricocheted past me to the right. I felt the wind from it. The ripping sound became a large, heaving growl and I jumped back behind the boulder. The growl became a roar and all hell broke loose. The rocks became missiles, larger and larger ones shooting past me, and if I hadn't pressed myself against old 88, I would have been hamburger.

Now I knew what was happening. I'd been told those crags were old, unstable rock and could avalanche. I was in one. When I called Blair to tell him I was leaving for Shasta, he'd said, "You're going to kill yourself on that mountain, friend," and he was right. Here I was hiding out behind a rock twice my size, 9,500 feet up, and part of the mountain was whistling through the air trying to kill me. I began to laugh. This was crazy. I might die in five more seconds if a big hunk of granite came rolling down and crushed 88 and me. The roar became symphonic thunder and I laughed and hooted until gradually the rocks sped by more slowly and the roar subsided to a growl and then odd belches of sound. I was alive. To every life there is a season, and mine was not over yet. Thank you, Lord, I guess this is what you call a second chance. I must remember that. When the last rock bounced by I came out of hiding and started down the ravine. What could harm me now? Bears? Hell. Let them come.

This bravado lasted all the way down to where the clouds parted and the cabin appeared below me. It should have been a happy sight, but the timberline was dark and quietly menacing. There was

that dash to the woodpile in the dark if I wanted a hot dinner, and I very much wanted it. Breakfast on the train and cold soup in the cabin and a pretty busy day on only a couple of hours of sitting-up sleep on the train: suddenly I was exhausted. The inside of the cabin was dark and I had not thought of candles. Feeling around in the blackness of that rustic shelter stirred up a panic in me. I had to find candles. I got two stubs, one on the wall shelf and another on the floor under the table. Now the fire. I coaxed up a small flame and teased it with a log and when the pinesap ate away at it I was able to add a second log. Then I unbarred the door and made a dash for the woodpile, grabbed the ax and whacked the hell out of an upended pine log, grabbed the split pieces, and ran to the cabin. The fire had gone out. Damn. Jack London would know how to get one hell of a blaze started, but in his absence I coaxed a small flame into dancing around the logs again and piled my two new ones on top and ran back to the woodpile, keeping a mighty sharp eye on the timberline, which was a black, unfriendly wall now. Between footraces I managed to cook up a minute steak, and with a nice hunk of French bread doused in oleomargarine I was feeling revived. It was necessary to make one more trip outside to clean the mess kit in the tiny stream. I scrubbed it with sand while the moon came up above the trees and lit the awesome white silhouette of Shasta.

By the light of the dying embers I worked in semidarkness, stowed the food, got my sleeping bag out, and gratefully climbed into it on an upper bunk. It was turning very cold. My brain had not yet gone off alert when I heard little feet overhead on the wooden beams. It was not hard to guess what they were. I was hoping chipmunks. I zipped the bag up to my face and swore to myself that if one of those creatures came nosing around, I would not let him in. I fell asleep. Then I woke up because something was outside, rubbing up against the cabin, moving and stopping and moving, and I heard heavy breathing. I got down from the berth and checked the bar across the door and then went to the little window and looked out. I could see nothing but the white mantle of Mount Shasta in the moonlight, like a warrior waiting. I found my knapsack and got the

pint of whiskey I'd purchased for cuts and bruises. Two good swigs of that and I was in the sleeping bag again and that's all I knew until eight in the morning.

To my surprise it had snowed while I slept. The cabin was now in an uneven landscape of white, the larger rocks had white caps on them. Two hours later I had produced breakfast and studied the topographical map for the best route up the glacier to that red cliff. That would be the toughest challenge, getting up that wall, and I hoped it would not be too steep. A history of Mount Shasta on the wall described its features and informed me that a nine-year-old boy had climbed to the summit. I hated him right away. Damn kid. At least it proved this was not a hard mountain to climb. I had mixed feelings about that, but it cheered me up a bit and I felt fit and ready this morning. I was going to the top.

Four minutes up the hill I was gasping for breath again. What in hell was wrong? Endurance was my long suit, I ran distance in school, and here I was flailing around like an eighty-year-old cripple two hundred yards from the cabin. Why couldn't I breathe? I stopped on a big, flat rock to have a talk with myself. Now, Holbrook, you must not allow this mountain to conquer you. Stop flinging yourself at it, take your time, you can't beat up an obstacle this big. It's a gi-ant. You are David. Don't grapple with it. I started up again, slowly. Methodically.

About two hours later, on my hands and knees, I crawled over the edge of the glacier. I'd been crawling that way from the cairn. It was time now for deep breathing exercises, but I couldn't breathe deep. Only shallow. The red cliff was up there, two thousand feet higher across the big white glacial basin. I'd better eat something, I thought. I wasn't hungry but I needed strength, and bouillon soup would do it, so I got out my mess kit and tried to dig snow into it, but it wasn't snow. The glacier was white like snow but solid, even when I kicked at it until my foot hurt. Climbing mountains was a mean business, just one damn thing after another. I got out the Swiss army knife and scraped at the glacier, but all I got was a little white fuzz. So I used the water in my canteen and it took a half hour for

the Sterno can to get it hot because the wind was fierce and getting fiercer. It was cold. I zipped my parka up around my face and put on the mittens and dark glasses to prevent snow blindness and finally dropped a bouillon cube into the water. The warmth felt good. What a gift!

I checked out my position. There were the black crags where the rocks had fallen and I saw how they had piled up in a deep ravine between me and the crags. That saved my life. Way down below was the cabin, a lonely little sight. And way, way down, a thousand miles away on another planet, was Shasta City, with the sun glancing off a tin roof. Would I ever get back? I might die up here. This morning in the snow outside the cabin where I had heard something moving last night were the prints of enormous feet. Was it a bear? Or was it Big Foot? Warning me that he was on my trail and had been watching from that line of dark green spruce. He was tracking me.

Oh hell! Cut it out, Holbrook. You think too damn much. Get off your butt and move on. I stowed the mess kit in my knapsack and got to my feet. The glacier ahead of me was like a big frozen lake of white ice, and it looked level. Why didn't it feel level when I started walking? I didn't slide backward, but according to my legs, which had gotten heavy, I was going uphill. I knew it was going to be rough, but this was unfair! "This hill where there is no hill is unfair," I said, gasping it out. Way up the slope was that big rock, the one the Lindbergh guide hit when he lost his footing, and you could see it was steep there, yeah, but not here! Wait a minute. Let me strap the clamp-ons on. That should make it easier. I had slipped twice now and fallen flat and it was hard to get up. Falling was bad. Bad. Bad! I'd have to watch out for that crevasse. What was a crevasse, anyway, come to think of it. An open hole? Or covered? I suppose you just fell down in it and froze in position.

Come on, up! Walk! Only another two hundred yards until it started uphill toward the cliff, right by that big boulder, but I didn't appear to be getting closer and my legs were so heavy and numb. I think my knees were detached from my thighs, because when I lifted my thigh the leg below it didn't move. It stayed where it was. It was

so still up here. Except the wind, which came slamming across the ice, angry at me, pounding my parka and burning my face. And my heart, I could hear that, too. Loud. It had never beat this loud before. I heard crackling. God! Big Foot? I looked around; there was no one coming. Great. But when I moved, there was the crackling again and it seemed to be coming from me. Around my heart, crackling. I unzipped the parka and felt around my chest pocket and pulled out a half-eaten Hershey bar. The loose paper—such a sound! So loud up here!

I was on the hill now, trying even harder to get enough air; my lungs must have shrunk. I began to count my steps. Fifteen, then stop. Ten. Stop. Maybe the air I took in was freezing the walls of my lungs and that was why they felt smaller. Less room in there. Five steps and rest. My heart was getting louder, terribly loud, warning me. Better rest a bit. First I'll crawl. There was the heart-shaped basin and the big rock the guide had hit. If I could get in behind it, maybe I could rest awhile, but first I've got to get up this hill. Careful now, stand up. Crampon in, step forward, crampon in, step and don't fall. This is where that pickax would help. The wind was trying to knock me down. If you fall, Holbrook, it's a long slide down to those rocks. Crawl, like in Jack London! Okay. Resting now. The ice so cool on my cheek. I thought of all the times I'd been knocked down—at that school where the Headmaster smashed me in the face; the football coach at that school in the Arkansas mountains who said Ruby and I hadn't tried hard enough to give a good show; Mike Carpenter calling me a quitter; that son-of-a-bitch casting creep at CBS. This was life, wasn't it? And now this broken marriage and my kid. Get up, Holbrook. Get up. I pushed myself up on my arms and held myself there until I felt a surge of power and threw myself forward and fell flat on my face.

I awoke to the raw sound of wind, with my face on the ice, numb, and when I raised my head, the boulder was a little ahead of me. That was as far as I got. The mountain had beaten me and I knew it.

Harold

The next day I brought my skis up there and skied on the icy surface very carefully. It was not a good idea. One fall and I would slide into one of the big swales that emptied onto the rocks below, and that would be as bad as a crevasse. Maybe. But I felt better. I could breathe and fill my lungs and finally I understood. *It was the elevation!* The thin air two miles up. I had adapted to it. It took me until the third day to realize this simple fact.

And other facts, too. There were limits. And there was loneliness, the terrible loneliness that could crush me and was going to be stalking me until I found a safe place to lay it down someday, in trust. Maybe with someone. I looked up toward the summit and thought, I could make it today. But I didn't have the heart for it. Snow was in the wind and the mists were gathering around that lonely peak.

There were still the trees and the no-man's-land between the cabin and the clearing. And those bear tracks in the snow. The weatherman was supposed to be waiting down there. From a distance it looked as if the clearing were empty, but when I got past some of the larger redwoods there it was, the station wagon and my savior standing next to it. It was a strange feeling to be carried out of the wilderness in a machine. The sound of my voice was strange to me, an unfamiliar sound. I had hardly spoken out loud for four days. And now I was laughing, too. I had not laughed, except when the avalanche was trying to get me. Al, the weatherman, quietly asked me questions and I responded by joking about the trip and telling him I had never climbed a mountain before. I described everything, the woodpile, getting lost in the clouds, the avalanche, passing out on the glacier—I made it all humorous, but he did not smile.

"The ranger was worried about you when the blizzard hit."

"What blizzard?"

"Monday night."

"I saw snow in the morning. That was a blizzard?"

"Straight from Alaska. Up where you were."

"I'll be damned. I just thought it was something normal. You know, snow on the mountain."

He was silent again. "What did you get out of it?"

"I was scared all the time. I never spoke a word and now I'm talking a blue streak. It wasn't funny to be up there, now I'm laughing." He didn't respond. "To tell you the truth, I thought I'd get closer to God. I'd get some answers. But all I found out was, I'm a coward. I didn't make it to the top. The mountain licked me. Or maybe I licked myself."

"You're no coward."

When we got down he invited me to his home for dinner with his wife, Dolores, and his son. We had a trout he'd caught right there in the stream behind his house. They listened to my stories without much response and drove me to the station, and when we said goodbye they said they hoped I would remember them once in a while. I said I would.

In San Francisco I stowed my gear at Lovey's place and she let me sleep on her couch. I caught her show again, and the sensation of being safe in a magical hiding place from the hardhanded world outside, safe in my tree house, piano chords rising and falling and the deep pulse of the bass and the sorrow in Lovey's voice, these sounds undid something in me. I felt free to dream. I was not a club crawler, I didn't have the money for it; it had always seemed like a frivolous activity. But in this club it was different. I felt some nobility there, where the communication of the spirit was welcomed. For the price of a few drinks in a dark room where black paint hid the flaws, you could feel things.

"There's a new group playing a midnight show down under the bridge," Lovey said. "You want to come with Keith and me?"

"Sure, love to."

The place was so crowded we had to sit on the floor. Clubs in those days were small. No screaming loudspeakers, just heart to heart. Sitting on the floor in that tiny space, we heard a young man

from the college in Berkeley, Dave Brubeck, and his backup, with Paul Desmond on saxophone, playing a new sound. A quiet, reflective, and intricate sound, and a year later this unknown would be on the cover of *Time* magazine. North Beach, San Francisco, 1954. I wasn't going to forget them, either.

31

The mountain had made me restless. I wanted to stop hiding out, acting the husband and father to conceal a dishonorable secret life. I was locked in a marriage I could not defeat. Would not. But I had no open road ahead. I was planted on the rim of an ordinary life with a wife and a baby, and the gate was slowly closing on my misadventure. It was exhausting my conscience, sneaking around to hotels, feeling shoddy when I headed home. Wondering if that studious gaze in my daughter's eyes could mean she had found me out. And Ruby—what was she thinking? I didn't want to know. So I tried to repair things. Tried to be thoughtful and revive our lost intimacies. My escape from the mountain had freed me up and my hormones got loose. We were able to resume occasional lovemaking. It relieved my conscience somewhat and reduced tensions in the home.

Then in late November, Ruby told me, "You're going to be a father again." I felt as if a lasso had looped around me and she had pulled it up tight. Roped and checkmated. I would have to scramble for money again because we would need a bigger place to live in. I tried to be happy and proud, but I was not ready for it. How could I handle the future—the self-conscious drama that had become our family existence? Dreams of success expired in the face of the responsibility I saw grinning at me now. Thought you were going to make it, didn't you? Think again, pal.

New Year's Day came, 1955. In one month and a half I would be

thirty years old, and what had I accomplished? There were actors my age who were achieving notable careers in the theater and I was a daytime soap opera actor. I had steered myself into a corner. One hundred and thirty performances of *The Brighter Day* in 1954, plus twenty-five shows on the road including the one Twain solo, and several minor radio and television jobs, and that was it. I was going down Also Ran Street.

In late January the phone rang. It was Lovey. She was singing at a place on Sixth Avenue called the Purple Onion—the North Beach club had planted a flag in New York.

"Hal, our comic Milt Kamen is leaving for three weeks and Jorie and Keith are auditioning to replace him. Why don't you try out for it with Mark Twain?"

"What? In a nightclub?"

"Sure."

"Lovey, are you kidding?"

"No, really. Try it."

"Twain in a nightclub?"

"It's cabaret, Hal. Anything goes."

Many times I had thought of boxing up the costume and forgetting about it, but I couldn't bring myself to do it. There was life in the character and since I was hoping for a chance to try it again, why not this place? A scary idea. I called her back.

"Okay. I'll do it. When?"

"Tomorrow. Around three p.m."

I found the club down a staircase on the corner of Fifty-first Street and Sixth Avenue, dark and dusty. In the miniature dressing room at the rear I got into my white suit and wig and mustache, walked through the audience space, took a good grip on a cigar, and mounted an eight-inch platform in front of two spindly music stands and a piano. I felt foolish, but it was too late to run.

"I wish to present to you a man whose great learning and veneration for truth" (in a nightclub, this is nuts! Nuts!) "are only exceeded by his high moral character and majestic presence." (Good God!) "I was born modest but it wore off." (Was that a chuckle or did some-

one choke?) "Last year I celebrated my seventieth escape from the gallows . . ." (I think it's someone choking.) "I never smoke when asleep . . ." and so on. Lovey was out front with Keith and Jorie and a couple of strays off the street and I'm sure they didn't know what in the name of Austrian bell ringers I was doing down there in front of two music stands, so it was one awful shock when Jorie said, "We can use you."

Christ! I'd taken the leap again and now my goose was cooked. But that was nothing compared with the striptease sensation I had the first night I went on. I'd watched Milt Kamen slam-dunk the audience a couple of times before he left and it was clear that I was going to feel as nude as a tulip when I took his place in front of people who were just looking for fun and a few drinks. "This weird thing in a white suit and fuzzy hair, where did they get him? Mark Twain? What planet are we on? Let's go down to the Village where they have acts that are strange and unusual, but nothing from Mars."

I played the Purple Onion for three weeks in February. When I think of the suicidal leap of faith it took for me to go down those stairs and face that Left Bank audience I wonder if I was entirely sane at the time. If it had not been for Lovey's encouragement and for the wildly improvisational situations in which I had performed our two-person show, I wouldn't have tried it. But there was a strange lure in it, the forbidden urge to join up with this unconventional pack of strays who didn't belong to any tribe I'd ever held membership in. I knew I didn't belong there, but I wanted to go out on an edge of life and be with people who dared.

The first night they announced me I walked in darkness between people at tables up to the little platform, turned and faced them, and pitched in. This was not regulation theater. You didn't get laughs like the ones in a theater where it all comes together in a big sound; you worked for chuckles and short explosions and you could see the people and read their faces if you dared, because that could throw you. Especially someone new like me. Confidence was the intoxication you needed for this job, and if I saw someone looking for the

waiter or whispering to his date, it could deflate the balloon of courage I had pumped up on the way to the stage. Settling down took time, lots of time. I had to just talk to them, pick 'em out and talk the stuff, stop worrying about myself and cut the acting, it didn't get me anywhere. And slow down, don't fear the pause. A pause could have some kind of power.

In those three weeks I got a disease called "lemme out, lemme out." It was telling me I could go on looking for trouble and try the Left Bank. Split from the conventional life on 108th Street and go on skirting the safety of traditional boundaries that had tried to capture me in Cleveland and at Culver, and in some quixotic way it might free me from my attachment to the redhead on the soap. Suddenly I had a couple of buddies, Lovey and Brooks Morton, the young piano wizard from Indiana. We started talking up Lovey's dream of having a club of her own and I got to be a part of it. This was far-out dreaming because New York was a big, tough town.

Lovey had changed. At Granville in the summer theater, where I had cast her as the daughter in *The Winslow Boy*, she had been a beautiful young woman with a mass of dark curling hair and eager dark eyes. She had wiped that image away. Her hair was short on her head like a black cap, she wore a plain, flat dark dress, she was removing her femininity. What she was doing was going out on the edge.

Perhaps it was what inspired me to want to sing, too. Watching and listening to the vocalists in the clubs we were visiting to get ideas had started my imagination running wild. I secretly saw myself as an undiscovered Frank Sinatra. The only trouble was I didn't know anything about singing and was afraid to do it in public. So I started taking singing lessons on my days off from *The Brighter Day*. I learned all about shooting the sound up through the top of my head, on top of the breath my diaphragm was pumping up from below, instead of lodging it in my throat. I'd imagine it coming through my eyeballs. Thinking ahead of the lyric, which helped keep the sound afloat and steady, such as on "My funny valentine . . ." I had to be thinking ahead to "sweet, comic . . ." or I'd sag. You see? It was a lot to remember.

After a few weeks I felt ready to sing in public. I had paused at the Lighthouse Café on upper Broadway several times because they had a sign in the window: MONDAY NIGHT, SING YOUR HEART OUT or something like that, and this is where I made my debut. The first Monday I got scared and turned back, but the next week I sneaked down, not telling Ruby, and waited my turn to sing. There were some sour-looking male animals crouched over the bar, clutching glasses. In a wee corner to the left as you entered this watering hole was a tiny platform with a piano on it and not much room to stand. Forget choreography, because you would fall off the stage and knock the glass out of the paw of a member of your audience. I figured this all out while I watched a guy with a twitch in his shoulders sing "Summertime" under the baleful gaze of the bar guys. Then it was my turn. The emcee, Mister Oily Hair, asked me my name and leapt onto the platform like a cat.

"Okay, folks. Now we got a treat! Make way for Hol Halbrook. Let's hear it for Hol."

There wasn't a sound. My heart had already sunk so there wasn't any lower it could go. I got up on the platform and wrapped a sweaty hand around the microphone and waited for the piano player to start. But he didn't. I looked at him and said, "I'm ready."

"So am I."

"Go ahead."

"What tune?"

"What?"

"Tune. What song are you singing?"

"Oh. Ah . . . 'I Got Rhythm.' "

"If you say so."

My hands were so sweaty the microphone on a pole kept sliding away from me and I had to grab for it to keep the whole rig from striking the spine of one of the guys on the barstools. They hadn't turned around. I don't know how I made it through "I Got Rhythm"; it had never seemed such a long song, endless is what it was, endless and pointless and medieval torture. As the last quavering note died the master of ceremonies bounced back on the stage, launched part

of his drink onto my shirt, and said, "There you are. Let's hear it for Hol." Nothing. "What's the next number going to be, Hol?"

" 'Smile.' "

"Try to do that, kid."

Anyone with a capful of intelligence would have quit, but actors are driven by some renegade spirit of daring that requires them to humble themselves dozens of times before they finally give in and try break dancing. If you keep singing, something good might happen or something bad, with the wind of chance blowing toward number two.

On June 5 Grandma died in Cleveland. The sudden news shot a bolt of guilt through me. I had visited her so seldom in the last years of her life and that must have been a cruelty to her because she had doted on me so possessively when I was under her care. It had been too smothering and I quietly backed away from it and she must have known that, too. Making me sit in that chair under the fringed lamp in her bedroom before our dinner dates, waiting for her to finish making up her ancient face, clad in corset and pink bloomers under a thin, flowered silky robe—it had revolted me. Her behavior with my father had bothered me, too, the times I had seen them together. Now she was gone out of our life and out of my father's life. Who would send him money?

He got to Cleveland before me. How my father found out she had died no one knew. He just appeared, from out of the West I suppose, ready for the funeral and in a controlled state of mind, which was not the case with Uncle Al and Aunt Merce. Lord knows what he might do! And some of the silverware was already missing. Of special concern was a soup tureen and ladle worth a flock of dollars. Vanished. Dad got to the apartment first and must have made a few bequests for himself before the will could be checked over. Now his main concern was for his mother and the funeral preparations, in which he took an active interest to the dismay of Aunt Merce and Uncle Al. They could see trouble coming, maybe a fistfight over the coffin, or Dad might try to get in it. Experience warned them that

anything could happen, most likely something bizarre, so they took care to warn me aplenty. June was there, still sort of married to strange Mr. Nile Nyles and living in that house with the corridors running through rooms stacked to the ceiling with newspapers and tin can labels.

I stayed at Grandma's apartment in what used to be my room and Dad occupied his mother's room. He was usually offhand and remote, but now he was concerned about the coffin, the funeral home, the preparation of the body, what Grandma was wearing. It was a new kind of father I was experiencing, one who involved himself in life, so this made it more difficult when Uncle Al took me aside and told me that June and I were going to have to put him back in the insane asylum.

"Why?"

"You can't have him wandering around all over."

"Why not? I mean, that's what he has been doing for quite a few years now."

"But he escaped from the asylum here and he should go back where he can get proper care."

"He looks pretty good. Pretty calm, too."

"That won't last. You don't know what he's up to. You can't tell what he's thinking."

"Well, I don't know. He's been taking care of himself on the road. Somehow. It doesn't feel right to lock him up."

"Who's going to send him money?"

"I don't know . . ."

"When the police call, they'll have to call you when they pick him up, Harold."

"Yeah."

"It's up to you and June now. He can't be calling Merce and me; we've put up with him all our lives, and now we need some peace from all that."

"Sure. I understand."

June was adamant against putting him away. I tried to explain the

argument for it, that he could get sick out there on the road somewhere and die or get injured and we might not find out about it until
it was too late. She said he would be better on his own—free to
roam—and in my heart I felt the same. But the threat of becoming
responsible for the uncharted life he'd be leading—the image of him
found dead on a cold street like that man I'd seen on the pavement
in the West Village one frigid night—worked on my mind. I tried to
consider Uncle Al's arguments and what being responsible for our
father would mean to me. It was clear that I would be "it," the responsible party, not June. The police chief in Tucson would call me.

There was no church service for Grandma. The family was unfamiliar with churches, it was a detail of life we never got around to, so
when the time came to need religion, uncertainty reigned. In Grandma's case there was too much uncertainty about everything, so the
viewing was held in a funeral home on Detroit Avenue. That affair
had its share of drama, and the ratcheting conflict that ensued de-
rived from my father's desire to press a rose into his mother's hands.
Aunt Merce was against it. When the rose went in she exhorted
Uncle Al to pluck it out. Dad put it back again. It got to be pretty
breathless what with Uncle Al inching close to me and whispering,
"Harold, you've got to get that rose out of there."

"Okay."

"Do it quick before they close the lid."

June was all for letting Dad have his way. "Hal, let Daddy put it
in there, for heaven's sakes, if he wants to."

"Sure. Right."

"Look. There he goes. It's in again. Here comes Uncle Al."

"Harold, did he put it back?"

"I don't know."

"Well, go and see."

It was nip and tuck for a while, the crowd moving past Grandma's coffin, Uncle Al getting in line to take the rose out, and Dad
getting in line to put it back in.

"Harold, they are going to close the casket now. Merce has told

them to go ahead and close it up, so I'm going to take the rose out just before they close it, and you watch Harold senior, don't let him near Mother."

"Okay."

The black-suited guys were making their way toward the casket when Uncle Al plucked that rose out of there and moved away to show it to Aunt Merce. June and I saw our father advancing on the casket.

"Let him do it, Hal."

"I will."

Our father pressed a rose between Grandma's clasped hands, the funeral guys lowered the lid on the coffin, and she began her trip to the graveyard with our father's message of love in place. He slept on her grave that night. I thought he had left town when I got back to the apartment late that night, but the next day Uncle Al told us he had been found sleeping on her grave. While June and I spent the evening talking about our lives and the crooked path of our up-bringing and what we should do about Dad, he was in the graveyard with Grandma.

Uncle Al had arranged an interview for us at city hall with two men who had the authority to put our father back into a mental hospital. June hotly argued against it. I was uncertain. We told Uncle Al that we did not want to have him put in that dreadful, dirty white prisonlike building on Carnegie Avenue and he promised us that Dad would go to a new mental hospital in the country on the south edge of Cleveland, with green lawns and trees. We drove past it to check the place out. June was trying to give some deference to my opinion, but she was against the whole idea. My real motivation was hiding itself. I wanted out from under the responsibility for this man who was a wandering stranger.

The two men at city hall did not take kindly to us. They sat in a gray room with a file in front of them and observed us with suspicion. What kind of delinquent offspring were we, trying to put our father away? I decided right there to give them a clear idea of what our father had been to us.

Harold

"We are not happy about this situation."

"You're not?"

"No. Our father has been out on the road like a hobo for a long time. We've had no contact with him. Our grandmother—his mother—was the only one he wrote to. Usually a telegram, collect."

"He would ask Gram to send him a little money," said June.

"Yeah. Send fifty dollars. She was his main person."

"Minnie Holbrook? She passed away June fifth?"

"Yes."

"Daddy slept on her grave that night."

"I think we should explain to you that our father and mother left us—June here and our sister Alberta who died recently, very sadly, and me—when we were three, two, and one year old. They disappeared into the wild blue yonder."

"Our grandpa raised us. He took us to South Weymouth . . ."

". . . in Massachusetts, and raised us."

"Until he died. He was a good man. A good man."

"Yes, he was. I was twelve and June was thirteen and the three of us came to live with Grandma."

"Here in Cleveland?"

"Yes. Anyway, about the only times we saw our father were in the mental hospital here on Carnegie Avenue."

"We brought Lucky Strike cigarettes to him . . ."

". . . Yeah, a carton. With Grandma. They had to unlock two big iron gates to let us in."

"So you want to put him back in there again?"

"Not there. I understand he would go to that new place south of Cleveland. Somewhere toward Parma. In the country."

"Why are you so anxious to put him away?"

"We're not anxious! We don't like it," June said.

"No. We're far from anxious. We just don't know what's best for him and neither one of us has a home where we could take him in. I live in New York City in a small apartment with my wife and baby . . ."

"I could take him in."

"How, June? I mean, you have to go between walls of old newspapers in that house and you have two children."

"Well . . . I could."

"The point is, what are we going to do? Let him roam free and maybe die on a cold street somewhere? Or have him taken care of? He's a strange man. I mean, he doesn't really communicate. Forget that he has never supported us or tried to take care of us in any way. Not one dime. Hardly ever saw him except in the asylum. How are we going to take care of him? We're not rich."

The men looked down at the file on the table in front of them. Finally one of them said, "He should never have been put away. There was nothing wrong with him. I see that your grandfather had him committed to the mental facility in Taunton, Massachusetts. Was he the one who raised you?"

"Yes."

"There was nothing wrong with your father. Not enough to put him in a mental hospital. But I see that he went in there in 1931 and was in for three years, 1934, and he's been in the one on Carnegie Avenue for several years . . ."

The other man spoke up. "The fact is, he's become a mental patient. He's become one after all these incarcerations. He's going to be better off in the hospital."

The image of my father flashed before me. He didn't look like a mental patient. Just remote and hard to reach. June was sobbing. Why was I doing this?

"You'll have to have him picked up."

"What do you mean?"

"The police will have to bring him in."

"The police?" June yelled.

"Why? Why police?"

"Because it's the way the law works. He escaped from Carnegie, so now the police have to escort him back."

"They'll be pretty decent about it if he doesn't resist them. You just have to keep him in the apartment until they get there."

Our father was boiling water for a cup of tea when they came for

him. I stayed in the kitchen with him while June watched from the picture window in Grandma's parlor, waiting for the squad car to show up. I was nervous, and he sensed it, the jungle cat always on the run. He had been talkative when we arrived and just as normal as any father; it was as if he were showing us how sane he was, and I began to doubt what we were doing. He watched me go out of the little kitchen into the narrow hallway between the parlor and the bedrooms in back and I saw him turn off the flame under the teapot. He knew. June turned with a stricken, awful look on her face and I saw them through the window coming up the walk and the police car down at the curb.

"Let them in. I'll keep him in the kitchen." I walked back into the hallway and turned into the kitchen and my father was waiting for me with the strangest questioning look on his face.

"Harold . . ."

"Dad."

He pushed me aside and stepped into the hall, and a primal sound came out of him. I followed him and stepped in front of the two policemen as my father backed away toward his mother's bedroom, one long arm outstretched and his finger pointing at me. His eyes had turned coal black and in them was the fear of a trapped wild animal, staring at me in astounded disbelief and howling, "No! No! No!"

He never thought his son would betray him.

32

On July 1, 1955, David was born. A son. Now it was my turn to be a father to a son and I hoped a better one than the stranger I had sent to the mental hospital. The task seemed overwhelming. I would try to be the good father and keep everything going, but I felt like a lonely man. The affair with the Smoky Mountain redhead had worn itself down since I came back from Shasta. We saw each other less and less frequently and finally a wordless understanding grew upon us that what we were doing had to end, and we let it go. Then there was emptiness. Our intimacies had become a secret form of loving friendship and when that drew away I felt alone again in a marriage that did not replace it.

Ruby and I had found an apartment a block away at 245 West 107th Street, which had two bedrooms and a dining room. If we ate our meals in the hallway we could convert it into another bedroom. I think the rent was $130 a month, which nearly doubled what we had been paying on 108th Street. As long as the job on the TV soap stayed put, we'd make it, but I needed to find an alternative source of income, a backup in case the bottom dropped out. Worrying about money had become a continual habit, a response to the threat poised like a guillotine blade above the neck of every actor. Unemployment. I needed a task to fill the emotional loss the end of an affair had pinned on me, and the solo Twain was a potential dark horse to give us protection, but how to get it out of the barn?

Harold

There was something hopeful about looking for a place for our nightclub. With the three of us chasing ideas around town it got to feeling like a pioneering expedition, safer than climbing a mountain but still full of uncertainties. We checked out a room in the Hotel Mansfield on Forty-fourth Street off Times Square, but the large window on the street would distract from our intimate style of performing. Then Jimmy DiMartino hove into view. He owned the Duplex Bar and Grill on Grove Street. There was a small vacant room above it that looked promising. The entrance at street level was really a landing from which you either went down to the Duplex or up a brief flight to the clubroom, which had a service bar. Perfection!

There was a baby grand at the far end, and the room could hold fifty-nine people according to the fire law sign posted on the wall. The walls were black, a perfect dark refuge for our club. There was one problem: the noise from the bar down below would kill a show.

"Jimmy, you've gotta have a sound wall."

"A what?"

"The bar's too noisy to put a show on upstairs. That's why the place has never made it."

"So what?"

"So you've gotta have a sound wall."

"I ain't buildin' no wall."

"You want the place to be successful?"

"I ain't building no wall."

"What if we build it?"

"You wanna build it?"

"What if we did?"

"You wanna build it, you build it."

"How about materials?"

"I ain't payin'."

"You won't pay for the materials to build it?"

"I ain't payin' nothin'."

"Even though it will make this room work? Be a success?"

"Hey. You be a success. Leave me out."

"What about the construction?"

"Right."

"Right what?"

"You wanna build it, you build it."

So we built it. Brooks had a friend, Cary, who would be a perfect maître'd' for us, and he had a friend who was good at remodeling things and had tools, so we made a deal with Jimmy. For $75 a week each we would run the room and perform in it. Jimmy's take was off the drinks from the service bar and the food from the kitchen below. We pitched in on the wall, put up another layer of two-by-four studs and stuffed fiberglass pads between them to baffle the sound, reset the door with padding, and painted everything charcoal gray. We had a club of our own in Greenwich Village!

The opening was set for the last week of September, but first we needed a press agent. I don't know who came up with Betty Lee Hunt, but when this tall, long-legged woman with the look of business in her eye showed up, we were partnered with a dynamo.

"You need a name."

"We know."

"Get one. We need to put a listing in *The New Yorker*, that's going to be our crowd, and get 'Pops' Whitaker to cover you."

A name escaped us. While we walked the blocks around the club, checking out our competition, we tried variations on the North Beach scene.

"Purple Peacock."

"No, no. God!"

"Well, how about the Golden Pheasant?"

"Above the Duplex bar? Please."

"The Hungry O."

"Nope."

"Lovey's Loft?"

"Well . . . maybe. How about Mark Twain's Pilot House?"

"C'mon. Cripes. Why don't we just call it Upstairs at the Duplex?"

"Upstairs at the Duplex?"

"Yeah."

"Hal. It's so . . ."

"Nothing."

"Yeah. Blah . . ."

"Besides, it's too long."

"But that's where it is. I mean, we've been calling it that. 'I'll meet you upstairs at the Duplex.'"

"Too many words. We need something more sophisticated."

We were running out of time and running out of names and when Betty Lee said, "Noon tomorrow, the name goes in," Lovey and Brooks abandoned the search for something exotic and Upstairs at the Duplex became the name of our club.

Betty Lee Hunt's fee was $75 a week. We each put up $25 out of the $75 Jimmy was paying us and another $5 each toward the *New Yorker* listing. We'd do two or three performances a night, Monday through Saturday. Daytimes I'd be doing *The Brighter Day* two or three times a week, with the radio show mornings and the television show in the afternoon. Some mornings I had jobs on other radio soaps, *Our Gal Sunday*, *Right to Happiness*, *Whispering Streets*, so not much time was left over for being a father and a husband. It allowed me to escape the day-to-day responsibilities of a father, which Ruby had to assume while I was burying myself in the mines and hoping to find a vein of gold. But it removed me from my children.

We opened on a Monday night late in September. Our stage entrance was through the door at the far end of the room behind the piano and we worked on the floor in the curve of the baby grand. The audience was three feet away. There were no announcements, we entered and began, first with Brooks doing a lush, reflective set on the piano, then a pause for drinks. We established a rule that no drinks or food would be served during the performances. After the audience renewed their martinis and Scotches I walked on. The audience had no idea who I was except that I looked like nothing they expected to see in a nightclub.

"My God! It's Colonel Sanders!"

I had to establish who I was pretty quick before the audience

began asking for fried chicken. Thus the self-introduction technique came into being and remained a part of every show. I had worked out three different fifteen-minute routines that I hoped would grab and hold an audience and get them laughing once they got over being bewildered. Mark Twain was rolling in his grave with merriment, or maybe he wasn't. Once I departed, the audience was in pretty severe need of another round of drinks, and then Lovey Powell came on. A tall, dark figure clad in a black jersey, without feminine curves, and her face was a pale mask. She applied a subtle clown-white makeup so that her hypnotic dark eyes glistened in the tiny spotlights and held the room in thrall.

> Some homemakers from San Francisco have taken over a small room above a bar on Grove Street in Greenwich Village, and turned it into a dimly lighted but smart-looking night club called Upstairs at the Duplex. Now and then a modest entertainment takes place in front of a baby grand. I think you can overlook the young man who comes on first and impersonates Mark Twain. Things pick up when, this ghost having vanished, a young man sits at the piano and strikes up the opening measures of Noel Coward's "If Love Were All," and a tall, slim, and handsome brunette with the disturbing name of Lovey Powell strides briskly into view and delivers a group of superior songs in husky tones. Miss Powell is really no great shakes as a singer, but she is a talented actress, and I am certain you will have no fault to find with her delivery of "Ten Cents a Dance," "Stay Well," and several other attractive things.

This was from *The New Yorker* of November 5, 1955, and was penned by Rogers Whitaker or Douglas Watt. I think Watt, who would review me again at a later date. Was I cast down by this notice? Can't remember. You receive so many blows to the head it destroys the memories of what hurt. I do recall that I'd assumed Lovey was the star attraction and I was the warm-up act and I never expected to move higher than that. I just worked on material and tried things. I learned about the pause and how to handle the audience and hold

their attention and how to deal with distractions. Say a drunk broad from Texas was confused about where she was—"Jesus, Harry, is this still New York? I thought you said we were in New York, Harry. This can't be it. I saw that fried chicken guy outside the restroom. Oh, my God, there he is again!"

That would be my entrance. The door we used also led to the ladies' room. They caught me in the little hallway outside, waiting to go on.

"Hey, honey, aren't you the cute one! Who are you, anyway?"

"Mark Twain."

"Who?"

"Mark Twain."

"I'm Eleanor Roosevelt. You wanna have a little fun?"

If a lady in the audience packing her third martini became desperate to make the restroom during our performance, she had to cross through the act and back me against the piano. It could kill a laugh line dead, coming and going.

We had to do something about that door so we decided to move it six feet toward the corner and lock it when we came out to do our act. On our day off we worked like slaves to carefully dismantle the door, because we didn't have money for a new one. We cut a hole in the wall for it and patched the hole where it had been. On Monday afternoon we got it painted just before showtime. Locking the door ensured that ladies coming out of the restroom wouldn't walk through the act. That also required them to wait out there. Sometimes quite a while. The sign outside the ladies' room telling them to go downstairs through the kitchen and the bar and come back into the club through the front door usually went ignored. Instead they would rattle the knob and pound on the door. Depending on how many drinks they'd had, the pounding would get very loud and so would the victim trapped outside.

"Open this goddamn door or I'll break it down!! Police! Police! Harry, I'm trapped out here, come quick! Help, help!"

It was hard to hold the audience's attention with this clamor going on behind and occasionally I had to unlock the door and let her in.

"You weird-looking son of a bitch, how dare you keep me out there like that. I coulda fallen down the stairs. I'm gonna sue you. Harry, let's get outta here!"

And then there were the ones who thought they had stumbled into a homosexual haven on the side streets of Greenwich Village. They got a whiff of it from Cary, who was light of foot but quick on the retort if challenged.

"Say, is this a homo club?"

"No, sir, but if you're looking for that sort of thing, there's one two blocks from here."

Once they got inside, the buffalo hunters from Oklahoma had a field day with my curly white wig. "John, damned if it ain't my aunt Harriet. You reckon she rides sidesaddle?"

"Hell, she can ride me any side she likes."

I had to figure out how to stop rubes like this and get the audience under control, so I researched for lines in Twain I could use in tough circumstances. "It's a comical invention the human race. But sometimes it does seem a shame that Noah and his party did not miss the boat." It could get a laugh from the rest of the room and mute the distraction. Or if it was a real mean bastard out there, I could use "Concerning the difference between the man and the jackass, some authorities say there isn't any. Occasionally this wrongs the jackass."

I had to keep my cool, keep the comments oblique to avoid confrontations, and stay in character, and I rarely allowed myself to ad-lib anything that wasn't written by Twain. The more I read of his work the more I respected him and admired the uniqueness of his genius with words and phrases. I wanted to be authentic, and I saw that his casualness could hide a stiletto.

"Man is the Deity's favorite, you know. After the housefly."

And the pause. That was an instrument of many uses, the variations were sometimes subtle, but I slowly became aware of its effectiveness to quiet an unruly crowd as well as to time a funny line. The pause is a personal kind of contact with the audience, a way of establishing intimacy with them because it causes them to wonder what

you're going to say. And if you hold it long enough, there is the suggestion of danger in it. You can isolate a troublemaker with it and cause him to become embarrassed and then slug him with a barbed line. Sometimes nothing worked and I had to fight my way to the end of the act and retire in disgrace.

During my seven months in the club I developed the first two and a half hours of the Mark Twain repertoire. I tried everything and failed or succeeded. I even put on the Sherburn-Boggs shooting incident from *Huckleberry Finn* and followed it with Colonel Sherburn's speech to the lynch mob, all in the curve of the baby grand. It rang bells because this was 1955 and churches were burning down south. Daring to try a variety of stuff was the key to getting somewhere, that and endurance.

I got to the club at 7:30 p.m., checked the bar setup with Cary, and then went to the dressing room and made up for two hours. We did two or three shows a night and I didn't get home until two or three o'clock in the morning, sometimes four when there were problems with the management of the club. After the last show I added up the receipts at the bar, and I remember Marlon Brando watching me intently one night from a table with Maureen Stapleton, Eli Wallach, Anne Jackson, and Wally Cox. I've always wondered what Brando was thinking. If I had *The Brighter Day* the next day, I had to learn my lines on the Seventh Avenue subway from Sheridan Square to 110th Street. I learned the new Twain material on that subway, too. Researching it took hours, even two or three minutes of new stuff, so I was a tired man. I got thin and so did my patience, but I hung on, hoping for something good to come along.

I think Ruby accepted my nightclub run as a career investment, but the isolation she and my young children endured through all this was profound, and I think it continued to erode the heart of our marriage. For my children, I'm not sure. Victoria was confident and unstoppable, but my son was quiet. By nature, I think, but my absence from him in those early years and later made him quieter and more pensive. He needed me.

Lovey and Brooks Morton were serious people. When they en-

tered the spotlight at the end of that dark room they weren't there to kid around. They were focused, and if the audience was not ready to listen, they made them listen by the intensity of their conviction. I saw Lovey take control of a distracted audience simply by the fierceness of her belief in the lyrics. Her gut belief in what she was singing had such conviction that they stopped and listened. It was a lesson I was learning, too. The audience may like you or dislike you, but if they know the conviction is in you, they will listen. In that club I learned to believe in Mark Twain.

Connections can become miraculous. Who would have thought that David Rounds, whom I had cast as Lovey's brother when I directed *The Winslow Boy* at the summer theater in Granville, would lead Ed Sullivan to Grove Street? David was a handsome, deceptively thoughtful human being and I am ashamed that I never got to know him better. One night he brought his friend, the director Fred Carney, down to our little club, and Fred had a brother named Art Carney who was Jackie Gleason's sidekick on television. Art was also a friend of Ed Sullivan's and one night Ed came to the club with an old pugilist friend and sat four feet in front of me. Sullivan's show was the most coveted variety show on television. The greatest names in the business had been on it—Bob Hope, Irving Berlin, Buster Keaton, John Gielgud, Alfred Lunt, you name it, Peggy Lee, Charles Laughton, Humphrey Bogart, that boy from Memphis who sang "Love Me Tender" and stunned the whole of America. I was making up in the boiler room when Cary came down to the cellar and said, "Ed Sullivan is upstairs waiting for you to go on."

There had been no warning. I never knew he was coming and I wouldn't have believed it if I'd been told. What in hell should I do for him? The Accident Insurance number got the biggest laughs, so I decided to do that even though an instinct warned me this was not a safe selection. The suicide impulse took over and I went up and did it for him. It was the early show, only four or five people in the rear of the club, and Sullivan sat right in front of me, and if ever there was the sound of a chuckle, that was all the response I got. I walked back down to the boiler room in disgust.

"Ed wants to talk to you. He says can you come up and sit with him?"

"Yeah, sure, yeah, cripes. Hell." I took off the wig and the mustache and climbed the two flights of stairs. They were waiting for me.

"Sit down, Hal."

"Thank you, Mr. Sullivan."

He introduced his friend. "Hal, you got any other material?"

"Yes, sir. That's a number I probably shouldn't have done. I have four other routines."

"What have you got?"

"One of them is the seventy-year-old birthday speech, how to get to be seventy, smoking and drinking. It's pretty funny."

"Would you come to my apartment at the Delmonico tomorrow and do it for me?"

"Sure. Sure. When—"

"About one o'clock."

"Yes, sir. Thank you. Thank you for coming down here. My gosh. Where is that?"

"Park Avenue and Fifty-ninth Street."

"Right. Okay. Oh, we'll take your check for the drinks."

What was happening was impossible. Maybe the best-known name in television was going to audition me in his apartment. Judas Priest! When I arrived the doorman called upstairs and ushered me to the elevator in a lobby made of white and black marble slabs. Mrs. Sullivan opened the door. "Come in, Hal." She called me by my first name. "Ed is in the parlor." She had to point the way, and there he was, sitting in a chair waiting for me.

"Thanks for coming, Hal. Have a chair." He pointed to one opposite, a French type of chair, elegant, with gray silk upholstery. The room was elegant.

"You find us all right?"

"Yes, sir."

"How long you been working in that club?"

"Since last September. Lovey and Brooks and I opened it."

"Yeah?"

"We run it, too."

"What's her name?"

"Lovey Powell."

"She's good with a song."

"Yes, sir. She sure is."

"What have you got for me, Hal?"

"Well, this seventy-year-old thing—"

"Why don't you just do it for me."

"Okay." I sat there and did the number for him and he smiled once in a while but made no sound.

"Can you cut that down to six minutes?"

I thought, "It won't be as good in six minutes, but the hell with it."

"Yes, I can."

"I think I can use that, Hal. Who's your agent?"

"I don't have one."

"You don't have an agent?"

"No, sir."

"All right." He waited, watching me. "How much do you want, Hal?" I had never thought of being paid. Money had never entered my mind.

"How much?"

"That's right."

"Ah . . . Ah . . ." My brain was whirling around, spinning from one dollar amount to another. A thousand? No, no, too high. Don't ask too much! Three hundred? Too low, too low! The Beatles got thousands, I'll bet. Thousands. But you're nobody, Holbrook. "Ah . . . Ah . . . How about . . . would . . . ah . . . would say . . . five hundred dollars be all right?"

He smiled at me. "You got a deal, Hal."

I floated out of there on a cloud, but I started worrying a block away. How would the makeup look on TV? I was going to turn thirty-one only five days after the show went on and I had to look seventy with just greasepaint and brushwork.

The result was pretty laughable and Ethel Merman nearly broke

down when she passed me in the hallway, but the curled wig and the mustache and white greasepaint in my eyebrows was about all I had to introduce Mark Twain to America, and this was certainly my introduction. It was much bigger than I had any idea of. Ed Sullivan was generous and delivered it with his famous immobile face and the final wave of the arm, like a gate opening at a railroad crossing. There were a few laughs from the audience, but when I passed Ethel Merman on the way out she hadn't changed her expression. Still disbelief. I'd heard she was tough with the quips, so I raced past, relieved to get away from her and back in my dressing room, where I felt safe. What a night.

When I try to recall Ruby's reaction to these early successes, reserved is the word that comes to mind. She was supportive but quiet. She must have been thinking of her own lost career—I would have been, in her shoes—and worrying about how to restart it. She needed an acting job. She was a reserved person, mostly, unless "onstage" in conversation with friends, and she was ambitious for herself. There was iron under Ruby's composure, as there had been in my grandmother. I was not the only star in the family. I think that this iron emerged when the joy had been bleached out of our marriage and that it caused me to draw away and look toward the attractions of a more available kind of woman.

Here I want to take a moment to raise my hand and salute Lovey Powell and David Rounds. Lovey's call to me got Mark Twain into a nightclub. David Rounds got me on the Ed Sullivan show. Without Lovey and David it is likely that none of what followed would have happened. I owe them my career. David Rounds played in a remarkable number of New York theater engagements between 1964 and 1981: for *Child's Play* he won the Theatre World Award, he played Mercutio in *Romeo and Juliet* at the Circle in the Square, and he won the Tony for Best Featured Actor as Homer in the acclaimed revival of *Mornings at Seven*. Not one of them did I see. How in the name of God Almighty I could have been too self-involved to see David perform in these roles I do not know. It shames me. David Rounds created a solo show entitled *Herringbone*. It received enor-

mous praise from the press and I never saw it. I believe it was in the middle of his New York run that I was told he had become ill and had to close his show. I wrote him and in his response he was courageous and generous and strong. He had AIDS. He died from it.

Success doesn't happen right away, but it happens. It is like a grid, the connections are made by the mysterious paths circumstance travels. An early connection for me was the arrival at the Duplex one October night a few months before the Sullivan show of an intense young actor whom I had met at the Lambs Club. I had become a member of this theatrical club and late one afternoon when I stopped in I got to telling Jerry Guardino about my Mark Twain experiences working above the bar on Grove Street. He came down to the club, liked what he saw, and talked to me.

"I'm directing a play at the Lambs, but it's only an hour long. I need a half hour to kick the evening off. Can you do it?"

"I think so."

The Lambs had a beautiful theater on the third floor, and Jerry told me that some great people had worked there, like John Barrymore and George M. Cohan.

"Wow!"

"Yeah."

I put a thirty-five-minute show together and rehearsed it on that stage, and on October 30, 1955, Mark Twain played uptown. The poet story, accident insurance, and the Italian Guide all went so well I was called back for an encore, and the seventy-year-old stuff capped the evening. Bobby Clarke, the classic Broadway comedy star, was reported to be leading the laughter and applause. This sent a shock through me. I was onto something bigger, maybe, than I had bargained for. I had scored in front of an audience of pros a half block off Times Square. It set me thinking about a longer show somewhere. Bookings on the road. Who knew?

The grid kept forming, and in February, a week after the Sullivan show, I got a call to do *The Tonight Show* on NBC in March for

Harold

Steve Allen. I believe it was the most watched show on late-night television. Not bad for a new guy with no agent. Steve was a gentleman and a scholar and truly interested in Mark Twain during our interview portion and he gave me eleven minutes to establish the character during the act. I began by working in the reference to his white suit ("Clothes make the man; naked people have little or no influence in society"), then the story about the poet who wanted to commit suicide (Twain helped him), and a mix of other stuff. I was learning to connect Twain's material into logical sequences, like chromosomes, and this would become the method by which I would lengthen the performance and create the illusion of a seamless event.

In April and May, Lovey and I accepted an engagement at the Cherry Lane Theatre a few blocks from the Duplex. It was called *Cherry Lane at Midnight*, and we dovetailed it in between weekend shows at the club. A pretty breathless affair, running through the Village streets as Mark Twain, but a job was a job. I stayed onstage for half an hour. Even in the middle of the night it seemed to hold attention. I told myself, Holbrook, maybe this baby gets better on a longer track. It's time to let it out of the barn and see how she runs. So I called Pryor-Menz and Higgins and Ricklie and told them to look for Mark Twain dates. I'd had a call from a lady at the Mark Twain Library in Hartford to do Twain in his old hometown. Edith Salsbury. Would I do a benefit for them in May at a school auditorium? They would pay me $500 for a one-hour show.

The lineup for this one-hour show followed the chromosome pattern, link by link, one selection blending into the next in what I hoped were natural transitions. I found stray lines in Twain's writing to splice it all together. I was adamant about not departing from Twain's own words, because I could not match him, nor did I want to try. I looked for the gems, the golden nuggets in his books and speeches and essays, so the show was not a "now for my next selection" sequence of presentation; it was one long talk, a stream of consciousness that never stopped moving, and it came from the wealth of his own experience. He had done all of it, or said he had, so it was a personal story in which he was somehow included, and

the stuff came out of his head. The show ended with the golden arm ghost story, and how the audience loved it! When this performance was over I knew I had found a thoroughbred, thanks to Mrs. Salsbury and the remarkable people who saved the great Mark Twain mansion in Hartford.

Another piece of the grid moved into place when Harry Byrd Kline stepped forward again, spurred into action, I suspect, by Ed Wright—who never stopped working on my behalf—and proposed that I do Twain at the International Platform Association convention in Lakeside, where Ruby and I had made our start eight years before. If I could pull that off for all those booking managers, I'd be on the track and running. Pryor-Menz had already opened the gate and were booking the Louisiana to Minnesota territory, which included Iowa, Missouri, Kansas, Wisconsin, and a piece of Oklahoma, all dates that were set for the fall. I had asked the producers of *The Brighter Day* to let me out for two and a half weeks in the fall to do Twain, plus selected weeks in the winter and spring, and they agreed to it. The bookings began to come in.

I had a talk with myself. It had become clear that I was splitting myself off in too many directions and that it would slow me down and dull my chance of succeeding in any direction, so I gave up the Duplex. Working those late hours week after week was exhausting me and I needed time to research new material and to pay attention to my family. I decided to give up the singing lessons, too. I'd enjoyed them, and my teacher, George Griffin, had brought me along to where I had auditioned for some musicals, but I needed to concentrate on building Twain now and stick with the soap for the security it provided.

Hollywood made a call. They were planning a television series based on *You Can't Take It with You*, and the studio was trolling around for an old actor to play Gramps. Mark Twain and Grandpa Vanderhoff, what a connection! A partially blind casting director must have spied me on Sullivan or Steve Allen and through the blur of glaucoma or whiskey deduced that I would be a perfect candidate for Grandpa. When I arrived at the Fifth Avenue office of the movie

studio and was ushered into a replica of the Oval Office, its portly immigrant success story behind the desk said, "Where is Holbrook?"

"He is me."

"Me? Who is me?"

"I'm Holbrook."

"You're Holbrook?"

"Yes, sir."

"Wait a minute." Buzz, buzz on the intercom. "April, did Bert get the wrong guy?"

(Intercom: "No, sir.")

"This kid is Holbrook?"

(Intercom: "Yes, sir.")

"Is this a joke?"

(Intercom: "No, sir. Bert sent him.")

He hung up. A long silence ensued and a searching look. "I'm looking at the guy who plays Mark Twain on television?"

"Just *The Ed Sullivan Show* and *Tonight*."

"That's you?"

"Yep."

"You're young."

"Yes."

"We're looking for a seventy-year-old guy. There's been a mistake."

"Sorry to disappoint you."

"That's okay, kid. Maybe in forty years."

"Thank you. I'll see you then."

33

In the summer of 1956 our family's fortunes turned a corner. Ruby went back to work at Holyoke in *A Roomful of Roses*, so she had overcome the worst of her depression. This was a promising event, tempered by the necessity of finding someone to take care of our young children. I was of small use in New York with *The Brighter Day* schedule and there was no room in the apartment for a live-in nanny, so Ruby took them to Holyoke for the two weeks and got help there. How to take care of our children with both of us working at the same time was going to be a problem. We needed more income to solve that.

But with the money from Grandpa's will we had been able to put a down payment on a cottage on the Housatonic River in the far northwest corner of Connecticut. Falls Village was the name of the small two-store settlement a mile or so up Route 7, and when Ruby and I were not working, we all headed up there in the station wagon. The little red one-bedroom cottage cost us $6,000 and I made the down payment out of the money from Grandpa—about $1,500— which I'd been stuffing in the bank for the past year and a half. The following year we would add a two-room extension off the back of the little place, bedrooms for Victoria and David. It was to become a refuge happily sought, perched daringly on a high bank of the Housatonic where the river broadened and slid beneath the canopy of overhanging trees. Across the stream cows grazed in a meadow.

Harold

The only sounds were from airborne creatures. We were hidden away at the end of a dirt track that ran alongside the river past three other cottages of spontaneous design. It was as close to heaven as we could get, and it put me in a place where I could be in constant contact with my children.

There were jobs to do which denied them my full attention, like restoring the cabin's rotten underpinnings, but I could beguile Victoria into "assisting me" while I worked. She was eager to be with me unless our neighbor's collie dog, Bruce, came over to play. She was four years old and could be my intelligent companion, ready for any adventure, so I took her with me. One morning I awoke her to watch the dawn come creeping along the edges of the river and filling the sky with its pure and stunning glory. The river was life in motion and I had bought a canoe so we could quietly drift on its benevolent surface. Victoria wanted to know where the river came from, so we stroked the canoe slowly upstream against the current to discover the answer. When a rapids challenged us below the dam, we made a tactical decision to turn for home, but the voyage of discovery had been successfully completed.

The energy of purpose crept into us again. We all had projects going. Ruby had begun working. Victoria was blessed with an unguarded heart and an inquisitive humor and David was celebrating the end of his first year on earth by trying to stand up. They were the innocent soul of a family that had lost its way while Ruby had been ill and I was philandering and working twenty-four-hour days, and this little clearing in the woods offered us a possibility of repair. For me it stirred up memories of that farm at the other end of the state where I had spent my barefoot summers, and it inspired in me a hopefulness to relive them with my children. Victoria and I visited the old-timey hardware store in Falls Village and purchased tools for making things, including a small child's replica of a toolbox so that she could work beside me in the grassy dirt while I constructed a dock. We would lower it down to the river by block and tackle off the high branch of a tree, with the other end of the rope tied to the station wagon. We were construction engineers and drafted our

plans in consultation. David's interest was in contemplating the possibility of a dive down the ten-foot embankment to the river. We tied a rope around him to keep him on land.

It was the right place for Tom Sawyer and Huck Finn to spiritually take possession of us and we could glide downstream by canoe in and out of the shade from the extended arms of elms and maples and swamp oak that formed the corridors of our dreaming. In those sleepy Connecticut summers the spirit of Mark Twain's boyhood floated into us in a natural way; it just hovered there as easily as the bees and dragonflies and exploring birds did, cruising in the drowsy air. It put my mind in gear for the performance late in August at Lakeside for the assembled gentry of the IPA. The future of the Twain solo rode heavily on that night.

Sometimes the cost of pursuing a career was too great, especially when it made me impatient at being reined in by my children. I had been left alone with Victoria and David one Saturday while Ruby was out for the day. I needed to take an important letter down to the post office at 104th Street in time to catch the afternoon mail. Should I get the children dressed and take them with me or race down the three blocks myself and leave my one-and-a-half-year-old son in the care of his four-year-old sister? It would take ten minutes. Victoria was on the couch in the living room watching television and David was crawling around on the floor.

"Victoria, I have to run down to the post office before it closes and mail this letter. Can you watch David for ten minutes?"

"Huh?"

"Can you watch David for ten minutes? I have to mail this letter."

"Sure, Dad."

"Just ten minutes. Keep an eye on him."

"Uh-huh."

David sat on the floor observing this exchange as if he understood the conversation. Smart kid, I thought. I moved fast. Long

strides, a guilty heart beating out the tempo, mailed the letter and walked back, fighting off bloody images with hope that all would be okay. Victoria was still watching television.

"Where's David?"

"What?"

"David—where is he?"

"I don't know. He was here."

I turned into the kitchen. He was headfirst inside the cabinet under the sink and when he turned around, his mouth was covered with a white powder.

"David—what have you—" I pulled him out and looked inside. The only white powder in the cabinet was around the holes in the top of a can of Comet cleanser.

"David, let me look—open your mouth!" I had to pry it open and he started crying. I couldn't tell if he'd swallowed the stuff or not.

"Vicki, for God's sake, I told you to watch him. Look what he's done! You were supposed to watch him!" She started crying. I was terrified that David had swallowed the stuff, but what if he hadn't? I read the label and it was serious.

"Come on, we're going to the hospital. Now!"

The children were crying, I was out of control. I grabbed Victoria's wrist and their coats and swung David under my arm and bolted out of the building with them, waving frantically at a cab. The hospital was up toward Columbia University and when we got there, a decision had to be made whether or not to pump David's stomach out. They couldn't be sure if he'd swallowed the stuff. It was an awful choice. I couldn't take a chance, so I told them to go ahead.

I blamed Victoria for this terrible ordeal and she never forgot it. I had put mailing a letter ahead of the responsibility of taking care of my children. It was unforgivable. Sometimes the cost of pursuing a career causes you to become way too single-minded. There can be no excuse for putting your children in danger or neglecting them, and my intense pursuit of success damaged this family. When I put my head down and tried to blaze a successful path through the mine-

field of showbiz, we all became casualties in different ways. But the one common denominator was loneliness. We all felt it and our children lost some of the joy of childhood.

I wish I could say our marriage had come through the fire in a much braver shape, but that would be untrue. Ruby and I couldn't reclaim the joy of our love affair. For me she had become a faraway person and I had pulled back from her. Asking who bore responsibility for this separation could lead to the riddle of the chicken and the egg. Ruby's loss of confidence in our marriage had only partially healed and I could not find the inspiration to mend it. Whenever a spontaneous emotion of love burst out of me it could no longer find the mark, so it slowly retired. We kept our marriage intact, but our happiness in each other had expired and it harmed our children. I could count only on Twain to fire up my mind and incite my passions, and his explorations of truth and justice became my new companions. I was heartened by the realization that he did not spare himself. He was often a man in pain and his frequent visitor was self-doubt. I was only an actor looking for a show to put on, but the man I was pursuing was edging up on me.

Playing that three-thousand-seat hall at Lakeside in August with a one-man show was no pushover. The microphone setup did not pick up my voice as loudly as it should have, which warned me to learn more about sound systems if I played houses that big. Otherwise the response was favorable. In September, Ricklie booked me for a luncheon on a platform in the Rainbow Room of the Hotel Carter in Cleveland to see how the solo Twain would do with an audience clanking silverware and glasses. In those days I said yes to anything for $250. They appeared to enjoy the performance when they weren't mopping up the aging lemon meringue pie.

Back in New York I found two more books at Argosy that further opened up the gold mine of Twain's mind. His autobiography and a leather-bound edition called *Chapters from My Autobiography*, pieces that had run in the *North American Review*, such as the great anti-imperialist essay "To the Person Sitting in Darkness." This book contained some of the material in the fourth volume of Albert Big-

elow Paine's official biography that I also found at Argosy, stuff supposedly suppressed, but there it was as clear as day, and the nuggets glittering on the pages of these books helped me sharpen the laughter onstage and weave material in a tougher pattern, questioning man's love affair with himself. "Man is the noblest work of God. Who found that out?" The autobiography was a beaut, an uncovered visit into the darker realm of Twain's mind, unknown to me and unsuspected by most Americans, and I began to sense the size of the Klondike I had fallen into when I innocently stepped forth to portray a humorist. "I wish I had the human race in the Ark again, with an auger."

My first tour with Mark Twain began on October 25 in Shreveport, Louisiana, at a fee of $500 (Pryor-Menz got half). An evening show in two acts that ran one hour and twenty-two minutes with a twelve-minute intermission. The response was continuous and enthusiastic, but the bigger surprise was the applause at the end of Colonel Sherburn's speech to the lynching mob. Down south. I had not expected that. The next morning I had a performance at the State College in Natchitoches in a beautiful theater, and everyone was as happy as ducks over the show. And so was I. It worked like a charm and the fee was $400, of which I got half. This was a money-maker, too. What a shock! It was *The Ed Sullivan Show* that allowed them to raise the fee so high.

I traveled more than a thousand miles north to Winona, Minnesota, for a show Monday morning at the State Teachers College (split $300 with P-M) and had to work hard on the 850 northerners to rouse them up to par, then plunged south to Mount Pleasant for a show that night in the chapel at Iowa Wesleyan. Five curtain calls and two encores. What was happening? I was adding new material, editing it during these long drives across the farmlands with the book open on the passenger seat and a tablet on my right knee, ducking around the bare teeth of farm equipment hogging the road, and chancing my luck across the double line on blind curves and hills. I learned to accelerate and tuck in fast or yank myself back in line when I guessed wrong and a head-on collision was coming at me. It kept the adrenaline flowing. The Advice to Youth speech went in, as

did the burlesque of the Wagnerian opera, and I began switching material around to test it in different positions. That kept me keyed up, but the big reward was that audiences found this man funny. They liked him, too. I just couldn't get over it.

I couldn't believe the names of some of the towns, either. Menominie, Wisconsin, between Eau Claire and St. Paul, three hundred–odd miles to the north and a whole day to make it. I headed through back roads to the Mississippi River across from Prairie du Chien and drove north through the river towns. I was revisiting the vast spaces out there where the people lived that he wrote stories about. His core people. You really had to get out there and spend time listening to them, talking to them, to understand the layers in the body of America. If you stayed locked up in the stone canyons of New York between two local rivers and thought you knew the American character, you were reducing the periphery of your mind.

To some, the spectacle of this kind of solo touring, crossing great distances of the country's midsection at speed and using the automobile as a mobile writing room, will seem loony and fraught with instant risk, and I suppose it was that, but for me it was the cauldron in which my mind could create. The intensity of concentration was almost bulletproof. Ideas sprang out of the risks I took and kept me at work on my show, pruning it, adding to it, arranging and shaping it, testing it in front of the next audience down the road, and then moving on with more ideas. I was never tired, not in that trance of creation, and I put a show together in an atmosphere of danger.

The clue to getting a good show knit together was the editing process, as well as the selection of material, splicing in the insights and bits and pieces that revealed Twain's developing mind. I had barely begun to think about that. I was relieved to find that Twain had altered his literature for the lecture platform, too. He had a great ear, the makings of a great actor, Henry Irving would say, so he knew the difference between storytelling on the page and storytelling on the stage. The actor is an adjective, so you lose some of the literary adjectives and give the actor room to do his work. My system was to dog a routine to death until I knew past certainty that the

material needed cutting, out of respect for Twain's great literary talent and a gaping uncertainty about my own. Finally I would gingerly operate on it and splice in a sudden laugh line to surprise them, like "By the end of this year I shall be sixty-seven years old, if alive. About the same if dead." Only I changed it to "seventy-one years old" because I was playing him at the age of seventy.

One more big jump three hundred miles to the end of the Oklahoma Panhandle at Goodwell, a tiny western cow town where a baby in arms gave a running commentary on the show. Its crescendo came during Colonel Sherburn's speech to the lynch mob. I worked on the floor of the gym and the audience was not bad considering the Bible Belt territory and the baby's admiration. The final show of the tour came two nights later, a long seven hundred miles northeast to Ed Wright's hometown of Marshalltown, Iowa.

So the tour was over, twelve shows and a booty of almost $2,000 in less than three weeks' traveling. Suddenly I had a new source of income. It was this first tour with Twain that taught me that I might have a Derby winner. So I began dreaming. What if I could do it in New York someday as Emlyn Williams had just done with Charles Dickens? Hah! Now there was a wild notion, good for a laugh or two. The Oklahoma Panhandle was a long way from Broadway, baby, but just in case, I acted on a hunch. I wrote Carlton and Jean about the show: Would they consider booking me to open the first week of the summer season at Holyoke? If I could extend the show to three acts and run it a week in that theater to good reviews, well . . . we would see.

I noticed that the show got stronger as it got longer. The more I showed the radical lights and shades in him, the more the performance had something to say. But I didn't have it right yet, far from it. I was still knocking off a laundry list of selections and jamming new numbers into the repertoire to explore possibilities, using this short tour to try out new stuff as fast as I was able to get it on, so the material was not well rehearsed and it was still a selection of stories by Twain, not a show. I had to build one and I needed to know why I was out there doing this man. Why? The performance needed an

arc: a takeoff, a critical highpoint, and then a descent and a landing. By the end of the week a letter came from Carlton: "The light is green."

I talked to the producers of *The Brighter Day* and got permission to leave the show for several weeks in late March and April and the week in June at Holyoke and then told Higgins, Ricklie, and Pryor-Menz to start booking. On November 30, Mark Twain's birthday, I played a benefit performance at the Lighthouse, the organization devoted to the blind that Twain had helped establish out of his admiration for Helen Keller. He had become her champion.

Somehow the news of what I was doing had reached Angels Camp, California. I got a request from the folks out there to appear as Mark Twain at the annual Calaveras County Fair and Jumping Frog Jubilee. They wanted to pay me $650 for two nights on a variety show, emcee the Frog Jump, and walk around the fairgrounds as Twain. I had never seen a "frog jump," nor had I walked around as Twain like a clown in the circus. This was all pretty intimidating and a far cry from what I intended to do with the show, but they said *Life* magazine wanted to cover it, and I couldn't turn down 650 whole dollars. At least I would learn something new. Oh yes, indeed.

People were getting wind of what I was doing. Another benefit in New York, at P.S. 135 for a cerebral palsy group, and the Hannibal, Missouri, Chamber of Commerce was interested in having me come out that summer for the Fence Painting Day parade and maybe do a show. I had the feeling that yes was the right answer to every chance I got to do Mark Twain. It might discourage other itinerant actors from staking a claim on the gold mine I'd stumbled into and that put a charge of urgency into my pursuit of him. I combed his books for material to improve the show and to use in odd circumstances. One laugh line in a letter or a story that I could edit into the show or use at a frog jump, that laugh was worth its weight in bullion. You could almost put a price tag on "Man was made at the end of the week's work, when God was tired," so I kept hunting through his books.

I was anxious to build a longer show for Holyoke, and the boys

in Council Bluffs had put together a rigorous two weeks in April, with a preamble of three dates for Ricklie and one for Howard Higgins.

March 14—10:30 a.m. Indianapolis, Marian College $250.
March 15—8:15 p.m. St. Louis, the Wednesday Club $275
 The *Post-Dispatch* took a series of pictures here.
March 18—Oklahoma City. 7:30 p.m. Men's Dinner Club $450, in the Persian Room of the Skirvin Tower Hotel.
March 19—Newark, Delaware. 7:30 p.m. The University of Delaware $300.

Even I could not have driven the fifteen-hundred-mile jump from Oklahoma City to Delaware in one day, so I must have adopted the airplane and flown to these engagements.

After the University of Delaware I had ten days off to put in a few shows on *The Brighter Day* and get out to St. Joseph, Missouri, for a morning show at the junior college. I shifted material around but couldn't break through the Missouri solemnity, and the performance lost steam; then they gave me an encore. There was an impregnable quality about Mark Twain. Warrensburg was next, for $300 and another solemn gang fifteen hundred strong who "loved the show," and the next day another struggle with the Missouri mule at Springfield for $300. The sure-thing numbers were getting to be the Interviewer, the Italian Guide, and the Golden Arm, and Seventy always scored. Mileage records were set from Billy the Kid country in New Mexico to Fargo, North Dakota, then twelve hundred miles south the next day to Seguin, Texas, and homeward bound halfway across the United States with $3,000 in the back pocket. Mark Twain had become a serious contender in the bread-and-butter department and I wondered if I would have to stay with *The Brighter Day* forever. Maybe I could move on.

I had less than two months to get ready for the big test at Holyoke and the Frog Jump at Angels Camp in between. The threat that *Life* magazine might show up at Angels Camp with cameras made

me get more serious about the makeup for Twain. I had Oscar and Maria Bernner study the wild silhouette of his white head more carefully before dressing the wig, and knowing I'd be working up close and in daylight, I changed the colors of the makeup to match normal skin color and took more time with it, teasing the lines and shadows into my thirty-two-year-old face so they would be more convincing at short range. The makeup preparation grew past two hours at Angels Camp and the results seemed to convince most of the customers, or scare them into amused respect, and my own sober belief in the character helped. I wasn't kidding.

But the gods were. It rained, poured down on us, and on Saturday night the show had to be moved indoors, where I tried to entertain an audience that could barely hear me above the clamor. On Sunday the variety show went outside, rain or no rain. I performed in the band shell on the infield of the racetrack and the seven thousand people sat in bleachers on a hillside across the track. I was a stand-up comedian with a mike and hundred-year-old material; the rain came down in torrents and the audience ran up the hill and watched me from under the pine trees two hundred yards away. I looked down at the puddles on the racetrack and up at my audience at the top of the hill and died like a soldier.

Three more shows had come in before Holyoke and they tested the mood changes I was building into the show. The performance was acquiring a progressive shape, but I still needed to know *why* I was doing this man. What message was he delivering that would stay with the audience going home? My goal was a laugh every fifteen seconds in the first act because it was important to break down any audience resistance early and get them on his side with no time for doubting, and by the time I got to the naked native girls in Hawaii and the Interviewer and the Italian Guide we were on a roll. But I still needed to find the sources of anger in him to spread danger in act two.

On June 6, just before heading to Holyoke, I got another appearance on NBC's *Tonight Show* with Jack Lescoulie as host. Would

that help me fill the big open-sided Mountain Park Casino in Holyoke? I wondered.

On June 11 Louise Mace wrote a review of it in the *Springfield Union*.

The Valley Players opened their 16th season last night at Mountain Park Casino, Holyoke, with a unique and rewarding program—a one-man show entitled "Mark Twain Tonight." And, in all life, so it seemed, there was Samuel Langhorne Clemens himself, complete with immaculate, comfortably wrinkled white suit, brisk red tie, drooping white moustache, ample white headpiece and the inevitable cigar . . . Technique never obtrudes, but it is there: in the stiff, weighted walk, the relaxed stance, the restless hands, the mannerisms, the clipped drawl and the quiet approach to the humorist point which Mr. Holbrook so deftly and significantly lights with the pause.

Mr. Holbrook's Mark Twain is richly and lovingly embodied, a re-creation of a man and a mind, a deeply kneaded personation . . . Mr. Holbrook makes him live again.

The road ahead was open. Now I had to find my way up it.

34

I think it was in the summer of 1957 when June showed up in Canaan, Connecticut, a few miles up the road from our cottage on the Housatonic. No warning; she just let us know she was there, working in a bar, and had her two children with her. Nile Nyles had run down his welcome and my sister was on the loose again, full of good cheer and confident that God would provide. If not, she'd find someone. Cheryl was a redhead, as thin as her mother and about to enter her teens. Kathy was a quiet little doll four or five years old who spent a great deal of time observing the uncertain world around her. June had tracked me back to New England and we saw them that summer when we could leave New York for the cottage and slow our pace to match the quiet drift of the river. Having my sister and her children near was something new and a good feeling. Maybe I could help her settle down and our children would get to know one another.

That fall another piece in the jigsaw grid of chance fell into place when Jerry Guardino introduced me to John Lotas at the Lambs Club. John had seen the Twain performance there two years before and we began planning for an off-Broadway production. Our first step was a backers' audition. A press agent named Maxine Keith came to our rescue and we lined up a small banquet room at the Hotel Astor and talked forty-five people into coming, but the rain came first and washed our hopes down the drain when only twenty-

five people made it. The $2,000 we wrung out of them was far short of the $9,000 we needed.

A little over three weeks earlier I had come home to Granville with Mark Twain to perform at Swasey Chapel, where as a student I had seen Cornelia Otis Skinner and Robert Frost and where Ruby and I had driven the great Ruth Draper up the hill for her show. I hoped to make Ed Wright proud. I did a morning show to a full house of fourteen hundred—a grand welcoming applause after Ed's introduction, laughs so long I didn't need much material. In the afternoon I spoke to the literature classes for an hour in the science lecture hall, where I had stumbled over physics nine years before, and that night, I performed the full show for an hour and forty minutes to an audience of three hundred. Game but tired out. My teacher was pleased.

This surprising year of 1957 ended with a performance on December 5 at the Lotos Club, a New York men's club established in 1870. Mark Twain had been one among its celebrated members. It was a productive year, fifty-three shows including the free ones and nearly $10,000 earned with the solo, plus eighty-two shows on *The Brighter Day*. We were making a good living now and there was a feeling in the wind that Mark Twain could give us the security we needed.

I was beginning to see his world as a template for mine. Literary critics like Dixon Wecter, Bernard DeVoto, Arthur L. Scott, and Philip Foner directed my mind into the audacious channels of his thinking, and the voice of Twain was beginning to rise: his disenchantment with the self-serving image we have of ourselves and the hypocrisy of our behavior.

Early in 1958 another link in the chain of circumstances moved us forward. The Lambs Club had given John Lotas and Jerry Guardino permission to put the full show on their stage if they could find a charitable organization to sponsor it at twenty-five bucks a seat and guarantee 250 people. Those guys found one—the Ophthalmological Foundation for the Blind. Mark Twain's championing of Helen Keller made him a symbol for them and a stroke of luck for

us. The performance on January 16 felt like the most exciting I'd ever had, a Broadway benefit crowd in full dress shouting "Bravo" and "More!" The show worked, the three-act format worked, and John and Jerry got permission to do a performance in the club theater on my thirty-third birthday, February 17. We could use it as a backers' audition.

In the audience that night was Madame Eliat, a psychiatrist Ruby had been going to. Ruby had requested me to accompany her on some therapy sessions, an uncomfortable task for me, but to help her I agreed to go. Madame Eliat turned out to be an interesting person, a petite French lady past middle age who lived on Washington Square. She had known the literary cognoscenti of the Paris Left Bank crowd as well as Sigmund Freud, and there was an intellectual mysterioso about her. I felt I was talking to someone thoughtful who did not come to quick conclusions. Not long afterward I started seeing her myself. I liked her. She let me talk out my feelings without judgment and I felt she understood them. Ruby's psychiatrist became mine. The grid of life was at work again.

We had gone into furious action to persuade anyone with an extra nickel to attend the Lambs performance a mere month away. John and Jerry did the heavy calling while I hit the road for five more shows. At the big Music Hall in Houston on the fourteenth I drew eighteen hundred people. It was the first time my name had ever been on a marquee. Next stop New York and our big night at the Lambs, or so I thought until the plane put down at Birmingham and I saw snow on the ground. Snow in Alabama? They grounded the plane at Atlanta and I had to stay overnight in a hotel. The next day was the sixteenth. I got an early morning flight for Newark and landed in the worst blizzard to hit New York in years. A path had to be shoveled through snow to bring the stairs out to the plane. In Manhattan there were no taxis running. The streets were adrift in white. The next day it snowed again and that night I did my birthday backers' audition at the Lambs. Forty-four prospects had pledged to attend. Three showed up.

We would do no more backers' auditions that year. Jerry Guar-

dino, who got it all started and had toiled for many hours to move my show forward, was going to California to look for work. He had just been married and could no longer live on bread and water.

In late September 1957 nine black students had waited on the steps of Central High School in Little Rock, Arkansas, protected by a thousand soldiers from the 101st Airborne Division of the United States Army; then they entered the school. President Eisenhower had sent the 101st in response to a telegram from the mayor of Little Rock, who was attempting to follow the orders of the United States Supreme Court and his city's school board to desegregate the schools. You could sense the tide of America's social conscience beginning to turn. In ten years it would rise to the flood, but early that September, Governor Orval Faubus had called out the state's National Guard to stop the students from entering the school. A federal judge and certain of Little Rock's leading citizens overruled him and the school took the black students in. Lost in the fury of news reporting was the fact that among the two thousand white students, even those who did not favor desegregation felt it was their duty to obey the law. It was a dress rehearsal for the drama the nation was going to live out in the decade to come, stirring emotions that would reach down to the primal gut of the country and force it to face the unfinished birth pangs of 175 years ago.

The drama would build throughout that school year, and in March I had a show forty miles up the road from Little Rock in Searcy, Arkansas. My instincts were in the liberal camp ever since I had stepped forward to volunteer as the sole white soldier to bunk with the black troops on the top floor of the Broadway Central Hotel, but I was not one of those who went around preaching to the choir in New York. The group thing bred too many opinions, the point got buried under noise and fury and made me want to go off and think by myself, so that's what I started doing. How could I say something and be *listened* to? I realized I had a trumpet in Mark Twain. Maybe not a trumpet. An oboe or a clarinet, but he could

make you turn around and listen. I would fly to Little Rock and drive up to Harding College in Searcy and do—what? What selection would update itself without my interfering with it and yet seem to refer to Little Rock forty-seven years after Mark Twain died? I had but one thing, and its dramatic line was somewhat off target— the scene where Colonel Sherburn faces down the lynch mob in *Huckleberry Finn*. It was Twain facing the Klan, and maybe the message would come through. A mob of a thousand people had surged around Central High when the nine black students were escorted into the school and they had to be slipped out a side door to safety. Maybe Sherburn's speech to the mob would ring bells.

There were a thousand people in the theater on a rainy night in rural Arkansas and the response was big and gratifying. When I got to the *Huckleberry* number, which starts off with a satiric description of a river town in Arkansas, its locals lounging around with the stray dogs and pigs, and then moves to the shooting of Boggs by Sherburn, the crowd took it in and responded, but when the lynch mob comes for him and he faces them down, there was deep and utter silence.

" 'Now the thing for you to do is to droop your tails and go home and crawl in a hole. If there's going to be any lynching done around here it will be done in the dark; and they'll bring their masks and fetch a man along. Now leave—and take your half 'a' man with you!' "

The whole speech dramatizes Twain's contempt for the Klan, and I forced the message into the darkness of the theater. The intensity of my thoughts willed it out there and I believe it landed. They did not talk about it afterward and I realized this was going to be expected: the silence was the response. I was learning that when you tread severely upon people's feelings it's wise to leave them alone with their thoughts and not preach to them.

That was the year I got my hands on Philip Foner's *Mark Twain: Social Critic*. More than any other study of Mark Twain's searching, iconoclastic view of America, this book laid it out plain for me and spurred my curiosity to follow the paths of Twain's appraisal of our

society—the corruption of gigantic corporations and the politicians who serve them, the dismemberment of our ideals by intolerance toward the slaves we had imported to toil in the fields and toward the immigrants from Europe flooding in after the Civil War to work the steel mills and coal mines powering the industrialization of an agrarian society. Our treatment of these strangers ate away at the dream of a democratic society. New ingredients were altering the social recipe. The land of the pioneers had moved west, but even there the ideal was being corrupted by the treatment of the Chinese.

Mark Twain had been out there and done that. The riverfront youth who left home and got Mr. Bixby to teach him how to pilot a massive steamboat up and down the treacherous north-south highway of America had seen from those floating palaces of sin and innocence the black men on the docks, muscles glazed in sweat, heaving five-hundred-pound bales of cotton on board. The Great War came and killed the river trade and the young man tried soldiering, but he could not take heart in "the killing of strangers against whom you feel no personal animosity; strangers whom, in other circumstances, you would help if you found them in trouble." He went west to the wild-hearted goldfields and the roaring bohemian society of San Francisco—"that was heaven on the half-shell"—and out there he saw intolerance in a new form, the singling out of Chinamen to carry the slave's burdens and suffer the whip and the dogs. It disturbed his fun. The frog story got him fans back east, and when his dispatches from the Hawaiian Islands trumped the coverage of a disaster at sea, Twain's visibility rose. He came home and tried the lecture gambit out west in imitation of his idol Artemis Ward. The earnest deadpan delivery, the daring pauses. The big East called him and he booked passage on a ship bound for the isthmus at Nicaragua and caught a disease-riddled vessel on the Caribbean side and somehow escaped death on board from yellow fever and made it to New York. A job he'd engineered to accompany a boatload of religious-minded gentry across the Atlantic to the Holy Lands and describe their adventures produced a big book, *The Innocents*

Abroad, and now he was Somebody, a new face in the eastern literary mecca of America.

Then he met the Langdons and their daughter, Olivia. She was beautiful and fragile and pure and lived according to the precepts of the Bible, and the Wild West traveling man fell in love with her. The father was a rich coal dealer in Elmira and they put up with this eccentric from God knows where until they couldn't resist him anymore and took him in. It was five years after the end of the Civil War and Elmira had been a major stop on the Underground Railroad for slaves escaping to the North, and Mr. Langdon had been part of it. He helped a black slave working in the Baltimore shipyards escape to the North and get an education; Frederick Douglass would then become the leader of his people. One night Douglass came to sup at the Jervis Langdon table. One of the Irish servants refused to serve Douglass and Mr. Langdon fired her. This is the family Mark Twain married into, the same Sam Clemens, born and bred in a slave state, and what do you think they talked about at the Langdon dinner table that night? About what did they converse? In five years he would begin *Huckleberry Finn*.

Change. No one with a head that big stays the same from year to year. The eyes—look at them—piercing, gray-dark, lurking under brows. The eyes of a hawk "hanging motionless in the sky," watching us. It was time for me to get to work and find out how many fathoms down this man went.

Traveling through those southern towns, I was watching, too. My trips into the South had a special feeling now. Rosa Parks had declined to move her seat on that bus in Montgomery and a fellow named Martin Luther King was preaching an interesting message. He was against violence. He did not want his people to imitate the physical violence and hatemongering some white people used against them on their marches and sit-ins. "We must forever conduct our struggle on the high plane of dignity and discipline," he said. Hmm, I thought. He had discovered a weapon and the weapon was his adversary: they would do the job for him. We would watch the lynching and police dogs and our shame would teach us to think it

over. He was a preacher, King, but he was going to let the racists preach his sermon. I thought, That's right off the pages of *Huckleberry Finn*.

I began to open up the show now in the middle section, around the Sherburn piece, to make the message tougher. Tried the piece of satire about Satan, suggesting that he was the model statesman on the planet and I was looking forward to meeting him and shaking him by the tail. I thought it was a long fly ball to the outfield that might land on somebody's brain. It was mostly work because many audiences would not loosen up and give you the rolling ride you needed to feel you had scored. But it toughened me up and I'd need that when I got to New York.

The tour wound up at Carbondale, Illinois, for a captive morning audience of fifteen hundred and I counted up the take, $3,900 for nine dates, of which I got half. The Pryor-Menz fifty-fifty deal was pretty tough compared with Ricklie's and Higgins's 20 percent, but they did get the bookings. The next day I was back on *The Brighter Day*.

The soap opera had become such a confining cage it drove me to consider the Actors Studio. Much as I was put off by their self-indulgences, maybe I should audition for it. They were getting all the jobs. Paul Newman had done *Cat on a Hot Tin Roof*, and my sister on the soap, Lois Nettleton, had taken over Maggie from Barbara Bel Geddes one night. I saw it, and Lois astonished me. It was an intricate and deeply emotional performance. The soap opera actress had disappeared. Could I connect like that?

I got an appointment with the stand-in for God down here on earth, Lee Strasberg. I didn't like what I'd heard about him. He lived in a handsome old building on the Upper West Side and when I rang the doorbell his wife let me in and I immediately felt like a Gentile. There was a hallway and then a door that opened onto a large room where His Highness was crouched behind a desk facing the door. Like the Oval Office. The phrase "on the carpet" came to mind. I was motioned to a chair in front of the desk and his pale blue eyes regarded me without any cheer. Silent scrutiny was my

welcome. He finally asked me to describe my acting experience, so I made as handsome a presentation of it as I could in the pale light of his indifference, my spell in the nightclub and on the road with Shakespeare and all, watching those pale eyes closely for any clue of interest or even humanity. Not a flicker. Another empty pause.

"Is that it?"

"Yes."

Another pause, which got so long I deduced it was his wordless way of dismissing me. So I got up and turned for the escape hatch when a thought struck me and I swung back.

"Oh. I've also done six years of summer stock."

"We'll try to overlook that."

I should have left, just smiled or grimaced and gone, but some kind of anger nailed me to the spot.

"I don't know why you should. It's some of the best training I've ever had." We stared each other down and then I left. I felt dismissed in the same way I had been by the CBS casting king, Robert Dale Martin, four years before when he tossed the brochure of our show back across his desk and said, "Did you get paid for that?"

It was not an auspicious way to treat the boss, fool though he might be, before my Actors Studio audition, but what the hell, I went ahead with it. Mona Bruns played Aunt Emily on the soap opera. She was a pro and so was her husband, Frank Thomas, Sr., a veteran actor of many years' service. And so was her son, Frank Thomas, Jr. They were an acting family and Mona was kind. We'd had a scene on *The Brighter Day* in which I came home late one night, drunk and uncertain of Sandra's behavior, and it occupied nearly the entire show and played well. I didn't want to audition for the Studio with the usual stuff—Miller, Williams, or Bill Inge. Everybody did them, so I asked Mona if she would do that drunk scene with me from the soap. When Mona and I stepped on the small stage at the Studio and played it together, one of those rare moments in actor's life happened when you nail it. There were three people out front, Cheryl Crawford and a director with a name something like Stix and a third person who is a blank now. When we finished,

there was some half whispering among them and then a voice said, "Will you come down here, Mr. Holbrook?"

I stepped off the stage into a diminutive seating area and was asked to join them.

"We like what you did. Where have you studied?" I gave them a short sketch of my history with Ed Wright and the boondock audiences of America.

"We may be able to offer you a place, but where did you find that scene?"

I thought, Tell them it's from an obscure play called *Brighten the Day*, but I figured what the hell, go for the truth. "It's from a soap opera I'm on. CBS."

The faces lost color and I could see brains dodging around this desecration. Pregnant looks, teeth lightly clenched. "Hal, we'd like you to come back with a scene from Miller or Williams or Bill Inge. Something where you haven't been drinking."

I never went back. I was wrong to let the shadow of hypocrisy set me down like that, but it just tasted bitter and I couldn't rise above it. I wonder where I'd be if I had gone back. If I hadn't chosen to go it alone.

35

In the summer of 1958 John Lotas and I formed a company and grandly called it Mark Productions. We rented a one-room office on the third floor of a run-down building on West Forty-fourth Street and put our desks in front of the two windows. We each had a phone with a button that turned from one line to the other. It worked until a call came in on John's phone for me and at the same time one came in for John on mine. Then we had to switch chairs. But we were so close to the heart of showbiz that if you leaned way out of the window, Sardi's could be seen on the other side of Times Square, and directly across the street we had a picture-window view of an Afro-American dance studio with continuous bongo drums. Our object was to get *Mark Twain Tonight!* on a stage in New York.

But I needed the strongest show I could edit together, material that would shift unexpectedly and keep the audience guessing. Suspense was important, and the pause—it could move their minds from one place to another, such as the shift in material at the end of the *Huck* numbers (I had two by now) when I let a big space of silence hang in the air while Twain takes out a match and relights the cigar. In that long silence the audience has to face its complicity in the plight of black people, past and present. Here the audience is doing the work for him, as the racists do for Martin Luther King. Then Twain says, "Man is the Deity's favorite, you know. After the

housefly," and he is steering us toward another tangent that unravels belief in our impregnable goodness.

I was still feeling my way along. When I hit the trail for two weeks the Council Bluffs twins had booked for me in the midsection of America's dozing corpus, I had new stuff I'd worked on to the beat of the bongo drums. *The Brighter Day* had released me for three weeks so I could fly to South Dakota and start a tour, which looked like this:

October 27—Brookings, State College, 11 a.m.
    " 28—Warrensburg, Mo., Central Missouri State, 10 a.m.
    " 29—St. Cloud, Minn., State College, 8:15 p.m.
    " 31—Superior, Wis., State College, 9:50 a.m.
November 1—Wahoo, Neb., Luther Jr. College, 8:15 p.m.
    "   3—Ada, Okla., East Central State, 11:00 a.m.
    "   4—San Angelo, Tex., San Angelo College, 8:15 p.m.
    "   5—   "   "   "
November 7—Silver City, N.Mex, New Mexico Western College,
              10:00 a.m.
    "   8—Santa Fe, N.Mex., Theatre Intime Series, 8:30 p.m.

I had finally adopted the airplane, more precisely the DC-3, a fine small air transport with two engines to keep it up and a civilized interior in which you could stand to your full height. It flew in every kind of crazy weather and somehow got you there, but I usually had to take two a day to carry me around this nutcase circuit. Try figuring how you'd fly from Brookings, South Dakota (heard of it?), to Warrensburg, Missouri (heard of that?). From Brookings you got yourself driven fifty miles to Sioux Falls by someone at the college, caught a DC-3 to Omaha or Chicago, another DC-3 to Kansas City, and then a sixty-mile drive east to Warrensburg off old Route 50. This was accomplished after a morning performance in South Dakota, and Warrensburg was at 10:00 a.m. the next day. The hand of God had to be close by.

I started laying down new material by the yard. Move forward, I told myself, experiment! Wagnerian Opera went in at Brookings ("rather weak") and the Evolution material from Paine's biography; I ended the show at Warrensburg with man's idea that in heaven you progress and progress and progress "and if that isn't hell I don't know what is"—for a big laugh to take me off. For St. Cloud's thousand strong I tried the Watermelon story and the Searching for Truth stuff, moving material around in different combinations. The Evolution routine really woke them up in Superior. I tried out a new *Huck* number in Wahoo, Nebraska, the "you can't pray a lie" sequence, but it needed work. At Ada, Oklahoma, for "the largest crowd they ever had"—twelve hundred—I tried the routine about the Ant again, but it did not hold up well.

The final paid show of the year was at West Liberty State College in West Virginia, where one hundred people were turned away. On November 30, Mark Twain's birthday, I did a short freebie for the Mark Twain Association of New York and some of the elderly crowd were shocked by his "irreverence." Ha!

So 1958 ended with thirty-seven solo shows plus two television appearances and ninety-one shows on *The Brighter Day*. I got close to $20,000 that year, but no closer to an engagement in New York. Damn it.

In the middle of February of the new year John got a call from a friend named Bunker Jenkins who suggested that we do another backers' audition in his living room. I did my makeup in his bedroom and made an entrance into the living room for a short two-act show lasting an hour and thirty-five minutes. There were six men there and their wives. At the intermission one of them asked for a pen and wrote out a check for $4,500. Half the money we needed. His name was Malcolm Pennington. After that the rest of the money came quickly. Then John made one golden decision: he went out and hired Harvey Sabinson, the ace press agent and fine human be-

ing whose company was preeminent on Broadway. Then John started looking for a theater.

I never stopped working the show. I'd played three times in January at Hartford, Flint, Michigan, and Syracuse University, where only 183 people showed up. And I had twelve shows booked in March. We were trying for an April opening in New York. Would anybody come? One afternoon I walked across Times Square on Forty-fourth Street and looked at the theater marquees lined up like the Russian army—at the Shubert, Gertrude Berg and Cedric Hardwick in *A Majority of One*; at the Broadhurst *The World of Suzie Wong*; at the St. James *Flower Drum Song*; at the Majestic, Robert Preston in *The Music Man*. I turned around and headed for our office across Times Square where I could hide out, but I paused at Shubert Alley and made a fateful turn to the left into Forty-fifth Street. At the Booth *Two for the Seesaw* with Henry Fonda and Anne Bancroft; at the Music Box *Rashomon*; at the Royale *La Plume de Ma Tante*; and on the other side of Eighth Avenue I could see the Martin Beck marquee announcing the opening of Tennessee Williams's *Sweet Bird of Youth* with Paul Newman and Geraldine Page. That finished me. I went no farther, but I knew that Helen Hayes was doing O'Neill's *A Touch of the Poet* on Forty-sixth Street and down the block John Gielgud had just closed in *Ages of Man*. I was going to commit suicide.

I had a hard time finding the curb into Times Square because someone was speaking to me. It was Chamberlain Brown. I hadn't seen him for two years. He looked older and tired and his clothing needed attention.

"Chamberlain! Hello!"

"I've been thinking of you."

The DC-3 had trouble finding the airport in La Crosse, Wisconsin. "Worst snow in thirty years," said Ruth Nixon as she drove me to the college theater, where five hundred people turned out. "Wonderful response," my notes say, "and remarkable turn-out" for this first

show of my final tour before going off the high board in New York. At Lubbock, Texas, where the original Hilton Hotel looms above the plains, I drew four hundred people in the three-thousand-seat Civic Auditorium, but got a much better response from a thinking crowd at Drake University in Des Moines. The new *Huck* number with Pap's inflammatory speech about the "free nigger from Ohio" was gaining confidence (I always felt ashamed playing him) and I moved the programming around, testing combinations for opening night in New York. The return engagement at Iowa State "even topped the first appearance," say my notes, and the Twain scholar Fred Lorch, who was writing a book on Twain's lecturing, was there again. We had 250 standees and Fred was very complimentary. You can imagine how it plucked up my confidence.

Worthington, Minnesota, deflated it again. I played on a gym floor with the houselights on to be seen. Dreadful response. Kidding the Christian missionary's attempt to civilize the naked natives in the Sandwich Islands brought the show down again, so at Saint John's University I figured they might burn me at the stake. Nope. We had good fun with the Catholics in the theater that night, so the religious stuff was hard to predict out there. Maybe it would be okay in New York? At Duluth I played the National Guard Armory. Without a brass band you're a loser there. In Dubuque, once again the grim clouds of reticence hovered over the mating of humor and religion.

The tour ended on March 23 at a college in tiny Lamoni in southern Iowa and kidding the missionaries in Hawaii cooled them down early. I began wondering if my show could make it in New York. When I got home, an extra date had suddenly reared its head at New York University in the Bronx just two days before I would open at the Forty-first Street Theatre, and the head that reared up got pretty ugly. Despite a beautiful small theater and stage, Ira Klugerman, the student booker, refused to move the set that was onstage for a play to make room for me. I worked on a tiny apron in front of it. They were condescending, as they had been at the Brooklyn Academy. The turnout was poor and the response dull. I did the full three-act show I was expecting to open with in two days. This

sudden uppercut to my ego right before facing the Broadway critics was fortified by a review from the student critic on the university paper. It was a deadly, deadly pan.

I've heard they've invented a pill for stage fright. It won't work. First they need a pill to get you to the theater on opening night. Then another pill to get you up that day and maybe another one to help you get dressed. Of all the fears that can change the course of your life, stage fright is a killer because it can immobilize you or elevate you toward brilliance. You never know which way it is going to go until you take the dive.

I would have only part of a day to settle my guts after that devaluation by the students of higher learning and their critic north of Manhattan, and on Sunday I found that getting up in the morning and jamming on my socks kept some of the devils out of my brain. I could have gone up to Riverside Church and fallen on my knees in supplication, but God would have been amused. It was too late. I'd been using Twain to deflate the hypocrisy of self-serving soldiers of God for too long.

The selection of stage props and furniture had been left to me because everything had to be the right height, period, and character, and only I knew what to choose. I had found the armchair and a marble-topped Victorian table at the Salvation Army the week before and I also bought a short dictionary stand there. At an antiques shop in the Village, run by the folksinger Susan Reed and the actor Jimmy Karen, I saw an ornate mahogany hat stand and bought it. I cut three feet off the top of the post, separated the desk of the dictionary stand from its legs, and bolted the desk to the hat stand post. The result was an ancient lectern upon which Twain could lay down his notes. It leaned just a bit to port. On the afternoon of the opening, April 6, I went down to the antiques shop in the Village again and found a cut-glass pitcher, an old tumbler, and an ashtray that had a receptacle for wooden matches. Now I felt ready. I went to the theater and started my makeup.

The Forty-first Street Theatre was the old recital hall in the base-ment of the Wurlitzer Building between Sixth Avenue and Broad-way, one block south of Times Square. It could seat 208 people. My dressing room was small, an airless cubicle into which we'd crammed a longish table, and on it sat one-half of the traveling show box I'd built to carry "Mark Twain": his wig, mustache, eyebrows, makeup supplies including spirit gum, makeup remover, and acetone to dis-solve the glue after the show, and a mirror built into the box with a lightbulb on each side. The other half of the box contained his three-piece suit (getting pretty full of holes I had mended), the pad-ding, congress gaiter shoes, socks, garters, shirt, and tie. Unpacking all this, carefully laying it out on the table, and hanging up the suit and padding and shirt settled me down. Then I sat in front of the familiar mirror and began what had become a three-hour-and-fifteen-minute session of making myself up to look like Mark Twain, the old man, thirty-six years older than me. If I could get into that disguise, maybe I wouldn't be afraid, maybe my hands would stop shaking, especially when I raised the brush from the glue pot to my eyebrows. If I could get old, old like my grandfather and like Uncle Sabe on the farm in South Woodstock where I went barefoot, if I could get back to them I'd be safe.

The hand holding the brush when I drew the age lines around my eyes and along my jaw and neck with a flat artist's sable brush had to be steady. I thought of the little headmaster at the junior school in Connecticut who beat me up so many times, who hit me in this face I was trying to age. I'll get back at him, the son of a bitch! And the cold-eyed bastard at CBS who said, "Did you get paid for this?" And the stand-in for the Almighty, Strasberg—all those guys who know it all. They've got all the answers and they sit in judgment and try to crush you, the lousy sons of— Hold it! Hold it! Calm down, calm yourself, Holbrook, keep your anger at bay, keep that hand steady, you're highlighting the lines and the brush cuts side-ways along them, you can't smudge or blur your work. Run a high-light down the nose to make it longer. Remember Ed Wright, the professional, and Elmer Wartz—those awful orange eyebrows and

the orange wig he put on before he turned and grinned and you saw the huge buck teeth he'd slipped in while his back was turned. Corny, corny—Twain was way more subtle than that; but how Ed could hold a pause and drop the punch line. He was going to be out there tonight, watching me.

Telegrams kept coming in and my stage manager, Joe Keating, brought them down to me in my little room. There were so many. I put the padding on and the shirt, tie, and suit so I'd be ready and then I sat down and opened the telegrams one by one. They were from all over, all over America, from my friends and classmates, from people I didn't know, people who had booked me into their schools and auditoriums in Texas and South Dakota and Georgia, people all along the trails I had come. They were out there thinking of me. I started to get a big lump in my throat and began to cry. I had never thought so many people would wish me luck.

At 8:35 it was time to go backstage. My dressing room was on the far side of the lobby, so I had to wait for the doors to close and slide down a narrow corridor along the right side of the auditorium to get backstage. That's just a phrase, "backstage"—there wasn't any, only a one-foot space between the back wall and the old black drapes we had rigged for the backdrop. I slid sideways through there to get to the opposite side of the stage, where I would make my entrance. The space there was one foot, so the stage manager and I hid in the folds of the black side drapes to wait for the cue to start. I could hear them out there, and in that part of my mind I was unsure of the beast that was waiting. My armor protected the rest of me. For five years I had felt it, way back in Lock Haven before I stepped onstage the first time in this disguise, that feeling of being impregnable in Twain's suit and wig and brooding mustache. There had been bloodshed onstage, but the armor always pulled me through. Now it had gone dark out there, the beast went quiet, then suddenly it was bright and Joe said "go" and I walked on with the shambling gait.

I looked up in surprise at the sound of applause. Oh, I have guests. Yes, pal, you do and this is not Tonkawa and it ain't Wahoo. That's when I stopped pretending. It hit me like a spear in the gut—

this is *New York*! The armor slid off and I was naked, found out, me, Harold, waiting to be punished again. The words started coming out—"Lays and gen'l'men, I wish to present to you a man . . ." Who do you think you are, Harold? That's a beast out there. This is not some hick state college in the far Midwest, this is *New York*—critics are out there, important, angry ones, and you are wasting their time with your impertinent road act. What? Yes, that was a little laugh you got just then, yeah, but tentative, from your friends, who must be as frightened as you are. God, my knees are shaking, really shaking, and they can see that out there. I can't make them stop. That was another laugh—right? Not big but . . . hell, I've dropped the match—damn, screwed up my timing and the laugh died like a skunk. My fingers won't get hold of a match, damn it. They're shaking. Can't stop the shaking—Harold, you'll spill them all over the floor if you don't—how am I going to light the cigar when I'm shaking like this? It will kill the show. Kill it. You're dead already, kid, and you've just started.

I was back on the glacier at Shasta, my body weak and out of control. The words were coming out rote, another person speaking my lines, and he sounded unconvincing. After all this time the character of Twain had not taken possession of me. This clown onstage tonight had no authority, he was a windup thing that was just unwinding. I was shocked that I could not get hold of myself and my show after all those miles of training myself in every kind of playing space—gym floors, the curve of a baby grand, a platform in the banquet room of hotels, on real stages in real theaters—what had happened to me? My confidence had fled.

At the end of the first act Ruby came back. "Where's the fire? Slow down." That helped some. I was rushing, okay, that was it. I was letting Ruby down, too. After all we'd been through together, those dark roads in Mississippi, speeding along in the station wagon, dressing behind temporary screens set up in the corners of God knows where, forcing the audience by sheer will to listen to us—that's what I didn't have: the will. That beast out there was stronger than me and it had the last word. I had to *please* it or else. No, that's

not the attitude you need, Holbrook. Let them come to you. Let them come to you, *goddamn it*.

Easier said than done. Act two. I tried to drag my mind away from the audience to Twain's material and believe in it. A simple acting dogma you learn in stage kindergarten, but not simple on the New York firing line. The satiric message in Advice to Youth gave me a better handle to life-raft myself out of the helpless feeling because I could put my mind on the subtext of Twain's message, the corrosion of social standards for the young. I had personal angry thoughts about that and the laughs that were there began to rise. The *Huck* number came next and that was the big challenge of the night, an acting one. In it I had to assume several voices—six, including Huck, who was telling the story—but they all bled through the character of Twain. Twain had acted out selections himself on the stage, so I was acting Mark Twain who was acting Huck who was impersonating a couple of Arkansas loafers and Boggs and Sherburn and a voice in the lynch mob, a triplex of impersonations for a thirty-four-year-old actor, and control was important to get it near to being right. My mind had to be on it, not the critics, and that was a battle royal for me. Then came the Evolution routine, which I personally adored whether they did or not. I may have found a groove there that got me through the act. John came back, smiling, and said I was doing fine.

"You're kidding!"

"No, they're enjoying it." I didn't believe him, but it gave me some hope.

The ghost story kicked off the third act with spooky lighting and voice pyrotechnics; its insane craziness stirred up the insanity in me as it had at Culver when I nearly strangled Ollie Rea. I just let go and hoped the critics wouldn't kill me. Things calmed down after that. The trembling had stopped. Before the Seventy-Year-Old selection that would end the show came the story of how Mark Twain got his name—"markin'-on-the-twine," two fathoms, safe water—how he stole it from the old river pilot he had mocked, Captain Sellers. I could put my heart into that, too, and then sit on the table and spin

Hal Holbrook

out the spittoon humorist, the country iconoclast from Hannibal. It was always a sure thing, too late to help now, I thought, but I looked into the audience and found the faces I knew—Jimmy and Agnes Wells, Bim Pond, my aunt and uncle from Cleveland, Ruby, and Ed Wright, my teacher. I thought I saw victory there.

We went to Bunker Jenkins's apartment and waited for the reviews. We didn't have to wait long. I had taken off the makeup and dissolved the glue, and shortly after Ruby and I arrived, Harvey Sabinson came in with some papers and read them to us.

"The New York Times, April 7, 1959
THEATRE: 'MARK TWAIN'
Holbrook Reads from Works of Humorist
By Arthur Gelb

"An extraordinary show called 'Mark Twain Tonight!' slipped into the Forty-first Street Theatre last evening. There should have been posters up all over town to herald its arrival.

"'Mark Twain Tonight' is a reading from the works of the American humorist by a young actor named Hal Holbrook. Mr. Holbrook, who is 34 years old, has got himself up as Twain at the age of 70 and portrays him as the roaming platform entertainer . . . The result can only be described as brilliant.

"Everything about the evening is perfect—the intimate theatre, Mr. Holbrook's faultless characterization and the uproariously funny selections from Twain that he has chosen. An inordinately skillful and inventive actor, Mr. Holbrook has every gesture, inflection and pause under control."

It went on. When Harvey finished, everybody started clapping. I was stunned. Stunned. Then Harvey read Walter Kerr's notice.

"New York Herald Tribune, April 7, 1959
'Mark Twain Tonight!' in a One-Man Presentation
By Walter Kerr

Harold

"For the first three seconds of 'Mark Twain Tonight' you are inclined to think monologist Hal Holbrook may have made a tactical error in electing to spend an entire evening with the vocal quaver, the possibly arthritic fingers, and the duck-like shuffle of the Twain who was already in his seventies. Will all of the youthful reminiscences, . . . and the salty moral lectures really survive the faltering mannerisms of a man who may not make it to the cut-glass water pitcher?

"They will, and they do. For Mr. Holbrook has discovered something that I, for one, didn't know. Age is the most flexible—perhaps even the most delectable—of comic accents."

Kerr spent time on the acting in *Huck Finn*:

"Through the quaver comes a second voice: the sleepy, callow sing-song of a river-bank adolescent. Through the stiffish bones comes a second teetering image: Huck walking a line, none too skillfully. And through the knowing, sardonic glance comes a wide-eyed, impervious innocence—a Huck who looks without emotion and without moral horror on the shooting of a town drunk and the attempt of a mob to lynch the killer. The new impersonation is all the more effective . . . for having been filtered through a distorting glass . . . gives to youth a fantastic, strangely real form . . . 'Mark Twain Tonight' is rich, robust, and mightily entertaining stuff."

People were congratulating me, some were crying, everyone was happy, I was in turmoil. Relieved, yes, I felt that, but most of all I felt disbelief. They were talking about someone else. Walter Kerr had understood everything I wanted to do on that stage, but I hadn't done it. How could he not have perceived my terrible fear, the dry mouth, and the shaking? Okay, he had mentioned my tremor, but that wasn't right—Twain didn't shake like that. Oh hell, let it pass. But all the rest, how could it be true? And *The New York Times*! I just didn't believe it. I'd been reviewed by small-town papers across

the country and only Louise Mace in the *Springfield Union* and *The Emporia Gazette* in Kansas had ever given me a review within miles of these two from New York's major theatrical pages. There had to be a mistake.

But the mistake kept building on itself. Francis Herridge, *New York Post*: "Irresistible. Priceless. Something like a combination of Bob Hope and Jack Benny, with their superb timing, only with comments covering a wider and deeper field." It was a ten-strike. John Chapman, the New York *Daily News*: "If you want to realize the awful artlessness and pitiful poverty of many of our film, radio and TV comedians, pay a visit to the 41st Street Theatre." Richard Watts, *New York Post*: "Unforgettable. The most fun I've had in the Theatre for ages. Whatever ecstasies of enthusiasm you may have heard over Holbrook's 'Mark Twain Tonight!' I can assure you they haven't been exaggerated." Every one of the New York newspapers gave the show a rave review. *Newsweek*: "One of the biggest surprises in the New York theatre this season has been a 34-year-old actor named Hal Holbrook, doing a Mark Twain impersonation which the rest of the country has seen and enjoyed for twelve years." All the magazines.

The only dissenter was the aforementioned student critic on the New York University paper in the Bronx. I'd give anything to find that review. I've thrashed through my notes and scrapbooks like a thirsty man in the desert but I cannot lay my hands on it. I must have burned the damn thing. I hope he reads all this.

Ruby and I went home happy that night. It felt like a shared victory. Together, we had laid the tracks for this evening. We had suffered all the sweat and the tiredness and humiliations and they did not seem so bad now. We had won at last. But the following day I was overwhelmed by another mountain to climb: eight performances a week plus *The Brighter Day*. That would be tough. But not as tough as living up to a reputation that I felt I had not really earned. I had to earn it now.

It was about a week later when the playwright Paul Osborn brought Margaret Sullavan to my dressing room after the show. I was dazzled to see her, the actress I'd fallen in love with when I attended

the out-of-town tryout of *The Voice of the Turtle* in Boston during my army days. They complimented me and then Miss Sullavan locked her candid eyes on mine.

"Mr. Holbrook, what can you do now?"

"What?"

"How will you ever find another character as rich as this? How will you be able to top it?"

That was going to be the real mountain. Nobody knew who I was. Mark Twain had become the star, not the thirty-four-year-old actor inside him. I was going to have to bring him out now, that kid named Harold who hid behind disguises, who had gone it alone too long, wondering who he really was. He would have to step forward. Mount Shasta would be cake beside that one.

Epilogue

How do you sum up thirty-four years of living when there are fifty-two more on record? With luck, that could increase. What has been accomplished in this half a life and was it worth it? And would I go that way again? What about the crippled figures? The Headmaster, the Man with the bullet-hole hat? And the new one. Myself. Are they staring at me?

I see now that I was a crippled figure. No one approaches the halfway point in a life without regrets, even those who have been taught not to question themselves. We have the stain of regret in us and it will not rub out. Maybe the Headmaster had it, and the sergeant, and that casting director. For me they were the face of evil, but there are so many of them out there, you have to survive them and try to pass them by.

But what about me? The mind flows back along the road I've taken. If I had it to do over, I would not give in to the harsh disciplines of my people and send my father back to the insane asylum. I would follow my own heart and let him go free, hit the road, live or die on it as June wanted him to do. They let him out of there a few years later, and he disappeared into the West. Our only umbilical cord was the postcard from Seattle or Sacramento or Tucson, but he didn't ask for money. Twenty years later I found him in a beat-up hotel on Mission Street in San Francisco and introduced him to his

granddaughter, Victoria, who was singing in a bar on the corner of Haight and Ashbury.

My children. What a mess. I dropped the ball there, put them in a lifeboat of their own and let them drift off to sea while I was fighting it out with Harold to find out who the hell he was and what he was made of. It took twenty-five more years. My children took the same and that's a story in itself. It will be told. My sister June. What a life! How did she go through the agonies and keep smiling? And hoping?

Should I have tried to find our mother? She made the choice to disappear and I let her do that. I wish I had tried to find her. Now I want to know what she was like. Like me? Was she the imp in me, the suicide gambler, the boy who danced alone? Was it my mother trying to come out? She danced into oblivion and I got lost, too. Something was missing. Always missing. I wish now that I had found her. What I didn't know about was being loved and loving in return. It was always a word to me. It was not a voice that sang to me and said, "It's okay. You're a good man. I love you." That took a while.

Was it worth it, this awful struggle to keep going, to survive, no matter what the cost to others, especially my children? I am much older now and I see the full span of that life I started out with and I feel the pain of it in me and the loss to others, and the desperation and the shame. And I am left standing here with one answer: you go down the road your gut tells you to travel. To ignore it is suicide. But you have to try much, much harder not to harm people, not to forget them, and not to let those loved ones drift away. We have just so much strength for that, and when we cannot hold on any longer, we still have to go. Searching, searching for that one true thing you didn't get long ago when it could have been your companion while you put a life together. That act of kindness that never goes away.

Acknowledgments

To those people who have helped me so much, thank you from my heart.

My teacher, Ed Wright.

Thomas LeBien, my editor at Farrar, Straus and Giroux, who has taught me how to put a book together and been my champion.

Billy Squier has taken dictation for every page and sent it back to me for revisions through the magic of electronic wizardry. His devotion to this project—and Joyce Cohen's, my assistant and my friend—will never be forgotten by me.

Vernon Burton started the book's journey to publication, and Phyllis Wender helped me early on. My pals Mark Dawidziak, who read some early chapters and greatly encouraged me, and Shelley Fisher Fishkin at Stanford University were always cheering for me. Mark and Shelley agreed to read *Harold* and offer their opinion, and so did Annie Potts, Woody Harrelson, Jack O'Brien, and Robert Redford. Thank you from the heart.

Lovelady Powell (Lovey) and her accompanist, Bruce Morton—my cabaret partners—and David Rounds, who engineered the feat of getting Ed Sullivan to our little nightclub. And thank you, Ed.

Bert Tanswell and Dick Corson and my dear friends from Denison University, Gordon Condit and Leah Ashbrook, who were so much a part of my early nurturing—and so were Luke and Dixie Campbell Utter and her sainted mother, Dixie. Ev and Gay

Acknowledgments

Reese, our constant supporters, and Ace Morgan, who lit a flame in me.

James B. Pond (Bim), son of Mark Twain's lecture manager, Major Pond, who told me I should do the solo and people would book it. Ricklie Boasberg, my fairy godmother. Phil Pryor and Cliff Menz; Harry Byrd Kline.

Devon Duncan of the Holyoke Library gave such generous research assistance. Carlton and Jean Guild.

Klaus Kolmar has booked me as Twain for fifty-two years, mostly without a contract between us. Joe Keating stage-managed my show for six years, and Bennett Thomson toured with me for thirty-four. Now Rich Costabile, Kurt Wagemann, and Jim D'Asaro are keeping it going. Harvey Sabinson and John Lotas, who got me onstage in New York.

And how can I properly thank my first wife, Ruby Johnston Holbrook? Our early career together was a shared one, and the success I have achieved goes back to her. My children, Victoria and David, had to sustain the stress and strain I put upon them, striving for success. Their contribution is beyond any measure.

My wife, Dixie Carter. Her kindness and beauty of soul, her belief that there was goodness in me and that it would thrive with encouragement, have been the gift of my life.